The Barbarians Speak

*

The Barbarians Speak

HOW THE CONQUERED PEOPLES

SHAPED ROMAN EUROPE

✳

PETER S. WELLS

PRINCETON UNIVERSITY PRESS

PRINCETON AND OXFORD

Copyright © 1999 by Princeton University Press
Published by Princeton University Press, 41 William Street,
Princeton, New Jersey 08540
In the United Kingdom: Princeton University Press,
3 Market Place, Woodstock, Oxfordshire OX20 1SY

Third printing, and first paperback printing, 2001
Paperback ISBN 0-691-08978-7

*The Library of Congress has cataloged the cloth edition
of this book as follows*
Wells, Peter S.
The barbarians speak : how the conquered peoples
shaped Roman Europe / Peter S. Wells.
p.   cm.
Includes bibliographical references and index.
ISBN 0-691-05871-7 (cl. : alk. paper)
1. Rome—Provinces.   2. Romans—Europe.
3. Germanic peoples—Europe—Influence.
I. Title.
DG59.E8W45   1999
936—dc21   99–12193

British Library Cataloging-in-Publication Data is available

This book has been composed in Baskerville

Printed on acid-free paper. ∞

www.pup.princeton.edu

Printed in the United States of America

3   5   7   9   10   8   6   4

✳ *Contents* ✳

CONTENTS

* *List of Figures and Tables* *

TABLES

* Preface *

THE HISTORY of Europe north of the Mediterranean begins with Julius Caesar's accounts, composed between 58 and 51 B.C. We possess very little written information about the peoples who lived in what is now France, Germany, the Low Countries, the British Isles, Scandinavia, and eastern Europe, before Julius Caesar led his Roman army against the Gauls in 58 B.C. and left us descriptions of his campaigns and of the societies he encountered. Caesar and subsequent Roman writers, together with a few Greek observers, are the sources of all of the written history of Roman Period Europe. The indigenous peoples, with no written tradition of their own, left no literary record of their perspectives and daily existence.

The subject of this book is these native peoples of temperate Europe and their experiences during the Roman conquests and the centuries of domination by that imperial power. By examining the material record that these peoples left behind—their settlements, graves, ritual places, pottery, and personal ornaments—we can learn a great deal about how they responded to the Roman incursions into their lands and how they created their own accommodations to the changing circumstances. My argument is that the native peoples played a much greater role in the formation of the societies of Roman Period Europe than we would think from relying on the written accounts of the Roman generals, administrators, and other commentators. Only by consulting the material evidence that they left can we let the indigenous peoples speak for themselves.

Most people today, unless they have made a point of reading about prehistoric archaeology, know very little about these natives of pre-Roman Europe. In our modern world we tend to think of nonliterate peoples as fundamentally different from us. Yet as I hope this book shows, Iron Age Europeans, though they left no written accounts of their lives, were like us in important ways.

Archaeologists working in Europe have conducted thousands of excavations and published thousands of site reports, scholarly papers, and books that pertain to the indigenous peoples before and during the Roman Period. But these are almost all specialized studies, aimed at professionals in the field and advanced students. This book is the first attempt to use the results of these investigations to examine on a broad scale the processes of response and accommodation by the natives of temperate Europe to the Roman presence in their lands. My aim is to present a synthesis and interpretation that will be of interest and accessible to the general reader, and at the same time to offer scholars and students a new perspective on Roman Period Europe.

New discoveries every year contribute to the growth in our knowledge of the native peoples of Europe and of their interactions with the Roman Empire. Understanding the period during which European societies were in the process of formation is thus a dynamic enterprise. I hope that I convey some of the excitement of this endeavor in the pages that follow.

European measurements are in the metric system. Since I have written this book primarily for an American audience, in most instances I first provide measurements in the traditional system—feet, miles, and pounds—but I include the original metric figures in parentheses. The metric measurements in the text are precise; the traditional measurements are approximate.

* Acknowledgments *

T HIS BOOK is a result of well over a decade of research into the indigenous peoples of Europe before, during, and after the Roman expansion north of the Alps. I have benefited from the support of numerous institutions and from the generosity and good advice of many people.

Excavations at the Late Iron Age *oppidum* settlement at Kelheim in Bavaria, and the subsequent analysis of the results, were supported by the National Science Foundation (BNS-9004164); the College of Liberal Arts, the Graduate School, and Research Explorations, all of the University of Minnesota; and by Earthwatch and the Center for Field Research. Research travel during several summers was supported by the National Science Foundation (SBR-9506958), and by several units of the University of Minnesota, including the College of Liberal Arts, the Graduate School (McKnight Summer Fellowship Program and Grant-in-Aid of Research, Artistry, and Scholarship), and the Institute of International Studies. Final preparation of this book was aided by a Scholar of the College award from the College of Liberal Arts. I thank all of these institutions for their generous assistance.

A great many individuals provided excellent advice in all stages of my research, from developing my themes at the outset to commenting on the manuscript. Others sent publications, aided me in examining museum collections, guided me around archaeological sites, and provided hospitality during my travels. I thank the following persons for their various contributions to the effort:

David Anthony, Oneonta, NY; Jörg Biel, Stuttgart; Peter Bogucki, Princeton; Olivier Buchsenschutz, Paris; Ingrid Burger-Segl, Bayreuth; James and Anne Coone, Oberursel; James Cusick, Gainesville, FL; Michael Dietler, Chicago; Stephen L. Dyson, Buffalo; Bernd Engelhardt, Landshut; Brian Fagan, Santa Barbara; Franz Fischer, Bonn; Jean-Loup Flouest, Glux; Otto-Herman Frey, Marburg; Dietmar Gehrke, Lüneburg; Olivier Gosselain, Brussels; Ulla Lund Hansen, Copenhagen; Colin Haselgrove, Durham; Lotte Hedeager, Göteborg; J. D. Hill, Southampton; Jonathan Hill, Carbondale, IL; John Hines, Cardiff; Jürgen Hoika, Schleswig; Werner Hübner, Landshut; Steen Hvass, Copenhagen; Jørgen Jacobsen, Odense; Henrik M. Jansen, Svendborg; Hans-Eckart Joachim, Bonn; Zbigniew Kobylinski, Warsaw; Scott MacEachern, Brunswick, ME; Orla Madsen, Haderslev; Jes Martens, Copenhagen; Karsten Michaelsen,

Odense; Rosemarie Müller, Göttingen; Matthew Murray, Mankato, MN; Harold Mytum, York; Oliver Nicholson, Minneapolis; Bernhard Overbeck, Munich; Johannes Prammer, Straubing; Michael Rind, Kelheim; Nico Roymans, Amsterdam; Peter Schröter, Munich; Susanne Sievers, Frankfurt; Gil Stein, Evanston, IL; Berta and Per Stjernquist, Lund; Martha Tappen, Minneapolis; Jiří Waldhauser, Prague; Günther Wieland, Stuttgart; Colin Wells, San Antonio, TX; David Wigg, Frankfurt; Willem Willems, Amersfoort; Greg Woolf, Oxford; and Werner Zanier, Munich.

Throughout the writing of the book, I have benefited greatly from the enthusiastic encouragement of my editor, Jack Repcheck of Princeton University Press. Jack has also provided excellent advice on both major issues and details.

Finally, I thank my wife, Joan, and my sons, Chris and Nick, for joining me on frequent research travels, for sometimes helping with the fieldwork, and for providing good cheer and support.

The Barbarians Speak

✳

Natives and Romans

ROMAN DISASTER IN THE TEUTOBURG FOREST

Today the countryside east of the small city of Bramsche on the northern edge of the Teutoburg Forest in northern Germany is a quiet rural landscape of small villages, open fields, and patches of light woodland. But in the year A.D. 9, one of the most important battles of the ancient world took place here, in which a powerful Roman army was ambushed and annihilated. Since 1987, archaeologists have excavated remains of swords, daggers, lanceheads, slingstones, shields, helmets, and chain mail in this bucolic landscape. These weapons, together with over 1,000 coins, fragments of military belts and uniforms, and bones of humans, horses, and mules, are all that survived of some 15,000–20,000 Roman soldiers who were waylaid by bands of warriors from small communities of peoples whom the Romans called Germans. Their leader was Arminius from the Cherusci tribe, who is thought to have served earlier as an auxiliary commander in the Roman army. But he changed his allegiance. In late September of that year, he led the attack on three Roman legions—the Seventeenth, Eighteenth, and Nineteenth—together with three cavalry units and six cohorts of accompanying troops as they marched through a narrow passage between a steep hill to the south and a swamp to the north. According to Roman written accounts based on reports by a few men who escaped, the battle raged over three days. As the Romans realized that they were beaten, the commander, P. Quinctilius Varus, and other leaders committed suicide, and the local warriors accomplished a complete rout.

This event shocked the Roman world, and played a decisive role in the future configuration of the Roman Empire and in the subsequent course of European history. Prior to this catastrophe, the Roman armies had won a series of stunning victories in Europe as elsewhere, conquering all of continental Europe west of the Rhine and south of the Danube. This disaster in the Teutoburg Forest two thousand years ago was so devastating to the expansionary vision of the Roman leaders that it effectively ended Roman designs on territory further north and east. Shortly after the battle, the Emperor Augustus ordered his troops to strengthen the

Rhine defenses, thereby shifting the Roman policy emphasis from of-
fense to defense, and thus establishing a permanent imperial frontier
along this river instead of pushing ahead to create a new one on the Elbe
(Figure 1). Augustus's decision established one of the most important
cultural boundaries in world history, the effects of which are still clear
today among the nations of modern Europe.

The excavations of the battle site at Kalkriese, north of Osnabrück in
Germany, are revealing important new information about this critical
event, about which only the barest outline was recorded in the Roman
annals. Despite two centuries of searching, the site was only discovered
in 1987. Besides recovering large quantities of weapons, military paraphernalia, and coins, the archaeologists have discovered an extensive
fortification wall that the German attackers had built of sod, parallel to
the track along which the Roman soldiers would march. Apparently they
had planned their ambush well.

Why were some 20,000 Roman troops marching across northern Germany in A.D. 9? What did they hope to accomplish, and what does their
resounding defeat by local warriors tell us about relations between Rome
and the indigenous peoples of Europe?

THE WEAPON DEPOSIT AT ILLERUP

In 1950, workers digging to lay a new drainage pipe at Illerup near
Skanderborg in Jutland, Denmark, came upon hundreds of metal objects
from the Roman Period. Archaeological excavations between 1950 and
1956, and again between 1975 and 1983, uncovered a major weapon
deposit. Sometime around A.D. 200, people threw the complete weaponry of more than 150 well-equipped soldiers into what was at the time
a lake measuring about 1,200 ft. (400 m) long by 750 ft. (250 m) wide.
Excavations of 40 percent of the now dry lake bed have recovered nearly
500 spearheads, 500 lanceheads, 100 swords, more than 300 shields,
about 10 sets of horse-harness gear, along with bows and arrows and a
variety of tools. Some of the equipment was highly ornamented, with
gold and silver trim on harness gear, shields, sword belts, scabbards, and
hilts. Solid gold bars and rings were part of the deposit. Four of the
metal objects bore inscriptions written in runes, a new form of writing
in northern Europe at this time.

Extraordinary as this site seems, it is just one of some thirty known
weapon deposits in Denmark, northern Germany, and southern Sweden,

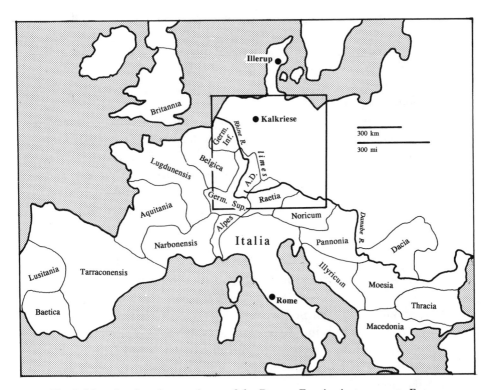

Fig. 1. Map showing the provinces of the Roman Empire in temperate Europe during the second century A.D. This map represents the situation as static, whereas changes took place in various boundaries over time. The rivers Rhine and Danube, and the *limes* boundary between them, formed the border between Roman territory and the unconquered lands. Sometimes Roman power extended beyond that border, as in the case of Dacia north of the lower Danube. The locations of Kalkriese, Illerup, and Rome, all discussed in this chapter, are shown. The square indicates the location of the map in Figure 2. Germ. Inf. = Germania Inferior. Germ. Sup. = Germania Superior. A.D. = Agri Decumates, a part of Germania Superior. Unless otherwise indicated, all maps in this book are oriented with north at the top.

most of which date between A.D. 200 and 400. They are believed to represent the victors' offering of weapons of defeated enemies to gods who helped them win the battles. The assemblages of weapons tell us much about military and political organization in northern Europe during this period. The Illerup deposit is thought to represent the equipment of an army that consisted of about three hundred infantry soldiers, forty heavily armed warriors, and five commanders.

Among the many surprises that have emerged from the analysis of sites such as Illerup is the fact that the great majority of swords are of Roman manufacture. Stamped marks, patterns of inlay, forging techniques, and shape all indicate Roman origin of the blades. The hilts, or handles, reflect a variety of traditions. Some are of Roman type, others of local Germanic character.

How did thousands, originally probably tens of thousands, of Roman swords come to be deposited ritually in Danish lakes, 280 miles (450 km) from the nearest Roman territory? We know from Roman writers that the defenders of the imperial frontiers feared groups to the east and north, who occasionally raided Roman territory. Why would Rome allow so many top-quality weapons to be in the hands of their potential foes to the north?

Kalkriese and Illerup are both outside the boundaries of the Roman Empire, yet the discoveries made at both sites show significant Roman activity. Surviving texts by writers such as Caesar and Tacitus tell us something about the Roman perspective on interactions with these indigenous peoples. But only the archaeological evidence lets us examine their experiences and their attitudes toward the Roman world. This book is about what archaeology can tell us about the native side of interactions with the Romans.

THE SETTING

Geography

This study focuses upon a single major region of the Roman Empire, the frontier provinces in temperate Europe—lands that are now in the Netherlands, Belgium, Luxembourg, Germany, France, Switzerland, and Austria (Figure 2). For the question I pose here—what role did the indigenous peoples play in the creation of the societies of the Roman Period?—such a medium-scale region is appropriate. Local societies varied greatly within the Roman Empire, and a more limited landscape might provide a too restricted and perhaps atypical picture of the processes of change during the Roman Period. A larger part of the Empire would be unwieldy, encompassing too much regional variety to handle in a study of this scope. The border provinces of Germania Inferior, Gallia Belgica, Germania Superior, and Raetia share certain essential features and form a coherent unit for the purposes of this study.

6

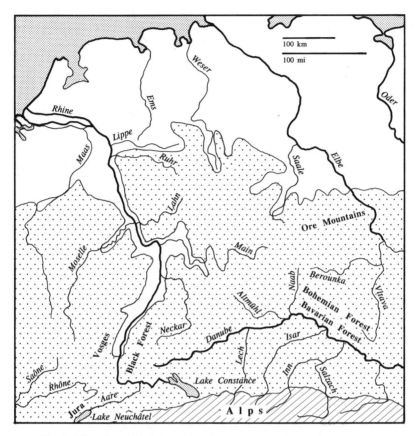

Fig. 2. Map showing the region of principal concern in this book,
with major rivers and mountains indicated. At the top are the North Sea
and the Baltic Sea. *White area:* North European Plain; *shaded area:* lands
over 659 ft. (200 m) above sea level; *hatched area:* lands over
4,919 ft. (1500 m) above sea level.

In this chapter, it is necessary to define the essential geographical characteristics of this region as they pertain to the Roman conquests and to
Rome's establishing of the provincial infrastructure and administration.
It is a truism that all human action takes place in a geographical context.
Many of the features of the geography of the border provinces are essential for an understanding of the processes of change that communities
experienced with the conquest and occupation.

The boundary of this region is defined by the two great rivers of Europe, the Rhine and the Danube. Julius Caesar in his conquest of Gaul
used the Rhine as the easternmost extent of his military conquests. The

importance of the Rhine in Caesar's mind is apparent in the number of times he refers to the river and particularly in his repeated emphasis that the Rhine formed the border between Gauls and Germans (see chapter 5). Long after Caesar's time, the Rhine remained a critical feature of the cultural geography of Roman Europe. The Emperor Augustus assembled the Roman legions on the left bank of the Rhine to prepare for the incursions across the river into the unconquered territories. After the defeat of Varus's legions in the Teutoburg Forest, Augustus and later Tiberius oversaw the strengthening of the defensive network on the west bank of the Rhine. Roman incursions across the river continued intermittently throughout the first century A.D. After Domitian's wars against the Chatti and the establishment of the Agri Decumates and construction of the *limes* boundary between the middle Rhine and the upper Danube, the lower Rhine remained the border of the empire for about four centuries.

The upper Danube was established as the imperial frontier following the conquest of southern Bavaria in 15 B.C. by the armies led by the Roman generals Tiberius and Drusus. After the construction of the *limes* wall, the uppermost course of the Danube from Eining upstream came to lie fully in Roman territory, but downstream from Eining the Danube remained the frontier.

We should not think of these two great rivers as impassible barriers, but rather as demarcations between Roman territory and the unconquered lands and as routes of communication. As major natural features in the landscape, they provided convenient lines along which the Romans arrayed their forts, but they offered little impediment to groups who wanted to cross them. As was the case everywhere before the development of motorized vehicles and the construction of railroads, transporting goods by water was much more efficient than over land, and the Roman authorities made full use of the Rhine and Danube waterways to move troops and materials along their frontiers. Recent discoveries of well-preserved wooden ships in both the Rhine and the Danube indicate the highly developed technology of river-going vehicles along these routes.

Topographically, we can understand our region in terms of three principal zones: the North European Plain, the hilly uplands of central Europe, and the Alps and their foothills. In the north, on both sides of the lower Rhine and along the shores of the North Sea and English Channel, the land is flat and the soil sandy; this is part of the extensive flat landscape known as the North European Plain. The sandy soils were not well suited to cereal cultivation, but these lands have a long tradition, from the Neolithic Period on, of cattle raising. Much of the land is damp meadow supporting rich grasses and other plants, well suited to the needs of grazing livestock. As we shall see, the specialized economy of this region played an important role in interactions between indigenous peoples and Romans. The branches of the Rhine, and other rivers that flow northward and westward through northern France, the Netherlands, and northwestern Germany, make this a landscape dominated by relatively shallow and slow-flowing water courses. Because of its alluvial character, this region offers little in the way of building stone or of ore deposits, except for bog iron ore.

Just south of the North European Plain, in the southern part of the Netherlands, northern Belgium, and northwestern Germany, loess soils cover the alluvial sands and offer much better conditions for agriculture. South of Cologne, the site of a major Roman center located on the boundary between the North European Plain and the hilly uplands of the central part of the European continent, the landscape is crossed by numerous rivers, including the Ahr, the Maas, the Moselle, and the Nahe, all of which flow into the Rhine, and the Doubs and the Saône, which flow into the Rhône. Much of the land, particularly on the river terraces and in valley bottoms, is fertile and productive of a range of crops. The hilly landscape offers a wide range of metals and building stone that were exploited in prehistoric and Roman times. The raw materials of the western Rhineland, including fine potting clays, limestone, basalt, and rich deposits of iron ore, made possible the great economic flourishing of this region during the first and second centuries A.D.

Most of the landscapes of eastern France and southern Germany consist of such hilly country with good agricultural land, river valleys providing routes for transportation, and substantial deposits of raw materials. The small mountain ranges of the Vosges and the Black Forest interrupt this general picture. They offered little in the way of farmland, but were productive of metal ores and of building stone. Much of southern Bavaria is flat open country lending itself to intensive agriculture, particularly around the city of Munich and along the Danube between Regensburg and Straubing. In the far south of Bavaria and in Switzerland, the Alps and their foothills comprise environments that include excellent pasturage for livestock and abundant mineral resources, but limited agricultural potential.

9

The landscape of this frontier zone of the Roman Empire was thus diverse in character, and it offered a rich variety of resources to the inhabitants of late prehistoric and Roman times, including good soils for agriculture, grazing land for livestock, metal ores, building stone, and fine clays for pottery and brick-making. Virtually all of the land was suitable for permanent habitation. Only the highest elevations of the mountains—the Vosges, the Black Forest, and the Alps—were unoccupied during the Late Iron Age and the Roman Period.

Changes since the Roman Period

The basic character of the landscape two thousand years ago was similar to that of today. Sea levels have risen along the English Channel and North Sea coasts, and the coastline is now a little over a mile (2 km) south and east of where it was in the Roman Period. (This change in sea level explains why the sanctuaries to the goddess Nehalennia at Domburg and Colijnsplaat, with their numerous carved stone altars, were discovered under water off the coast of the Netherlands.) Except for these coastal environments, the landscape of western and central Europe probably did not look very different in Roman times from today. It is likely that the region was more heavily forested then, but there is no general agreement among specialists on this point. The principal differences between the Roman and the modern landscapes are cultural. There are many more people in Europe now and much larger communities (see below), and of course motor vehicles have transformed the European countryside since the mid-nineteenth-century construction of railroads.

The Cultural Landscape

Humans have lived in western and central Europe for a long time (Table 1). Fossil bones belonging to earlier types of humans, *Homo erectus* and Neanderthal, indicate occupation for well over half a million years. Campsites of the Early and Middle Paleolithic periods attest to the hunting and gathering activities of these earliest Europeans. Around forty thousand years ago, modern *Homo sapiens* first appeared in Europe, and many sites of the Upper Paleolithic Period have been identified and excavated in this region. The material remains from those settlements demonstrate the more highly developed skills and cognitive abilities of ana-

TABLE 1
Summary Chronological Overview of Europe

A.D. 1914–18	World War I
A.D. 1790	Start of the Industrial Revolution
A.D. 1492	Columbus sailed to the New World
A.D. 1000	Vikings colonized Greenland
A.D. 800	Charlemagne crowned emperor
A.D. 450	End of the Roman Empire/start of Merovingian kingdoms
A.D. 200	Start of the Late Roman Period
25 B.C.	Start of the Early Roman Period
450 B.C.	Start of the Late Iron Age
800 B.C.	Start of the Early Iron Age
1200 B.C.	Start of the Late Bronze Age
2000 B.C.	Start of the Early Bronze Age
3000 B.C.	Start of Late Neolithic Period (Stonehenge)
5000 B.C.	Start of Early Neolithic Period (first farmers)
8000 B.P.	Start of Mesolithic Period
10,000 B.P.	End of Ice Age (warming of earth's climate)
40,000 B.P.	Start of Upper Paleolithic (*Homo sapiens*, cave paintings)
150,000 B.P.	Start of Middle Paleolithic (Neanderthal)
800,000 B.P.	First known humans in Europe
1,800,000 B.P.	First humans documented outside of Africa (*Homo erectus*)
2,600,000 B.P.	Earliest known stone tools (in Africa)
5,000,000 B.P.	Earliest hominids (immediate ancestors to humans) (in Africa)

Notes: Dates before A.D. 800 are approximate. B.P. = before present.

tomically modern humans, with more refined technologies for making stone tools, better strategies for hunting game and collecting plant foods, artistic expression in a wide variety of carved human and animal figurines, and the development of early systems of notation.

Agriculture was introduced around seven thousand years ago to this region. The principal crops, wheat and barley, were brought from the Near East where they were native, and cattle, pigs, sheep, and goats were introduced as well. We do not yet understand the precise mechanisms by which the plants and the technical knowledge of planting and cultivating were transmitted from the Near East to temperate Europe. Probably some groups migrated from the Near East into southeastern Europe, bringing with them their seed grain and herds of livestock, to establish the first farming villages on the European continent in Greece and Bulgaria around 6000 B.C. From there, others may have moved northward and westward, introducing the new economy and establishing new villages. Much of the change may also have happened through the gradual

11

transmission of seeds, livestock, and the technical knowledge of how to tend them, to groups that had been practicing hunter-gatherer economies in Europe. In any case, by about 4500 B.C., agricultural communities were predominant throughout western and central Europe, as far north as the English Channel and the North Sea.

The spread of the agricultural economy across Europe had important effects on the landscape. Farmers cleared forests in order to create fields for growing their crops, and the environment underwent substantial change from mostly forest-covered to largely open land. Many investigators believe that this initial clearing at the start of the Neolithic Period was a permanent transformation in the land cover of Europe—that the forest never grew back to the extent that had existed just before the Neolithic clearing.

During the Bronze Age, about 2000–800 B.C. in this region, the agricultural basis remained essentially the same as it had been during the Neolithic, but significant changes took place in society. Copper and tin, the metals that constitute the alloy bronze, are relatively sparsely distributed in nature, and the development of a metal-using economy necessitated the creation of extensive trade systems as well as mining operations. Soon not only the metals were circulating, but many other goods as well, such as amber ornaments, glass beads, and gold. Increasing wealth led to greater differences in social status within communities, and more complex forms of social stratification developed. During the final phase of the Bronze Age, 1200–800 B.C., many regions show an expansion of settlement and farming activity. More forested lands were cleared, in particular lands higher in mountainous zones than had been occupied previously. The traction plow came into general use, and metal sickles became a common tool that increased the efficiency of harvesting.

Thus, by the start of the prehistoric Iron Age, around 800 B.C., temperate Europe was very much a cultural landscape. Humans had long before cleared the forests and plowed the soils, thereby transforming both the surface of the land and the plant and animal communities that inhabited it. Clearing and cultivation also meant that topsoil erosion increased, further altering the shape of the land surface and the composition of its soils. The essential features of the food producing economy changed only gradually from the Neolithic Period to Roman times, with the introduction of some new plants and, especially during the Late Iron Age and the Roman Period, some new technologies applied to both agriculture and animal husbandry.

Demography

Before the Industrial Revolution of the nineteenth century, the population of Europe was much smaller than it is now. Estimating populations in earlier times is an extremely problematic exercise, but we can make reasonable estimates on the basis of excavated cemetery sites at which skeletons are well preserved, and from the sizes of settlements and the density of occupation debris. Different kinds of evidence suggest that the population of Europe during the Roman Period may have been about one-twentieth of the modern population. Population varied geographically, just as it does today. Italy and other regions on the Mediterranean shores were the most densely occupied parts of Europe, while Scandinavia was the least densely inhabited. The part of Europe with which this book concerns itself was one of the more densely occupied regions during the Roman Period; its population may have been between one-twentieth and one-fifteenth of today's. For example, the modern German state of Baden-Württemberg has a population of about nine million. During the Roman Period the population of that region may have been around half a million.

Not only was regional population smaller in the Roman Period than it is today, but individual communities were much smaller. Rome was an exceptionally large city for ancient times—estimates generally lie between three-quarters of a million and two million inhabitants for Rome at the time of Christ. But in the frontier provinces no towns—not even the great centers at Cologne, Mainz, or Trier—are likely to have had more than ten thousand inhabitants, and the populations as a whole were primarily rural. The vast majority of people lived in small villages or in isolated hamlets and farmsteads, or, in some parts of our region, in the new villas. Though the communities in the countryside were small, they were widely distributed across the landscape. All of the regions with good farmland were occupied. Except in the mountains, uncultivated and uninhabited regions were few and far between.

The Roman army bases represented the major exceptions to these generalizations. A legionary camp accommodated as many as 6,000 men, and it was frequently accompanied by a *vicus*—a settlement outside the fortress walls occupied by local indigenous people who supplied the needs of the soldiers. The great majority of the military bases were situated along the borders—the Rhine and Danube rivers and the *limes* wall. During the first and second centuries, some 110,000 Roman troops were

13

stationed in the forts along these frontiers at any one time. As we shall see, these large concentrations of soldiers had a very significant impact on the frontier regions.

ORIGINS AND GROWTH OF THE ROMAN EMPIRE

Origins of Rome

Two different kinds of information tell us about Rome's origins. Literary sources, composed during the second and first centuries B.C., offer legendary accounts of the founding of Rome. One legend links earliest Rome with the Homeric tradition of the Trojan War, making Aeneas, a survivor of that war, the founder of Rome. Another attributes the city's origin to the twin brothers Romulus and Remus, raised by a female wolf; according to this tradition, Rome was founded in the year 753 B.C. Some accounts link the two stories into a single foundation-myth. Historians regard these accounts as purely fanciful, but they do indicate how Romans of later times liked to think about their origins, just as later the Vikings of Scandinavia maintained a rich tradition of origin-myths to account for the world as they knew it.

Archaeological sources provide a different perspective on the beginnings of Rome and show that the original settlement was considerably earlier than the 753 B.C. date suggested by the legendary tradition. Excavations within what is now the city of Rome have uncovered remains of farmsteads and villages on the hills, dating back at least as far as the Late Bronze Age, before 1000 B.C. The hills offered dry land for settlement, while the low-lying areas between them were marshy and less hospitable for habitation. Postholes identified on the Palatine hill indicate small huts built of logs and branches, probably with roofs of thatched grasses. During the eighth and seventh centuries B.C. the settlements grew in size and in complexity. Objects recovered through archaeological research attest to the development of specialized craft industries and of trade with surrounding peoples, including Greek communities in southern Italy. Evidence for increasing social differentiation shows that status differences were emerging at this time.

Late in the seventh century B.C. the growing community of Rome entered the orbit of the Etruscan world. Our understanding of this process and of the following centuries is based both upon texts recorded later and upon archaeological evidence. The first literary sources concerning the history and development of Rome date to the end of the third cen-

14

tury B.C., but not until late in the first century B.C. do we find comprehensive accounts of Rome's history in such writers as Livy, writing in Latin, and Dionysius of Halicarnassus, writing in Greek. These writers recorded earlier traditions based on oral histories and documents such as laws and treaties, and also compiled surviving fragments of writings by earlier chroniclers.

The historical tradition informs us that during the latter part of the seventh century B.C., the Tarquin kings of Etruria gained political control of the growing community at Rome. The date suggested by the written sources is 616 B.C. Building traditions and landscape alterations that had been common practice in Etruria are apparent in the archaeological record at Rome from the end of the seventh century B.C. These include the draining and paving of the valley area that was to become the forum, construction of a temple on the Capitol, and the general use of stone for building foundations and tiles for roofs in the settlement. Early inscriptions indicate the use of writing before 600 B.C., perhaps stimulated by the Etruscan practice, but nevertheless in the indigenous Latin language. According to the tradition, the last Etruscan king, Tarquinius Superbus, was driven from Rome in the year 510 B.C., an event associated with the beginning of the Roman Republic, governed by a council of leading citizens, a precursor of the Senate.

Scholarly opinion holds that in general outline, these traditions probably represent the changes that the fledgling community of Rome experienced. During the late seventh and sixth centuries, the archaeology shows considerable growth in interactions between the inhabitants of early Rome and other peoples, including Greeks in southern Italy and Etruscans to the north. But the traditional dates are not supported by any firm evidence, and the term "king" used in the histories recorded during the second and first centuries B.C. must be understood in terms of the leadership structure likely in an expanding village. For the earlier period in particular, "village headman" might be a more appropriate designation. By the end of the sixth century B.C., the archaeology indicates an ever-larger and more complex community at Rome, coming into its own as a significant urban locus in central Italy.

Information about the Roman Republic is considered more reliable than that for the earlier development of Rome. It is based principally on the written histories of the final half of the first century B.C., which in turn derive from earlier written fragments, oral accounts, family traditions, and documents preserved in the form of inscriptions. In the early phases of the Republic, political power was held mainly by the patricians, the aristocrats of early Rome. Gradually over time, the plebeians—the common people—acquired power as well, and by the end of the Republic, a nobility comprised of both patrician and plebeian families ruled Rome.

Rome's Expansion

During the fifth century B.C., the city of Rome began to expand its territory and its power. Late in that century, Rome conquered southern Latium and established colonies there as means of securing the new lands and to provide some of its citizens with new farms. In 396, after ten years of war, Rome defeated the powerful southern Etruscan city of Veii—the first major military conquest by Rome. In 387 the city of Rome was sacked by Celtic marauders from across the Alps, an event that played a very important role in Roman thinking about northern barbarians for the next millennium. After that disaster, the Romans built their first major city wall, the Servian Wall, some six miles (10 km) in length. They became very concerned with the defense of Rome and, later, of Italy as a whole.

At this point it is worth introducing the major debate about Roman imperial policy, an issue to which we shall return later in this book. Did Rome have a long-term coherent policy of conquest and imperialism? Or are we to understand Roman conquests more in terms of defensive policy—seeking to establish secure frontiers and remove potential threats to Roman security? Some investigators see a concerted Roman policy of imperialism already in the fourth century B.C. as the city fought wars of conquest in Italy and in the western Mediterranean, while others regard these conflicts as essentially defensive tactics aimed at preserving Rome from future attacks. As the result of skillful use of diplomacy and warfare, colonization and alliance with local elites, Rome emerged from a series of conflicts as the principal power in Italy by the early third century B.C.

The beginning of Rome's overseas conquests, starting with the First Punic War against Carthage (264–241 B.C.) that resulted in Rome's winning Sicily and making it its first province, is commonly taken as the start of the accumulation of an empire by Rome. Roman armies defeated Hannibal's Carthaginian forces in 202 B.C.; one result was the acquisition of territories in Iberia. To the east and south, during the late third and early second centuries B.C., Rome fought wars and gained provinces in Illyria, Asia Minor, Macedonia, Greece, and Africa. All of these military victories resulted in great wealth coming to the Roman elites, and with it ever-greater political power on the part of the Roman nobility. The contacts with the Greek world to the east encouraged Roman imitation and borrowing of Greek arts, including architecture and literary traditions.

The final decades of the second century B.C. brought a number of problems throughout the growing empire. At Rome, social and political struggles resulted at least in part from growing differences between elites and the mass of the population. Wars and revolts erupted in Africa and Sicily, and between 113 and 101 B.C., the Cimbri and Teutones from northern Europe, and other peoples allied with them, swept southward and threatened Roman Italy. Gaius Marius, the general who finally led Roman forces that defused this threat, became one of several powerful military leaders, including Sulla, Pompey, and Caesar, who vied for power in Rome in the first half of the first century B.C. Julius Caesar emerged on top of these power-struggles, in large part because of his resounding and highly publicized military successes in the Gallic Wars of 58–51 B.C., and also because of his successes in battles against his rivals in the civil war that developed in Roman Italy in 49 B.C. Following the defeat of Pompey's forces in 48 B.C. and other military victories, Caesar, despite strong objections in the Roman Senate to the rule of one man, was appointed dictator in 44 B.C., only to be assassinated a month later by a conspiracy of Senators. A new series of civil wars erupted, culminating in Octavian's forces defeating those of Antony at Actium in 31 B.C., leaving the way open for Octavian to become the single ruler of the expanding empire.

The Empire

As noted above, as early as the late fifth century B.C., Rome began expanding its territory through conquest, and by the start of the second century B.C., Rome was the capital of an empire. But until Octavian was given the title "Augustus" and officially endowed with single-man power over Rome in 27 B.C., Rome had had no effective emperor. From Augustus on, the Roman Empire had a constant succession of individuals who ruled in the role of emperor. Augustus had won a critical victory at Actium in 31 B.C., and he skillfully negotiated power from the Senate and the equestrian elite as well as support from the army and the people of Rome. At the same time that he acquired exceptional powers from the leading institutions and families, as well as popular support, Augustus

17

also devoted considerable effort and resources to public works in Rome. He built aqueducts to provide the city with adequate fresh water and assured supplies of grain for the city's poor. Augustus also initiated a program of monumental public architecture to celebrate major military victories and to proclaim through these visual means the greatness of the empire.

Augustus's relationship with the army was particularly significant. Military leadership and success were of vital importance in Roman ideology, and Augustus's successful conquest of much new territory, particularly in continental Europe, during his forty years of reign was critical to his popular success. Augustus oversaw the development of a professional army with specified pay and conditions of service. He established a policy of granting land or retirement cash bonuses to veterans. These policies served well in maintaining a relatively loyal army with high morale, providing Augustus with a motivated and well-organized fighting force of about 350,000 men. Roughly half were legionaries and half auxiliaries.

The Roman army is of particular importance to the concerns of this book, in part because it was responsible for the conquest of territories in Europe and elsewhere, and because the army was the principal mediator of contact between Rome and indigenous peoples. During Augustus's reign between 27 B.C. and A.D. 14, Rome was engaged in extensive conquest of territory in continental Europe (see chapter 4). After that, Rome was concerned primarily with maintaining secure borders and responding to incursions by foreigners. The principal exceptions were the conquest of part of Britain in A.D. 43, the lands between the upper Rhine and upper Danube in A.D. 83, and Dacia by Trajan in A.D. 106.

WHY THE ROMAN EMPIRE MATTERS TODAY

The Roman Empire was one of the world's greatest unifying forces, linking peoples militarily, politically, economically, and culturally, from northern Britain and the Straits of Gibralter in the west, to the upper Euphrates and southern Egypt in the east. Rome's trade connections reached even further afield—north to Finland, south to sub-Saharan Africa, and east to India. The empire's effects are apparent in the languages, customs, and legal systems in many European countries today and in other parts of the world where Europeans have settled or where indigenous peoples have borrowed ideas from ancient or modern Europe. All of the Romance languages—Italian, French, Spanish, Portuguese, and Romanian—are descendants of the Latin of the Roman Empire. In the English-speaking world, we use many Latin expressions, particularly in the fields of law and medicine; *habeas corpus* and *quid pro quo* are familiar examples. The physical remains of Rome, particularly its stone architecture, serve modern peoples throughout the lands of the empire, whether as residents or tourists, as constant reminders of the power and durability of the 500-year empire.

Many aspects of the Roman Empire were similar to features of our modern global world system. Linkages of economic and political systems over vast expanses of space were common. When we find the same types of Roman *terra sigillata* pottery and glass beakers beyond the imperial frontiers in northern Scotland, Finland, India, and sub-Saharan Africa, we cannot help but think of the current worldwide distribution of Coca Cola, McDonald's, and Levi's jeans. The patterns in the distribution of Rome's influence and its products represent universal desires for metropolitan goods emanating from centralized and highly productive economic systems.

Even more important than the identifiable remains of Rome's power and influence in the modern world is the place Rome occupies in our imagination. Rome is the archetypal empire. It is the best known of the ancient empires, because the Romans kept written accounts of many of their imperial activities, and because the Western world has been interested in learning more about both the surviving texts and the standing ruins left from two thousand years ago. Renewed interest in Classical Antiquity during the Renaissance led to the discovery of large numbers of manuscripts preserved in monasteries throughout the continent containing the texts written by Roman and Greek writers about Rome and its empire. Many of the European countries in which the scholarly traditions of the Renaissance flourished had been occupied by Rome, and from the fifteenth century on researchers in them took a strong interest in the study of the Empire, especially as it pertained to the history of their own countries. During this awakening of serious interest in Classical Antiquity, educated Europeans began a systematic inventory and study of Roman remains on their lands. In early modern times, Edward Gibbon's *Decline and Fall of the Roman Empire*, published between 1776 and 1788, became popular with the reading public and made Europeans and Americans all the more aware of the Roman Empire. Post-Renaissance empire-builders of Spain, France, and Britain viewed their actions in terms of their perceived predecessors in ancient Rome.

Barely a generation ago, large numbers of school children in America and Europe learned Latin and with the language much about the world of ancient Rome. In the modern West, the Roman Empire plays a major role in fiction, cartoons, film, and other aspects of popular culture. Historical fiction about the Empire has long been popular, and in the 1970s the British television series *I Claudius* provided entertainment and food for thought throughout the English-speaking world. Hollywood productions such as *Ben Hur, Antony and Cleopatra,* and *Spartacus* created vivid images in the popular imagination of the Roman world and its peoples. The Roman context was used in comedy, notably in the musical *A Funny Thing Happened on the Way to the Forum.* Children all over the world delight in the comic series *Asterix,* about Gauls forever fending off the invading Romans.

No other empire plays such a powerful role in our imaginations, and our ideas about the Roman Empire form a major component of what we think we know about "the past."

EMPIRES IN WORLD PERSPECTIVE

The phenomena of military conquest and of political and commercial expansion, and concommitant changes in both indigenous groups and the conquerors, have been widespread through time and space in human experience. We can trace the phenomena of imperial conquest and colonization back at least to the Uruk Period in Mesopotamia, 3800–3100 B.C. Recent archaeological investigations have explored the relations between an Uruk colony at Hacinebi in southeastern Turkey and the indigenous peoples of the region during this early stage in the development of civilization.

Several early empires are well documented by both textual information and archaeological evidence, and the study of these, together with information from the more recent empires of the modern world, forms the basis for our understanding of imperialism as a human phenomenon. In the ancient Near East, the Akkadian Empire of the third millennium B.C. and the Assyrian of the early first millennium B.C. are among the best understood early empires. The Roman Empire thrived in the greater Mediterranean world from the first century B.C. to the fifth century A.D. From the thirteenth to the seventeenth century, the Mongol Empire controlled the lands from eastern Europe to China. The Mogul (also Moghul, Mughal) Empire dominated southern Asia, lands that are now India and parts of Pakistan and Afghanistan, from the early six-teenth to the mid-nineteenth century. In the New World, the Aztecs ruled central and southern Mexico from the fourteenth century until the ar-rival of the Spaniards in the early sixteenth century, and the Inca Empire, centered at Cuzco in southern Peru, gained control of the entire western seaboard of South America from the middle of the fifteenth century until the Spanish conquest early in the sixteenth. In modern times, the Spanish, British, and French had the most extensive empires, domi-nating different regions of the world from the early sixteenth century on, while other European nations, including the Portuguese, Dutch, and Germans, played smaller roles in modern empire-building. In some ways the former Soviet Union and the modern United States have played roles during the twentieth century similar to those of empires of the past.

All of these empires, in both the Old and the New Worlds, were multi-ethnic in character. They comprised diverse peoples, all of whom under-went profound change in the course of conquest and incorporation into the imperial systems. In the cases of European empires of the last five centuries, we have extensive documentation concerning imperial expan-sion, interaction with indigenous peoples, and associated changing pat-terns of society, economy, and identity among both indigenes and con-querors. Historians, anthropologists, and literary scholars utilize the records preserved in archives of the respective nations to study the changes brought by the empires and their administrations. Less studied, but equally significant, have been the effects of indigenous peoples on the imperial societies that conquered them.

The focus of scholarly attention has shifted in recent years from the traditional concentration on the imperial societies and their perspec-tives, to the indigenous peoples and their perceptions and experiences in the contexts of conquest and assimilation into the empires. Important recent examples include Eric Wolf's highly influential *Europe and the Peo-ple Without History,* Nancy Farriss's *Maya Society Under Colonial Rule,* and Nathan Wachtel's *The Vision of the Vanquished: The Spanish Conquest of Peru Through Indian Eyes, 1530–70.* Related studies in fields as diverse as an-thropology, literary theory, and marketing examine similar issues in the responses by indigenous peoples to the spread of political and military power by the former Soviet Union and of commercial products by the United States.

The most important result of such studies of indigenous peoples in imperial contexts is the demonstration that they were not and are not passive recipients of change brought to them by larger and more com-

21

plex societies, but rather active participants in interactions, from initial conquests through the end of imperial domination. Modern research thus focuses not just on the effects of conquest and imperial administration on indigenous peoples, but rather on the active roles played by those indigenes in the construction of the new societies that form in colonial contexts.

The new field known as postcolonial studies contributes useful theory to this approach. Literary and historical analyses of postcolonial literature emphasize the experience of the colonized in the interactions. Recently archaeologists have devised means of letting indigenous conquered peoples speak for themselves in earlier contexts, where no colonial or postcolonial literature developed.

The new approaches are also stimulated and informed by current events. Much of the turmoil in the world today, such as the emergence of independent states from former parts of the Soviet Union, the ethnic violence in the former Yugoslavia, and the massacres in Rwanda and Algeria, can be understood in terms of the same framework of analysis as the interactions between indigenous peoples and Roman empire-builders two millennia ago. The analysis of modern conflicts and comparison with the events of that era helps to shed light on both periods. The processes of human interaction are universal—the past informs the present, and the present informs the past.

DIFFERENT WAYS OF KNOWING THE PAST

Texts and History

Written texts provide information about the past, as it was interpreted and represented by individual writers. Critical theory has been valuable in showing that every text must be evaluated critically, and deconstructed. We need to ask why the author was writing a particular text, who the intended audience was, why the writer interpreted things in a particular way, and what bias and what agenda the author may have had. Until relatively recently, Greek and Roman texts were generally accepted by modern scholars at face value. The authors' assertions were taken as "fact," and the texts were used as the bases for interpreting other information, such as archaeological data. Recent approaches have demonstrated that they cannot be accepted as statements of fact but must be critically analyzed in their cultural contexts in order for us to understand their real significance.

22

For the past, including the distant past of ancient Rome, texts provide information about some categories of people and not others, and about some aspects of life but not about all. In early societies, texts almost exclusively concern elites—members of the wealthy and powerful groups. We learn very little about typical members of societies from textual evidence, until very recently in human history. Early texts usually concern political, military, sacred, and sometimes economic matters, but they very rarely inform us about everyday life.

In using textual sources of information to study the past, we are dependent upon the accidents of survival. Texts from ancient and medieval times are preserved only if they were written on material that did not decay or burn, or if they survived in exceptional circumstances. Such circumstances include the very arid environment of the mountains on the Levant coast, where the Dead Sea Scrolls were preserved, and the waterlogged, oxygen-poor conditions at Vindolanda in northern Britain where hundreds of thin pieces of inscribed wood survived. Most of the Roman texts that pertain to the expansion and administration of the empire in temperate Europe were preserved through copying in European monasteries, where they were discovered by Renaissance scholars late in the Middle Ages.

What Archaeology Can Tell Us

Archaeology is the study of the human past and of human behavior through collection, analysis, and interpretation of material remains left by people. Archaeology is able to study communities about which no written texts survive, and also to examine aspects of past human behavior that texts do not mention, including such subjects as everyday life and ritual practices. Roman authors rarely wrote about the indigenous peoples of temperate Europe—the "barbarians"—peoples whom the Romans considered to be less civilized than the Mediterranean societies. But the results of intensive archaeological research over the past two centuries permits us to study them in considerable detail, as we shall see in chapters 2 and 3. Archaeology enables us to examine what people ate, how they raised and processed their foods, what they made and what they acquired through trade, what kinds of houses they built, and how they represented status through their burial practices. Even much official Roman activity is not recorded in surviving written texts, but it can often be studied through the archaeological evidence. For example, civilian settlements, and some military bases, unrecorded in the written sources,

23

are discovered through archaeological investigation, even in the imperial frontier zone of temperate Europe, one of the best-researched regions of the world.

Archaeological evidence is different from textual in a number of important ways. Textual evidence always entails one individual's (the writer's) interpretation and selective recounting of information that we, the modern readers, must grapple with to understand. In working with archaeological evidence, on the other hand, we do not deal with someone else's interpretation, but we confront directly the surviving material evidence left by the people we study. As in the case of texts, elites tend to be better represented than nonelites in archaeology. They usually had bigger and more substantial structures, including houses, palaces, and tombs. But archaeology allows us to examine the lives of the majority of people in ways that textual documents generally do not. In most societies, all members leave material traces in their dwellings, their everyday material culture, their ritual sites, and their graves. Archaeology collects information from these categories of evidence and analyzes it in order to understand the people and their behavior.

For examining the native peoples of temperate Europe with whom the Romans interacted, the techniques of archaeology offer unique insight into everyday life, farming economy, manufacturing practices, trade systems, social organization, ritual activity, and even ways that people thought about the world and their places in it. By examining patterns before the Roman conquest and after it, we can ascertain the effects of that series of events on the indigenous peoples. Since the archaeological chronology of Roman Period Europe is well developed, we can study change over relatively brief periods of time and thus discern in considerable detail the indigenous peoples' responses to the processes resulting from Roman activity in their lands.

Like the interpretation of historical texts, the interpretation of archaeological evidence is complex and contentious. In the chapters that follow, I shall frequently discuss graves and settlements, and a number of specific categories of objects, among which pottery and fibulae are especially common. Here by way of introduction I shall say something about what we can learn from these categories of finds.

A grave can tell us a great deal about the status and wealth of the individual buried in it, and about the way that person was regarded by the community. Graves are complex artifacts of human activity, and every detail of their location, structure, and arrangement can be significant—depth, orientation, covering, arrangement of the body, character of

24

grave goods, and position of the goods. Graves represent the final stage in the funerary ritual, and often the character of a grave informs us about the nature of the ritual. Some aspects of graves indicate the cultural group to which the buried individual belonged, while others tell more about the way the individual chose to represent himself or herself. In most societies—including those of temperate Europe and Rome—funerary rituals and burials were very important events, not only for the individuals most directly connected to the deceased, but for whole communities. What the archaeologist finds in a grave embodies the most essential values and beliefs of the society to which the buried individual belonged.

While graves are intentional deposits structured to convey meanings about individuals and their communities, what archaeologists find on settlement sites is debris left by the people who once inhabited them. From foundations, whether postholes or stone and mortar walls, we can ascertain the arrangement and character of buildings. Broken pieces of pottery and fragmentary implements of stone, bone, bronze, and iron indicate when and for how long the settlement was inhabited, and they can tell us what kinds of activities people carried out on the site. Activities such as harvesting of crops, grinding of cereal grains, and cooking and serving of meals may all be represented. Fragmentary animal bones and charred seeds tells us what people ate and how they prepared their food. Debris from manufacturing processes, such as kiln waste, stone scrap, and metal slag, can reveal to us what industrial processes took place on the site. Foreign substances indicate that the community traded with peoples in other regions.

Pottery is important to archaeologists for several reasons. Pottery that has been well fired survives indefinitely, and potsherds are often the most abundant material on a settlement site. Even small fragments of pottery can tell us a great deal about the techniques used to make the pot and about the cultural tradition of the potter. Different communities made different kinds of pottery, but potters often borrowed ideas about form and decoration from other groups. Thus pots, or the sherds from them, embody a great deal of information that the archaeologist can extract to learn about the people who made and used them.

During the late prehistoric and Roman periods in Europe, personal ornaments made of metal were ubiquitous. They survive well in the ground, and we find them in graves, on settlements, and in ritual deposits. In this book, the most important category of personal ornament is the fibula. Fibulae are metal pins that worked like modern safety pins, and were used to hold together garments, typically attached at the wearer's chest or shoulder (see examples in Figure 22). They first became common during the Late Bronze Age (1200–800 B.C.) and were used throughout the Iron Age and Roman Period into medieval times. Fibulae are important chronologically, because their style changed relatively rapidly. Over the past century, European archaeologists have developed good fibula chronologies for most regions of Europe. Thus, when a grave is discovered that contains a fibula, we know immediately the period to which the grave dates.

Fibulae were often highly ornamented, and different styles of ornament were characteristic of different groups. Thus, like pottery, fibulae can tell us something about the group to which the wearer belonged. But also like pottery, people often borrowed ideas about making fibulae and combined traditional and adopted themes in new products. The varied styles of fibula that were used during the Roman Period in Europe are important for our interpretations of the changes that were taking place then.

The fact that fibulae were worn in locations on the body where they could be seen easily by others—like a brooch that a woman today wears on her lapel and like a necktie worn by a man—meant that they were used to communicate information about the wearer. Modern guides that advise women and men in the business world what kinds of clothing they should wear show that this link between personal ornamentation and communication has a long history.

Analogy in Interpreting the Past

Since we can never actually experience a past event or observe a process in the past, all interpretation of the past must be made by analogy with something else. In earlier scholarly traditions, investigators used what we call a "common sense" analogy. They assumed that once the investigator learned the "facts" through study of the historical and archaeological sources, then the interpretation would be self-evident.

The principal problem with this approach is that it assumes people in the past behaved in ways very similar to those of the modern researcher. On a very basic level, all humans today are similar to one another in the ways they think about things and organize their lives, as anthropologists and psychologists have shown. Yet there still exist important cultural differences between the world's peoples. Since humans two thousand years ago were physically like us, and their brains were structurally very similar to ours, it is reasonable to assume that they were as much like us as we are like all other humans on the earth today. But there are some ways in which our lives today are quite different from those of earlier peoples. We are accustomed to instantaneous communication via telephone, radio, television, e-mail, and the Internet. We travel at speeds unimaginable to people living before the twentieth century. Through the use of antibiotics, we assume that most children will live to adulthood. Science has changed the way we understand the natural world in which we live.

Thus analogies from the experience of modern everyday Western life may not always be the best for understanding conditions during the time of the Roman Empire. But we can employ analogies from other historical and ethnographic contexts to help us understand choices and decisions made by people two millennia ago. Analogies can help us as interpretive tools as they suggest possible ways of interpreting evidence that otherwise might not occur to us.

Europe before the Roman Conquests

DISCOVERY OF A PREHISTORIC CITY

IN THE FIRST weeks of excavation at the Late Iron Age site of Manching in Bavaria, Germany, archaeologists made discoveries that revolutionized our understanding of prehistoric Europe (Figure 3). The fieldwork from that first research season in 1955 and subsequent excavation campaigns has produced more new information than any other Iron Age site about the societies that inhabited temperate Europe before the arrival of the conquering Romans. When excavations began, Manching was already known to archaeologists and to local residents. An earth wall 4 miles (7 km) in length still enclosed the circular area of nearly 1,000 acres (380 ha), and objects had been found in Iron Age graves uncovered inside the enclosure. On the basis of the wall, archaeologists had classified Manching as an *oppidum*, one of numerous large fortified Late Iron Age settlements similar to those west of the Rhine in Gaul, where they were described by the Roman general Julius Caesar in his account of his conquests of the Gallic tribes in the years 58–51 B.C. But before 1955, no archaeologists had attempted extensive excavations inside the enclosing walls in order to study the structure and organization of the Late Iron Age settlements.

The circumstances surrounding the start of the Manching excavations were as unusual as the new approach and the extraordinary finds that were made. In 1936 a military airfield had been constructed in the enclosed area, and although no systematic archaeological excavations were conducted at that time, an alert archaeologist named Josef Reichart collected finds from the construction site and deposited them in the museum in the nearby city of Ingolstadt. In 1944, near the end of World War II, the airfield was heavily bombed by Allied aircraft. After the end of the war, in 1955, the United States Air Force decided to rebuild and expand the severely damaged facility to use as a base for jet fighters. With only a few months' advance notice, German archaeologists under the leadership of Werner Krämer organized a four-month excavation campaign during the summer just before the construction was to begin. The United States Air Force provided DM 100,000 from its construction budget for this rescue excavation, at the time a large sum for archaeology.

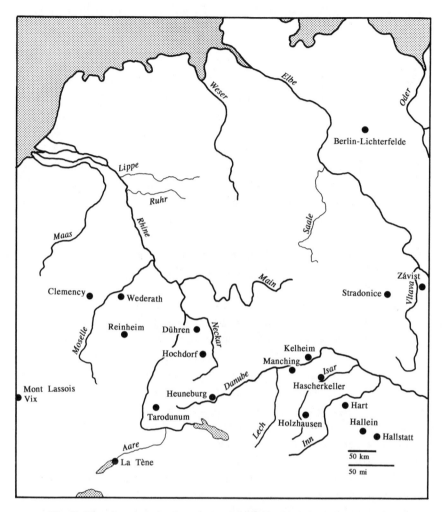

Fig. 3. Map showing the locations of the principal sites mentioned in chapters 2 and 3.

From May through August of that year, Krämer and his colleagues pursued a strategy aimed at ascertaining whether the enormous area enclosed by the wall contained remains of a permanent settlement. With the limited time available, they used a backhoe to excavate six 80-cm- (about 32 in.)-wide trenches across the land where runway construction was to take place; altogether they dug 4 1/2 miles (7.5 km) of trenches. Near the middle of the site, they excavated a contiguous area about 72,000 sq. ft. (6,680 m²) in size. Never before had archaeologists ex-

29

plored the interior of an *oppidum* so extensively, and what Krämer and his team found revolutionized our understanding of the pre-Roman peoples of Europe.

Except for a strip of land up to 1,500 ft. (500 m) wide just inside the enclosing wall, all parts of the site that the archaeologists explored yielded evidence of dense human occupation. The backhoe trenches and the open area revealed an unusually thick cultural layer made up of rich organic residue from human habitation along with great quantities of pottery, metal objects, animal bones, and other occupation debris. Postholes representing foundations of buildings, ditches that divided parts of the settlement, and storage pits for grain and other foodstuffs were everywhere, all containing Late Iron Age artifacts. Industrial debris attested to smelting and forging of iron, casting of bronze ornaments, manufacture of glass jewelry, even the minting of coins. Imports from the Roman world indicated long-distance trade, and many different materials showed active exchange between this community and neighboring regions of Europe.

Besides all of this evidence for a settlement much larger and more complex than the investigators had anticipated, they encountered another wholly unexpected phenomenon. In the cultural layer all over the settlement, and in many pits and ditches, they found human skeletal remains, sometimes whole skeletons, sometimes separate skulls and other parts. Many of the bones bore severe wounds. In the same locations were fragmentary weapons, iron swords, shield bosses, and lance points. All together the remains of over 420 individuals were collected and identified. The evidence suggested a massive battle on the site. But already after that first season of fieldwork, Krämer recognized that the battle could not have been part of an attack by Roman armies when they conquered southern Bavaria in 15 B.C. The form of the swords indicated that they had been made during the third or second centuries B.C., over a hundred years earlier than the Roman arrival. The problem of the supposed great battle of Manching, and how it fit into the history of the Late Iron Age occupation, became one of the many intriguing questions surrounding this extraordinary site.

As Krämer's reports about the early excavations appeared in scholarly publications, understanding of the Late Iron Age communities in this part of Europe changed radically. The Celtic peoples east of the Rhine River could no longer be regarded as simpler societies living in smaller, less complex communities than their counterparts west of the Rhine in Gaul. The emerging evidence at Manching made clear that this settlement was urban in character, it had a population much larger than anyone had imagined for a prehistoric community north of the Alps, and it was much more complex economically and socially than scholars had believed.

Since that first exploratory excavation in 1955, teams of researchers have been working almost every summer at Manching. Werner Krämer and his successors have published their ongoing results in exemplary fashion, so that the information is readily available to scholars and other interested readers all over the world. Reasonable estimates place the population of Iron Age Manching at between three thousand and ten thousand people, and the very abundant evidence for industrial activity shows that a large number of specialized industries operated on the site. Over two hundred different types of iron and steel tools have been identified, designed and used for a wide range of manufacturing and processing tasks. The community had a money-based economy. It minted coins made of gold, silver, and bronze, and traded widely with other communities throughout Europe. But with all of the evidence of urban living and a highly complex economy, the people of Manching left no written records to tell us about their traditions or their experiences.

The results from the excavations at Manching have stimulated many other investigations in countries where *oppida* occur, including Austria, Belgium, the Czech Republic, France, Hungary, Luxembourg, Slovakia, Switzerland, and Yugoslavia. But none has been as extensive as the Manching excavations. As of 1998, about 37 acres (15 ha) of the site have been intensively explored, an extraordinarily large area for any one locale, and the quantities of pottery, metal tools and jewelry, animal bones, glass ornaments, and coins recovered from Manching dwarf collections from all other sites of the period. Manching is the standard against which all new finds are compared.

By 15 B.C., when the Roman armies under the command of the generals Tiberius and Drusus marched into the lands south of the Danube that now comprise southern Bavaria, Manching had already declined in importance and retained only a fraction of the population that lived there at its peak, around 120–50 B.C. What happened to all of the people who had lived in the city, and to those in outlying communities who had depended upon the industries at Manching for their manufactured goods? What role did the descendants of Manching's occupants play in the creation of the societies that developed under Roman domination? New discoveries from all over temperate Europe, and new ways of interpreting the evidence, are helping us to answer these questions.

New Perspectives on Indigenous Europeans

The Greek and Roman texts that described the late prehistoric peoples of temperate Europe are typical of accounts written by members of complex literate societies about nonliterate, less complex groups whom they encounter. The texts portrayed the indigenous peoples as static, with no apparent history of social or economic change to account for their present condition. They represented the indigenous peoples as divided into discrete, well-defined groups, referred to in the modern literature as "tribes," to each of which the Classical authors assigned a name, such as Aedui, Boii, Helvetii, and Treveri. Prehistoric archaeology, as well as Roman Period archaeology, developed in the context of the Classical textual sources, and archaeological research has long been guided by the texts. In fact, most research on the Late Iron Age and on the beginning of the Roman Period in temperate Europe is still preoccupied with attempting to match the material evidence with the portrayals in the written sources. But now that we have a better understanding of the nature of such texts, both from recent critical analyses of the Greek and Roman writings and also from broader anthropological studies of the nature of imperial texts in general, we can take a different and more theoretically informed approach to the relation between the texts and the archaeological evidence.

When Roman armies invaded the peoples of temperate Europe, beginning with Caesar's campaigns in Gaul in 58–51 B.C., the communities they encountered belonged to dynamic, open societies that were undergoing profound cultural changes. Roman writers often portrayed the Roman conquest as a transformation in otherwise changeless societies, but the archaeological evidence shows that this event was only one in a whole series of changes experienced by the peoples of temperate Europe. Communities throughout Europe had maintained contact with the Roman world for over a century before the conquests; the interactions are clearly evident in the large quantities of Roman goods on settlements and in burials during the final century of the prehistoric Iron Age. It could be argued that the conquest was just an intensification of interactions that had taken place for generations.

We are sometimes told by modern investigators, especially those with a perspective based on the Mediterranean civilizations, that Rome brought urbanism to temperate Europe. But many of the large and complex settlements known as *oppida* of the Late Iron Age were urban in form and function (see chapter 3). Some of the indigenous peoples of Europe were beginning even to adopt writing before the Roman arrival (see chapter 5). In his account of his campaigns, Caesar mentions the use of writing by the Helvetians.

The Late Iron Age peoples of Europe were certainly not static in the way they are often represented. In order to understand the dynamics of interactions that took place during and after the Roman conquest, we need to take account of the changes that happened before the arrival of the Roman armies, and to view the subsequent changes in the context of those earlier ones. In an important sense, many of the innovations that Rome is credited with introducing had already been adopted well before the Roman arrival.

The archaeological evidence from Late Iron Age Europe shows that the peoples were not clearly delineated into specific groups that might correspond to the tribes named by the Roman and Greek writers. Rather than being long-term social or political entities that had developed during late prehistoric times, these tribes probably represented divisions between groups that had formed in response to the Roman incursions. Thus what the Roman writers perceived as fixed, historically developed entities were in fact short-term creations generated by the Romans themselves (see chapter 5).

This chapter examines the principal changes that were taking place in the societies of temperate Europe shortly before and at the time of the Roman arrival. The essential point I shall be making is that these peoples were dynamic and creative, and when the Roman armies arrived on the scene, they represented one more element—albeit a powerful and persuasive one—in the overall pattern of change that the societies were undergoing.

COMPLEX SOCIETIES OF LATE PREHISTORY

In archaeology, as in all historical social sciences, researchers divide the past into specific "periods"—Stone Age, Bronze Age, Iron Age, Roman Period—and subdivisions within them. Such division is necessary as a means of organizing research and fostering discussion between investigators, but we need to be cautious to remember that the periods are arbitrary categories that we impose on the data. Too often people forget the artificiality of these designations and write as if they had some reality in the past.

I begin my discussion here with the period known as the Late Bronze Age, which archaeologists date to the period 1200 B.C. to 800 B.C. Between the Bronze Age and the Roman Period there are no major discontinuities in the archaeological evidence in temperate Europe—no breaks in the pattern of development that would suggest major migrations in or out. At least from the beginning of the Neolithic Period (around 5000 B.C. in temperate Europe) on, the evidence shows gradual change in all of the regions of Europe, with no abrupt shifts that might indicate large-scale invasion or abandonment of landscapes.

From the Late Bronze Age to the end of the prehistoric Iron Age, we can identify an overall gradual, but not always regular, growth in cultural complexity. Over time, the number of settlements increased, some communities became much larger than any earlier ones, and the sizes of cemeteries indicate an overall growth of population from the Bronze Age to the Late Iron Age. Burial evidence suggests that social differentiation increased; over time, there is a general trend toward greater differences between the richest and poorest burials, but with considerable local variation. The sets of tools available for food production and manufacturing became more complex over time; by the end of the Iron Age, there existed a rich variety of iron tools designed for a multitude of special tasks, such as plowing the soil, harvesting crops, forging iron, casting bronze, carpentry, and leather working. I emphasize that this pattern is apparent only on a broad scale. If we examine in detail changes in individual landscapes, we find some periods with relatively large populations, other periods with smaller ones. For some early centuries we can identify a number of relatively large towns, while for later ones there seem to be fewer. We must avoid viewing later prehistory in terms of "progress." There was no single, universal process of growth in wealth and complexity, but instead many ups and downs at different times and in different places. But viewed from the vantage point of the year A.D. 1999, the evidence shows an increase in the number of people and communities, in the size of settlements, and in the complexity of social arrangements, tool technology, and economic systems during the Iron Age.

From the Late Bronze Age through the Iron Age and into the Roman Period, we can identify certain consistent patterns of behavior among the peoples of temperate Europe. These include wearing particular types of personal ornament, use of specific symbols, practices of funerary ritual and burial, and ways of representing the identity of individuals and groups. These patterns changed over time and varied over space, but certain regularities show the maintenance of specific traditions, behaviors, and values over time. These will be important when we come to consider interactions between indigenous peoples and Roman representatives, and questions concerning the creation of the societies of Roman Period Europe. Such recurring patterns of behavior are an aspect of what has been understood as "culture," a term that anthropologists once used widely but now employ only with great qualification.

By 1000 B.C., the peoples of temperate Europe were practicing a varied agricultural economy. Excavations carried out at hundreds of settlements and cemeteries of this period provide detailed information about the communities. Wheat, barley, and millet were cultivated as cereals, lentils and peas were common legumes, a variety of plants were exploited as sources of oil, and fruits, berries, and nuts were gathered from trees, probably both wild and partly domesticated. Apples, pears, cherries, grapes, raspberries, strawberries, and hazel nuts are well represented by their seeds and shells on settlements. Domesticated animals raised included cattle, pigs, sheep, goats, horses, and dogs. Although there is evidence of hunting on a small scale, indicated by the bones of animals such as red deer and wild boar, most of the meat protein came from the domesticates. Traction plows were in regular use by this time, bronze sickles increased the efficiency of harvesting cereals, and systems of maintaining soil fertility were in use, perhaps manuring and crop rotation.

This broadly based subsistence economy was relatively secure. If a blight affected one crop, or a disease killed one species of livestock, others survived. The basic subsistence economy of temperate Europe did not change substantially from this time until the sixteenth and seventeenth centuries, when New World crops such as potatoes and tomatoes were introduced into the European diet.

Late Bronze Age communities were small. The best evidence for population size comes from cemeteries, and the evidence is consistent in indicating very few communities of more than fifty individuals. Today we would call such communities hamlets or very small villages. Houses were rectangular, built of shaped logs and wattle-and-daub. Some were similar to log cabins of modern times, with walls of horizontal logs, the whole structure lying on a foundation of horizontal sleeper beams resting on the ground. Others had a vertical post construction, with corner and wall posts set in holes dug into the subsoil, and between these posts walls of branchwork (wattle) packed on the interior and exterior with clay (daub). In a few cases where preservation has been exceptionally good, we even find indications that people painted their walls. At Hascherkeller in Bavaria, at least some of the houses had walls painted white with red stripes, evidence for a much more colorful settlement than most reconstructions suggest.

The most common burial practice during the Late Bronze Age was cremation, with cremated remains often placed inside a ceramic urn together with one or more small vessels and small quantities of ornaments, such as pins and bracelets. But some graves were considerably more elaborate in their structure, and more lavishly outfitted, than the majority, and these suggest that substantial differences in wealth and status between individuals had developed by this time. A richly outfitted man's grave at Hart an der Alz in Upper Bavaria, dating to about 1200 B.C., is representative of this group. Unlike the majority of graves of the period, this one was covered by a stone cairn and a mound of earth. The cremated remains of the man had been placed on a four-wheeled wagon, represented in the grave by its many ornate bronze fittings. Accompanying the man was a set of bronze weapons—sword, knife, and arrowheads, as well as a small gold wire fingerring. Also in the grave was a set of seven ornate ceramic vessels of different forms for different purposes. Completing the grave inventory were three vessels made of hammered sheet bronze—a pail, a cup, and a strainer. We know from later contexts that sets of this type were associated with the drinking of wine imported from the Mediterranean world (the strainer was used to filter out spices frequently added to wine in the ancient world), and the possibility of wine trade from the south has been raised in connection with the Hart burial. The four categories of objects placed in the Hart grave that distinguish it from the majority of burials—weapons, gold, feasting equipment, and a wheeled vehicle—remain symbols of elite status throughout European prehistory, during the Roman Period, and in early medieval times. Women's graves of comparable wealth contained quantities of personal ornaments, including pins, bracelets, fingerrings, and head ornaments; occasionally these were of gold. These particular ways of expressing special status in the societies of temperate Europe will be important in later discussions of interaction and change following the Roman conquests.

The fibula as a clothing attachment and as a medium of personal expression (see chapter 1) came into common use during the Late Bronze Age and remained an essential part of personal ornament through the early Middle Ages. Fibulae were made in a variety of different shapes and styles. Often individual fibulae are unique; other times they were mass-produced and large numbers of them are nearly identical. Like modern wedding rings, earrings, and belt buckles, fibulae communicated information about the wearer to others in the society. Research into the meaning of different types of fibulae in different contexts in prehistoric Europe is still in its infancy, but Ludwig Pauli was able to show that in southwestern Germany around 500 B.C., specific kinds of fibulae accompanied women of different statuses in their burials.

Other important devices for communicating information about individuals were also used in the Late Bronze Age. Sheet bronze belt plates, worn by both men and women in some communities, were highly individualistic; no two are identical, though all share the same repertoire of symbols. The cast bronze handles of swords often bear intricate incised linear ornament; as in the case of the belt plates, all are different, though the elements that make up each design are similar. Thin-walled ceramic cups display unique compositions made of arrangements of incised lines, dots, and other shapes. In these three cases, the evidence suggests that the specific pattern—on a belt plate, sword hilt, or cup—represents the individual who owned the object. Perhaps as research progresses on these questions, we shall gain understanding of the specific meanings behind the symbols.

I must say a final word about ritual practice before leaving the Late Bronze Age. I have mentioned burial ritual above, but communities were also engaged in another important category of ritual behavior—the making of offerings. The interpretation of ritual behavior in archaeology is always complex and problematic, and in prehistoric contexts we must be careful not to impose our interpretations too forcefully on the evidence. But we find recurrent patterns of behavior that can best be understood as ritual, and, as we shall see, they correspond closely to behaviors documented from later, historical times.

The most common and readily identifiable ritual practice in the Late Bronze Age was the depositing of valuable objects in places associated with water. Often fine pottery was dropped into disused wells. At Berlin-Lichterfelde, for example, over one hundred intact ornamented cups, many of them containing food and drink, were dropped into a disused well. At many locations along rivers and lakeshores, bronze objects were tossed into water. Hundreds of instances of bronze objects recovered at particular places in rivers and other bodies of water have been recorded throughout temperate Europe, from the Bronze Age through the early Middle Ages. The nature of the occurrences makes it apparent that the

37

majority were not lost accidently, but were deposited purposely. These practices were carried out throughout later prehistoric and historic times and indeed into the present day. The wishing well of folk tradition, into which the wisher drops a coin, is a continuation of this practice. It is interesting to note evidence of the observance of this ritual in fountains in the suburban malls of modern America.

Communities larger and more complex than farming villages first developed in the hilly upland regions of temperate Europe after around 600 B.C., during the period known as the Early Iron Age. Archaeological research carried out at the salt mine complex at Hallstatt in Upper Austria and at fortified hilltop settlements such as Mont Lassois in eastern France, the Heuneburg in southwest Germany, and Závist in Bohemia, reveal the habitations of communities with considerably more members than those in the farming hamlets and villages, and with a substantial proportion of them actively involved in manufacturing and commerce. The populations of these new centers, including both the fortified inner areas and outlying open settlements, may have been in the range of three hundred to five hundred—still a small community by twentieth-century standards, but an order of magnitude larger than any communities before this time in temperate Europe. Excavations at the Heuneburg, Mont Lassois, and Závist reveal dense settlements of closely packed rectangular timber buildings; debris from manufacturing in a variety of materials, including bronze, iron, gold, coral, bone, antler, lignite, and jet; and trade goods from many different regions, including the Greek and Etruscan societies of the Mediterranean basin.

Associated with these centers are indications of increasingly complex social hierarchies in these larger communities. Wealthy burials in this period contain categories of objects similar to those in the preceding period, but the grave assemblages are often considerably more lavish. The richest men's and women's graves contain ornate gold neckrings; bronze feasting equipment, often imported from the Mediterranean world; gold jewelry; and vehicles. The woman who was buried about 500 B.C. at Vix at the foot of the Mont Lassois settlement in eastern France wore an exquisitely crafted gold neckring weighing about 1.06 pounds (480 g) and fibulae adorned with gold ornament. She was accompanied by a four-wheeled wagon, locally made pottery, and a lavish set of feasting equipment from the Mediterranean world. This set included an Etruscan bronze wine jug, two Etruscan bronze basins, two fine painted wine cups from Athens, and a unique 458-pound (208 kg), 5-foot-5-inch (1.64 m) high bronze mixing vessel made in a Greek workshop, probably in a colony in southern Italy. The man buried at Hochdorf near Stuttgart in southwest Germany, dated at about the same time as the Vix grave, was interred on a bronze couch wearing gold fibulae, bracelet, and neckring, his dagger sheath and handles were coated with gold, and even his shoes had gold covers. Besides a wagon laden with dinnerware, he had a bronze cauldron from the Greek world, a gold dipping bowl, and nine drinking horns of iron with gold bands (Figures 4 and 5).

These Early Iron Age centers were all in contact with the complex societies of the Mediterranean world. Excavations of the settlements have yielded quantities of ceramic amphorae used to transport wine and fine Greek pottery, particularly the ornate Attic wine-consuming equipment represented by the two cups in the Vix grave. Like the Vix burial, all of the richest graves at the centers contain some Mediterranean imports, mainly fine pottery and bronze vessels. These vessels are all part of accoutrements of the wine-drinking ritual in Greek and Etruscan societies, a practice documented in Greek texts and in pictorial representations on Greek pottery and on Etruscan wall paintings. This wine-drinking ritual played a special role in status display and social competition in those Mediterranean societies. The occurrence of sets of such equipment, including mixing vessels, serving jugs, and drinking cups, in the wealthy graves of temperate Europe suggests that those elites were borrowing not only the objects, but also some aspects of the behaviors with which the objects were associated in Greece and Etruria. The outfitting of the rich Early Iron Age graves with ornate imported feasting equipment compares closely with feasting behavior among elites in many other societies. This expression in the burial ritual of feasting activity will be a subject to which I shall return in subsequent chapters.

The precise nature of the interactions between communities in temperate Europe and the Mediterranean societies is not well understood, but they are currently thought to have revolved around trade. Temperate European societies had access to a range of forest products and other raw materials that were in short supply in the Greek world at this time. The Phocaean Greek colony of Massalia, on the site of modern Marseille, was established around 600 B.C., about the same time that the centers in temperate Europe developed and that substantial quantities of Mediterranean imports began to arrive at communities north of the Alps. Etruscan commercial centers were also expanding their activity during this

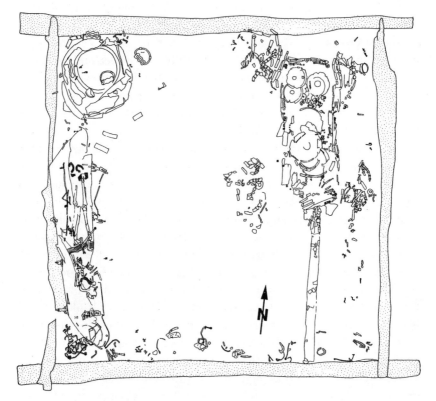

Fig. 4. Plan showing the arrangement of feasting objects and other grave goods in the burial at Hochdorf near Stuttgart. This is one of about forty richly outfitted graves from 550 to 500 B.C. in western central Europe, and is one of very few that had not been looted before its excavation by archaeologists in 1979. Along the west wall *(left)* is the skeleton of a man, and at his feet *(upper left)* a bronze cauldron. On the east wall *(right)* are the remains of a wagon with bronze vessels on it. Along the south wall *(bottom)* are fragments of drinking horns. From Biel 1985b, p. 78, fig. 78. Used by permission of Jörg Biel, Landesdenkmalamt Baden-Württemberg, Stuttgart.

period; many of the imported wine vessels found in temperate Europe originated at the Etruscan bronze-working center of Vulci.

Certainly the interactions between elite groups in temperate Europe and communities on the Mediterranean coasts were more complex than commercial trade, however. The patterning of the Mediterranean wine-consuming equipment—ceramic cups and mixing vessels, as well as bronze jugs, basins, and cauldrons—in the graves and on the settlements

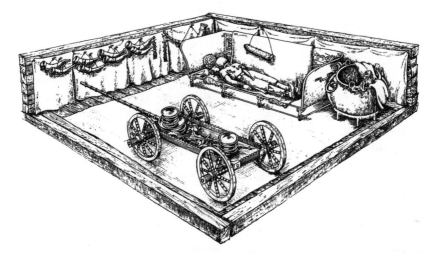

Fig. 5. Reconstruction drawing of the arrangement of the grave goods in the Hochdorf burial. Skeletal remains of a 30-year-old man, outfitted with elaborate gold ornaments and an ornate dagger, lie on a bronze couch. At the foot of the couch is a bronze cauldron from a Greek workshop, and on cloth draped over it, a locally made gold drinking bowl. The wagon holds stacks of bronze vessels. Along the south wall are the fragmentary remains of nine drinking horns, one much larger than the others, all made of iron and decorated with gold bands. This elaborate set of feasting equipment emphasizes the role of the deceased man as a host who distributed food and drink to his followers. From Biel 1985b, p. 102, fig. 119. Used by permission of Jörg Biel.

strongly suggests that not only the objects, but also information about how they were used in ritual was transmitted from the Mediterranean world to temperate Europe, whether through Europeans observing the customs in the Mediterranean world, or Greeks or Etruscans visiting temperate Europe and demonstrating their customs. A Greek-style wall of clay bricks at the Heuneburg, and several life-size sculptures of local stone expressing Mediterranean sculptural styles, further attest to the transfer not just of objects, but of technical know-how. The most significant aspect of all this evidence for interaction is that some people, at least, in temperate Europe—in the lands to be conquered by Rome five centuries later—were becoming familiar with aspects of Mediterranean society and lifestyles and clearly found them very attractive.

In the northern part of the region we are considering in this book—on the North European Plain of northern Germany and the Low Coun-

41

tries—there is little indication either of the formation of larger communities or of the development of interactions with peoples of the Mediterranean Basin. Cemetery and settlement evidence both indicate that communities remained very small, at most a few families living together practicing agricultural and livestock-raising economies. Craft production remained largely domestic in its organization, with little evidence for specialization. Mediterranean imports in this part of Europe are rare, and no burials have been found that compare in wealth with Vix, Hochdorf, and the other elite graves at the centers to the south.

La Tène Style and Celts

During the first half of the fifth century B.C., a new style of ornament appeared in temperate Europe. Early La Tène (La Tène is the name of a site on the shore of Lake Neuchâtel in Switzerland) ornament is characterized by curving forms based on plant motifs, rather than the geometrical straight lines, rectangles, rhomboids, triangles, and circles that formed the decorative repertoire of the preceding centuries. The new ornament occurs particularly on metalwork, including ring jewelry, fibulae, bronze vessels, and weaponry, but also on other ornaments, pottery, and stonework. Many of the earliest examples are on gold objects and bronzes of exceptionally fine workmanship, and they occur in especially rich burials in the middle Rhine region.

The range of materials in which the Early La Tène style is expressed, with similar motifs often represented in different materials, attests to a high degree of craft specialization. But we know little about how craft production was organized. Considerable discussion has revolved around whether the objects were manufactured in fixed workshops, or by craftworkers who moved from place to place serving customers. Since there is little direct evidence for workshops—such as structures containing the debris from metalworking—most studies rely exclusively on comparisons between final products and on their geographical distributions. The lack of substantial physical evidence for workshops, and the small size of known implements used in the process of making ornaments, such as those found close to the burial at Hochdorf, strongly suggest that many or most objects were made by mobile metalworkers who carried their tools and raw materials with them. On the basis of the tools for fine metalworking that were recovered in the rich grave at La Gorge Meillet in eastern France, it has been suggested that members of the elite group, with whom most early examples of the new style have been found, actually produced many of their own ornaments.

Many archaeologists believe that the new style was developed in conjunction with the emergence of a new identity for people who came to be named *Keltoi* (Celts) by Greek writers in the fifth century B.C. Current interpretation suggests that the Early La Tène style was developed sometime around 480–470 B.C. in the middle Rhineland, perhaps specifically in the Hunsrück-Eifel area. This is the region in which many early and highly distinctive specimens ornamented in the new style have been found, and it is also a region in which large numbers of Etruscan imports, particularly bronze vessels that form parts of feasting sets, have been recovered from rich burials. The motifs that characterize Early La Tène ornament and distinguish it from that of the preceding period were adopted by the local craftworkers from objects made in the Mediterranean region. The motifs had been current in the arts of Greece and Etruria well before they appeared in temperate Europe, and the new style appeared in the middle Rhineland at the time that numerous objects bearing such motifs were transported from Mediterranean lands to that region. The local craftworkers did not simply copy motifs from southern models, but selected certain ones for adoption and transformed them into distinctive local patterns.

This new style may have been a vehicle for establishing the identity of the elite groups who created and used it. As they rose to wealth and power in the middle Rhine region during the fifth century B.C., they created these signs of a new identity to distinguish themselves from the elites to the south, at the old centers such as Mont Lassois and the Heuneburg. Early on, the new style was restricted to small groups of elites represented in wealthy burials, but after a generation or two, it was adopted more broadly. This style became popular at this time probably because there were good reasons why the peoples of southern temperate Europe wanted to differentiate themselves from their neighbors to the north and to the south. They were interacting increasingly with groups on the north European plain at this time (see below), and interactions with peoples of the Mediterranean lands were also growing in intensity. Such situations of increased extra-group interaction commonly create the need to develop signs of identity to serve as boundary markers between "us" and "them."

North of the central uplands, on the North European Plain, the character of the material culture was different. Just as this northern region differed from southern temperate Europe in the Early Iron Age in that it lacked centers, craft specialization, wealthy burials, and Mediterranean imports, during the fifth century B.C. it remained separate in maintaining its own distinctive style of ornament, known as Jastorf after a cemetery in north-central Germany. During the fifth century B.C., the new La Tène style of ornament spread from the middle Rhineland throughout the central regions of the continent. By about 400 B.C., metalwork especially, but also some other aspects of material culture, shows a strong degree of uniformity throughout the hilly upland regions. This stylistic divide at the boundary between the North European Plain and the central uplands of Europe became increasingly marked during succeeding centuries (see map, Figure 16).

MIGRATION AND INTERACTION

The Early Iron Age centers declined and were abandoned sometime around the middle of the fifth century B.C., at which time the series of wealthy burials associated with them also ended. Archaeologists disagree about the reasons for this decline. One possibility is that the trade connection along the Rhône River with the Greek colony at Massalia was disrupted, perhaps because of political changes in the central Mediterranean region, perhaps because Greek merchants found more accessible supplies elsewhere. Following this argument, since the centers had developed around that trade, when the trade ended, the centers collapsed. Another model posits internal unrest among people at and around the centers, leading to popular uprisings that overthrew the elites in power. In this scenario, proponents point to the increasing social distance between elites and others implied by the ever-richer graves dating toward the end of the sixth century B.C. It is possible that both of these mechanisms played a part in the demise of the Early Iron Age centers. Along with the breakdown of the centers and of the regular trade with the Mediterranean world, we also observe a sharp decline in the manufacture of fine craft products of gold and of hammered bronze and a return to a more domestic, rather than specialized, system of manufacturing.

The series of rich graves containing objects of Early La Tène ornament ended by around 400 B.C. The cultural landscape of the fourth and third centuries B.C. was characterized by small agricultural communities and relatively little social differentiation reflected in burials. There were no towns known comparable to those of the Early Iron Age, and very few unusually rich graves.

The burial evidence indicates that communities were small, with usually fewer than fifty people living in farmsteads and hamlets. The predominant burial practice was inhumation in flat graves. Almost half of the men were buried with iron weapons, particularly swords and spears, sometimes shields, and occasionally helmets, and sometimes with one or two personal ornaments such as a fibula or a bracelet. The prevalence of weapons as burial goods suggests that men's status as warriors was a particularly important social factor at this time. Many bronze scabbards bear ornamentation, and each is decorated differently. Just as noted above for the sword hilts of the Late Bronze Age, here too were signs of identity of individual warriors.

Women were buried with bronze jewelry, including neckrings, bracelets, legrings, and fibulae. Women's burial equipment was usually much more ornate and complex than men's. The bronze neckrings were often highly ornamented, and each specimen was unique, suggesting that these objects bore signs pertaining to the identity of the wearer. Probably neckrings were selected as the principal bearers of such information, because they were worn where they could easily be seen and "read" by others. Most women were buried with fibulae, sometimes one or two, other times many. Like the neckrings, many of the fibulae bore complex and unique ornament; they too probably played a role in communicating information about the wearer.

The number of Mediterranean imports in temperate Europe declined sharply during the fourth century B.C. But ancient textual sources inform us of two important mechanisms through which individuals and groups from temperate Europe interacted with peoples of the Mediterranean region. One was migration, the other mercenary service.

Textual sources by Greek and Roman writers inform us that the fourth and third centuries B.C. were a time of active emigration of people from central regions of temperate Europe westward, southward, and eastward. The archaeological evidence for these migrations is sparse and ambiguous. Ancient writers, including particularly the Roman historian Livy, indicate that groups from central Europe crossed the Alps to raid and to settle in Italy. Some moved through eastern Europe and southeast to Delphi, and others pushed on into Asia Minor, where they became known as Galatians. The majority of such migrants probably came as settlers in search of new farmlands, but the raiding parties made a stronger impression on the ancient writers. Attacks on Etruscan communities in the Po Plain of northern Italy, the sacking of Rome in 387 B.C., and the attack on the Greek sanctuary of Delphi in 279–278 B.C. were important in creating a generalized and long-lasting fear of northern peoples on the part of populations of Italy and Greece.

While it is apparent from the historical sources that some groups of people moved from central and western Europe into southern and eastern parts of the continent, it is very difficult to estimate the scale of these migrations. There is no archaeological evidence in temperate Europe, such as major breaks in settlement or cemetery sequences, to suggest substantial depopulation of landscapes because of out-migration. One reason may be that many of the migrants returned to their homelands after a time. A recent examination of migration as a universal phenomenon found that a majority of migrants returned to their homelands, sometimes after only a short stay abroad, sometimes after a longer absence. If this pattern obtained in Iron Age Europe, then the textual accounts may be accurate, but incomplete; the writers may not have known about, or failed to describe, return migration.

In some cases, as in northern Italy, archaeological evidence supports the ancient writers' accounts of migration. Cemeteries in the Po Plain and along the Adriatic coast of northeast Italy indicate the arrival of groups from north of the Alps, bringing with them their characteristic burial practice, long iron swords, and jewelry ornamented in the La Tène style. It is significant that many of these groups continued to reproduce the La Tène style in their ornament, apparently as a means to re-create and reemphasize their identity as distinct from those of their neighbors. Rather than blending into the local context of their new homelands, they chose to maintain their separate identity as Gauls. In fact, many of the objects that best exemplify the extreme expressions of La Tène art originated during this time not in temperate Europe, but in peripheral areas newly settled by emigrants from there. These include a large number of ornate bronze helmets, fibulae, ring jewelry, and appliques from northern, eastern, and central Italy, and even the extraordinarily richly ornamented Canosa helmet from southern Italy, as well as the comparably extravagant helmet from Ciumeşti in Romania. Such extreme expressions of style are characteristic of situations in which people living removed from their homelands, among groups of different cultural traditions, display exaggerated forms of their traditions in order to emphasize their distinctive identity.

Numerous Classical authors tell of Celtic mercenaries serving in armies of Mediterranean peoples during the fourth and third centuries B.C. The accounts record their service in various Greek and Carthaginian armies, and places mentioned in which they saw mercenary duty include southern Italy, Sicily, Corsica, Sardinia, Greece, north Africa, and Egypt. It is not always clear from the accounts where the particular contingents of Celtic mercenaries came from. In some instances the sources indicate origins north of the Alps, but other times the troops came from Gallic groups in northern Italy and southeastern Europe. Details about the hiring arrangements and systems of payment are not clear, but at least one account mentions payment to them in gold coins. Such mercenary experience was important in familiarizing many young central European men with the Mediterranean world. Most probably returned home after their service, though the texts tell little about that aspect, and when they did, they brought with them wealth, including their pay in the form of gold coins; knowledge about lifestyles, languages, and ideology of Mediterranean peoples; and, at least in some cases, desire to emulate aspects of the Mediterranean way of life. To judge by the surviving textual sources, Celtic mercenary service in the Mediterranean world declined around the beginning of the second century B.C.

CHAPTER 3

Iron Age Urbanization

URBANIZATION AND COMPLEXITY

Beginning in the second century B.C., textual sources written by Greek and Roman writers about peoples north of the Alps become much more abundant and more detailed than ever before, and they provide some important background information against which we need to interpret the archaeological evidence. Texts inform us that Rome became actively involved militarily and politically in southern Gaul, particularly in the area around Marseille, during the second century B.C., and these actions culminated in the establishment of the Roman province Gallia Narbonensis around 120 B.C. This military, political, and administrative presence of Rome in southern Gaul meant intensifying interaction between the peoples of temperate Europe and the expanding Roman world.

Greek and Roman texts tell of migrations of peoples within temperate Europe from the latter part of the second century B.C. on, starting with the Cimbri and the Teutones, and including the Ambrones, the Boii, the Helvetii, the Suebi, and others. The earliest of these was the migration of the Cimbri, people said to be from the north of Europe (modern interpretations place them in the northern part of Jutland), who moved southward in 113 B.C., and, joined by the Teutones, also from the north, engaged and defeated a Roman army near Noreia, most likely a site in what is now Austria. From there they moved to Gaul, where, at Arausio (modern Orange) in the south, they delivered another major defeat to the Roman armies in 105 B.C. These victories over Roman forces alarmed Rome, especially since the sites of the battles were close to Italy, and the memory of the sacking of Rome by barbarians from the north in 387 B.C. was still powerful. The Roman consul Marius reorganized the army to meet the threatening groups, and in 102 B.C. finally beat the Ambrones, and then the Teutones, at decisive battles at Aquae Sextiae, modern Aix-en-Provence. The next year, 101 B.C., he led Roman troops in a crushing defeat of the Cimbri at Vercellae on the Po Plain, the precise location of which is unclear.

There is not a great deal of information in the Classical sources about the migrations of these peoples nor about the size of the groups on the move. The ancient writers indicate that the Cimbri were in search of new farmlands and that their migrations included their families and portable possessions. At Aquae Sextiae, the total number of barbarians, including women and children, is estimated at around one hundred thousand, the Roman troop strength at about thirty-two thousand. It is difficult to know whether these numbers are close to the actual counts, but even allowing for considerable exaggeration, the accounts suggest massive military confrontations. We are informed that Marius organized a rush by his cavalry down from a hilltop location against the Teutones, together with an assault by the infantry. The Roman legionary soldiers were outfitted with helmets, mail shirts, javelins, shields, short swords, and daggers. According to the accounts, the Cimbri and Teutones were similarly equipped with helmets, iron body armor, shields, and javelins, but they carried long swords instead of the short Roman type. While we do not know details of tactics and battlefield organization, it is apparent that battles were sometimes on a large scale and resulted in decisive outcomes.

These and the other recorded migrations, whatever their scale, contributed to the breaking down of existing boundaries between peoples, and the bringing of groups from different parts of the continent into close interaction, sometimes peacefully and sometimes not. The migrations had an important immediate effect on the Romans, reminding them of the sacking of Rome by Gallic marauders two and a half centuries earlier and the settlement of bands of northerners in the Po Plain and along the Adriatic coast of northern Italy. Caesar was strongly influenced by the historical tradition surrounding the Cimbri and Teutones when he embarked on his military campaigns against the Gauls half a century later. Like other migrations mentioned in the ancient texts, those of the Cimbri and Teutones, and the subsequent migrations by other groups, are not readily apparent in the archaeological record. There is increasing evidence for interaction between communities in northern and southern parts of temperate Europe, but it is difficult to distinguish results of migration from those of trade, gift exchange, and other kinds of interaction.

LATE IRON AGE CENTERS: THE *OPPIDA*

Beginning sometime around the middle of the second century B.C., a new type of settlement was established in temperate Europe in the regions in which the La Tène style of ornament was prevalent. The new settlements are known as *oppida*, after Caesar's use of that term (Figure

49

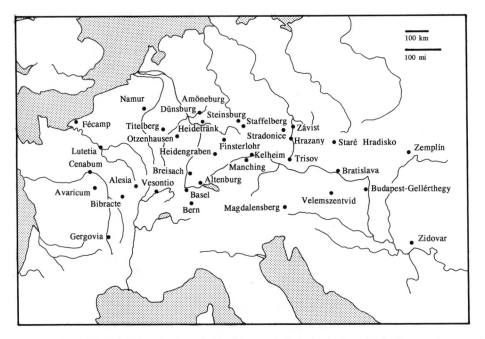

Fig. 6. Map showing the locations of some of the principal *oppida* in Europe.

6). They were large settlements, fortified with extensive walls, and usually situated on defensible hilltops. In the size of the enclosed areas and in the quantities of debris from industrial activities that had been carried out inside these settlements, they were much bigger and more complex than the Early Iron Age centers that had flourished between about 600 and 450 B.C. (see chapter 2). The Greek and Roman writers provide no information about the origins and development of these new, larger settlements, and all of our knowledge about them derives from the archaeological evidence, until Caesar encountered these centers in Gaul during his campaigns of 58–51 B.C. Although each *oppidum* was unique, there are significant similarities between them across the whole of their distribution from central France in the west to Slovakia in the east. Similar details in the structure of walls and gates and in organization of the interiors indicate the exchange of information and sharing of architectural knowledge across the continent. The similarity of the material culture recovered in the settlement deposits—pottery, iron tools, bronze ornaments, glass jewelry, and coins—also indicates strong contacts between communities that inhabited the centers.

The appearance of the *oppida* is an important sign of increased organizational complexity and formation of settlement hierarchies. Many inves-

Fig. 7. Map of the town of Manching in Bavaria, Germany, showing the remaining portions of the wall (semicircle in right half of map) that enclosed the Late Iron Age *oppidum* settlement. Parts of the prehistoric settlement investigated as of 1985 are indicated as follows: *shaded gray:* areas excavated; *hatched:* surveyed; *parallel lines within the enclosing walls:* trenched. From Maier 1986, plan 1. Used by permission of Susanne Sievers, Römisch-Germanische Kommission (RGK), Frankfurt.

tigators consider the *oppida* to have been the first urban communities in temperate Europe. This conclusion is based partly on the now abundant archaeological evidence from many excavated sites and partly on Caesar's statements about the tribal centers of Gaul. The massive walls that surround the *oppidum* settlements enclose areas much larger than any earlier sites. Many are between 100 and 250 acres (50–100 ha) in area; Manching in Bavaria (Figure 7) is nearly 1,000 acres (380 ha) and Kelheim nearly

1,500 acres (600 ha). Many of the investigated *oppida*, such as Bibracte in central France, Manching in Bavaria, and Stradonice in Bohemia, have yielded evidence for communities much larger than those at earlier settlements—with populations in the thousands, and extensive indications of manufacturing and trade. Large quantities of iron-working remains have been recovered at many of the sites, including Manching and Kelheim. Bronze-casting, coin-minting, glass jewelry production, leather-working, and the processing of a range of other materials are regularly represented. The *oppida* were also centers of commerce, both within their regions and beyond. Each *oppidum* minted distinctive types of coins, and at some *oppida* thousands of coins have been recovered by archaeologists. Analysis of these finds by numismatists shows that coins were circulating widely all over Europe. *Oppidum* communities were also engaged in interaction with the Roman world. Ceramic amphorae, fine pottery, bronze vessels, coins, writing implements, medical tools, and a variety of other objects from Roman Italy have been recovered at *oppidum* settlements. Significantly, the most common imports are those associated with feasting behavior, and especially with wine-drinking, as was the case four centuries earlier at the Early Iron Age centers (see chapter 2).

But excavation results show that not all of the settlements inside the walls were as dense as those at Manching, Stradonice, and other major sites. Some, such as Tarodunum near Freiburg in Germany, have yielded only sparse traces of habitation. Such sites must have been constructed to serve as defensive refuges in times of invasion, but not occupied permanently.

Explanations for the establishment of these large defended settlements have tended to emphasize their military and economic character. In light of the trends identified above—increasing interaction with peoples to the north and to the south, and formation of larger and more hierarchical social and political structures—an explanation for the *oppida* in terms of political and ideological processes is worth exploring. Rather than reflecting primarily specific defensive needs or responses to economic intensification, the *oppida* may be the physical outcome of trends toward the formation of larger and structurally more complex communities, and of the need to concentrate production of goods—for economic and for expressive purposes—that were required to support the newly centralized political and social system. A number of archaeologists argue that the *oppidum* walls were constructed not only for defense, but largely for expressive purposes, to emphasize the power of the community over its territory. In his commentaries Caesar portrayed the *oppida* of Gaul as political centers of tribal territories, but of course it is unlikely that he understood the larger processes of political change of which they were a part.

Contemporaneous with the *oppida* and similarly distributed in temperate Europe are rectangular enclosures defined by banks and ditches known by their German term *Viereckschanzen* (literally, "rectangular enclosures"). Many hundreds have been identified, often close to *oppida*—in a few cases even inside them—but also frequently in areas far from the large fortified settlements. There has long been debate about the function of these enclosures, but most archaeologists now accept the interpretation that the majority were ritual places of some kind. Excavations have shown that many have in them deep shafts in which various objects have been recovered. Some investigators interpret these objects as offerings purposefully dropped into the shafts, while others argue that the shafts were wells and that objects found were part of the apparatus for raising water. These interpretations need not be mutually exclusive, since wells have long served ritual functions, as they have into modern times in the form of the wishing well (see above). The enclosures often include, in one corner, postholes from substantial structures, indicating walls of house-like buildings, and smaller posts outside them suggesting supports for a roof covering a passage around the outside of the building.

Klaus Schwarz, who excavated the important *Viereckschanze* at Holzhausen south of Munich, linked the enclosures with the Greek term *temenos*, meaning sacred space, and argued that the enclosures were the material manifestation of ritual places among the people of temperate Europe mentioned by Classical authors. Current discussion of these sites often focuses on finds that do not suggest a strictly ritual function but rather a more secular one. Many investigators take too normative an approach to the interpretation of the enclosures. They do not all need to adhere to precisely the same pattern in order for them to have a general significance as ritual places. According to all of the information currently available, the most likely interpretation is that they were primarily used for some kind of ritual activities, whether religious, celebratory, or even political. This interpretation does not exclude the possibility that some enclosures were used for different, or even multiple, purposes.

GROWTH OF COMPLEX ECONOMIES

Coinage is a good indicator of the integration of communities in Late Iron Age temperate Europe. The minting of coins coincided with the distribution of the *oppida*. Many were the sites of mints, but coins were also minted at other, smaller settlements in the same regions. The first indigenous coins in temperate Europe were minted during the third century B.C., and the designs were based on Greek prototypes. Researchers agree that the idea of coinage was introduced into the region by mercenaries returning from Greece (see chapter 2). The gold staters that served as models for the first coins minted in temperate Europe probably represented about a month's pay for an average soldier. We cannot consider such gold coins as money in the sense of a standard value for use in everyday exchange, because they were so valuable. More likely, a gold coin constituted a form of treasure or wealth that could be accumulated.

Around the time the *oppida* developed during the second century B.C., silver and bronze coinages appeared, modeled on Roman currencies (Figure 8). With the addition of silver and bronze coins, we can speak of a true money economy at the *oppida*. Numismatists can identify the origin of individual coins—different regions and different *oppida* minted their own specific types, and the distributions of the hundreds of thousands of known Late Iron Age coins show that they circulated widely between the different regions of Europe. The standardization of their weights indicates a common system of value among the communities that used them across the continent.

Other kinds of evidence demonstrate other aspects of the fundamental changes indicated by the emergence of the *oppida*, the enclosures, and coinage. Objects made at the centers show that a fundamental shift took place in the organization of manufacturing, from a pattern in which production was primarily domestic and family-based to one in which it was largely specialized and intended for commerce rather than just domestic consumption. Before the appearance of the *oppida*, we do not have evidence for mass production of pottery and iron tools. The potter's wheel was first used on a large scale at the time of the *oppida*, and mass production of iron implements began at the same time. The result was a new level of standardization of products manufactured at the centers and distributed to outlying communities through a commercial network.

This change is also apparent in personal ornaments, such as fibulae. Previously many objects that were worn on the person, such as fibulae, were unique in their form and ornamentation (see chapter 2). In the course of the second century B.C., a change took place, and the majority of fibulae became more standardized and less ornate. The Nauheim fibula, the most common type between 150 and 50 B.C., is a good example. It is a form that was mass-produced and usually carried very little ornament. The range of variation among Nauheim fibulae is slight compared

Fig. 8. Four Celtic coins from the *oppidum* settlement at Kelheim in
Bavaria. *(1)* and *(2)* are silver-covered copper, *(3)* and *(4)* are bronze.
Photographs by Bernhard Overbeck. From Overbeck and
Wells 1991, plate 11. Used by permission of Bernhard Overbeck,
Staatliche Münzsammlung, Munich.

to that of earlier types. The proliferation of this new form suggests a
change in the relationships between people and the ornaments they
wore. The decrease in the amount of individualized information transmitted by unique objects suggests that individual identities were becoming less important in social interaction, and membership in larger corpo-
rate groups more important. This shift coincides with the increasing
degree of homogeneity in the material culture as a whole, discussed
above. Larger social and political systems require disproportionately
more energy than smaller ones for information processing and decision
making. In this sense, we can understand the changing patterns of manufacturing and new types of fibulae, pottery, and other goods in terms of
a fundamental shift in the relationship between people and the objects
that they made and used, and between individuals and groups in Late
Iron Age societies.

During the second century B.C., evidence for interaction between peoples in northern Europe, particularly Denmark and southern and central
Sweden, and the central regions of the continent increased greatly. Metalwork ornamented in the La Tène style appeared more frequently in
Denmark and surrounding lands, particularly in the form of fibulae, belt
equipment, ring ornaments, and animal figurines. Until recently, much
of this metalwork was interpreted as the products of metalsmiths in central Europe that were imported into Denmark. But recent analyses have
shown that though the style of many objects clearly derives from the La
Tène style of the south, the objects show distinctive features indicating
local manufacture. Most likely, local metalworkers adopted elements of

La Tène style that they observed on imported objects, and transformed those elements to suit their own products. Likewise, blue glass bracelets very similar to those manufactured at the *oppida* became common in the Netherlands during the second and first centuries B.C. It is not clear to what extent these objects were imports from the *oppidum* workshops and to what extent local products.

In many of the northern regions of Europe, where these growing contacts with central Europe are particularly evident, processes of formation of larger, more hierarchical communities are in evidence at the same time that the *oppida* were emerging to the south, though the northern communities remained much smaller. Excavations at Hodde on Jutland revealed a village substantially larger than earlier ones, with some twenty-eight farmsteads enclosed by a common fence. One farmstead, with its own fence separating it from the other twenty-seven, was distinguished by more substantial buildings than the rest and by pottery of notably higher quality. The fortified settlement of Borremose similarly shows a trend toward the development of some farmsteads that were larger and better constructed than the majority and whose occupants had access to finer goods than others did. Jes Martens has referred to these as "magnate" farms and interprets them in terms of the rise to power of a small number of families concerned with drawing distinctions between themselves and other members of their communities. Even before the Roman conquests in temperate Europe that started with Caesar's advance into Gaul in 58 B.C., a few Roman bronze vessels were brought as far north as Scandinavia, where they have been recovered in contexts of this late pre-Roman Iron Age. At Gudme on the Danish island of Fyn, both the settlement remains and the burials in the Møllegårdsmarken cemetery attest to the early stages in the formation of a center that played a major role in long-distance interactions during the Roman Period, as we shall see below (chapter 10).

SOCIETY AND EVERYDAY LIFE

Archaeology enables us to reconstruct the basic economic character of daily life of Iron Age Europeans with some confidence, while for matters such as social organization and religious belief, the archaeological evidence is more difficult to interpret. On these issues we must cautiously consult the problematic evidence in the writings of Greek and Roman commentators. The archaeological evidence makes clear that different individuals possessed different status in late prehistoric society. From the Late Bronze Age on, the burial evidence makes clear that some individuals were accorded considerably more elaborate burial monuments and much richer grave goods than others. But in Europe, no prehistoric burials suggest the great social distance between individuals that is represented in some other ancient societies, such as in Mesopotamia at the Royal Cemetery of Ur, in China at An-yang, or in Peru at Chan Chan. European Iron Age societies were smaller-scale than those, and the social system was less hierarchical.

In his description of the Gauls at the time of his conquests, Caesar wrote that their social structure consisted of two categories of people, an elite of druids and knights, and everybody else, who had very little status compared to the elite. The burial evidence does not suggest such a straightforward division, but instead a wide range of variation without any distinct breaks in wealth or status. The tribes that Caesar and other authors described may have been very recent formations, created in response to the Roman advance (see chapter 5). Many investigators think that before the Roman arrival on the scene, the peoples of temperate Europe were organized in small-scale, family-based territorial units. This idea would correspond well with the archaeological evidence and its lack of a stratified hierarchy extending beyond the local community. According to the burial evidence, each territorial unit had elite and non-elite individuals, but there is no indication of any overarching leadership structure to integrate multiple units. The tribes or nations described by Caesar and Tacitus are likely to have formed only when communities were faced with outside threats, and then the elites of the communities coming together would have been likely to choose a leader—chief or king—to oversee their responses to the threats.

Excavated settlement sites inform us about the existence of large centers—the *oppida*, some of which had populations in the thousands, smaller towns of several hundred inhabitants, villages and hamlets, and farmsteads—agricultural complexes inhabited by single extended families (up to perhaps fifteen people). The vast majority of people in temperate Europe lived in hamlets and villages, probably communities with populations between twenty and one hundred. They built their houses by first sinking trunks of medium-sized trees into the ground as corner and wall posts, then bending branches (often hazel wood) between them and packing outside and inside with clay—the technique known as wattle-and-daub. The branchwork created the wall's strength, the daub sealed the wall against moisture and wind. Roofs were thatched of straw.

Houses were rectangular and typically between 200 and 600 sq. ft. (20–50 m²) in area. Each house had a hearth inside. A pit for storing food—a necessity before artificial refrigeration—was situated under the floor or just outside the house.

In general, each house was occupied by one family, though of course family size varied. The archaeological evidence suggests that marriages for the most part were monogamous. Though the vast majority of graves contain a single individual, some have in them one man and one woman, suggesting the burial of man and wife together. Graves that contain one woman and more than one man, or one man and more than one woman, are very rare. What little information we have about the customs of the Iron Age peoples in the writings of Greek and Roman authors also suggests that monogamy was the rule, though there is evidence that some elite males may have had more than one wife.

Animal bones recovered on settlements indicate that people relied principally on cattle and pigs for meat, cattle for dairy products, and sheep for wool. Preserved seeds and other plant parts show that spelt, emmer, and einkorn wheats, along with barley and millet, were the principal cereal crops, and lentils and peas were significant legumes. A wide range of fruits and berries were gathered around the settlements, and some hunting was done as well. Most of people's nutrition came from agriculture and from domesticated livestock.

By the Late Iron Age, iron production was widespread. Most communities larger than hamlets had on-site iron-working, and by this time iron was in use for a wide range of purposes, including for plowshares to break the soil, scythes for harvesting hay for winter fodder, and nails for building houses, furniture, and wagons. Bronze was still used for ornaments, as were gold and silver for people who could afford them. Glass bracelets and beads were much in favor as ornaments, especially by women, and imported amber was also valued for beads. Wood working, bone carving, and leather working were important for a variety of household purposes.

Most settlements yield evidence of weaving, in the form of ceramic loom weights used to hold taut the fibers on a vertical loom and spindle whorls (weights to keep the spindle turning while fiber was spun). Both wool and linen garments are well attested at sites where unusual chemical conditions resulted in the preservation of organic fibers. In burials and bog offerings in northern Germany and Denmark, lakeshore settlements in Switzerland, Germany, and other circum-Alpine countries, and in the salt mines at Hallstatt and Hallein in Austria, numerous items of clothing have been preserved in remarkably good condition. We have evidence of tunics—loose, shirtlike garments—for both men and women, trousers for men, shawls for women, and cloaks for both sexes in cold weather. Women's hairnets survive on some Danish sites. Caps of fur and of sheepskin are known from Hallstatt and other places. Both men and women wore leather shoes. Some textiles show that garments were colorfully decorated with plaid patterns. Rare finds of silk and of gold threads indicate how wealthy individuals displayed their status in their clothing.

It is very difficult to reconstruct religious beliefs in Iron Age Europe. We have good evidence for the practice of rituals—I have mentioned water offerings, deposits in shafts, and the *Viereckschanzen* above, but what these rituals meant to people is not at all clear. Among the most striking sites of Late Iron Age ritual behavior is Gournay-sur-Aronde in northern France. Between the fourth century B.C. and the Roman conquest, hundreds or thousands of animals seem to have been sacrificed there, and over two thousand fragmentary weapons attest to the intentional destruction of implements for deposition on the site. Ironically, it is not until after the Roman conquest that we learn the names and attributes of indigenous Celtic and Germanic deities; and of course, then we must ask the extent to which these conceptions had already changed as the result of contact with the Roman world. Caesar and a few other commentators mention druids as members of a priestly class among the Celts (Caesar tells us that the Germans had no druids), but we learn very little about beliefs or practices from those references. There is no clear archaeological evidence for druids.

The evidence that we can extract from the Classical sources and from early medieval Irish mythological tales suggests that the Iron Age peoples believed in the existence of numerous spirits and minor deities in the natural world, along with a few more substantial, inter-regional deities such as mother goddesses and sky gods. It is possible, but cannot at present be demonstrated, that the numerous offerings deposited in rivers, lakes, shafts, and pits were intended as gifts to these various deities, in requesting favors or in gratitude for favors granted. This is an area in which systematic research in the future is likely to be very productive of new understanding.

A few Classical accounts mention human sacrifice, but there is little archaeological evidence for this practice. In assessing such accounts, we must bear in mind that the Greek and Roman authors usually disdained the barbarians and were eager to transmit any bizarre and negative information about them. Furthermore, at the time of contact with the Classical world, when the authors heard stories about them, the indigenous European societies were undergoing extraordinary stress.

During the final century of the prehistoric Iron Age, burials provide important evidence linking the communities of this period with earlier traditions in the region, and also with subsequent developments during the Roman Period. During the second century B.C. the dominant burial practice changed from inhumation with relatively abundant grave goods, to cremation with relatively few. For many parts of temperate Europe in this period, the number of burials known is very small, indicating that changes took place in the methods of disposing of bodies. But in the northern part of the regions of concern here, between the middle Rhine and the English Channel, the practice of including grave goods continued in the cremation graves.

A small number of richly outfitted burials from this time provides important information about tradition and society. The character of the grave goods shows that communities identified strongly with the traditions and practices that had been established in the Late Bronze and Early Iron Ages. For example, a woman's burial at Dühren in Baden on the upper Rhine, dated around 140–120 B.C., contained Roman luxury imports, including a bronze wine jug and pan and two bronze mirrors; precious metal ornaments of local manufacture, including two gold fingerrings, two silver fibulae, and a silver coin; a large bronze cauldron and iron hanging apparatus; and a substantial quantity of personal ornaments, including four bronze fibulae, four glass bracelets, six glass ring beads, a bronze locket, and amber ornaments. The fibulae, fingerrings, bracelets, beads, and locket are all objects that were traditionally placed in women's burials in temperate Europe. The bronze vessels and iron support constitute the feasting equipment characteristic of rich burials. The practice of including a bronze mirror in a woman's burial began earlier; two mirrors were in the woman's burial at Reinheim, from about 400 B.C. Coins occur with some frequency in wealthy women's graves during this final phase of the prehistoric Iron Age.

Grave 1216 at Wederath near the middle Moselle valley contained a double burial. The burial was found within a rectangular enclosure defined by a ditch. The grave pit was rectangular and contained a wooden chamber roughly 6 1/2 by 5 1/4 ft. (1.95 x 1.60 m) in size. In the grave were found, in two deposits placed close together in the eastern corner of the chamber, the cremated remains of a man aged forty to sixty and of a woman aged eighteen to twenty. Recovered in association with the

Fig. 9. Reconstruction drawing of the inside of the burial chamber at
Clemency in Luxembourg, from around 70 B.C. Note the Roman transport amphorae, ornate textiles on the walls, ceramic and bronze vessels,
and animal parts that accompanied the burial. From Metzler et al. 1991,
p. 160, fig. 109. Used by permission of Jeannot Metzler, Musée
National d'Histoire et d'Art, Luxembourg.

man's remains were eighteen ceramic vessels, remains of wooden vessels,
an iron sword, two spearheads, a shield boss, an axe, a belt hook and
two belt rings, and an iron bracelet. The weapon set and belt parts are
characteristic of rich men's graves, and the large vessel assemblage suggests a role in social interaction in the same way that the feasting equipment in the Dühren grave does. Figure 9 shows the arrangement of objects in a grave at Clemency in Luxembourg, also from this period just
before the Roman conquest and containing numerous objects representing the feasting ritual.

INTERACTION AND IDENTITY

As this and the preceding chapter indicate, the late prehistoric peoples
of temperate Europe, including the groups that Caesar and his armies
encountered in Gaul, belonged to dynamic societies in which complex
changes were taking place in economy, political organization, and social
structure. Especially important for our interpretation of the Roman conquests and subsequent events is the increasing evidence for interaction

between peoples inhabiting different regions of Europe during the final century B.C. I have noted above the growing quantities of Roman goods that were arriving in communities north of the Alps, ultimately to be deposited in burials or on settlements. The increasing desire to acquire such objects, and their increasing availability, led to growth in the networks along which they were transported from Roman Italy into central and western Europe, and even northward to communities on the North European Plain, Denmark, and as far as Gotland and central Sweden. Another indication of this broad expansion in interregional interaction is the sharp increase during the second and first centuries B.C. in La Tène–style metalwork in the north, especially well represented in Denmark and on the island of Gotland.

The richly equipped men's graves of this final stage of the prehistoric Iron Age display what has been called an "international warrior style." A number of well-outfitted men's graves throughout the whole of temperate Europe contain very similar objects, including long iron swords, scabbards decorated with elaborate openwork ornament, and ornate spurs. This particular set emphasizes these individuals' status as elite, horseback-riding warriors, a status that achieved special prominence during the Roman Period. Significantly, these graves occur both in the landscapes to the south, which are characterized in this period by the *oppida*, rectangular enclosures, coinage, and mass-produced wheelmade pottery, and to the north, where those signs of organizational complexity do not occur and where settlement and economy remained much smaller in scale. The striking similarities among these graves in different regions indicate that social ties connected elite individuals over long distances, and across apparent cultural boundaries delineated by the distribution of particular kinds of settlements and manufactured goods.

This same interregional sharing of material culture during the final decades before the Roman compaigns in Gaul is also apparent in some everyday objects, most notably fibulae. For the first time, a few standardized fibula forms became common both in the southern and in the northern parts of temperate Europe. This pattern contrasts with that of earlier fibula types, which are restricted to either southern or northern Europe.

These signs of linkage between individuals and groups across great distances in Europe—expressed both in the well-equipped elite men's graves and in the everyday fibula forms—are new phenomena in Europe during the final century B.C. Above I drew attention to the boundary between the landscapes characterized by the La Tène style of ornament to the south and the Jastorf style to the north, which constituted a significant cultural divide during the preceding centuries. Besides the differences in ornamental style, this division also separated the landscapes characterized by the more complex societies centered on the *oppida*, from the less complex ones based on much smaller communities.

Thus the pattern of societies in temperate Europe at the time that the Roman armies of Julius Caesar made their first foray into Gaul was complex. Regional distinctions existed in the degree of centralization of political and economic life, but there are also strong indications that the boundaries across these divisions were being crossed increasingly by individuals, manufactured goods, and ideas. Caesar's commentary does not suggest that he was aware of the changes that were taking place in the decades before his arrival. Yet these changes greatly affected the progress of the Roman conquest and the character of subsequent developments in temperate Europe. Recent analyses of the archaeological evidence for interactions between groups in different parts of Europe before the Roman conquest of Gaul provide important new information for the interpretation of Caesar's commentaries and those of the other Roman and Greek writers.

❋ CHAPTER 4 ❋

The Roman Conquests

Roman Conquests in Perspective

WHEN ROMAN armies invaded lands in temperate Europe, beginning with Caesar's campaign in Gaul in 58 B.C. (Table 2), they encountered complex communities, many living in large urban settlements, most of which had been in trade contact with the Roman world for generations (Figure 10). The interactions surrounding the Roman conquests thus were fundamentally different from many other imperial expansions in world history. Although Roman imperialism bears some similarities to the Spanish conquests in the New World during the sixteenth and seventeenth centuries, a major difference was that Rome and people in Gaul had been in contact long before the conquest; the Spaniards had had no previous contact with central or south Americans. Much of the imperial expansion of European powers in modern times brought Europeans into contact with smaller-scale societies, often comprised of hunter-gatherers, for example in Australia and parts of Africa. In contrast, the peoples in Late Iron Age Gaul lived in permanent agricultural communities, some even in the urban *oppida*, at the time of Roman expansion. In many respects, Rome and the Gallic peoples were much more alike than other imperial powers were like the peoples they conquered and colonized.

As I have shown in the preceding chapter, the societies of temperate Europe were dynamic and heterogeneous when Roman armies marched into central Gaul. There was a wide range of community size, from urban *oppida* to isolated farmsteads. Architecture and burial practice indicate substantial differences in status and wealth between individuals. Many elite persons in Gaul had become familiar with aspects of Roman society through importation of goods, and perhaps through visits to Roman towns in southern Gaul or Italy, while others had had no direct experience of things Roman before the conquest. We need to bear in mind that the interactions that ensued cannot be understood in simple terms of Roman armies conquering and subduing masses of indigenous peoples. Some groups allied with Rome, others opposed Roman expansion. Some individuals saw benefits in Roman takeover, others did not. The experience of large urban communities was different from that of fami-

TABLE 2

Important Historical Dates in Roman Europe

A.D. 239	Alamanni and Franks crossed frontiers into provincial Roman lands
A.D. 166–80	Marcomannic Wars
A.D. 83–89	Conquest of lands between upper Rhine and Danube
A.D. 43	Conquest of Britain under Emperor Claudius
A.D. 16	Emperor Tiberius recalled Germanicus back to Rome
A.D. 9	Varus's three legions destroyed in Teutoburg Forest
15–12 B.C.	Emperor Augustus in Gaul and on Rhine
15 B.C.	Conquest of lands south of Danube
27 B.C.	Octavian designated "Augustus" and made emperor
31 B.C.	Octavian victorious over Antony at Actium
58–51 B.C.	Gallic Wars waged by Julius Caesar
113–101 B.C.	Battles with Cimbri, Teutones, and their allies
264–241 B.C.	First Punic War—start of Rome's building of empire
387 B.C.	Gauls sacked Rome
396 B.C.	Rome defeated Etruscan city of Veii
510 B.C.	Traditional date for end of Etruscan rule, start of Roman Republic
616 B.C.	Traditional date for start of Etruscan rule over Rome
1000 B.C.	Approximate date for early villages on site of Rome

lies living in farmsteads. The impact of the Roman armies and subsequent administrators differed also according to native individuals' gender and status in their society.

The Roman conquests in temperate Europe have been the subject of extensive research and writing, and I provide only a brief summary of complex and much-studied events. The citations in the bibliography will lead the interested reader to the more detailed literature.

Sources of Information

Our information about the Roman conquests comes from three principal sources: texts written by people who lived at the time; inscriptions on tombstones, military diplomas, and monuments; and the material evidence of archaeology. Some of the writers of the surviving texts were directly involved in the military campaigns of the conquests. Julius Caesar is the best example; he wrote an extensive commentary on his campaigns in Gaul between 58 and 51 B.C. that provides detailed information about such subjects as alliances between different groups in Gaul, Roman military tactics, and indigenous peoples he encountered and fought with or against. Most writers whose texts recount the Roman conquests were

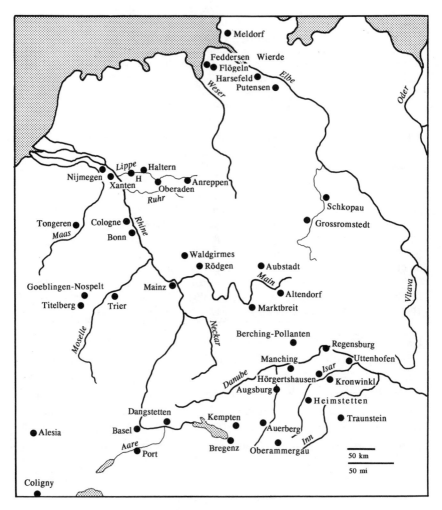

Fig. 10. Map showing the locations of places mentioned in chapters 4 and 5.
H = Holsterhausen (on Lippe River).

not as directly involved as Caesar, but instead recorded information learned from others who had participated in the events.

The information that such texts provide is mostly descriptive rather than interpretive. Authors tell us which Roman generals and which legions were involved, where they went on their campaigns, and what peoples were conquered, but they rarely include detailed information about the native groups they encountered. The purposes of the texts were military and political, and they conveyed information exclusively from the Roman point of view.

66

Epigraphic sources—inscriptions—also play an important role in documenting the experience of individuals in the Roman army. From specific inscriptions we can often generalize about the composition of the military units and about their movements. Inscriptions on gravestones often inform us about the campaigns in which individuals participated. For example, the stone marking the cenotaph (grave containing no body) of Marcus Caelius, a soldier in the Eighteenth Legion who was killed in the Battle of the Teutoburg Forest in A.D. 9 (see chapter 1), was found at Xanten on the lower Rhine, site of the Roman base at Vetera (Figure 11). On the 4 1/2 ft. (1.37 m)–high tombstone, the soldier is portrayed in relief, with honorific oak-leaf crown, medals on his armor, and a switch, sign of his rank. The inscription indicates that he was a fifty-three-year-old centurion from Bologna, Italy. It states further that the stone was commissioned by his brother Publius Caelius, and that the body was not buried but left unrecovered on the battlefield.

Military diplomas frequently yield similar information. Those recovered are typically incised on bronze plaques, and they document the career of a soldier upon completion of his service. They tell where the soldier came from, in which units he served, and often where he was stationed.

Monumental inscriptions on buildings often indicate the presence of particular legions and provide information about the course of campaigns. The well-preserved block from the east gate of the military base at Regensburg (Castra Regina) indicates a date of A.D. 179 for the completion of the defensive wall around the site and the carving of the inscription. It designates the Third Italian Legion as the principal unit resident at the site.

Compared to the amount of information provided by the surviving texts and by the epigraphic sources, the archaeological evidence that has been collected for the actual process of conquest—the physical remains of battles—is sparse. Most such evidence has been gathered in the last few years, and ongoing research is likely to generate much more data pertaining to the conquests of different regions of temperate Europe.

In Gaul an international team of archaeologists has evaluated recently the archaeological evidence at Alesia attesting to the battle between the inhabitants of the *oppidum* and Caesar's forces in 52 B.C. The great majority of the weapons recovered through excavation—helmets, shields, swords, lances, spears, and arrowheads—are of types made and used by Gallic peoples. Weapons of clearly Roman form are fewer, and most of them are weapons propelled from a considerable distance, such as spears, rather than implements used in hand-to-hand combat. As we

Fig. 11. Photograph of the gravestone of Marcus Caelius, found at Xanten; now in the Rheinisches Landesmuseum in Bonn. Height 54 in. (1.37 m). The inscription indicates that this Roman soldier was killed in the battle of the Teutoburg Forest in A.D. 9, in the service of the general Varus. Photograph courtesy of Rheinisches Landesmuseum, Bonn.

would expect, a large proportion of the weapons at Alesia show nicks and dents resulting from use. Coins recovered in association with the weapons support the connection with Caesar's attack on Alesia. The Roman coins, which can be precisely dated, are all from the year 54 B.C. and earlier. The Celtic coins, which cannot be dated as precisely, are consistent with the Roman series.

The first archaeological evidence for the Roman conquest of the regions south of the upper Danube, in modern Bavaria, in 15 B.C. has only recently been identified in the Alpine foothills near Oberammergau. Excavations in 1992 and 1993 at the site of two chance finds of Roman daggers yielded over three hundred Roman weapons and large numbers of indigenous weapons, personal ornaments, and tools. The Roman weapons include an iron catapult bolt point with a stamp indicating that it belonged to the Nineteenth Legion. One interpretation of the site is that the weapons all derive from a single major battle between invading Romans and native defenders. I shall say more about this site later in this chapter.

Among the most spectacular recent discoveries in European archaeology was that of the site of the Battle of the Teutoburg Forest, mentioned at the beginning of chapter 1.

Such archaeological evidence for the conflicts between Roman armies and native defenders would not permit us to do a very thorough reconstruction of the progress of the Roman conquests. The historical sources provide a more detailed and coherent picture of the campaigns and of their chronology. However, the available historical texts do not provide a full account of Roman military activities in Europe. For example, new military bases are often discovered archaeologically that are not mentioned in the written sources. Recent examples include camps at Marktbreit on the Main River and at Waldgirmes on the Lahn. Even where the texts give us the broad outline of campaigns, the archaeological investigation of specific military bases frequently tells much more than any of the written sources do about the size of forces, the economy of military communities, and the daily life of the troops. Excavations since the middle of the nineteenth century in the Netherlands, Germany, and Austria provide a detailed view into the character of the Roman bases, including their architecture, size, and internal organization. The associated pottery, ornaments, and coins inform us about the date that specific forts were established and abandoned. They also provide important information about the lives of the soldiers who staffed the forts and guardposts and about craft and trade activities through which they created or acquired the necessities of daily life and of their military campaigns.

CONQUEST OF GAUL: HISTORICAL ACCOUNTS

The history of Caesar's Gallic Wars is known to us from written sources, especially Caesar's own descriptions. Much excellent critical scholarship has been done recently on problems of interpreting Caesar's and other Roman accounts, and some of the issues raised will be noted here. The following brief summary of our understanding of the Gallic Wars is based on the ancient authors and must be considered in light of the perspectives, assumptions, and biases of those writers.

Rome in Southern Gaul

Rome had special connections with the Greek city of Massalia, on the site of the modern French city of Marseille, for over a century before Caesar entered Gaul. Historical accounts record the participation of Roman military forces in a number of engagements concerned with protecting Massalia from indigenous groups in southern Gaul that were growing in size and power and were threatening the city. Rome had become actively involved in military and political affairs in southern Gaul early in the second century B.C., and by the end of that century had established a solid foothold in what became, around the year 120 B.C., the province of Gallia Narbonensis. In the course of these machinations, Rome established friendly alliances with some of the native peoples of the area, while developing enmities with others. The lands to the north remained relatively unknown to most Romans at this time. The Roman perception of interior Gaul was that it was, by Mediterranean standards, a wild country, but one highly productive of foodstuffs and raw materials. No doubt the lively trade between Rome and peoples of the interior provided interested Romans with ideas about the economic prosperity of peoples to the north.

Caesar's Campaigns, 58–51 B.C.

The factors recounted by Roman writers that led to the wars between Rome and Gaul were many and interrelated. Several of the most apparent were the establishment of Roman political and military interests in southern Gaul during the second century B.C.; migration of peoples, including incursions into the lands of nations friendly to Rome; the arrival in Gaul of Ariovistus and the Suebi; and the political rivalry in Rome between Caesar, Pompey, and Crassus for control of the fledgling empire. In the final decades of the second and at the beginning of the final century B.C., Rome was called upon to assist allied peoples in dealing with a series of disturbances, resulting in part at least from incursions by a group called the Cimbri from northern Europe, believed by modern

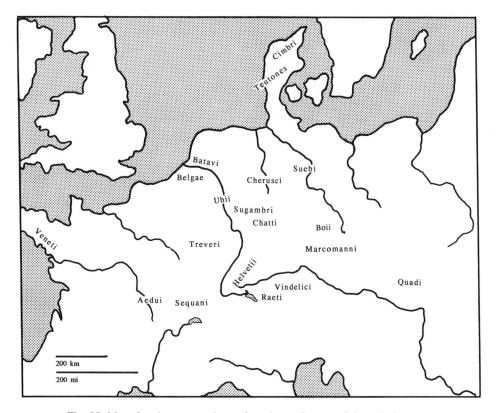

Fig. 12. Map showing approximate locations of some of the tribal groups mentioned by Roman and Greek writers from the time of Caesar to that of Tacitus, according to the descriptions in the ancient texts.

scholars to have come from northern Jutland. According to the accounts, another northern people, the Teutones, joined in these attacks. Roman historical tradition records that as a result of these movements of peoples, the Helvetii, a Celtic group that inhabited lands in central Europe, moved south and west into what is now Switzerland, then in the 60s B.C. moved on toward central Gaul in search of new lands where they might settle (Figure 12). According to the account preserved in Caesar's commentaries, Gallic peoples of eastern and central Gaul requested aid from the Romans in order to repulse these incoming Helvetii from their lands.

These events recounted by Caesar and other Roman writers were taking place at a time of fierce rivalry between different Gallic peoples, some of them declared allies of Rome and others sworn enemies. According to the Roman and Greek written sources, a great deal of disagreement

71

and fighting was taking place in Gaul from the end of the second century B.C. on. These conflicts were surely in part stimulated by the Roman military and political activity in southern Gaul, though it is quite possible that the writers were unaware of the fact that Rome's actions affected peoples far off in the interior of the continent. The Sequani, among the nations opposed to Rome, allegedly offered attractive land to Ariovistus, leader of the Suebi in central Germany, if he would lead his warriors against the enemies of the Sequani. Ariovistus accepted the offer, led his armies in victory, then seized lands from the Sequani themselves. Again, the Romans were called into Gaul, this time to help the surrounding allies of Rome in their new struggle against Ariovistus. In the year 61 B.C., the Roman Senate passed a resolution in support of the Aedui, one of Rome's principal allies involved in the strife. Conditions were ripe for more extensive Roman military intervention.

In 60 B.C. Caesar, Pompey, and Crassus held power in Rome. According to recent interpretations, Caesar probably was looking for some spectacular achievement that would give him the political influence to rise above his two rivals. Caesar's entry into the conflicts in Gaul thus was not simply a matter of coming to the aid of allies besieged by enemies, as Caesar states in his commentary. Rather, Roman intervention was the result of carefully calculated planning by the savvy politician Caesar as a means of enhancing his standing in Rome. In fact Caesar may have in some way goaded the Helvetii and Ariovistus into hostilities to provide a pretext for him to lead his armies into war.

After having first entered central Gaul to help the Aedui and other allies stop the Helvetii, Caesar was asked by the Aedui and other Gallic groups to aid in expelling Ariovistus and the Suebi from the land, and again he was successful. Different Gallic groups took sides with or against Rome. In 57 B.C. Caesar's forces defeated the people known as the Belgae, in the lands of modern Belgium. In 56 B.C. he fought the Veneti and their allies on the Atlantic coast of France. The following year Caesar led his forces against raiding parties, whom he called Germans, in the lower Rhine region, and that same year built a bridge across the Rhine, perhaps, as some investigators have suggested, near the modern city of Cologne, and brought his troops across to the east bank of the river, which he reported was German territory. He crossed the English Channel to attack Britain in 54 B.C. and defeated groups in the southern regions, but did not conquer the whole island. The following years he was largely occupied quelling rebellions among peoples in Gaul, culminating in the defeat of Vercingetorix and his forces after an extended siege at

Alesia in central Gaul in 52 B.C. In 51 B.C. Caesar's troops dealt with the last vestiges of rebellion in Gaul, completing the conquest and establishing peace for the newly acquired Roman territories.

Caesar's commentaries include detailed descriptions of his tactics in a number of major sieges against native strongholds. Besides that at Alesia (see above), he recounts the progress of his army's attacks on the centers at Avaricum, Gergovia, and Uxellodunum. From these accounts, we learn much about Caesar's reasoning, the enemies' strategies, and the weaponry used by the opposing sides.

Caesar's Army

Initially Caesar had at his disposal a military force of four Roman legions, each with around 3,000 or 4,000 active troops, some 2,000 auxiliary cavalry from Spain and Gaul, as well as special archers and slingers from other regions. By the time he completed his conquest in 51 B.C., ten legions were based in Gaul under his command, and he employed many more auxiliary troops. Legionary soldiers were men from Italy and citizens of Rome, while cavalry units and other special combatants were usually drawn from peoples allied with Rome who were especially skilled at particular tasks such as fighting on horseback or shooting the bow and arrow. Legionary soldiers were infantry troops, typically outfitted with helmet, chain mail tunic, shield, spear, and sword. Caesar deployed his legions according to the characteristics of the landscape in which they were fighting and the nature of the enemy's forces; their flexibility was a highly valued asset. Auxiliary cavalry and other troops fought with their native weapons and tactics, thus complementing the standard Roman techniques. In the course of the Gallic War, Caesar employed cavalry troops from Germanic peoples in the Rhineland, regarded as particularly skillful horsemen. Thus from an early stage of Roman involvement in temperate Europe, Caesar and other generals took advantage of indigenous military practices to further the imperial aims of Rome. Caesar seems to have designed his battle tactics in ways that enabled him to integrate the capabilities of his infantry and those of his cavalry to great advantage. In sieges against Gallic strongholds, such as Avaricum and Alesia, the Roman army used complex structures including portable towers to overcome the defenses.

Some numbers in Caesar's account give us an impression of the scale of operations. In his battles against Ariovistus in 58 B.C., Caesar had about 20,000 legionary troops and 4,000 auxiliaries, including cavalry.

In the attack on Avaricum, the Roman force comprised some 30,000 legionaries and 8,000 auxiliaries. In the final showdown with Vercingetorix at Alesia in 52 B.C., Caesar's troops consisted of about 40,000 legionary soldiers and 10,000 auxiliaries. In each case the enemy's forces were somewhat larger than Caesar's, according to his account. The accuracy of Caesar's numbers has been the subject of considerable scholarly debate, but they at least provide a rough idea of how many soldiers were probably involved. Certainly if the Gallic peoples had united against the Romans, they could have defeated the invaders. Caesar's success depended upon building and cultivating alliances with many of the Gallic groups who helped him defeat the others.

Recent Critiques

I need to say a few words about current thinking concerning the texts and their accounts of Roman policy and conquests. One major issue concerns the question of a grand strategy of the Roman Empire. In studies conducted during the nineteenth and twentieth centuries, the Roman conquests have frequently been portrayed as parts of a grand design, or overall policy of conquest and expansion. Individual campaigns have been interpreted as specific strategic actions within this larger conceptual framework. An example of this perspective is Edward Luttwak's influential study *The Grand Strategy of the Roman Empire* (1976). Much has been made of the effects of the early migrations of the Cimbri and the Teutones and the impact of those migrations on the thinking of the Romans. Many investigators have viewed the Roman conquests in temperate Europe as primarily defensive in aim, to establish borders that could be well fortified against other such incursions.

More recent studies challenge these assumptions and in particular show how ideas about Roman imperial strategy and frontiers were influenced by the political and military concerns of Britain, France, and Germany during the nineteenth and twentieth centuries and, in the case of more recent studies such as that by Luttwak, by Cold War thinking. Benjamin Isaac's *The Limits of Empire* (1990) has been instrumental in advancing this new perspective. Through thorough examination of the ancient texts that pertain to the Roman conquests, Isaac shows that there is no evidence that Roman emperors or anyone else had a grand strategy of imperial expansion. Roman knowledge of geography of lands beyond the imperial domain was too incomplete, and it simply was not part of the Roman mindset to conceive of a grand coordinated strategy that extended over generations. From the time of Augustus on, the emperor was the principal decision-maker for Rome, and he was supported by the army. The texts report repeatedly that the Roman emperor decided to launch an offensive in order to defeat a tribe that invaded Roman territory. Isaac argues that this set of actions is described so frequently and in such a similar fashion that it seems to be a trope—a standard explanation applied to any military venture the emperor chose to undertake. The textual sources indicate that striving for honor and glory were appropriate justifications for offensive campaigns, but that there is no indication that Rome went to war to defend endangered provincial populations. Isaac describes Roman expansionary policy as "opportunistic."

Recent studies have emphasized the importance of military ideology among the Roman elite for our understanding of the process of the army's involvement in Gaul. In the competition for status and political power among the leading families of Rome, success in military ventures may have been a necessary qualification for the top ranks. This argument provides a consistent model for understanding Caesar's actions in Gaul and his accounts of them, and it obviates the need to find some direct economic motive for those wars of conquest.

Current critical studies of Caesar's commentaries emphasize the need to interpret them in the context in which they were written. Caesar, the general, was writing reports about his campaigns in order to gain popular and senatorial support in Rome for his expanding political career. His perspective was that of an elite Roman military man, and his depictions of the Gauls were much affected by his background and his purposes in writing. Some scholars view his work principally as propaganda to excuse his actions and to portray himself in the best possible light to Roman sensibilities. As several investigators have noted, he carefully and subtly manipulated Roman fears of invasion by groups from the north, thereby gaining favor for his actions, which he represented largely as defensive in nature when in reality they were offensive.

NATIVE SOCIETIES EAST OF THE RHINE

As we have seen in chapter 3, at the end of the prehistoric Iron Age when Caesar began his campaigns in Gaul, the cultural landscape on both sides of the Rhine was relatively homogeneous. In the hilly upland regions of central Europe, people made and used objects ornamented in the La Tène style. *Oppida* dominated the settlement pattern, the manufacture of iron tools and of pottery was increasingly specialized, and a money-based economy had emerged at the centers. The uniformity of the material culture of communities west and east of the Rhine indicates that they maintained active contacts across the river. The thousands of Iron Age coins recovered yield precise information about the trade patterns across Europe. Coins from many different parts of Late La Tène Europe are represented at all of the major *oppida*.

When the Roman armies entered Gaul, they disrupted these interactions. Caesar's account shows that the years of the conquest, 58–51 B.C., were a period of intense military mobilization and stress throughout Gaul, with Roman troops and their Gallic allies attacking and ultimately defeating their common enemies. These events had powerful effects on the peoples east of the Rhine, but there has been surprisingly little research attention paid to the changes that took place there. Most investigators focus on the Roman activity and do not ask what happened across the river from Gaul. In approaching this question, recent studies of indigenous societies on the peripheries of conquered territories offer useful ideas. For example, research on indigenous peoples in Yucatan and in the Caribbean region shows that even peoples living a great distance away from the areas under conquest by the Spaniards in the sixteenth century were strongly affected by the military actions. The reason is that they had been in contact with the conquered peoples, and the military and political changes severely disrupted those interactions. We might expect a similar impact of Roman military activity in Gaul on the peoples east of the Rhine.

According to his account, Caesar made two forays across the Rhine into what he said was German territory. The locations of these incursions are not known; no archaeological evidence of Caesar's Rhine crossings has been identified. Recent investigators have suggested possible crossing places ranging from the Taunus Hills in the south to the Ruhr River valley in the north. These advances had no discernible effects beyond increasing the natives' awareness of the proximity of Roman troops and their alarm at the prospect of attack.

Framing the Question

Textual information pertaining to those landscapes in this period is sparse. Caesar and other chroniclers name several groups who, they say, inhabited the regions east of the Rhine. In the context of his descriptions of the Gauls, Caesar also informs us about peoples east of the Rhine whom he calls Germans. According to his account, the Germans did not live in large and complex communities, but only in small ones. Their economies and political systems were less complex, and their religious traditions were simpler. (I discuss Caesar's distinction between Gauls and Germans in detail in chapter 5.) The archaeological evidence shows that Caesar's remarks may well apply to the peoples east of the Rhine during the Gallic Wars. By Caesar's time the inhabitants lived in communities that were much smaller than *oppida* and than many of the open settlements of pre-Caesarean times. They had less developed craft industries, no coinage, and a general lack of the special economic features associated with the *oppida*. Major changes seem to have occurred in the cultural landscape between the time when the *oppida* were thriving and the time of the Gallic Wars. These changes may have been similar to those documented on the peripheries of Spanish conquest in the New World.

End of the Oppida

Current interpretations of the archaeological evidence suggest that many of the *oppida* east of the Rhine declined precipitously in population and in economic activity at the time that the Gallic Wars were raging west of the Rhine, in 58–51 B.C. The evidence for this decline is the very sparse representation of objects that belong to the chronological phase that begins about the middle of the final century B.C. (Figure 13). Fibulae of the arched type and Beltz Variant J, and belthooks of the perforated triangular and rod types (all shown in the box labeled D2 in Figure 13), are characteristic objects of this post-*oppidum* phase, and they are only very poorly represented at the *oppida*. There is no evidence for a violent end to the *oppidum* occupation at Manching (though damaged weapons on the site attest to an earlier conflict there), and recent investigations at Kelheim similarly failed to produce any indication that the settlement was abandoned as the result of military action. Noteworthy is the dearth of large tools and complete ornaments left on the sites, which we might expect to be left behind or overlooked if the inhabitants were overwhelmed by attackers or fled in a hurry. All indications suggest that the people moved from these settlements in an organized fashion and took useable objects with them. Not everyone left—a small number of metal ornaments and sherds of pottery attributed to this later phase attest to a small community that remained at Manching. But with the departure of the majority of the population and the end of Manching's role as a center of production and commerce, the *oppidum* came to an end. Why did Manching and other *oppida* cease to function as centers?

While present information does not allow us to answer this question in detail, it appears increasingly likely that the decline of the *oppida* resulted from the breakdown of the economic systems that had sustained the specialized communities resident in them. The functioning of these centers depended upon political authority to oversee and protect manufacturing and distribution systems, and on economic networks to provide required raw materials, labor to process them, and channels to distribute the products. In the absence of any apparent evidence for military defeat at *oppida* such as Manching and Kelheim, the most likely cause of the demise of those communities was disruption of the economic systems that supplied materials, labor, and markets or of the political authority that protected the operations. Roman intervention in Gaul, beginning with Caesar in 58 B.C., was probably the principal factor in the disruptions.

Caesar's account of the Gallic Wars, comments about them by other writers, and the archaeological evidence for the armed conflicts such as that at Alesia, make clear that the military conquest of Gaul was a major undertaking for the Roman army and for the peoples of Gaul. Tens of thousands were killed in battle and in reprisal actions by the Romans, and probably many more died of starvation and disease during the war. Caesar writes about destroying crops to hinder the communities against whom he was fighting, and surely such actions and others associated with large-scale war had broad demographic, social, and economic repercussions. Commerce between communities in Gaul and other parts of Europe surely declined or ceased. The interregional trade between *oppida* in different parts of La Tène Europe, through which coins, personal ornaments, bronze vessels, amber, graphite, and other goods flowed, was linked to local trade systems between *oppida* and smaller communities around them that supplied agricultural products and raw materials to the centers. Disruption in the interregional commerce caused breakdown of local systems of goods circulation. Without the inflow of goods obtained through interregional trade, the *oppida* could not maintain the industries that operated at them, nor the relations with outlying communities that supplied them.

Studies of the breakdown of complex cultural systems show that predictable changes take place in material culture when social and economic systems disintegrate. Similar patterns can be recognized in a wide variety of contexts, from the collapse of ancient civilizations in the Near

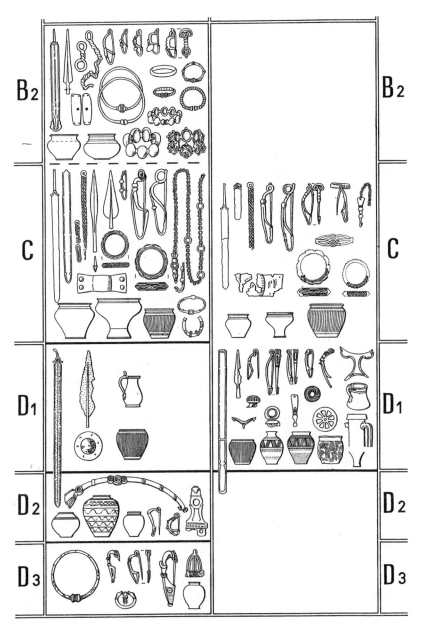

Fig. 13. Chronological chart showing the types of objects that archaeologists use to define the phases in the relative chronology of the Late Iron Age, also known as the La Tène Period. The right column shows representative objects from the *oppidum* of Manching; the left column, objects from graves in southern Bavaria. The linking of these phases with calendrical dates is still under debate. Currently accepted dates for La Tène C are 250–125 B.C.; for D1: 125–55 B.C.; for D2: 55 B.C.–A.D. 10; and for D3: A.D. 10–60. From Krämer 1962, fig. 1. Used by permission of Susanne Sievers, RGK.

East, to the decline of Roman authority and power in Europe during the fifth century A.D., to the disintegration of the Teotihuacan state in the Valley of Mexico in the seventh century. Among the common patterns are abandonment of major centers that had served to coordinate economic, social, political, and religious functions; dispersal of previously concentrated populations into small communities in the countryside; shift from centrally produced, highly specialized goods to largely domestically made, nonspecialized goods; and greater diversity in form, technology, and decoration of objects manufactured in the small communities than in the centers.

These are precisely the characteristics we find in the landscapes east of the Rhine after the demise of the *oppida*. For this period, only a handful of graves and settlements are known from the region of southern Germany where *oppida* had existed, and all suggest very small communities and economies much simpler than those at the *oppida*. Among the best documented sites are 11 burials in southeastern Bavaria, at the sites of Hörgertshausen (5 graves), Kronwinkl (2), Traunstein (1), and Uttenhofen (3), and small cemeteries in northern Bavaria at Altendorf and Aubstadt. These graves are distinguished by a particular set of metal ornaments, fibulae of the arched and Beltz J type and belthooks of the perforated triangular and rod types, all of which seem to be later in date than the principal occupations at the *oppida*. Pottery in the graves also reflects some significant differences from that at the *oppida*.

Most of the settlements identified from this post-*oppidum* time are represented by very sparse remains, such as single storage pits that contain pottery and small quantities of metal objects. A larger example is at Regensburg-Harting, an open settlement comprising two or three farmsteads. Three rectangular sunken floors could be identified, measuring about 16 by 11 ft. (5 x 3.5 m), perhaps remains of workshops. Iron slag and charcoal in one indicate iron-working. Foundations of two houses were found, both post-built, one about 33 by 33 ft. (10 x 10 m), the other 36 by 20 ft. (11 x 6 m). Pits on the settlement contained pottery, animal bones, metal objects, slag, and stone implements. Of the roughly 1,100 sherds of pottery recovered, about 90 percent consist of a ceramic described as very coarse, hand-made pottery. About 10 percent of the sherds are from wheelmade vessels, and that pottery matches ceramics from *oppida* such as Manching and Kelheim. Among the few metal objects found were three fibulae of the same types as those in the graves of this period—a Beltz J fibula of bronze and two iron arched fibulae.

Settlement remains from other sites of this period are similar in character, but even scantier than those at Regensburg-Harting.

If we compare these grave and settlement finds with the archaeological evidence at the *oppida* and at smaller sites contemporaneous with them, we find significant differences. The *oppida* housed large communities, and other contemporaneous settlements, such as Berching-Pollanten in central Bavaria, were substantial in the numbers of houses and quantities of pottery, iron tools, bronze, iron, and glass ornaments, and coins recovered. The subsequent settlements like Regensburg-Harting and the few graves known from this post-*oppidum* time indicate much smaller communities. At Manching and other settlements of the period, most of the pottery was wheelmade. Iron tools at Manching were manufactured in a system of serial production, with large numbers of nails, knives, axes, chisels, and other implements made in very similar forms. Even the fibulae, the most common personal ornaments, were made in series. Technical analyses show that the Nauheim fibula, the most common during the time of the *oppida*, was designed to be mass-produced (see chapter 3). At the later sites, most of the pottery is handmade rather than wheelmade. Iron implements are few in number, and they show no evidence of mass production. And the fibulae are of new types that were not mass-produced, but individually crafted.

For most of the *oppidum* settlements such as Manching, Kelheim, and Heidengraben, very few burials have been found contemporaneous with the principal occupation. Tens of thousands of graves, well outfitted with weapons and jewelry, have been excavated and studied from pre-*oppidum* times (see chapter 2), but around the middle of the second century B.C., burial practices changed, and the few graves that have been found for the *oppidum* period account for only a tiny fraction of the population that lived at the *oppida*. Physical anthropologist Günter Lange, who conducted the analyses of the human skeletal materials found on the settlement at Manching, suggests that they represent not the results of a great battle (see chapter 2) but instead the practice of exhumation and ritual manipulation of bones as part of new funerary rites. But excavations at Kelheim and Heidengraben have revealed no such human remains, except for part of a skull found just outside the inner wall at Kelheim, interpreted as a building offering. However, there is evidence that the funerary ritual changed from inhumation (burying the body) to cremation (burning the body) and that most cremation graves were no more than small holes in the ground containing ashes and burned bones. Such deposits would have been destroyed long ago by plowing. The graves from the post-*oppidum* time thus show a return to the pre-*oppidum* practice of burying the dead with grave goods. Most of these graves contain cremated remains, but some were inhumations.

Changes in burial practices are very difficult to interpret, and investigators do not understand why they changed so much between the start of the Late Iron Age and the beginning of the Roman Period. Besides being means of disposing of decomposing corpses, burial practices are rituals in which communities communicate information about group identity, family affiliation, social status, age, gender, and other aspects of individuals. Particularly in circumstances of rapid cultural change, variability in burial practice can be very complex.

Some investigators have suggested that the post-*oppidum* finds represent immigrants from regions to the north, and they connect them with the peoples Caesar referred to as Germans. These interpretations have placed heavy weight on Caesar's statements about migrations. Caesar described migrations of people he called Helvetii in 58 b.c. from central regions of the continent into what is now southwest Germany, then across the Rhine into Gaul, and finally back into southwest Germany. He further recounted migrations of other groups in central and north-central Europe, such as the Boii. Because the particular types of metal ornaments that characterize the post-*oppidum* graves and settlements in southern Germany are well represented in lands to the north, especially around the Saale River and the middle Elbe, some investigators argue that these graves and settlements are those of immigrant Germans from those northern regions who settled in lands vacated by groups such as the Helvetii. Some also draw attention to similarities between the pottery of these post-*oppidum* finds and that of the Saale–middle Elbe region.

My interpretation of these graves and settlements is different. None of the graves in southern Germany is just like any grave in the numerous excavated cemeteries of the Saale–middle Elbe region. If these graves were those of immigrants from that region who retained their traditions, then we would expect the graves to be outfitted like those in their homelands. The graves in southern Germany are diverse. They do not indicate any single set of funerary rules that we might expect among an immigrant population maintaining its traditions. Although the metal types in the southern German graves are well represented in the Saale–middle Elbe region, Thomas Völling's comprehensive studies of fibulae and belthooks show that these types are widespread over much of temperate Europe, not concentrated in that one region. Furthermore, the style represented in a number of the objects in these post-*oppidum* graves belongs to the local La Tène tradition of ornament, not to that of the north. The clearest examples are the ornate rod belthook from Traunstein and the belthooks from Uttenhofen graves 2 and 3, both of which had enamel inlay. While some of the pottery in the post-*oppidum* graves has been compared to northern wares in shape and decoration, the pottery in the graves is mostly wheelmade, a characteristic feature of local production during the time of the *oppida*, but unusual in the northern region. On the settlements such as Regensburg-Harting, the pottery is mostly coarse and handmade, but some vessels closely resemble those at the *oppida*. The most striking feature of the pottery of this period is its diversity.

I offer an interpretation of these finds that is more consistent with current understanding of cultural dynamics in situations such as that in temperate Europe after the decline of the *oppida*. When the centers declined in activity and population around the middle of the final century B.C., the economic systems centered on the *oppida* disintegrated. The majority of the residents abandoned the centers and moved to smaller communities in the countryside. They were unable to re-create the large-scale, specialized systems to procure raw materials, build manufacturing facilities, and maintain specialist craftworkers. Instead they had to make what they needed on a much smaller scale, in domestic or village settings. Manufacturing became primarily individualized—each object was made as demand for it arose, instead of in the serial production at the *oppida*. The result of this change was a greater diversity in products, because different communities created somewhat different goods; individually crafted objects varied more than serially made ones.

The archaeological evidence of the post-*oppidum* sites matches this model. On the settlements we observe a larger proportion of handmade pottery than at the *oppida*, consistent with small communities or individual households making their own ceramics, and the pottery is much more diverse in character than that from the central production facilities at the *oppida*. Pottery made of the graphite-clay mixture that had been much favored at the *oppida* for cooking vessels is very rare at the small post-*oppidum* sites, because the supply systems to and from the graphite sources had broken down. The small quantity of wheelmade wares very rarely bear the painted decoration that had characterized the finest pottery at the *oppida*. Glass production and coin minting are not in evidence in these small communities.

Hence these small, diverse communities of the post-*oppidum* period east of the Rhine can be best understood in terms of the changes that occurred with the decline of the *oppida*, not with reference to immigrants from the north. However, I do not imply that there were no migrations. As noted in chapter 3, there is considerable archaeological evidence for the movement of people and exchange of goods throughout temperate Europe during the second and final centuries B.C., and surely the Roman textual accounts of migrations reflect significant movements. But locating the origins of migrating groups mentioned in the Roman and Greek texts, and linking them with archaeological evidence, is much more difficult than many modern scholars admit. It is usually not clear when such migrations consisted of relatively small war bands, and when they were mass movements of entire families. Most migrations are followed by reverse-migrations—people return to their homelands (see chapter 2). In any case, I do not think that migrations that may have taken place during the second and final centuries B.C. were so extensive that they resulted in landscapes empty of human inhabitants.

While models such as this are needed for assessing our understanding of cultural processes in the past, we must not oversimplify the complex character of the cultural landscape in the post-*oppidum* period. There is clear evidence at Manching that some small population remained at the site. Perhaps some of the industries at the *oppida* were maintained on a reduced scale; that could explain why some of the materials in the post-*oppidum* contexts, such as pottery, are very similar to those produced at the *oppida*. Surely some of the occupants of the new small communities in the post-*oppidum* time had been skilled in manufacturing at the *oppida*, and they attempted to reproduce their products in the new contexts, without the industrial infrastructure that had existed at the *oppida*. Others who were less experienced produced pottery for domestic use. Some individuals probably had access to goods coming in from outside, such as pottery and ornaments from the north, while others did not. Some local craftworkers adopted forms and styles from such imports and integrated them with local traditions of manufacturing. All of these behaviors probably contributed to the manufacturing of the material culture of the post-*oppidum* time, and they would explain the unusually diverse character of the pottery and metal ornaments to which several investigators have called attention.

The re-creation of the ritual of burial in the post-*oppidum* contexts can be understood in terms of cultural dislocation and social stress typically suffered by people in circumstances when complex economic and social systems disintegrate. Some communities, such as those in southeastern Bavaria represented by the graves discussed above, re-created the traditions of burial that their ancestors had practiced a few decades earlier. The categories of objects placed in the graves were similar to those in pre-*oppidum* times. Differences in burial practice and in grave arrangement reflect the diversity of the communities in the post-*oppidum* circumstances.

While it is generally agreed among investigators that the earliest of these post-*oppidum* graves and settlements date to around 60–50 B.C., less clear is how late some of these finds may be. A settlement pit at the site of Eching north of Munich contained pottery characteristic of this group of sites, associated with a Roman coin minted during the reign of the Emperor Tiberius, in A.D. 14–37. The occurrence of very similar fibulae in graves of the post-*oppidum* group and at early Roman settlements such as the Auerberg and Kempten in Bavaria and Cologne in the Rhineland is further evidence that some of these complexes were contemporaneous with the early Roman Period.

CONQUESTS EAST OF THE RHINE

South of the Danube

During the two decades following Caesar's conquest of Gaul, Rome was largely concerned with power struggles between competing leaders. Caesar challenged his rivals by bringing his victorious armies across the Rubicon into central Italy in 49 B.C. After defeating Pompey's army in 48 B.C., Caesar rose to the position of dictator of Rome in 44 B.C. Very shortly thereafter he was assassinated. Rivalry between Octavian, Caesar's adopted son, and Mark Antony culminated in the defeat of the latter in 31 B.C. at the sea battle of Actium. In 27 B.C. Octavian assumed the title of Augustus and emerged as the first leader of the Roman Empire. These decades of civil strife distracted Roman attention from newly conquered Gaul. Minor disturbances regularly occurred within Gaul during this period, and textual sources report that groups east of the Rhine periodically crossed the river into Roman territory. Roman troops responded to quell the uprisings and repulse the incursions, but only limited Roman attention was devoted to Gaul during these decades.

Agrippa was appointed governor of Gaul in 39 B.C., and he led expeditions across the Rhine to punish groups there that had raided into Gaul. As a means to defend the Rhine border, Agrippa invited the group known as the Ubii to move across the river into Gaul and to settle at the site of modern Cologne. Agrippa began construction of the road system in Gaul, thereby making it possible to move troops quickly from the interior regions to the Rhine frontier when they were needed there.

A change in Roman policy on the middle Rhine occurred in about 16 B.C., apparently in response to an attack by a group known as the Sugambri that resulted in the defeat of a legion. Emperor Augustus traveled to Gaul and remained there three years to develop means for dealing with such crises, including making preparations for further action against the groups east of the Rhine. Beginning in 15 B.C. he established a series of military bases along the west bank of the lower and middle Rhine to serve both as defenses against incursions from across the river and as staging points for Roman invasions eastward.

Meanwhile, south of the upper Danube, in what is now southern Germany, the Roman army undertook more conquests of territory. In the summer of the year 15 B.C., the Roman generals Tiberius and Drusus, adopted sons of the Emperor Augustus, led Roman armies to conquer the lands between the Alps and the Danube. Various reasons are given in different accounts for this Roman campaign. According to several sources, including Cassius Dio and Strabo, the Raetians of this region had been carrying out raids into Gaul and Italy, and had mistreated travelers from Rome and its allies. Recent scholarship concerning Roman texts about military actions teaches us that we cannot accept such rationales at face value. Different interpretations can be offered for these actions, and it is unlikely that we shall ever arrive at a single one that all scholars accept.

The Roman writer Pliny reported that Drusus marched his army north from the Po Plain of northern Italy, over the Alpine passes, and into what is now southern Bavaria. Only recently have archaeological materials come to light that document the passage of Roman troops through the Alpine foothills en route into the heart of southern Bavaria. Excavations at the site of Döttenbichl near Oberammergau in 1992 and 1993 recovered over three hundred Roman weapons, as well as some eighty characteristic boot nails. The weapons include arrowheads, lanceheads, and points from catapult bolts, including one with the stamp LEG XIX, designating the Nineteenth Legion. The Roman materials were found in association with typical metal objects of the indigenous peoples, including spearheads, tools, and fibulae. The excavator suggests two possible interpretations of the site. It may have been the location of a battle between Roman and indigenous troops. Or, perhaps more likely, it may be an offering deposit set in place by indigenous peoples who won an encounter with Roman invaders. In either case, the connection of this site with

Drusus's advance from Italy into Bavaria in 15 B.C. seems clear, and the deposit demonstrates the existence of a native population in the upper Ammer Valley at the time of the Roman arrival.

According to contemporary Roman accounts, Tiberius advanced from the west, probably from Gaul. Archaeological evidence for Tiberius's advance is apparent west of Lake Constance at the military camp on the north bank of the upper Rhine at Dangstetten, excavated in the late 1960s and early 1970s. Smaller military posts at Basel, Windisch, Zurich, and on the Walensee in Switzerland also date from this time. Apparently the inhabitants were unable to offer any effective unified resistance, and the land was subdued during the single summer with relatively little military effort.

As noted above, according to the accepted chronological schemes, by this time several of the important *oppida* as well as other sizable settlements had declined greatly in population several decades earlier. There is debate among archaeologists and historians about the character of the cultural landscape at the time of the Roman conquest. No on-the-spot account by Roman generals survives comparable to Caesar's descriptions of his campaigns in Gaul. Instead, we need to work with brief accounts by Roman writers who were not on the scene, and with the archaeological evidence. Many archaeologists have interpreted the available evidence to indicate that the landscape was only sparsely populated in 15 B.C. when the Roman troops arrived. To explain this apparent scarcity of occupants, some have turned to the historical record of the movement of the Helvetii in 58 B.C. from southern Germany into Gaul, suggesting that a massive out-migration of people occurred at this time. But a number of statements by the ancient authors indicate that the landscape must have been substantially populated. For example, Cassius Dio reported that after the conquest, the Roman military inducted men into the auxiliary forces in order to prevent local rebellions. Texts mention the participation of Raetians and Vindelici—names of two peoples who inhabited the lands south of the Danube—in the Roman forces in the Weser region of northern Germany in the year A.D. 16. Strabo reported that Raetia regularly supplied tax payments to Rome; there must have been people there if taxes were being paid.

Several different kinds of archaeological evidence that have emerged recently support this view that the landscape was well populated at the time of the Roman conquest. One is the settlement evidence noted above; though the principal *oppida* had been abandoned, recent excavations have yielded numerous small settlements as well as scattered burials of the post-*oppidum* period. The recent discoveries at the Döttenbichl near Oberammergau provide clear evidence for local defenders in the upper Ammer valley at the time of Drusus's invasion. Siegmar von Schnurbein explains why the evidence for indigenous habitation at the time of the conquest has been less abundant in southern Bavaria—especially in the regions of Upper Bavaria just north of the Alps—than elsewhere. This land has not been cultivated as much in modern times as other parts of central and western Europe, thus archaeologists do not find surface traces of settlement activity—such as sherds of pottery, ornaments, and coins—on freshly plowed fields the way they do elsewhere. The land is largely given over to pasture, a use that does not lend itself to discovery of archaeological materials, because of the thicker ground cover and lack of regular plowing. Another major reason why the situation has appeared to represent abandonment to some archaeologists is that settlement and economic structures changed from a centralized system, with the *oppida* as prominent foci of settlement and economic activity, to a dispersed system of much smaller communities. These smaller communities are by their very nature much more difficult to find—and less likely to be identified—than large settlements with massive fortifications. Following the abandonment of the larger settlements, all inhabitants of the region lived in very small communities, with small dwellings and simpler material culture, as settlements such as Regensburg-Harting show. The specialization of production at the *oppida* and other large settlements meant much more efficient manufacture of goods—pottery, metal tools, bronze ornaments, and glass jewelry. With the abandonment of the centers, the specialized production systems came to an end. Small communities produced only what they needed, without the efficiency of scale that had existed at the centers. The people were making fewer objects than they had at the *oppida*, hence there is less evidence from this time for archaeologists to find.

Finally, there is clear paleoenvironmental evidence that the landscapes south of the Danube were not empty of human settlement at the time of the Roman invasion. In his studies of the pollen record in southern Bavaria, Hansjörg Küster demonstrates that the landscape was regularly cultivated throughout late prehistoric and early Roman times. The pollen evidence does not suggest any kind of break or decline in cultivation that we would expect if the landscape had been abandoned, even for just a few years. Such a decline might be represented by increased quantities of pollen from woodland vegetation or from plants that typically colonize abandoned fields. Clearly, people remained in the region and continued to plow the fields, sow their crops, and combat the spread of weeds and the encroachment of the forests.

Roman Military Activity across the Middle and Lower Rhine

There is considerable debate among historians as to the aims of Augustus in particular and of the Roman political and military powers in general at this stage. One side of the argument views the Roman actions as principally defensive, aimed at securing the borders—in this case the Rhine border of Gaul—against the incursions of bands from across the river. The other side believes that the Romans were undertaking a policy of imperialism, aimed at conquering more territory beyond the Rhine to add to the growing empire. Another position is that at this time—in the years 16–12 B.C.—the Romans had no unified policy toward the regions beyond the Rhine, but that subsequently, after uprisings of Germanic tribes in the year A.D. 1, Rome established the goal of conquering the lands east of the Rhine and creating a new province extending to the Elbe.

The following brief summary of Roman military activity in the lower and middle Rhine regions from the time of Augustus until the start of the second century A.D. is based on both textual and archaeological information. It will form the historical background to the chapters that follow.

From 16 to 13 B.C., the Emperor Augustus spent three years on the frontier in the middle Rhine region, overseeing the reorganization of the defenses of eastern Gaul and preparations for a major offensive eastward across the Rhine. During Augustus's reign, a series of military bases were established along the west bank of the river. Archaeological research has identified major forts at Nijmegen, Xanten, Moers-Asberg, Neuss, Mainz, and Bonn as likely sites of legionary camps at this time. Other smaller military forts were established at other locations. When Augustus departed from the Rhineland in 13 B.C. to return to Rome, he left his stepson Drusus in charge as governor of Gaul and leader of Roman forces on the Rhine. In 12 B.C. the Sugambri attempted another Rhine crossing, and Drusus began an offensive to defeat the attackers. He advanced across the Rhine from military bases at Vetera (Xanten) and Mogontiacum (Mainz). Drusus's forces reached the Elbe, where they met up with a Roman fleet that had sailed up the river from the North Sea.

As part of these campaigns into the lands east of the middle Rhine, the Roman forces established a series of bases along the Lippe River.

Archaeological excavation has revealed the locations, size, character, and chronology of forts at Haltern, Holsterhausen, Oberaden, and Anreppen. Chronological evidence from dendrochronology, coins, and pottery indicate that these bases were built probably between 12 and 7 B.C. Oberaden was abandoned about 8 B.C. Haltern was destroyed in A.D. 9, and Anreppen probably then too. Holsterhausen was a marching camp and not well dated. Perhaps by A.D. 9, perhaps slightly later, all Roman military activity at these forts had ceased. Further south, another series of forts was constructed across the Rhine from Mainz. One at Rödgen was built in 10 B.C. and abandoned two or three years later. Similarly short-lived bases were established at Bad Nauheim and Friedberg, as well as the recently discovered fort at Waldgirmes in the Lahn River valley.

The Romans constructed 28 military bases in the area during the time of Augustus (27 B.C.–A.D. 14), 16 during the reign of Tiberius (A.D. 14–37), and 9 that belong to one of those periods or the other. For the decades during which Claudius and Nero were emperors (A.D. 41–68), there are 6 legionary bases identified, 25 other forts, and 19 probable forts. For the early Flavian period, A.D. 70–80, there are 7 legionary bases and 58 other forts.

During this period of activity on the Rhine, the Romans established not only military forts, but also supply bases. Tongeren in Belgium was a supply base for the army but occupied mainly by craftworkers and merchants providing goods needed by the troops stationed in neighboring regions. Some already inhabited indigenous communities may have also assumed such a function during this period, as for example the *oppidum* settlement at the Titelberg in Luxembourg, where we have abundant evidence of Roman Period activity following directly upon that of the Late Iron Age. Other new foundations appear to have had soldiers in residence, but not to have been primarily military sites. The Auerberg and Kempten sites in southern Bavaria, and Bregenz in Austria, appear to have been mainly civilian settlements on the basis of the finds, but with some representation of military presence. Archaeology in Germany, in particular, has focused heavily on the Roman military bases along the Rhine and Danube frontiers, and hence we have a vast amount of data about Roman activity in this period. Yet so far we may have identified only some 10 percent of places occupied during the Augustan Period.

For our purposes here, the principal importance of the Roman military bases is in their bringing indigenous peoples into direct contact with Roman imperial forces. Even in instances in which bases were occupied for only a few years, the effects upon local populations of having hundreds or thousands of Roman soldiers stationed in their territories were profound. Economically, the bases created great demands for food products, raw materials, and manufactured goods. Politically, the presence of large military forces must have had strong effects on local political and social systems, whether or not direct military confrontation took place with local communities. In terms of personal experience, meetings between Roman soldiers and local individuals surely had a significant impact on all involved (see chapter 6).

Between 3 and 1 B.C., Roman troops made forays across the Rhine and marched to the Elbe, but still did not subdue the inhabitants of those lands. Around the time of Christ, a series of uprisings against the Romans began among the indigenous groups between the Rhine and the Elbe. In the year A.D. 4, Tiberius assumed command of the armies, and he achieved some success in campaigns against the peoples east of the Rhine. In A.D. 6 or 7, P. Quinctilius Varus took over command of the troops. Varus was by training an administrator, not a military man. In late September in A.D. 9 Germanic warriors under the leadership of Arminius ambushed Varus's three legions, three cavalry units, and six cohorts of auxiliaries, and wiped out about half of Rome's Rhine army (see chapters 1 and 10). The catastrophe was the turning point in the thirty-year Roman campaign to subdue the peoples between the Rhine and the Elbe. The Roman military abandoned its bases east of the Rhine, effectively pulling back to the west bank of the river.

The defeat in the Teutoburg Forest was of immense importance for the future course of Roman activity in Europe. The Emperor Augustus responded by increasing the number of troops stationed on the Rhine from five or six legions to eight. Although the Roman forces campaigned east of the Rhine for several more years after Varus's defeat, that event effectively ended serious Roman designs on the region. After Varus, Tiberius again resumed command of the Rhine armies, and in A.D. 12 Germanicus, son of Drusus, took over. Offensives in A.D. 14 and 15 resulted in considerable Roman losses and no effective gains. In A.D. 16 the then Emperor Tiberius called Germanicus back to Rome and ended Roman campaigning east of the lower Rhine.

It has always seemed ironic that the Roman armies were able to conquer the larger-scale, more fully integrated, relatively complex communities of Gaul, with their urbanlike *oppida*, their highly developed systems of production, and their advanced economies with coinage; but unable to defeat the much smaller-scale societies of the territories east of the Rhine. A major factor in the Roman inability to conquer Germany may have been the lower level of political and economic development there than in Gaul and south of the Danube. The communities in these lands showed nothing of the centralization of manufacturing, trade, and political organization characteristic of the *oppida*, and not the same centralized collection and storage of food and other goods. Hence the Romans could not acquire the sources of supply they needed in the field, as Caesar had been able to do in Gaul. According to this argument, it was the very underdevelopment of the lands of northern Germany, relative to Gaul and Germany south of the Danube, that made them impossible for the Romans to conquer with the resources available to them.

Following the annihilation of Varus and his legions and the failure of the Roman forces to claim any substantial victory in the immediately succeeding years, Augustus and his successor Tiberius's policy was to scale down the campaigns east of the Rhine and to build up the defenses along the Rhine. An important result was that eastern Gaul remained a militarized zone, with much of the local political and economic framework designed specifically to supply the garrisons defending the Rhine frontier. This arrangement was a critical factor in the creation of the frontier zone in temperate Europe. When it had become evident that the German campaigns were not going to succeed in annexing lands east of the lower Rhine into the Roman Empire, or in subduing the peoples there, the Romans stationed eight legions on the west bank of the Rhine as garrison troops to defend the river frontier. They established bases at Cologne and Trier, first as military posts, but they quickly became important civilian centers in which Roman and local practices and traditions interacted to create new amalgamations.

Under the emperor Claudius (A.D. 41–54) the province of Raetia was established, with the town of Augusta Vindelicum (now Augsburg) as its capital. New forts were constructed along the south bank of the Danube. When the emperor Nero (A.D. 54–68) committed suicide, the scramble among the potential successors Galba, Otho, Vespasian, and Vitellius led troops loyal to those men to leave their border stations and fight in support of their leaders. In the absence of the troops, local uprisings resulted in the destruction of many forts along the borders. Burned layers that include deposits of charcoal, ash, and debris reflect such activity at Mainz, Wiesbaden, Augsburg, Kempten, and Bregenz. On the lower Rhine, the Batavians staged a major uprising, led by Civilis, taking advantage of the temporary power vacuum on the frontier.

After Vespasian assumed the imperial throne in A.D. 69, uprisings were quelled, troops loyal to Rome were reinstalled in the border posts, and new forts were constructed, for example at Günzburg, Eining, and Regensburg-Kumpfmühl on the Danube. Between A.D. 82 and 90, the Emperor Domitian established the provinces of Germania Superior, with its capital at Mainz, and Germania Inferior, its capital at Cologne. Probably in the years 83–85, Rome began a systematic campaign against the Chatti who lived in the Wetterau region north of the Main River confluence into the Rhine. After the defeat of that group, Rome started the construction of the *limes* boundary, linking the middle Rhine frontier with that on the upper Danube, an undertaking that went on into the third century. At first, the *limes* was simply a road with wooden watchtowers along it. Later, a palisade was erected to mark the boundary between Roman and unconquered lands. Around the middle of the second century, stone guard towers were built. Toward the end of the second and beginning of the third century, a wall and ditch created a more substantial border marker.

Throughout the first century A.D., the Roman border had been regularly overrun by raiding parties from east of the Rhine and north of the Danube. Then the reigns of Trajan, Hadrian, and Antonius Pius (A.D. 98–161) were distinguished by peaceful conditions along these frontiers. In the middle 160s attacks on the frontier began again, from the Chatti and, more significantly, from the Marcomanni and Quadi north of the Danube. After the Marcomannic Wars of 166–180, relative peace reigned again until the 230s, when a series of incursions began that marked a turning point in the Roman Empire in Europe.

In most cases, new Roman military and civilian foundations did not take place in empty land, but in areas already occupied by indigenous groups. In some cases, Rome established its centers at existing important places, such as Cologne. By the middle of the first century after Christ, the Rhineland was becoming an economically active and wealthy part of the Empire, in part because of the large number of troops stationed there. The troops spent their earnings in the local environment in which they lived, and new markets developed around the military bases to serve the needs of the soldiers. In the Rhineland centers arose for the manufacture of a variety of goods, including ceramics, glass, and grindstones, and for extraction of materials such as building stone. Towns known by their Latin designation *vici* formed close to the military communities. These often developed into sizable manufacturing and commercial centers, and served both military and civilian customers. Rather than a hinderance to development, taxes charged to money-earners may have stimulated entrepreneurial activity by requiring producers to generate cash.

Incorporating Indigenous Peoples into the Empire

The summary above represents an outline of the progress of Roman expansion in continental Europe north of the Alps. Most studies of this process have focused on the military aspects of the conquests, including questions of strategy and motivation among leaders in Rome and generals in the field, reasons behind particular campaigns, tactics in battle, and policies toward defeated indigenous peoples. My concern here is rather with the impact of the conquests on the parties involved. The incorporation by Rome of lands in temperate Europe into its growing domains brought a number of significant results beyond the immediate political and economic changes. The Roman world had been in contact for nearly two centuries with the peoples that became incorporated into the empire with the conquests. From early in the second century B.C. on, Roman products attest to the importation of Mediterranean goods by central Europeans (see chapter 3). The burial evidence in temperate Europe indicates that Roman metal vessels were adopted by Late Iron Age elites as part of an elaborate set of display items associated with feasting ritual. Thus the change that took place at the time of the conquest was not in the establishment of contact and beginning of interactions between Rome and peoples who inhabited the lands north of the Alps. It was rather in a shift from interactions driven by economic factors to a situation in which Rome exercised some measure of political and military control over the European lands.

From the perspective of Rome, central and northern Gaul, the Rhineland, and the Alpine foreland of present-day Bavaria, all changed from little-understood, foreign, richly productive lands, to parts of the Roman world, administered by Rome. Even though the majority of the inhabitants continued to identify themselves as indigenous peoples, from Rome's viewpoint they had been incorporated into the Roman cultural sphere. They were within the political and economic boundaries of the empire, but culturally to some extent still outside of it. One result was the development of complex and conflicting understandings among different groups in the newly Roman lands. Through their incorporation they became part of Mediterranean civilization; but in their language, lifestyle, and material culture many remained barbarians. There was considerable potential for stress and tension in this new situation. The ways in which the indigenous peoples responded to the opportunities and the challenges tells us much about how they experienced, and how they directed, the processes of change. As we shall see, different groups, and even different individuals, among the indigenous peoples responded in different ways.

New approaches to the study of the indigenous peoples emphasize not how they were "Romanized" or forced to become "provincial Romans," but rather how they participated in the creation of the circumstances of interaction with Rome and in the construction of the new societies that emerged in the provincial landscapes. Recently a new focus of attention has developed on diplomatic, political, and social approaches to the issue of conquest, rather than on military perspectives. It is now understood that much of what Rome achieved in building its empire in temperate Europe was accomplished through alliances with native groups and through negotiation with indigenous elites. The Roman expansion into temperate Europe can be productively viewed as a process that involved interaction between peoples, negotiation with political leaders, and sometimes combat; but it was not a series of pitched battles. Viewing the Roman conquest from this perspective provides us with a different view toward the native peoples of the conquered lands, and toward interactions between incoming Romans and indigenous communities that led ultimately to the formation of new, multiethnic communities of Roman Period Europe.

In order to understand the Roman conquest from this perspective, we need to consider the indigenous peoples as decision-makers in the process. They were not simply hostile defenders, fighting to keep the Roman armies from their territories. In many instances, elites welcomed the opportunities offered by alliance with the Roman administration for increased status, power, and wealth. Analysis of elite burials from this period following the conquest provides valuable information about how they responded to these opportunities and how they constructed their identities in the incorporated territories.

Four well-outfitted burials at Goeblingen-Nospelt in Luxembourg excavated in 1966 are particularly informative. All date to the decades after the conquest of Gaul, between 50 and 15 B.C. All four were placed in wooden chambers similar to those of the Early and Late La Tène Periods, and all were covered with sizable mounds, another Iron Age tradition in the region. The corpses were cremated and the remains scattered on the floors of the burial chambers. Grave goods were placed, unburned, with the cremated remains.

All four graves contained objects that connect these individuals with the mounted warrior tradition of the Late La Tène Period. Each grave included iron lance points and one or two spurs. Three had long iron swords, and two had shields. In two graves, the well-preserved scabbards show the openwork ornament characteristic of many elite burials of prehistoric times. While these graves are united by burial practice and by the standard symbols of elite horse-riding warriors of indigenous tradition, they differ in objects from the Roman world that they contain. Graves C and D had indigenous fibulae and pottery of the post-*oppidum* period, between 50 and 30 B.C. Grave C contained no Roman objects; Grave D had a Roman amphora.

Grave A, dated between 30 and 20 B.C., contained both local indigenous pottery—some just like that in Graves C and D—and Roman vessels. These latter included early *terra sigillata*, imports from Italy, and products from Gallic potteries. A locally made pottery known as Belgic Ware that combined indigenous forms with newly introduced techniques of surface treatment and ornamentation appears in Grave A, represented by seven vessels. The grave also contained a Roman wine serving set comprising bronze dipper, sieve, and basin, probably made in Campania in Italy.

Grave B, dated between about 25 and 15 B.C., represents the most extensive transformation toward provincial Roman material culture, even though it contained an indigenous-style long iron sword with a scabbard elaborately ornamented with openwork. The weapons and horse-riding gear make apparent that this is the burial of an individual who was still identified with local tradition, but only three ceramic vessels out of forty are of indigenous character. A bronze cauldron and two wooden pails with ornamented bronze bands reflect local crafts, while five bronze vessels belong to the Roman wine service. The large number of Roman plates and dishes in Grave B may show that this individual had not only adopted many elements of material culture from the conquering society, but also Roman dining practices. The importance of feasting ritual among elites is represented in rich burials throughout the Iron Age, and here in Grave B at Goeblingen-Nospelt we see the continued significance of that ritual for the re-creation and expression of social status, now transferred from local equipment to the newly fashionable Roman tableware.

Three graves at Heimstetten near Munich that date to the decades just after the Roman conquest of that landscape south of the Danube provide instructive comparisons with the Goeblingen-Nospelt burials. All three were inhumation burials. Grave 1 contained the skeleton of a woman in her early twenties, Grave 2 of a girl about fourteen years of age; the skeleton in Grave 3 was not well preserved, but the burial goods were very similar to those in the other two graves and it is likely that that grave contained the body of a woman as well. All three graves were well outfitted with personal ornaments of kinds that characterize women's burials in Late Iron Age Europe—fibulae, bracelets, glass and amber beads, triangular openwork belthooks, and small rings with many decorative knobs on them. Grave 1 contained a Roman coin minted in the reign of Caligula (A.D. 37–41). That coin, and comparison of the style of the ornaments with those from other, well-dated contexts, indicate a date for the three graves between A.D. 30 and 60.

The fibulae are of several different types, representing a variety of forms that were circulating at the time. The bracelets, a neckring in Grave 3, and bronze objects called amulet-rings are distinctly archaic in character, closely resembling objects that were in regular use during the Late Iron Age. Some of the pottery, including a vessel in Grave 1 at Heimstetten and vessels associated with other finds of this group, bear strong similarities to the Late La Tène ceramics of the region.

In their studies of these Heimstetten graves and others of the same groups, some archaeologists interpret the metalwork and the pottery as developments of the styles of La Tène tradition. Others view the individuals buried in these graves as immigrants who settled in southern Bavaria during the reign of Tiberius (A.D. 14–37). As in the case of our earlier discussion of the post-*oppidum* graves in southern Germany, an interpretation in terms of cultural dynamics among indigenous peoples is more consistent with current understanding of changes in patterns of material culture in circumstances such as those that obtained in the region following the Roman conquest.

There is every reason to think that these graves represent indigenous peoples expressing conflicting identities in the process of change, rather than immigrants from outside. Probably the clearest indication is the connection between the pottery associated with these complexes and that of Late La Tène settlements in southern Bavaria. It was made by potters working in the local tradition of late prehistoric ceramics. The burial practice—inhumation with substantial personal ornaments in the form of fibulae, bracelets, neckrings, fingerrings, and belthooks—can be understood as a re-creation of indigenous traditions several generations old, from the practice of the great cemeteries that preceded the *oppida* throughout temperate Europe. This practice of re-creating earlier traditions is similar to the reuse of wooden chambers and burial mounds at Goeblingen-Nospelt.

At Heimstetten and at Goeblingen-Nospelt we see elite individuals buried in the decades just after the Roman conquests of the two regions, in funerary complexes that integrate new features introduced by the Roman presence with old traditions of the indigenous groups. These graves give us a special view into the ways in which elite members of the indigenous societies responded to the opportunities and challenges presented by the changes introduced with the coming of Roman military power and administration. The individuals in these graves were represented by the communities that outfitted their burials as eager to adopt goods from the Roman world, but not to give up important traditional signs of their status and identity in their native social systems.

✳ CHAPTER 5 ✳

Identities and Perceptions

T HE PRECEDING chapter has considered the evidence—textual, epigraphic, and archaeological—that informs us about the Roman conquests in temperate Europe and about some of the effects of those conquests on the native peoples. We need next to turn to a different set of aspects of the interactions, those of identity and perception. The ways in which the authorities in an imperial society view indigenous groups play a determinative role in the character of interactions and of the societies that develop in the colonial context. What did the Roman conquerors think about the indigenous peoples they encountered? What did the indigenous peoples think about the Romans? How did these perceptions affect the interactions, and how did the perceptions change through the process of interaction? What role did perceptions about the others play in the creation of new societies in the Roman provinces? To address these questions, I turn to four main categories of evidence—textual, pictorial, linguistic, and archaeological.

ROMAN PERCEPTIONS OF INDIGENOUS EUROPEANS

Texts

The Roman-native interactions in temperate Europe were classic instances of conquests of smaller-scale, nonliterate peoples by a larger-scale, literate society. The written records left by Roman generals, politicians, administrators, and others have been an immensely powerful force in interpretations of the progress of Romanization. If we are to try to achieve an unbiased view of the changes that took place during and after the Roman conquests, we must escape what Jonathan Friedman calls the dominant discourse of the conquerer. Conquerors' accounts—or indeed any accounts by members of one society about members of a different society—are notoriously biased. But if we can understand, and deconstruct, the biases, then we can make fruitful use of the texts. Texts are cultural constructs, and we need to treat them as such. To make sense of the Roman and Greek accounts, we must determine which of the assertions constitute stereotypes or tropes, then separate those and focus on the significant details left.

Roman writers represented the peoples of temperate Europe in terms of the characteristics with which they, as outside observers or compilers of information, were familiar. Before and during the Roman conquests in temperate Europe, this familiarity was most often in the form of interactions in military contexts. None of the writers whose works are preserved spent time living in an Iron Age village, nor were any of them merchants who traveled among the late prehistoric peoples north of the Alps. Hence we learn virtually nothing about everyday life from the textual sources. Some few remarks that the Greek author Polybius makes about appearance and habits of Celts pertain to the groups living in northern Italy, not in temperate Europe beyond the Alps. Instead, we read that the Gauls were brave, fierce, and very aggressive warriors and they used tactics and weapons different from those of the Roman armies. This information derives from a number of encounters, including the invasions of Italy during fourth and third centuries B.C., described by the later historians Polybius and Livy; the well-documented service by Celtic mercenaries in armies of Mediterranean potentates during the fourth, third, and second centuries B.C.; and the direct experience of Caesar and other generals fighting during the final century B.C. and, in the case of the peoples designated Germans, during the first century A.D. Most of the specific information about the native peoples north of the Alps derives from such confrontations. Hence it is highly military in nature, and it reflects the indigenous groups in circumstances of extreme stress, not in the course of daily life nor in circumstances before their conflicts with Mediterranean civilizations.

On a more general level, Roman and Greek writers perceived a fundamental difference between their literate civilizations and the groups they called barbarians—peoples of other regions who did not speak Latin or Greek and who practiced customs they regarded as peculiar. The ancient authors represented this difference in two opposite ways. Sometimes they portrayed barbarians as savage, uncouth, uncivilized peoples who behaved in unpleasant fashion. Other times, the authors idealized them as noble, simple peoples unspoiled by sophisticated lifestyles. But always they represented them as essentially different from the Romans and the Greeks.

Until quite recently, the great majority of modern studies treated the Classical texts as objective representations of the state of affairs in the European landscapes at the time of contact between the Iron Age peoples and the literate Mediterranean civilizations. But especially since the 1960s, a number of scholars have advanced more critical approaches to the texts, in concert with modern thinking and with anthropological models of interaction between more complex and less complex societies. In this section I shall address some of the issues raised in these studies.

In their descriptions of barbarians, the Classical authors almost invariably portrayed them in stereotypical ways, as unusually large, exceptionally strong and fierce, wild in nature, and childlike in many respects. The writers represented their lives as simpler than those of people in the Classical world, and the lands they inhabited were viewed as wilder and less transformed by cultivation than those of the Romans and Greeks. In the case of the peoples of temperate Europe, the further north they resided, the more extreme were these traits that differentiated them from the standard view of the Mediterranean cultures. Like most authors writing about different peoples and foreign lands, the Greek and Roman commentators were especially interested in portraying things they considered strange and outlandish. While Caesar drew a number of parallels between Gallic society and Rome, he also informs us about what he considered bizarre behavior among the Gauls, such as human sacrifice. When he mentioned Germans, he commented on practices that were probably exceptional, not typical. In the *Germania*, Tacitus distinguished groups among the native peoples by their peculiar customs.

There are two principal kinds of information transmitted by the ancient writers about these indigenous groups of temperate Europe. One concerns geography—where the groups lived. The other concerns their ways of life and character as peoples. The earliest known identification of the Celts is in Greek writers of the sixth and fifth centuries B.C. Hecataeus stated that *Keltoi* inhabited the lands around the Greek colonial city of Massalia (today Marseille on the coast of southern France), and Herodotus writing in the mid-fifth century B.C. indicated that the source of the Danube River was in lands occupied by *Keltoi*. Subsequent Greek writers, including Polybius, Posidonius, Diodorus Siculus, and Strabo, provide additional information about these peoples. But the most detailed account of the indigenous Celts of Europe, to whom the Romans referred with the name Gauls (*Galli*), was that of Julius Caesar, in his commentaries on the peoples of Gaul whom he conquered between 58 and 51 B.C.

In the case of Germans (*Germani*), Caesar is also our principal early source. The Greek geographer Posidonius may have written about the Germans a few decades earlier than Caesar, but his writings have been lost, though some of his observations survive as references in the subsequent works of other authors; it is not always clear which ideas came from Posidonius and which from later writers. The principal information that Caesar provides is that the Germans lived east of the Rhine River, while Gauls (Celts) lived west of it. Caesar went on to indicate that the Germans had a simpler and more rugged lifestyle than did the Gauls. To some extent, his portrayal of the Germans reflected a common attitude among Romans. Groups that inhabited lands near Rome were regarded as like Romans in fundamental ways, while peoples further away were considered more different.

Thus all of our earliest information about peoples named Celts and Germans comes from sources written by outside observers. The Greek and Roman writers defined the categories Celt and German, associated them with particular regions of temperate Europe, and ascribed specific characteristics to the peoples so designated. There is no reason for us to think that all of the groups whom the Classical writers referred to as Celts ever felt that they belonged to a common people, nor that those Caesar and Tacitus called Germans saw themselves as members of a distinct, super-regional population. Outsiders dominated the written discourse, and that domination persists today in the way most researchers approach issues of identity among the indigenous Europeans.

When the ancient texts were rediscovered late in the Renaissance, preserved in copies in European monasteries, the descriptions of the indigenous peoples of temperate Europe by the Greek and Roman writers were accepted as objective accounts of those prehistoric inhabitants. From the development of scholarship during the seventeenth, eighteenth, and nineteenth centuries on, the Classical writers' portrayals of the Celts and Germans have dominated the discourse of historians, archaeologists, and others concerned with the transition from late prehistoric to early historic Europe. In modern Europe, many nations look back for the definitions of their identities to the period in which their inhabitants were first named in written sources. The Gauls, as they were described by Caesar, are an essential part of France's modern national identity. In the minds of modern inhabitants of Great Britain and Ireland, the ancient Celts play a related, but not identical, role. For Germany, the *Germani* described by Caesar and by Tacitus form an important part of the national consciousness. In regard to modern scientific research, much of the archaeology of Iron Age Europe is still driven by the categorization of peoples created by the Classical writers, as a perusal of the many recent books about ancient Celts and Germans reveals.

The information regarding lifestyles of native Europeans is highly stereotypical. Descriptions of the Celts by Greek and Roman writers tell of a heroic, warrior-based society, with chiefs and followers eager for battle and just as enthusiastic about feasting and drinking when they were not fighting. Their courage has been described as reckless, and their politics as volatile. The men are portrayed as large, muscular, and fierce; the women as beautiful and brave.

During the first century B.C. and the first century A.D., when Germans entered the consciousness of Roman and Greek commentators, they were represented in similar terms, but with the frequent observation, especially by Caesar, that they were less civilized than the Celts, lived in smaller communities, and had less highly developed religious practices. Caesar informs us that the Celts had a designated group of religious leaders, the druids. The Germans had no such formal authorities nor did they practice sacrifice. According to him, the Germans were not farmers, but spent most of their time hunting or engaged in warfare. They had no permanent leaders, but elected temporary chiefs for military ventures. Caesar also informed his readers about the unusual creatures of the German forests, among them the unicorn and the elk, an animal without leg joints. Caesar explained that the elk could not raise itself from the ground and hence had to sleep on its feet, leaning against a tree. Locals captured the animals by sawing part way through a tree at its base; when the elk leaned against it, the tree fell over, and the animal fell with it and was easily dispatched. (These bits of fanciful natural history should caution us against relying heavily on details in Caesar's account of the Germans!)

Caesar's statements about the peoples he called Gauls indicate that he became somewhat familiar with their way of life through his experience during the campaigns. However, his portrayals make clear that he judged everything he saw in terms of his own background in Rome. He had none of the objectivity in his observations that we would expect of a modern anthropologist. His remarks about the groups he called Germans indicate that he was very poorly informed concerning peoples east of the Rhine. Even aside from his description of the bizarre forest animals, his statement about the lack of agriculture shows that either he was misinformed or was passing along false information.

The image that Caesar and other Roman writers had of the peoples beyond the Alps derived not only from their direct personal experience, but also from historical traditions of Rome. The migrations of the Cimbri and other groups from northern Europe at the end of the second cen-

tury B.C. (see chapter 3) played a major role both in Romans' conceptions of the cultural geography of temperate Europe and in Caesar's
attitudes and policies toward the peoples of Gaul and beyond the Rhine.
Those incursions were the second major episode of invasions from beyond the Alps, after the sacking of Rome in 387 B.C. by Gauls (see chapter
2), a tradition preserved in the writings of Polybius and Livy, and they
had rekindled Roman fears of barbarians from the north. As the peoples
of Gaul became more familiar to Rome, both through Rome's military
and political activity in southern Gaul during the second century B.C.
and through the growing trade from southern Gaul northward, Romans
developed a model of the European interior. According to this view, the
southern, more cultivated zone was inhabited by Celtic peoples; the
more distant, northern, more heavily forested region was inhabited by
other peoples. The Rhine River formed the boundary between these
imagined territories. In his accounts of the Germani living east of the
Rhine, Caesar connected the traditions about the Cimbri and the Teutones with the occupants of those landscapes in his time. In Classical
geographical thinking, rivers frequently were boundaries between peoples. Thus it may be that lacking a clear understanding of the character
of the peoples beyond the Rhine, Caesar followed traditional thinking
in making that river the boundary between the Gauls and the Germans.

Pictorial Representations

Representations of the indigenous Europeans in the art and iconography
of Rome provide another important source of information about perceptions. The earliest portrayals of Celts show battles between Gauls and
peoples of Italy and Greece during the fourth and third centuries B.C.
The Gauls of northern Italy are represented in heroic fashion as large
and muscular warriors, distinguished from their adversaries in being
partly or completely naked and sometimes wearing torques around their
necks. The great majority of these earliest representations of Gauls in
the Mediterranean lands and of later portrayals of Celts and Germans
north of the Alps revolve around the theme of war.

Every substantial victory won by Roman commanders against barbarian peoples was accompanied by public representations of the defeated
enemies. Some were in the form of monumental architecture on temples
and triumphal arches. Others were smaller in scale, such as individual
statues and altars. From the time of Caesar onward, coins were much
used as means of disseminating propaganda about defeated groups to
the wider Roman public (Figure 14). Domitian's victory over the Chatti

in A.D. 83 and Trajan's successes were particularly commemorated with the minting of new coins bearing stereotypical images of the barbarians.

The memorial columns erected under the reigns of Trajan (A.D. 98–117) and Marcus Aurelius (A.D. 161–80) are rich sources of information about Roman attitudes toward the barbarians beyond the Alps. Both bear long relief sculptures showing scenes of battles between Roman troops and barbarian peoples east and north of the Rhine and Danube frontiers. Both are idealized representations, showing heroic victorious Romans and defeated, humiliated barbarians. But there are significant differences in the portrayals that signal changes in Roman attitudes during the second century.

Trajan's column is an enormous monument, standing almost 140 ft. (43 m) tall and bearing a continuous narrative picture in the form of an upward spiral band. A statue of Trajan crowned the column, and the emperor's tomb was originally built into the base. The pictures portray wars against the Dacians in A.D. 101–2 and 105–6. The column may have served a purpose similar to that of Caesar's commentaries about the Gallic Wars—to present to the people of Rome an account of the military campaigns in which the leaders had invested so much manpower and resources. Just as Caesar told the Roman elites that his campaigns in Gaul were necessary to forestall future barbarian invasions on Rome, so too the Emperor Trajan represented the Dacians as a strong threat to Roman authority on the lower Danube. The barbarian enemies are represented in heroic fashion, as dignified warriors unable to resist the might of Rome. Their clothing, weapons, and the architecture of their settlements appear in realistic portrayals, and these representations match archaeological materials from these groups.

On the column of Marcus Aurelius, erected more than half a century later to commemorate the victories following the long and difficult wars against the Marcomanni and the Sarmatians, there is not the same indication of sympathy and admiration for the enemies. The portrayals do not emphasize as much their dignity and heroism, but rather the glory of the emperor and the invincible power of Rome. Comparison of these two columns, erected for similar purposes and representing similar themes, reveals important changes in Roman public attitudes toward the barbarian peoples on the European frontiers of the empire.

All of these public representations are important indicators for us in that they show how the Roman authorities transmitted information about the indigenous Europeans whom the empire was conquering to the people of Rome. The sculptures were all in prominent places, people saw them regularly in the course of their everyday lives, and the images

Fig. 14. Roman coins that portray victories over Celts. *(top)* Roman denarius from period of Caesar's Gallic Wars—*obverse*: head of a mourning Celtic woman, with a war trumpet (*carnyx*) behind her; *reverse:* female deity holding a deer's antlers in her right hand and a spear in her left. *(middle)* Roman denarius from 48 to 47 B.C.—*obverse:* female head with oak crown; *reverse:* trophy with Celtic weapons, including helmet, axe, shield, and war trumpet. *(bottom left)* Roman denarius from 48 to 47 B.C.—*reverse:* beneath a trophy sits a chained Celt with long hair. *(bottom right)* Roman denarius from 46 to 45 B.C.—*reverse:* trophy with Celtic weapons, below it a male and female Celt, mourning defeat by Caesar's army. Photographs courtesy of Bernhard Overbeck, Staatliche Münzsammlung, Munich.

must have become fixed stereotypes in the minds of the viewers. Coins were an even more immediate source of propaganda that confronted the public constantly. Regularly viewing pictures representing defeated peoples of Europe probably contributed to a widespread and unthinking acceptance on the part of the populace of Rome of the official attitudes toward the barbarians. The dominant content of that notion was that the peoples against whom the Roman armies were warring were different from Romans, and they were unattractive in their personal appearance and habits. These messages were very different from those that Roman soldiers stationed on the frontier received, as chapter 6 will show.

CELTS AND GERMANS: LINGUISTIC EVIDENCE

The linguistic patterns in Europe at the time of the Romans constitute an important source of information in the recognition of identities among the indigenous peoples. Language is a critical aspect of cultural and ethnic identity, though language and other aspects of ethnicity rarely overlap completely. The terms "Celtic" and "Germanic" used in designating early languages of temperate Europe are in themselves of complex meaning. These two categories are artificial creations by investigators working in the field of comparative philology in the nineteenth century. The categories "Celtic" and "Germanic" are based on study and comparison of known languages from later times, such as Breton and Irish for Celtic and English, German, and Gothic for Germanic. It is important that we bear in mind this fact that the categories are modern constructions imposed on early languages; the linguistic patterns in Late Iron Age Europe most likely did not correspond to the modern categories. Linguists can nonetheless distinguish between what they consider Celtic and Germanic languages at the beginning of historical times in temperate Europe.

The earliest datable evidence we possess for the languages spoken in temperate Europe is in the form of inscriptions from shortly before and around the time of Christ. Such inscriptions were first written in the context of intensifying contact between the peoples of temperate Europe and those of Greece and Rome, when writing was first introduced by those Mediterranean societies and adopted by some members of the indigenous groups.

For Celtic languages, the earliest datable traces are inscriptions written in Greek characters in southern Gaul, beginning as early as the third century B.C. Personal names that appear in those inscriptions correspond closely to names recorded later by Caesar, in the middle of the first century B.C. But some early inscriptions containing Celtic names occur in other locations. For example, two sherds of characteristic local pottery recovered at Manching bear incised Celtic names, written in Greek letters. At Port in Switzerland was found an iron sword with the name KORISIOS stamped in Greek letters onto the upper part of the blade. The name is believed to be Celtic. We do not know the significance of this stamp, whether it names the swordsmith or the owner. Latin writing was adopted by peoples considered to have been Celts by the first half of the first century B.C. Most common are inscriptions in the Latin alphabet on coins, for example among the Boii in central Europe and among some groups in east-central Gaul. The longest Latin inscription in temperate Europe from before the time of Christ is on the Coligny calendar found in Ain, France, a bronze tablet believed to date to the late second century B.C. and bearing calendrical information in a Celtic language.

The earliest datable evidence for Germanic languages is in the form of inscriptions of runes—short messages written in characters consisting of combinations of straight lines, a system common among Germanic peoples in the early Middle Ages. They include the inscription on the brim of the bronze helmet found at Negau (Ž
enjak) in Slovenia, probably dating to the second or first century B.C. Another early inscription is on the bow of a fibula from Meldorf in northern Germany, thought to date to the first century A.D., and an inscription from the bog deposit at Vimose in Denmark has been dated at about A.D. 160. By the end of the second century A.D., runic inscriptions were increasingly common. They occur mainly on small, portable objects such as fibulae and weapons found in northern Europe, especially in Denmark, southern Sweden, and northern Germany. Runologists suggest that runes of the late second and early third centuries display a level of skill and confidence indicating that they had been in use for a considerable period of time.

The distributions of early Celtic inscriptions in Gaul and runes mostly in northern continental Europe suggest a general geographical distinction between peoples who spoke Celtic and Germanic languages at the time of the Roman arrival in temperate Europe (Figure 15). Yet the evidence is complex and ambiguous. For example, the incised sherds from Manching with Celtic names written in Greek characters are far east and north of the great majority of early Celtic inscriptions. The Negau helmet is far south of the main distribution of early runic inscriptions. An analysis of early Celtic place-names suggests a distribution similar, but not identical, to that of the Celtic inscriptions. Names ending in -*dunum* attested in the ancient sources are concentrated in southern Gaul, but there are also examples in central and northern Gaul, in the Rhineland, and in the lands south of the upper and middle Danube, as well as in Britain. Names ending in -*magus* concentrate in southern Gaul and on the left bank of the Rhine.

In summary, this complex evidence of language suggests that at the time of intensifying contact with the Roman world during the second and first centuries B.C., peoples in Gaul spoke Celtic languages, and peoples in Denmark and adjoining regions spoke Germanic languages. But we are poorly informed about the languages spoken in other regions. Philologists know virtually nothing about the languages that were spoken in the lands east of the Rhine before the start of the Roman Period. Early Celtic inscriptions are even lacking from the Rhineland, though not, as the sherds from Manching indicate, from the lands east of the Rhine and south of the Danube. In the Roman Period too, names recorded from the province of Germania Superior are of Celtic character, like those of Gaul, not Germanic. In the Rhineland, personal names and names of settlement communities recorded during the Roman Period are mainly Celtic in character. But, curiously, names of deities, such as the mother goddesses that are common in the lower Rhine region (see chapter 9), are most often linked with Germanic personal names. This evidence may indicate the survival of Germanic name-elements in populations that otherwise were acculturated to Gallo-Roman society.

Wolfgang Meid interprets the linguistic evidence from the area between Gaul and northern Europe from which we have only sparse epigraphic evidence to indicate the existence of languages that combined elements of what we call Celtic and Germanic. He thinks that many people in this region probably spoke languages that modern linguists could not readily classify into one or the other of these modern categories. There is even evidence that personal names often included elements of what today would be considered Celtic and Germanic. Before the existence of modern political boundaries and language textbooks, linguistic patterns could vary much more widely.

ARCHAEOLOGICAL EVIDENCE

Celts

We can identify two extreme positions in the question of Celts and archaeology. One is represented by archaeologists who study the European Iron Age and who interpret literally statements by Greek and Roman

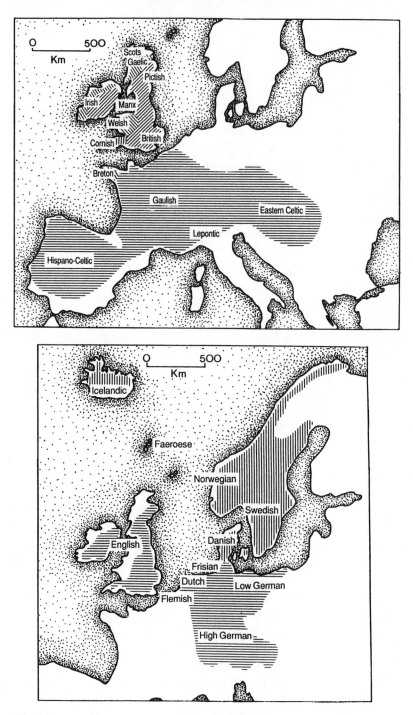

Fig. 15. Maps showing the distribution of Celtic *(top)* and Germanic *(bottom)* languages at the time of the Roman conquests, based primarily on evidence of place-names, inscriptions, and group and personal names. Note overlap in Rhine and upper Danube regions. The names identify languages recognized in later times. From Mallory 1989, pp. 85 and 95. Used by permission of Thames and Hudson Ltd., London, and J. P. Mallory, Queen's University, Belfast.

writers regarding the location and character of the Celts. According to this approach, the people who were living around the upper Danube in the middle fifth century B.C. were, following Herodotus, Celts. The peoples whose fourth and third century B.C. cemeteries have been excavated in northern Italy and whose grave goods are similar to those in eastern France and western Germany during the same period were, following Polybius's and Livy's accounts of the invasions across the Alps, Gauls (or Celts). The people inhabiting the lands west of the Rhine River in Caesar's time were Gauls, as described by Caesar. The statements by ancient authors concerning the society and behavior of the Celts can be linked to the archaeological evidence in the regions described as Celtic homelands. Proponents of this position view the Celts as a clear, unambiguous people whose identity as Celts was recognized both by themselves and by others.

The other extreme position is represented in a recent book by Malcolm Chapman entitled *The Celts: The Construction of a Myth* (1992). Chapman argues that the "Celts" did not exist as a recognizable group of people. The name was used by ancient writers to designate unknown peoples in the northern regions of continental Europe, beyond the shores of the Mediterranean and beyond the Alps. In modern times, the "Celts" were a construction by Romantic writers of the eighteenth and nineteenth centuries, seeking a unity among diverse groups that did not exist in any objective criteria.

How do we develop a reasonable research agenda in light of these two extreme and opposed positions? An important criticism by Chapman is that the ancient authors do not indicate the basis of their ascription of identity. They do not tell what criteria they use in identifying the people of one region as Celts rather than as another named group, such as Scythians. Instead, at least in the earlier texts of the sixth and fifth centuries B.C., "Celts" seems to refer generally to "those people beyond the Alps," barbarians that fit the stereotype. Similarly in Livy's account of the Gauls pouring across the Alps and into northern Italy at the start of the fourth century B.C., there is no reason for us to interpret this designation any more specifically than indicating peoples from beyond the Alps. Only in the final century B.C., when Caesar makes pointed distinctions between Gauls and Germans, can we constructively examine the archaeological evidence in relation to the designations made by the ancient authors. At that stage, it is useful to examine the relevant archaeological evidence first, then turn to the texts and ask what information could Posidonios, Caesar, Strabo, Tacitus, and the others have learned about the people represented in the archaeology that led them to make the assertions they made.

If we accept Herodotus's statement of the mid-fifth century B.C. that *Keltoi* lived around the headwaters of the Danube River, then we can link the name Celts with the material culture known as Early La Tène. This same link can be made another way, through the Champagne region of northeastern France and northern Italy. Greek and Roman texts concerning the fourth and third centuries B.C. refer to Celts living in the Po Plain and eastern central Italy, as the result of the much-discussed migrations across the Alps around 400 B.C. (see chapter 2). In the latter part of the nineteenth century, archaeologists working in Champagne noted that the style of decoration on objects in burials there, particularly metal ornaments, matched that on similar objects in the cemeteries in Italy. Thus the connection was made of *Galli* with peoples of northeastern France using the La Tène style in the fourth and third centuries B.C. But the problem with this approach is that the written sources of this period do not name any other peoples north of the Alps—any peoples with whom to contrast Celts. Just because groups producing objects ornamented in the La Tène style lived in regions where Herodotus and others say that Celts lived, does not mean that groups on the North European Plain making ornaments in the Jastorf style were not also Celts to the Greeks, if they were aware of them at all. Unfortunately, no other name for peoples in these regions north of the Alps appears in the ancient literature until Caesar's use of Germans. (Herodotus and other ancient writers knew of a group of peoples they called the Scythians, but they were placed far east of our regions, in the lands north of the Black Sea.)

For the early part of the La Tène sequence the connection between this style of ornament and the people known as Celts is problematic, since we know no other names to associate with other styles. In Caesar's time in the mid-first century B.C., the distribution of objects ornamented in the La Tène style does not correspond to the landscapes in which Caesar stated that Gauls lived. The La Tène style is well represented on both sides of the Rhine, both to the west where Caesar said Gauls lived, and to the east where he said Germans lived. This is the earliest clear assertion by an ancient writer concerning the location of Celts and Germans. The same material culture was in use on both sides of the Rhine—similar settlement types, house forms, burial practices, and similar pottery, iron tools, bronze and glass ornaments, and coins. Caesar's repeated assertions that the Rhine was the boundary between Celts and Germans has stimulated a vast literature in archaeology, but the apparent conflict between Caesar and the archaeology has not been resolved using traditional approaches.

Germans

The most important aspects of the Germans as they were described by Caesar and other ancient authors are that they, like the Gauls, inhabited lands beyond the Alps in temperate Europe; they lived east of the Rhine, in contrast to the Gauls; and their society was simpler and smaller-scale than that of the Gauls. But whereas in his account, Caesar emphasized differences between Gauls and Germans, Strabo, writing at about the same time, said that the Germans were very much like the Gauls and were closely related to them. The principal difference, according to Strabo, was that the Germans move more; he referred to substantial migrations that they undertook.

There is no evidence that in Caesar's time the myriad groups east of the Rhine that he lumped together with the term Germans felt any kind of common identity, such as we might recognize in common personal ornaments, designs on pottery, or burial practices. Furthermore, Tacitus, writing around A.D. 100, in the famous passage in the second section of his *Germania*, informs us that the name Germans had only recently come to be applied to the whole group of peoples. The issue is further muddled by the fact that the name Germani originally seems to have designated a much smaller group of peoples in northern Gaul, that is, west of the Rhine, not east of it. Caesar referred to this latter group as *Germani Cisrhenani* and said that they came into Gaul from lands on the other side of the Rhine. Caesar distinguished a small group called the Germani from the larger ethnic group he designated Germani, and that small group he said lived west of the Rhine, where, according to his general model, Gauls lived. Thus the name Germani is fraught with complications.

Caesar's several references to the Germani were all made in the context of his description of the Gauls, among whom he was leading the Roman military campaigns. As noted above, Caesar's account contains two important kinds of information about the Germani—they lived east of the Rhine, and they lived a simpler and less civilized lifestyle than did the Gauls, without towns, permanent governmental institutions, or organized religion. Before Caesar's arrival in Gaul in 58 B.C., the abundant archaeological evidence indicates very similar patterns west and east of the Rhine River. From the archaeology, we would never suppose that

113

the Rhine formed an ethnic boundary or any other kind of major division between peoples. The *oppida* are similar on both sides of the river. Pottery, iron tools, bronze and glass ornaments, coins, and other materials are very much alike in the two regions, as we have seen in chapter 3.

There are two contexts in which the archaeological evidence indicates groups that could be interpreted to correspond to Caesar's characterization of Germans. North of the central regions of temperate Europe, where the *oppida* existed and characteristic Late La Tène material culture was produced, small-scale groups lived. Their settlements were farmsteads and small villages, with no larger centers such as the *oppida*, and they did not produce wheelmade pottery, glass ornaments, or coins. Their iron-working technology was not as highly developed as that of their neighbors to the south, and they were not as much engaged in interaction with the Roman world, to judge by the dearth of Roman imports there compared to those in the *oppidum* zone. The dominant style of material culture in this northerly region is known as Jastorf (Figure 16). Much of Caesar's characterization of the Germans could fit what we know about groups characterized by Jastorf material culture. If Caesar had said that east of the *lower* Rhine the lands were inhabited by Germans, then this description could correspond to the archaeological situation. But Caesar did not make that stipulation in any of his remarks about the Rhine boundary.

Even more directly relevant to the issues we are considering are changes that took place in lands east of the upper and middle Rhine at about the time that Caesar conducted his campaigns in Gaul. As we have seen in chapter 4, many of the *oppida* east of the Rhine were abandoned, and considerable changes took place in settlement systems, manufacturing patterns, and burial practices.

DYNAMICS OF IDENTITY AND THE ROMAN CONQUESTS

The complexities of the Roman texts and of the archaeology can be better understood if we examine the evidence in the context of the changes in the archaeological material. Like most descriptions of indigenous peoples written by members of imperial societies, the Roman texts present the indigenous Europeans in static terms. Caesar, Strabo, Tacitus, and other writers seem to have been largely unaware that the Iron Age peoples of Gaul and Germany were undergoing substantial changes in their

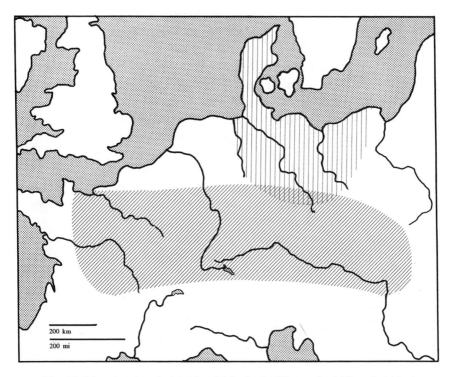

Fig. 16. Map showing regions in which the La Tène style *(oblique hatching)* and the Jastorf type *(vertical hatching)* material cultures were common.

social, economic, and political organization well before Caesar's campaigns in Gaul. Nor is there evidence in their writings that they knew that contact with the Roman world was profoundly affecting the structure and organization of those indigenous societies. Surprisingly, a similar lack of attention to the dynamic aspect of the indigenous European cultures characterizes much recent research in the fields of archaeology and ancient history.

As we have seen in chapters 2 and 3, societies in temperate Europe were undergoing significant changes for well over a century before Roman troops marched into Gaul under Caesar's command. Among the changes were the migrations southward and eastward, increased interaction with peoples in the Mediterranean region and in northern Europe, establishment of the *oppida*, and transformation of funerary practices. The arrival of the Roman army, first in Gaul and later east of the Rhine, was another of many factors that stimulated changes. In this section, we

115

need to examine evidence regarding the effects of the Roman conquests and of the establishment of provinces on the identities of the native peoples, both as they saw themselves and as the Romans saw them.

We know from more recent instances of contact between expansionary complex societies and smaller-scale indigenous ones that the latter groups typically change substantially as a result of the contact, frequently well before actual conquest. Studies in different parts of the New World show profound effects of interaction, both among the groups in contact with European explorers and conquerors, and among peoples living beyond the scenes of direct contact. In many of these cases, it is apparent that change brought about through mechanisms of contact took place before Spanish commentators gathered information about the indigenous groups. These well-documented instances in the New World raise the question for Roman Period Europe, how might the indigenous peoples have changed before Caesar and the other Roman writers arrived on the scene? When we pose the question this way, examination of the archaeological evidence in Europe makes clear that interaction with the Roman world had important dynamic effects on indigenous peoples before the Romans who did the recording came into temperate Europe. This observation makes all of the Roman accounts problematic. It is apparent that the writers were unaware of much that was going on around them. But with this question in focus, we can apply both the written and the archaeological sources of information to learn about Rome's early impact on the ways that native Europeans organized and represented themselves.

Tribalization and Rome

Recent analyses of ethnographic and ethnohistorical data show that the phenomenon we know as "tribes"—groups made up of thousands of people with a defined territory and a clearly designated leader—are characteristic of the peripheries of empires and other complex state-level societies. Tribes form in response to interaction between indigenous peoples and larger societies. Research in more recent colonial contexts in the Americas and in Africa reveals the mechanisms involved. When states expand through imperial conquest or colonization, they foster the formation of discrete political and territorial units among complex, multilingual, culturally diverse indigenous peoples. Such "tribal" units are easier for empires to administer than are the typical pre-imperial diverse societies, because they are usually accompanied by a leadership structure

116

that involves a single potentate. This individual can represent the tribe in dealings with the imperial state. Thus a colonizing power establishes static boundaries on groups that had been fluid and not easily understandable or administrable. Indigenous elite individuals play special roles in such tribes as mediators between the colonial power and the newly organized entities.

Jonathan Hill analyzes the process of tribalization in nineteenth-century North America. The conditions he describes are comparable in significant ways to those of indigenous Europeans at the time of the Roman expansion. From an early stage in interactions between colonial enclaves on the east coast of North America and indigenous peoples of the interior, a process began of what he calls the "geopoliticization of indigenous American cultural identities." In his model, the policies pursued by the expanding European state systems—specifically their concept of the nation-state—created tribal entities. The result was fixed tribes with specific territories and leadership structures that enabled interaction with the European American communities. This situation supplanted much more complex indigenous societies with less well defined boundaries and less institutionalized leadership structures. It was not until after 1860 that what we now regard as tribal names such as Cree and Ojibwa became associated with specific individuals and lands. Hill emphasizes what he calls the fluidity of groups before the tribalization process, and also the great extent of interethnic relations before the fixed tribal identities appeared. Both of these patterns could lie behind the archaeological evidence for very active movement and transmission of goods during the final centuries of the prehistoric Iron Age, and they may lie behind some of the phenomena that the Classical writers described as migrations.

The expansion of Roman activity in the south of Gaul during the second century B.C. (chapter 3) may have set in motion processes that contributed to the formation of the *oppidum* centers and of the tribal groups that Caesar and other writers describe. Significantly, the distribution of the *oppida* is very similar to that of Roman imports, including amphorae, bronze vessels, fine pottery, and coins. This is not to say that there were no self-recognizing groups in temperate Europe before the Roman activity in southern Gaul in the second century B.C. We know from the accounts by Polybius and Livy of the migrations into Italy that some of these peoples had group names and identified with their kinsmen back in Gaul. But the archaeological evidence shows that they did not have territorial centers comparable to the *oppida* and thus are not likely to have had as strong a territorial identity as tribal groups.

East of the Rhine during the latter half of the final century B.C. we can also identify evidence for a process of tribalization on the edges of the expanding world, but there it did not result in the formation of centers as large and complex as the *oppida*. Before the time of Caesar, the communities of what are now central and northern Germany had broadly similar, but locally varied, kinds of pottery, ornaments, and tools, and they practiced similar burial rituals, all characteristic of the Jastorf Culture (see chapter 2). At the time of the Roman military and political involvement in Gaul from the 60s B.C. on, the patterns in the lands east of the Rhine changed. Regionally distinctive groups became increasingly apparent, differentiating themselves from their neighbors by burial practice, pottery form, and other such material expressions. Even without the emergence of regional centers on the scale of the *oppida*, these changes appear to represent a process of tribalization across the new frontier of the expanding Roman imperial state. In his remarks about the lands east of the Rhine, Caesar names particular groups of peoples he calls Germans in the same way he describes the tribes of Gaul.

This change in the interregional patterning of material culture is accompanied by the emergence of communities larger and economically more complex than earlier ones. Before the time of Caesar's campaigns in Gaul, settlements in northern regions east of the Rhine were composed of loose agglomerations of farmsteads, typically comprising several buildings. Each farmstead was dominated by a three-aisled structure that combined human residence and livestock stalls. Other buildings included workshops and storage structures. But around the time of the Gallic Wars or shortly thereafter, new, considerably larger settlements were established, of which Feddersen Wierde and Flögeln, both in Lower Saxony, are well-studied examples. These settlements differ from earlier ones in their size and in their degree of economic integration.

The settlement at Flögeln began with four long houses set close together, and several outlying farmsteads. Near the settlement was a complex of fields, defined by walls built of earth and stone. Around A.D. 100, a more substantial village was established at the site, with six farmsteads enclosed within a fenced compound. Each farmstead had up to four house-barn combinations in it, together with other buildings. Altogether some fifteen or twenty dwellings were occupied at any one time during the second and third centuries representing a population of some 150 to 200 persons. The barns accommodated about sixteen cattle each, with a total of some 240 to 320 head at Flögeln. This new arrangement represents both a much greater population than any earlier settlement in the region and a much more highly integrated local economy.

These changes are also apparent in the burial evidence. Cemeteries that had been in use for some time earlier now were distinguished by some graves that were considerably more richly outfitted than others. At Harsefeld, for example, some men's graves during this period are characterized by weapons such as swords and lanceheads, spurs and other accouterments of horseback riding, ornate drinking vessels in the form of horns, and Roman bronze vessels used as urns.

In both of these instances—in Gaul during the second century B.C. and across the Rhine in Germany during the final century B.C. and the first century A.D.—the archaeological evidence suggests processes of change similar to the tribalization processes described by cultural anthropologists among indigenous groups in the New World during the Spanish imperial expansion. If this model is applicable, then in the formation of the *oppida* and of the regional groups across the Rhine we see the expression of new group identities among the indigenous peoples, created in response to Roman activity in the vicinity. There is also evidence that individuals responded to Roman categorization of them in the ways they came to see themselves and their roles in society.

Indigenous Responses to Roman Categories

During the preconquest decades of interaction, in the course of the conquests, and in the context of relations established after the conquests, there was abundant opportunity for indigenous peoples to become aware of their place in the Roman worldview and of Roman attitudes toward them. The natives surely must have responded to the categories in which the Romans placed them. The clearest archaeological expression of new identities created around Roman categories is in the practice of burying weapons with deceased men, both within the newly conquered lands and in regions beyond the frontiers. The practice of including weapons in graves first became a custom east of the Rhine shortly before the time of Christ. We know from the historical sources that this was shortly after the time when Germanic auxiliaries began serving in the Roman army (see chapter 4). Romans established the category of auxiliary soldier, and some indigenous men took on this category and were so designated by the weaponry placed with them in their burials.

There are good examples of this expression by indigenous individuals of their role in the Roman military framework. For example, at Wederath, Grave 1344 contained Roman-style weapons—a *gladius* sword, a *pilum* (spear), and a shield, all the typical equipment of an auxiliary soldier in Roman service. But Roman graves did not contain weapons, hence this burial was most likely that of a Treveri soldier who served in an auxiliary unit and after death was buried with the symbols of that role. Across the Rhine in unconquered territory there are numerous graves that contain Roman weapons and are believed to be those of Germans who served in auxiliary units, returned after their twenty or twenty-five years of service with their weapons, and were subsequently buried with these important signs of their relationship to the Roman world. Many such graves are in the large early Roman Period cemeteries in the lower Elbe region, including Putensen and Ehestorf-Vahrendorf. I shall say more about these burials in chapter 10.

Another important example of indigenous people's responding to Roman categorizations is in the practice of burying spurs, an essential piece of equipment for cavalry warfare. Ornate spurs occur in a significant number of men's burials dating to the final half of the last century before Christ, but rarely before this time. Very similar spurs have been recovered in graves within Gaul and beyond the Rhine frontier. In the Moselle River region, a landscape said to be the home of the Treveri, from whom Roman armies hired many cavalry troops, two warrior's graves at Konz, three at Goeblingen-Nospelt, and one at Thür exemplify this practice. Spurs of the type found in these graves also have been recovered in major cemeteries east of the Rhine, for example at Putensen on the lower Elbe and at Grossromstedt and Schkopau in central Germany. The practice of including spurs in warriors' graves just after the time that Caesar reported the employment of auxiliary cavalry troops strongly suggests that the individuals represented in these graves were responding to the Roman use of them as cavalry troops, thus creating for them identities as cavalry in Roman service.

Finally, we know from historical sources that it was Roman policy to establish friendly relations with leaders of peoples along the imperial frontiers, as a means of supporting the defense of the Roman territories. Caesar and other Roman writers mentioned a number of these "friendly kings" by name, but the texts provide little information about their status with respect to Rome or to their own communities. In 1988 a burial was discovered in the course of road construction work at Mušov in Moravia, just north of the Danube frontier, that may provide us with a detailed picture of the complex combination of cultural identities that such an individual encompassed. The excavation report describes a large wooden chamber measuring about 20 by 13 ft. (6 x 4 m) and covered with a stone mound, that housed the burial. Although the chamber had been robbed, an extraordinarily rich assemblage of grave goods was found by the archaeologists, including more than 150 objects of metal, glass, and pottery (Figure 36). This grave, situated about 35 miles (60 km) north of the Danube frontier, shows how local rulers displayed their status and wealth through both Roman imports and significant objects of local manufacture. The grave contained eight or more bronze vessels, a set of silver tableware, glass vessels, and ten pieces of provincial Roman pottery. Ornate furnishings also included a Roman bronze folding table and two-part bronze Roman lamp. Iron andirons, several weapons, numerous personal ornaments, sixteen spurs, and handmade pottery represent local craft industries. Some of the objects, such as the lamp and folding table, are characteristic of burial inventories of provincial Roman elites while others, such as weapons and spurs, are characteristic of indigenous, non-Roman traditions. The elaborate sets of Roman ceramic, bronze, and silver dinnerware suggest not just importation of goods or even receipt of diplomatic gifts, but rather a personal familiarity with Roman banqueting customs. This individual was thus represented in his burial as an elite Roman, but also as an elite native of the unconquered territories. His identity, as portrayed in the grave, was thus in part created in response to the Roman category of "friendly king," and in part the re-creation of the traditional position of the elite warrior in European society.

✳ CHAPTER 6 ✳

Development of the Frontier Zone

CHANGE AND DIVERSITY

THE NEXT FIVE chapters concern changes that took place in temperate Europe after the Roman conquests (Figure 17). It is important at the outset to recall that the societies of temperate Europe were undergoing substantial changes in economy, social structure, and political organization before the arrival of the Roman armies (see chapters 2 and 3). Thus we should not attribute all of the changes reflected in the archaeological material to the effects of Rome. Instead, we need to ask how ongoing processes in the indigenous societies and innovations brought by the conquerors contributed to the complex mix reflected in the evidence in the new provinces.

Typically the conquest of a region by Rome was followed by a period in which military bases were established for the stationing of troops who were charged with suppressing any residual unrest among the newly subjected peoples. After a generation or so, the introduction of new infrastructure began in earnest, with the laying out of major towns on grid plans and the erecting of public buildings in stone, construction of paved roads for moving troops and commerce efficiently, and official designation of territory as a new province. Aqueducts were constructed to provide towns with fresh water, baths were built, and temples erected. The timing and exact nature of these developments varied with region and with circumstances.

Viewed over the entire landscape we are considering in this book, the changes were complex and varied and cannot be reduced to any single formula. In every instance, the textual and archaeological evidence shows a complex pattern of combining indigenous traditions and elements introduced by the Roman military or administrative apparatus. Viewed as a whole, the dominant aspect is diversity. Our principal source of information is archaeological, because textual sources say little about the details of setting up provincial administrations and creating the infrastructure in the new territories.

The pattern of change in each region of the new provinces was different. Particular burial practices, ritual structures, pottery types, and orna-

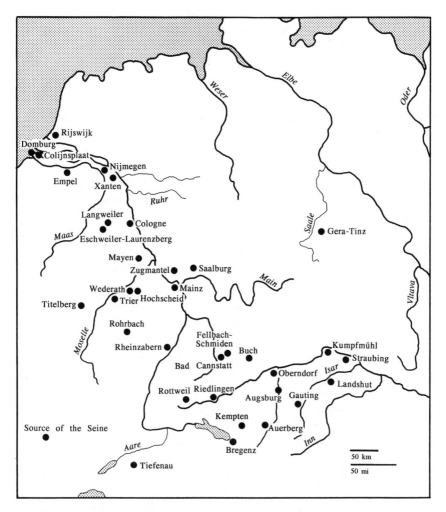

Fig. 17. Map showing locations of places mentioned in chapters 6, 7, and 8.

ments characterized some provinces, but not their neighbors. Each community experienced changes differently. Even on the level of the person, the structure and arrangement of burials and the inclusion of specific kinds of grave goods shows that we can distinguish differences between individuals in how they experienced changes in this period. Men and women in the provinces experienced them differently, as we would expect from recent studies of gender differences in colonial situations. For example, research into changes in clothing practices shows that men tended to adopt new fashions more quickly than women, who retained traditional garments well into the Roman Period. Status also affected how individuals responded to the new situation. Persons of elite status had different interests in adapting to the new Roman administration than did persons of lesser positions in their societies. The complexity of responses to the new situations of Roman domination that we can expect on the part of the indigenous peoples of temperate Europe—on the level of the individual, the community, and the society—is readily apparent in studies of modern colonial contexts.

The next four chapters examine changes that took place after the Roman conquests in the regions that became the frontier provinces. This chapter focuses on the early phase in the establishment of the frontier zone, especially concerning the most important element of Roman civilization there, the army. This early phase is defined by Rome's giving up its aim of conquest east of the Rhine in A.D. 16 and by the disruption of peace in Roman Europe by the Marcomannic Wars in A.D. 166.

Chapter 7 examines evidence for the persistence of indigenous traditions after the conquests. Its primary purpose is to show that the conquests did not result in landscapes devoid of indigenous populations, nor in subject peoples who quickly gave up their traditions to become provincial Romans. The evidence suggests that after the conquests, all of the landscapes of temperate Europe remained substantially populated by indigenous groups who had occupied those lands for generations. Despite the textual accounts about large-scale migrations, the archaeological evidence shows a much stronger element of in-place development. The migrations may have been on a smaller scale than many modern investigators have thought, and many may have included return migration (see chapter 2). As we shall see, after the conquest indigenous groups continued doing many things the way they had done them during the prehistoric Iron Age. This is not to say that they remained unaltered. Human communities are in a constant state of change, and much of the variation apparent in the archaeological material reflects gradual change in traditions, not abrupt shifts after the conquests.

In chapter 8 I examine the civilian aspects of change in the frontier zone during the early period, focusing first on towns and then on the countryside.

Chapter 9 focuses on the next century, from A.D. 166 to the middle of the third century. During this phase, changes in Rome and in other parts of the empire combined with increased pressure on the frontier in temperate Europe by groups to the east to bring about major changes in the provinces. Among those apparent in the archaeological material is the reemergence of symbols of local identity that had gradually fallen out of use during the first few generations of the Roman Period.

The penultimate chapter examines changes on the other side of the Roman frontier, among groups east and north of the empire. Peoples inhabiting those landscapes had important effects on the Roman provinces, just as the presence of the Roman empire west of the Rhine and south of the Danube had a substantial impact on the societies in those regions.

THE ROMAN FRONTIER IN EUROPE

The purpose of this chapter is to examine the ways in which the indigenous peoples of temperate Europe reacted to, and participated in, the Roman administration's establishment of its basic structures of defense, administration, and economy in the European frontier provinces. The focus here is on the period between A.D. 16 and 166. In A.D. 16, the Emperor Tiberius recalled his general on the Rhine frontier, Germanicus, thereby apparently giving up his designs on further large-scale campaigns eastward from the Rhine to the Elbe. From that time, we identify a consolidation of Roman military power along the Rhine border, and with that the political, economic, and cultural development of the Roman Period Rhineland. The Marcomannic Wars that began in A.D. 166 resulted from a variety of stresses in the lands north of the middle Danube and caused severe disruptions in the border zones of the Roman Empire.

Two problematic issues must be introduced at the outset—the concept of the frontier in relation to the Roman Empire, and the many processes commonly referred to as "Romanization."

The concept of the Roman frontier has been much discussed in historical and archaeological studies in Europe, especially in Britain and Germany, where physical remains of walls—e.g., Hadrian's Wall and the *limes* wall—and watchtowers encouraged an early focus on physical barriers between Roman territories and others beyond them. Studies of imperial Rome advanced substantially during the latter decades of the nineteenth century and in the early years of the twentieth century, before the First World War, at the same time that Britain and Germany reached the apogees of their imperial powers. Much of the thinking and writing about the Roman world by scholars such as Haverfield in Britain and Mommsen in Germany was deeply influenced by the contemporaneous imperial situations. Such investigators, living and working in imperialistic societies of the late nineteenth and early twentieth centuries, probably reacted to the unsavory aspects of the modern situation by idealizing the extent of order and organization in the Roman Empire. In modern times too, the boundary that separated western and eastern Germany, including the wall through Berlin, played a significant role in the conceptualization of the Roman frontiers, especially by German scholars.

Probably most important in the recent change of thinking about the Roman frontiers has been the growth in comparative approaches to frontiers as universal phenomena in world history. As a number of investigators have shown, Roman frontier phenomena can be productively approached through comparison with other frontiers. Among those most often brought into the discussion are the eighteenth- and nineteenth-century western frontiers in the growing United States and the frontiers of the British Empire in the late nineteenth and early twentieth centuries, both of which are abundantly documented with historical sources. Among the important ideas to emerge from such comparative studies is the demonstration that frontiers are not boundary lines that can be neatly defined by walls or even by natural features such as rivers. Frontiers are instead zones of interaction, broad areas of land on which peoples that live within the imperial territories interact with peoples living outside of them. This new perspective has greatly advanced studies of the Roman frontier, making many phenomena observed in the archaeological record understandable. In this chapter, I use the term "frontier" in this sense of a zone rather than a line. The frontier zone includes lands on both sides of the arbitrary lines that define borders. I focus here on the part of the frontier zone that was within Roman territory. This was a critical area in which Roman authorities gathered and processed information on the outer reaches of Roman imperial control.

The term "Romanization" has been used since the latter part of the nineteenth century to designate the spread of "Roman culture" to the peoples in the territories Rome conquered; its use implies that people who had been Romanized essentially became "Romans," culturally if not legally. The use of the term was based on a now outmoded concept of acculturation, whereby the representatives of the larger, more complex culture—the Romans—brought the obvious benefits of their lifestyle to more primitive peoples, who eagerly adopted it. It is easy to scoff at such simplistic notions of cultural process today, but even in the 1930s, when anthropologists and archaeologists were first beginning to deal systematically with issues of interaction between societies, such thinking was not out of place.

According to our current understanding based on studies in anthropology, history, and literature, processes of cultural change that take place when societies interact intensively over an extended period of time are much more complex than one society adopting cultural traits from another. When two societies interact, each affects the other. Yet studies of the Roman Period have tended to greatly overemphasize what have been interpreted as Roman effects on the indigenous peoples, and underemphasize—or completely ignore—effects of the indigenous societies on the Roman Empire. Aspects of Roman culture that were adopted by natives in temperate Europe are more obvious to us than aspects of the indigenous societies that were adopted by representatives of Rome, mainly because we have been trained to look for them. The whole purpose of this book is to focus on the other interchange—the impact of the native peoples on the societies that developed through the interactions.

The word "Romanization" implies a standard process. The reality is that in all contact situations, the character of interactions and of borrowing and adoption are different in different places and at different times. There is great variation, and the only way to study it effectively is to examine specific cases. Thus I focus my analysis in this book on specific archaeological sites and what they can tell us about the changes that were taking place.

Even the word "Roman" is highly problematical in reference to temperate Europe. Properly speaking, the word might refer only to individuals and objects directly associated with the city of Rome. When we discuss the soldiers, administrators, and merchants in temperate Europe, we must be cautious, because we know that many were not from Rome. Many were from northern Italy, or southern Gaul, or other regions that Roman armies had conquered. The Roman army comprised many auxiliary troops recruited from newly conquered lands and even from unconquered territories beyond the frontier. This issue of the use of the word "Roman" becomes critical when, for example, we read of the Roman army as a major force in "Romanization," or in bringing Roman culture to the provinces. In fact, in the frontier provinces, the majority of the "Roman" soldiers were auxiliaries; aside from their military equipment and presumably some of their training, there was nothing "Roman," in the sense of the city of Rome, about them. Similarly, we need to be cautious when we refer to "Roman pottery." The classic fineware used in the European provinces was *terra sigillata*, a style originally manufactured in central Italy but subsequently made in southern Gaul, central Gaul, and eventually even in Germania Superior and Raetia. To call *terra sigillata* manufactured at Rheinzabern or Westerndorf "Roman" pottery makes little sense, since the potters were most likely descendants of indigenous groups of the area. It is, of course, a moot question, whether they considered themselves "Romans" or "indigenous peoples." Most likely, they did not think in these categories at all. Perhaps "Roman-style" would be a better designation, since it recognizes that the style originally came from Roman Italy, and modern researchers perceive it as an indication that the consumers identified, on some level, with the cosmopolitan culture. But we must exercise caution in assuming that consumers in temperate Europe necessarily viewed such objects as linked to the Italian city of Rome in any way.

NEW APPROACHES TO THE FRONTIER

Once Rome had gained political control over the landscapes of temperate Europe, either through military conquest or through diplomacy and negotiation, its next task was to secure the lands and to introduce Roman structures and values. Past studies of "Romanization" have focused principally on the Roman side—the activities of Roman soldiers, administrators, and architects in re-creating Roman culture in the provinces. Roman forts have been described as microcosms of the Roman world, and the new cities, such as Cologne, Trier, Mainz, and Augsburg, have been compared closely with Roman cities in Italy. The written sources, composed by individuals who identified with Romanness, overstate the degree to which the lifestyle and material culture of the provinces became "Roman." The questions I pose are, how were the native peoples affected by the Roman arrival and the introduction of new structures and values, how did they act to adapt to the changes, and how can the material evidence inform us about their experience?

The past emphasis on the Roman side of the changes results from two main factors. As explained above, the literary tradition left by Roman writers has been very powerful in guiding thinking about the character of the Roman provinces. At the time when archaeology as a serious field of inquiry was developing, the practitioners were largely trained in the Classics. In the latter half of the nineteenth century, when Roman sites were first being systematically excavated and institutions were being established to foster further investigations, the groups that became involved in the discipline held the Roman and Greek writers in high esteem and accepted their accounts as objective statements of fact. This attitude was perpetuated in the educational systems of England, France, Germany, and other countries throughout the twentieth century, with the result that archaeologists, as well as historians, still tend to begin their research with the assumption that the written sources record facts, and the archaeology provides details that can be integrated into the framework created by the texts. Thus our perspectives on the changes that took place in the provinces have been determined substantially by the accounts left by Roman writers.

Another factor is the character of the Roman material remains. The Romans introduced stone architecture into Europe north of the Alps. Stone had been used in Neolithic times in the construction of the megalithic monuments, during the Bronze and Iron Ages for building burial chambers and mounds, and in the Late Iron Age for the facing of *oppidum* walls. But the prehistoric peoples in most of temperate Europe did not use stone for building houses, ritual structures, or public architecture. The Romans introduced stone architecture for city walls and gates, military buildings, public monuments, temples, villas, and bath complexes (Figure 18). Since stone architecture withstands the passage of time in ways that wood does not, many structural remains of Roman architecture survive on the surface, and the stone foundations of Roman buildings are much easier to find and follow than are the often obscure postholes from the indigenous, wood-based building techniques. Roman portable material culture is also more apparent than its indigenous counterpart. Roman pottery, glassware, bronze and iron implements, and coins were extremely popular in the provinces, and they are abundantly represented on archaeological sites. Indeed, Roman industries mass-produced basic goods for consumption both in the capital city and in the provinces. Excavation of Roman Period sites yields large quantities of Roman-style material.

This great flourishing of Roman architecture and abundance of the portable objects of Roman tradition in the provinces has led to the widespread and uncritical designation of the societies inhabiting the European provinces as "Romans." But this concept of Roman needs to be examined critically. Many recent studies have shown that most of what is regarded as typical Roman architecture—in temples, public buildings, and villas—was built under the sponsorship of indigenous individuals, adopting Roman fashions for their own purposes. Most of the Roman portable material culture in the provinces was used by indigenous

Fig. 18. The Porta Nigra at Trier, the northern gate in the Roman city wall.
The structure stands nearly 100 ft. (30 m) tall.

peoples, especially elites, in temperate Europe who wanted to display their familiarity with and access to the latest cosmopolitan fashions in architecture, pottery, glassware, and personal ornaments. Before the conquest, Roman imports were scarce and highly valued, and they are found almost exclusively in elite contexts. After the conquest, they became more generally available, and much greater proportions of people could acquire them.

ROME AND THE PROVINCIAL POPULACE

In contrast to some other imperial situations, such as the Spanish in the Americas, the Roman conquerors generally did not force indigenous peoples to adopt Roman religion or any other trappings of Roman civilization. But the archaeological evidence makes clear that Roman fashions were attractive to many people in the provinces. Many natives adopted the architecture, ceramics, metal vessels, and personal ornaments that Rome introduced. However, those who did not may have been more numerous than most investigators believe. As I demonstrated in chapter 4, communities that did not acquire Roman imports or otherwise adopt Roman fashions but instead continued to build their houses and make their pottery and jewelry in traditional ways are very difficult to distinguish from Late Iron Age communities. Recent studies in Hungary and Germany show that many communities did not adopt Roman styles as early as others in their regions did, either because they could not afford to or because they chose not to. To a large extent, in the early phases the adoption of Roman fashions was probably largely a matter of social status—individuals of exceptional status and wealth were able to acquire the accoutrements of the conquerors, others were not.

Roman authorities were concerned with winning the loyalty of the elites in native societies, because they could then serve as Rome's representatives in the countryside. We use the term "elites" in archaeology as a convenient idiom to refer to groups and individuals that possess more wealth or authority than the majority of the members of a society do. The word is purposely vague when we use it in this general sense. The character of elites—how they acquire their positions, how they use their wealth, how they exercise their authority—varies between societies and over time within communities. The concept can be broken down into subcategories, such as political elites, social elites, military elites, and religious elites. The origin and behavior of elites are important topics in the social sciences, but outside the purview of this book. In the case of natives in the new Roman territories, some elites probably derived their status from their ancestry in the local societies, some through economic success in the expanding commercial world of late prehistoric and Roman Period Europe, and some perhaps through distinguished military service as auxiliaries in the Roman army.

Rome's ability to integrate many diverse peoples on three continents into its empire was unique. Egon Flaig distinguishes three principal mechanisms the Romans used to achieve this aim. One was introducing what he calls the "Roman way of life," especially the urban lifestyle of the Mediterranean world. He suggests that new urban settings tended to break down traditional identities and encouraged those people affected—primarily elites—to partake of a whole series of new integrating activities. Numerous signs of Romanness permeated urban settings, including monumental architecture and heroic statuary. Public festivals and spectacles in the amphitheater served to transmit Roman values and ideals to the new urban dwellers.

Another mechanism was the granting of Roman citizenship to individuals of diverse backgrounds. The concept of citizenship developed in the Greek and Roman worlds at the same time that urbanism was growing. The Roman tradition differed from the Greek, for example, in frequently granting citizenship to many different groups within the empire. Thus Roman citizenship was not tied to a particular territory, but instead was connected to participation in Roman civic life and the sharing of a particular set of values. In practical terms, an individual who was granted citizenship in a province became exempt from the authority of the governor, and also gained advantages in tax payments. Rome granted citizenship to some members of indigenous societies, particularly to elites who had aided the Roman cause during the period of conquest, and significantly to auxiliaries after their period of service (see below).

The third mechanism Flaig identifies was the advancing of indigenous elites into the Roman imperial aristocracy, especially in the context of their service commanding auxiliary troops in the army. Through these latter two means, the indigenous elites became the focal points of the new order in the provinces. They became in effect "Romans" and faithful to Rome, but at the same time remained leaders in the local social systems. They thus served as bridges between the cultural traditions, while playing dual roles themselves. The latest two of the four graves at Goeblingen-Nospelt described in chapter 4 reflect this phenomenon in the decades immediately following the conquest of Gaul. An example of this representation of Romanized elite identity at the end of the first century A.D. is Grave 8 at Nijmegen in the Netherlands, discussed below.

The Army and Indigenous Peoples

Throughout the frontier zone that is the topic of this study, there was often a considerable time lag of a couple of generations between the conquest of territory and the establishment of the Roman infrastructure of government and building of towns, roads, and other manifestations of the imperial power. Caesar completed the conquest of Gaul in 51 B.C., but it was not until the time of Augustus (27 B.C.–A.D. 14) that the Roman administration undertook the organizing of the new provinces there, in large measure because of distractions of the civil wars in Rome. The lands south of the Danube were conquered in 15 B.C., but organizing and building projects in the province of Raetia did not begin until the second half of the first century A.D.

The Army on the Frontiers

In A.D. 100, the imperial Roman military forces totaled about 300,000 soldiers, roughly half legionary troops and half auxiliaries. Of this total, about 90,000 were stationed in the Rhineland and another 20,000 in Germania Superior and Raetia. During the first and second centuries, the majority of the troops stationed along the frontier were auxiliaries. By the third century the units stationed along the Rhine and Danube frontiers constituted the greatest concentration of troops anywhere in the Roman Empire. Their purpose was both to deter and, when necessary, to repulse incursions across the frontier by war parties from the unconquered territories, and to discourage and put down uprisings within the provinces. The Roman army was unlike any other in preindustrial times in that it was a highly professional fighting force, with soldiers who devoted twenty or twenty-five years of their lives to their military careers.

We have descriptions of fighting in the works of a number of Roman writers, most notably Caesar, Tacitus, Cassius Dio, and Josephus. The columns erected in Rome by the emperors Trajan and Marcus Aurelius include scenes of battle between Romans and barbarians (see chapter 5). These sources of information tell us about the appearance and equipment of soldiers in combat and about military tactics. But of course the great majority of soldiers spent most of their time doing things other than fighting. The majority of the frontier troops on the Rhine and Danube between A.D. 16 and 166 probably saw little military action. Since the Roman troops were the most important representatives of the imperial authority in interactions with the indigenous peoples, it is important for us to consider what we know about their experience, daily lives, and perspectives.

Information collected from a wide variety of sources enables us to put together a general picture of the lives of the troops on the frontiers. Roman soldiers had numerous tasks besides fighting and preparing for battle. They had to fell trees and prepare timber for construction, build and maintain fortification walls, and dig ditches. Tacitus reports complaints by legionary soldiers engaged in such tasks in Germania Inferior during the first century A.D. At the bases, many soldiers practiced specialized crafts; they included surveyors, blacksmiths, sword-makers, coppersmiths, woodcutters, carpenters, wagon builders, trumpet-makers, leather-workers, and butchers. But soldiers also had considerable leisure time, during which they were free to enjoy themselves. We know that they visited the baths and gambled, but we do not have much information about other ways they spent their free time, since this was not a matter of concern to the authorities who left the written records. Surely many soldiers must have established relationships with local women (see below). Overall, Roman soldiers occupied a relatively high position in their society. They were well cared for and well paid, and the individual soldier had opportunities to rise in rank and social status through diligent service.

Most of our information about the soldiers comes from documents written by Roman authorities. Inscriptions on tombstones and on military diplomas provide some information, but that concerns mainly specific facts regarding individuals' origins, places of service, and time of retirement. An unusual and highly informative source regarding soldiers on the frontiers is the discovery of wooden writing tablets at Vindolanda in northern Britain, preserved in ideal circumstances in a waterlogged environment. As of 1994, archaeologists had recovered over two hundred readable texts from the site. Most of them contain information about supplies for the troops, but many are personal letters composed in Latin by individual soldiers. It is not clear whether the soldiers themselves actually wrote the letters, or whether they hired scribes to do the writing. In any case, the texts indicate that the soldiers who composed them possessed considerable verbal ability in expressing their thoughts.

The army was the Roman institution that had the most direct and most profound impact on the indigenous peoples of temperate Europe. In sheer numbers of soldiers stationed along the Rhine and Danube Rivers, this institution was bound to have a major impact on the environments in which the troops were stationed. They created new demands on foodstuffs, raw materials, and manufactured goods that played an important role in economic change in the provincial landscapes and also beyond the frontier. Native communities resided near the forts, and frequently special settlements—*vici*—were established next to the forts specifically to provide goods and services needed by the troops. Thus there was considerable personal interaction between individual soldiers and natives, though this level of interaction is difficult to demonstrate archaeologically in the present state of our understanding of the material.

The Roman army was composed of two main categories of soldiers. The legionaries were Roman citizens. In the early days of the empire, they were recruited in Italy, both by volunteer service and by conscription, but during the first and second centuries A.D., legionaries were recruited increasingly from among citizens of the provinces. Even when legionary soldiers were not from Italy, as citizens they embodied at least some essential Roman values and attitudes, and for the most part they were able to speak Latin. Large numbers of recruits were drawn from southern Gaul, Noricum, and Spain. Over time there was a tendency to recruit from the provinces in which the soldiers were to serve, both to make recruiting easier and to ensure dedicated fighting in defense of home territory. In the year A.D. 5, the term of service of legionaries was established at twenty years, with another five years in the reserves. By the middle of the first century, their term of regular service had been extended to twenty-five years.

Unlike the legionaries, auxiliaries were not Roman citizens at the start of their service or while they were in the army, but upon completion of their duty they were granted citizenship. Auxiliaries were recruited in the lands that Rome conquered, and many even came from unconquered territories beyond the Roman frontier. Surely citizenship was considered an honor and a privilege by individuals who earned their status through two decades of military service. Early in the empire, auxiliaries were often led by their own leaders and were organized into "ethnic units"—units composed of soldiers from specific indigenous peoples. Auxiliaries most often served close to their home territories. Cavalry units in the Roman army, known as *alae*, were often composed of auxiliaries, hired because of their special skill at fighting on horseback. For example, some German troops from the Rhineland region were considered exceptionally able horsemen, and Roman commanders recruited them specifically for cavalry duty. Other auxiliary soldiers served in light infantry units. By the latter half of the first century, auxiliaries, who probably numbered roughly the same as legionaries, typically served a twenty- or twenty-five-year tour of duty.

Along the frontier in temperate Europe, the majority of the troops were auxiliaries. When Rome conquered a region, it was common practice to draft the men and boys into auxiliary units of the army. Service in the Roman army was an important experience in exposing these individuals to Roman practices and values and to the Latin language. Written sources do not provide much information about the experience of individual auxiliaries, but of the roughly 400 extant inscribed bronze military diplomas, some 260 are those of auxiliaries. The archaeological evidence of burials shows, as we shall see below at the cemetery at Kempten, that many of these individuals combined their experience serving in the Roman military with aspects of their traditional identity to form a complex amalgamation that constituted an important element in the cosmopolitan society of Roman Period Europe.

Frequently, as for example in the case of the province of Raetia, the men and boys inducted into the auxiliary forces were sent out of their homelands to be stationed elsewhere on the imperial frontiers, as a precaution against their participation in an uprising among their own people. (This practice varied with time and place.) The effects of such removal of the adult male portion of the population on the economy and society of the remaining indigenous peoples are apparent in one well-studied region. In the Dutch River area, the sending of the men off to Britain in A.D. 43 resulted in a gradual shift from a primarily livestock-raising economy to one in which agriculture played a larger role, and to a society with growing hierarchical organization.

During the first two centuries A.D., auxiliary troops frequently used the traditional weapons of their group, and often their traditional combat tactics as well, which could be advantageous to Rome in fighting other indigenous peoples. One sign of the degree to which auxiliary soldiers could adopt Roman values is the sculpting of gravestones for them in the provincial Roman manner, as exemplified by a stone from Andernach in the middle Rhineland commemorating Firmus, a member of the Raetian cohort, from the middle of the first century A.D. His tombstone shows Firmus outfitted in the characteristic military weaponry, with sword, dagger, two spears, and an oval shield, while the inscription makes clear that he was a Raetian and an auxiliary soldier.

Historical sources inform us that Germanic mercenaries often served the Roman army as scouts and spies, especially during the first century A.D. At some of the *limes* forts, notably Saalburg and Zugmantel, considerable quantities of pottery have been linked with ceramics in the unconquered lands to the east and interpreted, along with particular types of fibula found at the same forts, as evidence for Germanic mercenaries serving at those bases.

A good example of interactions between native peoples and incoming Roman troops is at the Titelberg in Luxembourg, the site of extensive excavations in recent years. The Titelberg was an *oppidum* during the Late La Tène Period and was situated in the territory of the Treveri, though Caesar does not mention any *oppida* in the lands of that people. After the Gallic War in 45 B.C., a mint on the Titelberg produced coins of Hirtius, governor of Gaul, indicating that the authorities at the site were supportive of the new Roman rule. The archaeological evidence shows no substantial changes in the Titelberg settlement in the two decades following the Gallic War, while large quantities of archaeological material and the presence of very wealthy graves in the vicinity—at Goeblingen-Nospelt and at Clemency—show that the Titelberg remained an important central place.

During the third decade after the conquest, however, there is evidence of major changes at the site. New luxury imports appear, particularly ornate *terra sigillata* pottery from Italy, wine amphorae from Spain, and new types of fibulae. Resident potters and metalsmiths began making new forms of pottery and ornaments. In the cemetery of Lamadelaine, just northwest of the Titelberg, a change in burial practice is reflected in the sudden appearance of new forms of tableware. These changes may reflect the arrival of Roman troops into the vicinity, and many objects recovered from the layers representing this period on the Titelberg attest to the presence of Roman soldiers, most likely legionary troops rather than auxiliaries. Roman pottery and other materials indicate a Roman site on the Petrisberg at Trier at 30 B.C., perhaps the remains of an early fort. These materials represent the beginning of Roman activity at the site that was to become the most important imperial center north of the Alps several centuries later.

At the Titelberg, the fortification walls of the Late Iron Age center were dismantled, and the houses of this new phase of construction were largely built using sill-beams rather than the traditional sunken-post frame. Two buildings of this period were accompanied by stone-lined cellars. Shortly thereafter, during the second decade B.C., the Titelberg was abandoned. The Late Iron Age center lost its importance to a newly established open settlement at nearby Dalheim.

Rebellions

Revolts staged by indigenous peoples are a common feature in imperial situations, and the rebellions that took place in the frontier zone of temperate Europe conform to a regular pattern of native uprisings. Our information about rebellions comes mainly from the surviving written sources. The Batavian revolt of A.D. 69 is a well-documented case, and it illustrates the pattern that many of these movements followed. The Batavians were characterized by the Roman writers as a Germanic tribe inhabiting lands around the mouth of the Rhine River in the present Netherlands. Since the time of Caesar, they were allies of Rome, and in that position they were not required to pay tribute. Their soldiers served as auxiliaries in the Roman army. As was usual for auxiliary units, the troops were commanded by members of the Batavian elite, who had themselves been made citizens and possessed equestrian status, and thus were members of the Roman imperial aristocracy.

In A.D. 68 rebellions broke out in Gaul and Spain, and during the year A.D. 69, four rivals vied for the title of emperor. Troops supporting different candidates fought, and in the course of the confused confrontations auxiliaries loyal to Vespasian fought against Roman legions and auxiliaries loyal to Vitellius. The description by Tacitus indicates that this revolt was led by Civilis, a local native who had served in the Roman army as commander of an auxiliary unit. This pattern of native identity and Roman military experience is a common one among leaders of such rebellions; Arminius was a similar kind of figure sixty years earlier (chapter 10). According to Tacitus's account, the rebellion began during a ritual celebration in a local sacred place, and in the course of the revolt a series of traditional native practices were carried out, often involving symbols of Rome now used to defy the imperial administration. In the early stages of the revolt, the Batavians undertook the destruction of Roman buildings, including all of the military bases from the mouth of the Rhine to Vetera, Xanten in present-day Germany. Many sites show evidence of destruction and burning at about this time, probably resulting from this period of rebellion (see chapter 4).

Forts and Natives

The most important medium for interactions between indigenous peoples and representatives of the Roman military was the forts in which soldiers were stationed along the frontier. The basic security system of the Roman provinces was the line of forts constructed on the imperial borders. The purpose of these forts was primarily to defend the borders from incursion from the outside—specifically from the east—but they also stood ready to put down rebellions within the provinces. The forts conformed, with minor variations, to a standard plan—rectangular in shape, with outer ditches, walls, four gates at the cardinal points, and interior arrangements of barracks, officers' quarters, and workshops. Legionary forts typically held one legion, totalling 5,500–6,000 men; forts of auxiliary troops housed about the same number or sometimes fewer. Smaller forts for cohorts, cavalry units, and other divisions housed between 50 and 1,000 men.

Our principal concern here with the forts is their relationship with the peoples in the landscapes around them, a theme that has been particularly developed by Dutch investigators but has recently gained attention in other landscapes as well. Forts were built in landscapes already inhabited by indigenous peoples, thus the occupants of the forts maintained relations with the surrounding countryside from the outset. Since most of the Roman troops serving on the frontiers were auxiliaries rather than legionaries, the interactions between troops and indigenous peoples were most often with noncitizen soldiers, usually not from Italy or the Mediterranean lands of southern Gaul or Spain. This point is important because it means that the indigenous peoples who lived near the forts were not interacting with "Romans" in the sense of citizens from Italy or one of the early western provinces, but rather with individuals from other parts of the greater Roman world and even from lands beyond the frontier.

The Roman military constructed forts typically several decades after a territory had been conquered and incorporated into the empire. Thus some forts in Gaul were constructed several decades earlier than forts in Raetia. While written sources from Rome inform us about specific campaigns undertaken by the various generals and troops, information about the location of Roman frontier forts comes principally from the archaeological evidence. Just in the past decade several new forts have been discovered, for example at Marktbreit on the Main in Franconia and at Waldgirmes in the Wetterau. In many instances, the first construction phase of a Roman fort was of wood and earth, a technique with a long history in temperate Europe. For example, the fort at Regensburg-Kumpfmühl in northeastern Raetia was first constructed of timber and earth, sometime around A.D. 70. A later rebuilding of the fort, around A.D. 150, was in stone, the characteristic Roman construction technique introduced into temperate Europe.

Vici

A category of settlement—the *vicus*—developed in the landscape next to the new forts in order to benefit from the economic needs of the troops. These were usually new foundations, their locations determined specifically by the situations of the forts. In some instances, however, as for example at Lahr-Dillingen, a *vicus* settlement seems to be a continuation of a pre-Roman settlement on the same site. The inhabitants of the *vicus* provided a range of goods and services to the fort and to individual soldiers stationed there. Soldiers were paid in cash, and their ability to spend money to purchase things played an important role in transferring wealth from the Roman imperial treasury to indigenous communities in the frontier provinces, particularly to the inhabitants of the *vici*. Thus the *vici* played a major role as vehicles for interaction between the troops and the indigenous peoples.

Excavation at the *vicus* associated with the fort at Regensburg-Kumpf-mühl recovered, in addition to wares typical of Roman military camps, pottery of Middle and Late La Tène character. This pottery may indicate Late Iron Age settlement activity in the vicinity, perhaps small units such as farmsteads that did not leave substantial structural remains. But the presence in the settlement features of the *vicus* of handmade pottery similar in both form and manufacturing technique to that of the pre-Roman communities of the region, suggests that indigenous peoples resident at the *vicus* continued to manufacture pottery in their traditional manner. This pottery is found in association with the characteristic wheelmade Roman-style wares.

Much of the architecture at Regensburg-Kumpfmühl consists of long rectangular buildings that are common at other *vici* in temperate Europe. They were arranged along streets, with one narrow end facing the street. Some were built of timber, similar in technique to local Iron Age building practices, others were built of stone. These structures typically served as dwelling places, workshops, and stores, all under one roof. Public buildings on the site included a bath complex and an inn.

This *vicus*, like most, yielded abundant evidence for manufacturing. Crucibles, molds, slag, partly made objects, and scrap metal all attest to bronze working. Significantly, both military goods and civilian objects are represented by the partly made pieces. Iron working, lead processing, and pottery production are attested by the finds. It thus appears that the community at this settlement produced a variety of goods of different materials, probably most of them for consumption among the troops stationed at the fort. These craftworkers were most likely mainly indigenous individuals who adapted their output to serve the needs of their customers.

Soldiers and Native Women

The *vici* associated with the military bases provided one means through which soldiers could meet local women. But there must have been a substantial amount of interaction between soldiers and native women generally, as there always is around military bases. We know that Roman soldiers had a considerable amount of free time, and it is very likely that many of them spent time courting local women. These close interpersonal interactions were extremely important in providing a vehicle for the transmission of much cultural information between natives and Roman soldiers, but we know very little about such relationships. When marriage entered the picture, then the interactions acquired an official significance, and we have some documentary evidence pertaining to liasons that reached that point. But of what were probably the vast majority of relationships formed between soldiers and native women, we know virtually nothing. They did not attract the kind of official attention that would have led to their being recorded in any way, and so far no one has identified archaeological evidence that might tell us something about such relationships.

Excavations of *vici* yield evidence that women and children lived in them, but there is no clear indication as yet to connect them with the soldiers at the bases. The best evidence we have pertaining to marriage between soldiers and native women is in the form of inscriptions—on gravestones and on military diplomas, in particular. In Egypt, writing on papyri yields exceptionally rich information about that issue, but we cannot assume that conditions on the Rhine and Danube were similar to those in the very different world of Egypt. Until the time of Septimius Severus (A.D. 193–211), Roman soldiers were not permitted to marry, but the literary evidence makes clear that many nonetheless entered into relationships with women that involved permanent unions and procreation of children. Inscriptions from military diplomas suggest that these relationships were often acknowledged without disapproval.

Thus the epigraphic and literary evidence makes clear that soldiers stationed on the frontier entered into permanent relationships with local women and fathered children, but the sources do not tell us how common such arrangements were. And there is no evidence for the fleeting, casual relationships that were probably much more common. In the present state of our understanding, we can only bear in mind that relationships, both temporary and permanent, between soldiers and native women were probably very important in exchanges of cultural information on the individual level between the representatives of the imperial power and the indigenous peoples.

Supplying the Troops

There is very little specific written information about how the troops stationed in the forts were supplied, but a good indicator of relations between the Roman frontier forts and the native peoples around them is in the archaeological evidence for economic transactions between them. Apparently the Roman government oversaw the procurement of food-stuffs for the military bases, and these requirements were vast. For example, a single legion needed more than two thousand tons of wheat per year. But at least in the early Roman Period, individual forts seem to have been required to obtain their own manufactured goods. The military bases could produce what they needed in their own workshops, or they could contract with indigenous potters, metalsmiths, leather-workers, and weavers. Roman soldiers required a wide variety of ceramic, metal, leather, and textile objects. They needed pottery for daily food preparation and consumption. Soldiers often used bronze pans for cooking. Iron and bronze were needed for military gear and for ornaments that formed an integral part of each soldier's outfit. Leather was required for various belts, straps, and for tents for use on campaigns. Textiles were needed for clothing. Written sources say practically nothing about how the military bases supplied these needs, but recent archaeological research provides useful information. Excavations at many of the *vici* have shown that they served as centers of manufacturing for the neighboring bases, as the industrial debris from Regensburg-Kumpfmühl illustrates (above).

Excavation of pottery-making facilities, and studies of the distribution of vessels manufactured at particular sites, shows that a wide range of different workshops, some large and some small, produced the ceramics used by the troops. Potters at the military bases covered some of the need, but most of the ceramics were brought in from outside sources. Some of the fine wares were imported from the Mediterranean Basin. *Terra sigillata*, the most popular fine ware, was first imported from Italy. As demand among both soldiers and the civilian population in the European provinces increased, new factories were established in southern Gaul to produce the ware, at La Graufesenque and at Lyon. Later, *terra sigillata* was manufactured in central Gaul at Lezoux, and finally at production centers as far north as the Rhineland and southern Germany. It has been estimated that the factories at Rheinzabern in the upper Rhine valley turned out about one million *terra sigillata* vessels per year.

Scholars disagree on the extent of governmental control over the circulation of pottery, particularly regarding supplies to the military bases. While some level of official oversight may have existed for the manufacture and distribution of ceramics from the large, specialized production sites, such as Lezoux and Rheinzabern, for the numerous small potteries that have been identified archaeologically such control is unlikely. Along with the *terra sigillata* and other Roman-style wares, the soldiers at the bases also used substantial quantities of local indigenous pottery, much of it made with the same fabrics, in the same shapes, and even with the same decorative motifs as Late Iron Age pottery. Much of this pottery at the military bases is indistinguishable from that at the prehistoric *oppida*, and it clearly indicates the persistence of local ceramic traditions at least several generations into the Roman Period.

In the case of metalwork, the archaeological evidence suggests that most of the soldiers' equipment was made outside of the military bases in civilian workshops, such as those at the *vici*. Some limited manufacture of weapons, tools, and ornaments was done by soldier-craftworkers, but much more metalworking debris and tools have been found in settlements near the bases than on the bases themselves. Soldiers required large amounts of metal objects for their weapons and for clothing attachments and ornaments (Figure 19). Swords, daggers, lanceheads, and spearheads consumed large amounts of iron; helmets and body armor required both sheet iron and leather padding; shields were made of wood, leather, and iron. Buckles, strap-ends, belt attachments, and ornaments were made of bronze; a recent study estimates that each soldier wore ten or more such objects. The total amounts of metal required by the soldiers at each base were enormous. The manufacturing evidence at the *vici*, in particular, gives us insight into how and where these materials were produced.

Thus even without good textual evidence for interactions between soldiers stationed along the frontiers and the indigenous peoples in the lands around the bases, this evidence for the supplying of critical goods to the troops provides a picture of intensive interaction and of military bases dependent upon the goods generated by the local industries. At one level, it might seem ironic that occupying troops relied upon manufactured goods—including weapons—produced by the populations of the conquered territories. But this system of supply is indicative of the complex relationships that developed over time between Roman troops and indigenous peoples.

These interactions had profound effects on all of the parties involved. In economic terms, they stimulated production among local communities and introduced into their economies a steady source of cash. The roughly 110,000 troops stationed along the frontier in the Rhineland, along the *limes*, and in Raetia constituted an enormous new market for the products of the indigenous industries, and they in turn increased production to meet the demand in pottery, iron, bronze, leather, and

1

2

3

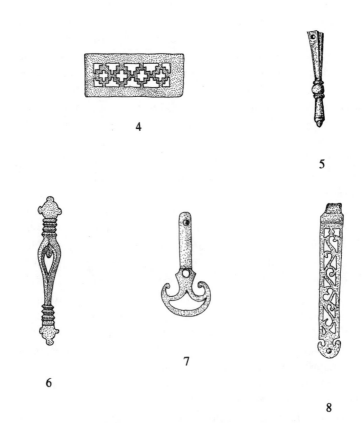

4

5

6

7

8

Fig. 19. Examples of bronze ornaments worn by Roman soldiers on belts, straps, and elsewhere on their uniforms. All found on military bases—*(1, 5)* Zugmantel. *(2)* Osterburken. *(3)* Feldberg. *(4)* Saalburg. *(6)* Straubing. *(7)* Weissenburg. *(8)* Pocking. All drawn to same scale; *(1)* measures about 3 in. (7.65 cm) across. From Oldenstein 1976. Used by permission of Susanne Sievers, RGK.

other materials. Larger amounts of iron meant more iron mining and smelting, and more trade systems for acquiring iron from other regions. More bronze meant more mining and smelting of copper and tin, and more transportation to bring the metals together for alloying and working into finished ornaments. The great demand for leather on the part of the Roman army required more cattle to be raised for their hides within the provinces, and intensive commerce across the frontier to acquire hides from other regions (see below). It has been estimated that a single legion required for the tents it used on campaign the hides of some 54,000 calves. If we calculate needs by all troops for all equipment of leather, the numbers of cattle required are staggering. These kinds of considerations make clear that the presence of the Roman army in the frontier zone served as a major stimulus to the local economies.

But the impact of these interactions was not only economic. The economic aspects show up well in the archaeological evidence, but along with them were also interpersonal relationships that developed and evolved as indigenous people interacted with soldiers. Above I have discussed soldiers' relationships with native women, but there must also have been many casual friendships established between soldiers and locals. As in all contexts in which people from different backgrounds meet, there must have been considerable sharing of information and of traditions, and surely the two parties influenced each other in ways that we have not yet begun to really comprehend. What little textual evidence exists on the subject, and the more abundant archaeological evidence, indicate that for the most part, such interactions were peaceful and cordial. During the early Roman Period, troops were stationed in the frontier zone for some 250 years. Only rarely did rebellions and other forms of conflict take place. On the whole, the indigenous peoples and the soldiers at the bases seem to have interacted successfully and in mutually beneficial ways.

The acquisition of goods to supply the material needs of the frontier troops also had significant effects in lands outside the imperial borders. Chapter 10 deals with this topic in some detail, but a few remarks are appropriate here. Many thousands of Roman objects found in the territories east and north of the frontier attest to regular interaction between peoples within and outside the empire. Frequently these objects occur in contexts that show profound cultural change, and it is apparent that such changes were closely linked to the interactions with the Roman world. A few Classical writers mention goods that peoples within the Roman empire obtained from peoples to the east and north, mostly foodstuffs and raw materials, but they provide little specific information about sources, quantities, or costs in exchange goods.

Archaeological evidence beyond the frontier attests to the growth in production facilities for commerce with the Roman provinces. For example, at Gera-Tinz in Thuringia, one of many iron-production facilities has been excavated that may have produced metal for export to Roman territories. In the Holy Cross Mountains region of southern Poland there is evidence for the growth of large-scale iron production linked to this Roman trade. At Feddersen Wierde in Lower Saxony, a community intensified its raising of cattle for Roman consumers, and was importing a variety of luxury goods from the provinces in exchange (see chapter 10).

Both within the new provinces of the empire and in places outside of the imperial domains, the demand for goods to supply the troops with foodstuffs, pottery, metals, leather, and other materials had the effect of stimulating local economies to produce larger surpluses to exchange for the new variety of attractive goods available through trade with the Roman world. In many instances, indigenous producers adjusted their crafts to suit the tastes of their customers, which included both the troops and other local groups that acquired the taste for Roman styles of pottery and metal goods. A good example of these changes is at the site of Schwabegg in Bavaria, where a prehistoric pottery industry continued to produce ceramics during the early Roman Period, shifting its output from typical Iron Age wares to Roman-style ones. Even several generations after the Roman conquest of the region, makers' names stamped into the Roman-style vessels suggest that the majority of the potters were local Celts.

Through their supplying of goods to satisfy the demands of the troops stationed in the frontier zone and of the general populace eager to acquire fashionable new objects, many craftworkers and merchants became wealthy and gained status in the provincial society. Some of the richly outfitted burials of the first and second centuries A.D. show us how such individuals displayed their status (see below).

Supply, Production, and Identity

The subject of indigenous groups manufacturing goods for troops in the forts raises important issues regarding identity. Insofar as the craftworkers in the *vici* were producing pottery and metal ornaments in their traditional techniques and styles, they were continuing to express their identity as indigenous peoples of the landscape. One way of viewing this persistence is in terms of resistance among native communities to the changes introduced around them. Studies of resistance and rebellion in the modern world show how indigenous peoples often express their dissatisfaction with regimes imposed by foreign intruders through seemingly small gestures, such as making pottery in their traditional way (see chapter 7).

On the other hand, as fashions changed, either because of customer demand or evolving tastes on the part of the manufacturers, the people who made the pottery changed their ideas about themselves and their crafts. In cases where indigenous craftworkers changed the character of their products to meet customer demand, as for example in the shift in pottery made at Schwabegg (see above), their ideas about their relationship to their customers—Roman soldiers or fellow indigenes who now preferred goods in the Roman style—inevitably changed too.

Many of the materials that the craftworkers in the *vici* made for the troops were dress paraphernalia—ornaments worn on the military gear, including fibulae, belt ornaments, enameled pins—and thus signs that soldiers chose to display as indicators of their personal identity. In a sense, then, the craftworkers in the *vici* were playing an active role in constructing the identities of the soldiers. Present evidence does not allow us to answer the important question of who chose the style of the objects of military dress paraphernalia—the craftworker in the *vicus* or the soldier-customer? No doubt the interactions varied in different situations.

CHAPTER 7

Persistence of Tradition

Postconquest Continuities

After the conquests of the different landscapes, and often after a period during which provincial administrations were organized, the archaeology shows the gradual introduction of Roman-style material culture—military camps, urban centers, public buildings, baths, villas, pottery, metalwork, and so forth. But at the same time, much of traditional material culture and behavior continued to be expressed, created, and used. The evidence suggests much more than simply a transition between preconquest indigenous traditions and postconquest Roman-introduced ones. Different kinds of evidence indicate instead a long period, lasting several generations, during which many different groups of native peoples in different parts of the conquered lands continued to practice their traditional behaviors and reproduce their traditional material culture, even while Roman styles and behaviors were being adopted around them.

The clearest evidence for the continuity of practice among indigenous peoples is in pottery. Archaeologists excavating Roman Period sites have long recognized the presence of Late Iron Age–style pottery on the settlements. Until recently, this pottery was usually dismissed with a brief remark about apparent pre-Roman occupation on the site. But during the past couple of decades, archaeologists have been paying more attention to this important evidence. Virtually all early Roman Period settlement sites in the frontier zone of temperate Europe, whether military or civilian, yield Late La Tène–type pottery. The coincidence is too strong to attribute all of it to earlier settlements.

For understanding the changes that are taking place in thinking about indigenous peoples in Roman Period Europe, it is worth considering why much of this material has been under-represented in past studies. Before the mid-1980s, only a few investigators drew attention to the existence of distinctive Late Iron Age cultural elements in Roman Period contexts. One reason for such neglect is the linear chronological thinking that dominates research in Iron Age and Roman Period archaeology. In the chronological framework based on typological change (see Figure

13), there is little consideration given to the problem of different lengths of time during which specific types of objects were in use. Particular types are used to define periods, and the method does not have good ways of dealing with objects that are found together with items believed to belong to a different period. According to a strict application of typological chronology, once the Roman Period began, Late Iron Age material culture ceased to be produced. This view of course sounds nonsensical— virtually all human practices change gradually, not abruptly, but strict application of the typological method would argue thus. Hence the discipline has had difficulty in dealing with Late Iron Age–style pottery on Roman sites.

The second reason that such pottery and other similar kinds of evidence have not gained adequate attention until recently is that Late Iron Age societies are studied by prehistorians, while Roman Period Europe is the focus of specialists in provincial Roman archaeology. In much of Europe these fields are surprisingly different in character; the background, assumptions, and interests of the investigators in the two disciplines are often quite different. Only a few individuals work comfortably in both subdisciplines.

In the discussion that follows, I examine evidence for such persistence of native traditions in several categories of archaeological material in the conquered lands.

SETTLEMENT ARCHITECTURE

There is considerable evidence for the persistence of Iron Age building techniques and settlements well into Roman times throughout the frontier provinces. Native settlements with characteristic post-build and wattle-and-daub architecture, distinct from that of the newly introduced provincial Roman type, have been identified throughout the frontier zone. Such settlements have attracted research attention in the Netherlands, Belgium, France, the Rhineland, and Hungary. Exceptionally fine research on this issue has been carried out in the Netherlands, where the settlement of Rijswijk serves as an example.

Rijswijk is situated in the western Netherlands, near the coast of the North Sea, in the province of Zuid-Holland, just southeast of the modern city of the Hague. It is the site of a settlement that was occupied continuously from early in the first century A.D. until the second half of the third century. In the years 1967–69 the settlement was entirely excavated, an area of 8.6 acres (3.5 ha). In its early phases it had the character of a typical pre-Roman farmstead—a farmhouse with ancillary buildings and nearby fields—on the North European Plain, as represented at other excavated sites such as Wijster in the Netherlands and Feddersen Wierde and Flögeln in northern Germany. In the first occupation, between A.D. 30 and 60, postholes indicate a wooden house of just 473 sq. ft. (44 m²), constructed in the three-aisle scheme, with humans residing in one end and animals, primarily cattle, kept in the other. The three-aisled pattern is recognizable by four parallel rows of postholes. The two outer rows held the posts that supported the exterior walls of the building, while the two inner rows supported the peak of the roof and divided the interior into three aisles running the length of the structure. After about a generation, the house was replaced with a slightly larger one on the same spot and with the same architecture, but now with the house divided into two distinct rooms, the larger of which served as a stall for livestock. In this phase, dated around A.D. 60–90, the material culture was richer than for the first phase, and more objects point to the use of Roman-style objects, though local pottery still predominated. Around A.D. 90, yet another, larger house with an area of 871 sq. ft. (81 m²) was constructed on the same spot, again with the same traditional architectural techniques. A second house may have been built at the same time; if this latter house belonged to this same phase, then it would indicate growth from a single farmstead to two.

Early in the second century the inhabitants expanded the settlement, to three farmsteads. One house built during this phase, on top of the original dwelling of the settlement, included a number of new features adopted from provincial Roman architectural traditions. These included partial architecture of stone, wall paintings in at least one room, and a heating system. But the basic architecture—still the traditional indigenous three-aisle post-built structure—and the predominance of indigenous-style pottery indicate that the population identified itself as indigenous. The inhabitants of the hamlet added buildings that have been interpreted as a temple and a granary complex.

The material culture on the site is dominated by indigenous pottery which remained remarkably unchanged from the early first into the third century A.D. The pottery belongs to the Late Iron Age ceramic traditions of the central and northern Netherlands, and it is very similar to pottery at many other sites of the early Roman Period in the region. Substantial quantities of Roman-style pottery also occur on the site, especially from the second century, with around 25 percent of the objects recovered having been identified as Roman. These include *terra sigillata* produced at Trier, *terra nigra*, and other styles of pottery. Other materials recovered during the excavations are typical of Late Iron Age and early Roman Period rural sites, including grindstones, whetstones, carved bone objects, and gaming pieces. Among personal ornaments, fibulae are most common.

The structure interpreted as a temple is so designated by process of elimination. Its structure is represented by a U-shaped arrangement of posts, measuring about 33 by 17 ft. (10 x 5.25 m) and opening to the west. The posts are believed to have formed the framework for a solid wall. Outside of the two long walls to the north and south were rows of seven postholes. At the western end, two posts between those of the two outer rows form with them a north-south line just in front of the opening. The excavators interpret the outer structure as a gallery around the inner structure, similar to that of Gallo-Roman temples (see chapter 9). (A second structure may have been similar in form, but its traces are much more fragmentary.) This arrangement is very different from all other remains on the site, but it matches those at a number of other excavated settlements, for example at Nijmegen in the Netherlands and at the Saalburg north of Frankfurt in Germany.

Rijswijk is informative about the continuation of traditional building and living practices by a native community within the imperial borders, and at the same time about the gradual and selective adoption of elements of the provincial Roman world.

Nico Roymans has suggested a model that helps us to understand the persistence of the traditional indigenous rural house architectural form and technology in terms of active decisions made by the inhabitants. He argues that traditional types of farmhouses are important symbols for people, not only of their traditional identity, but also of their value system and ideology. This perspective enables us to view settlements such as Rijswijk, which is not unusual, as showing that the inhabitants during the early Roman Period continued to re-create their value system and identity by rebuilding the same style of house using the traditional technology, but at the same time adopting certain elements that had been introduced to the region by Roman newcomers. These new elements were added to the houses only insofar as they did not interfere with the fundamental integrity of the traditional structure. In this sense, the persistence of the indigenous house forms can be understood as an active statement of the link between the occupants and their traditional values and beliefs. Another way of looking at the issue is to say that the continued re-creation of this powerful symbol of indigenous identity was a form of resistance to the imposing effects of Roman domination.

Recent field research in Hungary yields important new evidence for the persistence of native settlements well into the Roman Period there. The patterns are similar in essence to those at Rijswijk and suggest that such re-creation of indigenous house forms was practiced throughout the new provinces. Excavations at Réti földek near Szakály in the Kapos Valley revealed dwelling structures of characteristic Late Iron Age type on a settlement dating to the first and second centuries A.D. Some Roman products were found, and they provide the essential chronological information, but they were of modest quality and only sparsely represented. Aside from the Roman objects, the material culture of the community was indistinguishable from that of late prehistoric settlements well into the second century. Miscast and discarded jewelry indicates that metalworkers continued to make indigenous forms until the middle of that century. Even the animal bone assemblage demonstrates stock-raising and consumption patterns similar to those of prehistoric times.

Except in the Netherlands, Hungary, and Britain, where Roman-native interactions have long been a subject of research concern, such traditional indigenous sites have not yet attracted much research attention. There are several reasons for this state of affairs. Roman Period settlements with stone architecture are much easier to find than the indigenous type with only wattle-and-daub construction. Stone-built sites are often encountered by farmers, who report their discoveries to local archaeologists, and they are much more easily identified by archaeological survey, whether carried out on the ground or from the air. Indigenous wood-built settlements are more difficult to find. The wooden elements have long since decayed, leaving only postholes in the subsoil for identification by the archaeologist. Even when such a site has been found it is not always easy to ascertain whether it dates to the prehistoric Iron Age or to the Roman Period. Unless there are some datable Roman objects present, or substantial pieces of surviving wood for obtaining dendrochronological (tree-ring) dates, it can be difficult to demonstrate that such a settlement dates to the Roman Period. In southern Germany, wood-built farm dwellings frequently show that an indigenous component of provincial Roman society may be represented on many sites, but that they have been largely ignored in favor of the more easily recognized stone structures. Such post-built houses were in use as late as the second half of the second century A.D. at Langweiler 9 on the Aldenhovener Platte in northwestern Germany. The implication of these few recent observations is that indigenous-style wooden buildings were much more abundant than past studies have recognized.

Communities that resisted changing their architecture to new styles introduced by Rome and consciously continued to re-create their traditional Iron Age–type material cultures during the Roman Period would have been unlikely to adopt Roman-style objects such as pottery or metalwork. Thus from an archaeological point of view, they would look like Iron Age settlements. We might compare this problem with trying to establish the date, through artifact typology, of an Amish settlement of the late twentieth century in rural Ohio. Since the Amish reject most aspects of modern technology, including electricity and motorized vehicles, we might well think that an Amish farmstead was occupied several hundred years earlier than it actually was. An important example of an Iron Age–style settlement that may have been occupied during the early Roman Period is Eschweiler-Laurenzberg, east of Cologne. While most of the objects recovered at the site point to a typological association with phases La Tène C2 and D1 (see Figure 13), that is, probably before the middle of the first century B.C., some of the pottery is very much like that from early Roman sites. The settlement may have been occupied in the early Roman Period, and with some of the pottery made and used in the tradition of the prehistoric Iron Age ceramics. According to the standard chronology for the region, there are virtually no finds from the immediately postconquest period. But if there was little typological change in the area after the conquest, then many of the sites that look earlier according to the style of their pottery and metalwork may have been occupied during this post-Caesar time. As more investigators think about these issues and devote attention to questions about typology and chronology, we are likely to find many cases of such typologically "earlier" sites dating to "later" periods.

It is likely that the rate of typological change for indigenous-style materials decreased during the Roman Period. Styles probably changed much more slowly than they did during the final phases of the prehistoric Iron Age, and it is possible that some communities persisted in using pottery and ornaments that we would classify as La Tène D2 or D3 well into the Roman Period. The inhabitants of the small communities that replaced both the major *oppidum* settlements and the sizable unfortified settlements such as Berching-Pollanten probably had less access to new fashions in personal ornaments, pottery, and other goods than the populations of the centers had enjoyed. Communities that maintained La Tène–style material culture into the early Roman Period were more conservative than those that readily adopted the new fashions. Their continued production of ornaments, pottery, and other objects in their traditional style after the Roman conquest suggests that they were consciously re-creating that style as a means of asserting their identities as native peoples. In such circumstances they would be most likely to reproduce existing forms of decoration and morphology rather than create new ones or even develop variations on the traditional themes.

A situation similar to that at Eschweiler-Laurenzberg pertains in many other contexts, for example in the Isar River Valley of Lower Bavaria, part of the Roman province of Raetia. There we have evidence of substantial rural occupation just before the time of the Roman conquest, characterized by material culture of La Tène D2 character, and again evidence of abundant settlement activity in the second century A.D. Between these times, according to the standard typological chronological scheme, there exists an unexplained gap with no evidence of human occupation. Just north of the city of Landshut, on the lowest terrace above the Isar River, the sites of Hascherkeller, Ergolding Nord, Ergolding Ost I, and Ergolding Ost II all yield pottery and metal ornaments attributed to the phase La Tène D2. However, this material is heterogeneous in character and probably does not represent a single short phase of time, as the standard chronology would suggest. The middle Roman Period is well represented on this same terrace by a substantial number of villas and associated cemeteries, all thought to begin around the middle of the second century A.D. The same pattern of stylistically Late La Tène materials together in a landscape with middle Roman Period settlements occurs at Straubing on the Danube. There is a strong likelihood that some of the heterogeneous and "late-looking" pottery and metal ornaments in Late La Tène style actually belong to settlements that span the first century A.D. The gap between the latest La Tène occupation and the second century Roman Period occupation is only an apparent one, created by reliance on strict application of typological chronology as the only available technique of dating.

The purpose of the foregoing discussion is to show that it is likely that there are many more Iron Age–style settlements and houses than we currently recognize from sites such as Rijswijk. Many probably look very similar to typical Late Iron Age settlements and, because of conscious or unconscious reproduction of architectural technology and other goods in the styles of the Iron Age, they cannot be easily recognized as dating to the Roman Period. As archaeologists become more aware of this issue, and as they employ different techniques for establishing the chronology of sites—especially as more dendrochronological dates become available—the continuity in house type and settlement occupation from the Iron Age to the postconquest period will become increasingly apparent.

In some parts of the frontier zone, as for example the western region of the Rhineland, which was conquered by Caesar's armies during the Gallic Wars of 58–51 B.C., no such apparent gap exists. In Cologne and Bonn, for example, typical Late La Tène materials occur in association with the earliest Roman structures and objects. Throughout the first and second centuries A.D., indigenous-style pottery and metal objects continued to be produced. In some cases, they show substantial adoption of provincial Roman styles and forms, in other cases they do not.

Manufactured Goods

Pottery

Pottery is an important category of material to examine for the questions addressed here for several reasons. Pottery is the most abundant cultural material on sites of Late Iron Age and Roman Period date, because vessels break easily and the sherds are rarely reused. Communities need steady supplies of new pots to replace broken ones. A large number of attributes of pottery can be examined to ascertain techniques of manufacture and of decoration, and many of these elements can provide information about the choices made by the individuals who created the pots, concerning vessel form, firing techniques, and decorative methods and motifs. Unlike small, lightweight, less breakable objects, such as fibulae and belthooks, pottery vessels are less likely to be carried over substantial distances for use; thick-walled, handmade coarse wares, especially, are almost always found in the same region in which they were manufactured and used. From study of the handmade coarse everyday wares, we can learn much about local conditions of production and use.

Ethnographic, historical, and archaeological studies of pottery construction show that pottery is frequently employed as a vehicle for information about identity. Because of the wide range of choices open to the potter regarding techniques, forms, and decoration, pottery constitutes a particularly flexible medium for the communication of such information. Thus we can expect pottery to be particularly informative about the maintenance of traditions among indigenous peoples of Europe, and conversely about their willingness to adopt new elements introduced during the Roman Period. The indigenous wares recovered on Roman

Period sites include a variety of different types, encompassing a range of coarse handmade, undecorated wares, and fine, wheelmade pottery with painted bands in patterns of white and red. Such ceramics occur not only in very early Roman Period contexts, but throughout the first and second centuries A.D.

An important recent study of the handmade wares at the Roman town of Arae Flaviae, now Rottweil in southwest Germany, examined thirty thousand sherds from the Roman levels that match in form, style, texture, and decoration the pottery of the Late La Tène tradition of the region. Associations with well-dated Roman materials on the site show that most of the pottery dates to the second half of the first century A.D., but some is as late as the second half of the second century. The most common decoration on the pottery was vertical curved comb strokes. The handmade pottery did not imitate the wheelmade wares on the site, but constituted distinct forms, specifically for cooking and storage purposes, and also for table and drinking ware. Close parallels to the Rottweil coarse wares are evident at numerous other Roman Period settlements in southern Germany and Switzerland, including Hüfingen, Winterthur, Schleitheim, and Oberstimm.

Other types of pottery at Rottweil also suggest production by indigenous potters rather than by Roman newcomers. Fine wares with painted bands that replicate forms and decorative styles of the Late Iron Age remained in common use to the end of the second century, in some places in southwest Germany even into the third century. Even the forms of some of the polished black pottery known as *terra nigra* reflect local prehistoric traditions of potting. Two potters' names attested by stamps—Atto and Vattus—are Celtic in origin.

For some of the handmade pottery in the analysis, variations in shape from the Late Iron Age forms can be identified. Some forms seem to replicate those of Roman vessels rather than common prehistoric ones. This pattern is consistent with indigenous potters adapting their traditional technology to the new circumstances. Roman troops stationed at Rottweil, and civilians in the new town, may have wanted pottery in forms to which they were accustomed, but welcomed the practical advantages of the indigenous fabrics. The adaptation of traditional technologies to new demands is a common feature of interactions such as those between natives and Roman soldiers.

In those instances where vessels were manufactured that reproduced very closely Late La Tène forms and decorations, we could posit resistance to the changes brought by Roman conquest. But there is also abundant evidence for adaptation to the new circumstances. Importation of pottery from workshops in Gaul was one form of adaptation. Local manufacture of vessels similar to those being made in Gaul was another. Adopting some elements from new wares, and combining them with traditional styles, was another expression of the desire to adapt to changing circumstances.

Fibulae

As in the case of pottery, in the early Roman Period we find a diversity of fibula forms in use, some of local origin and others introduced from outside. But in contrast to pottery, with fibulae there are no types that were clearly introduced from Roman Italy or Roman southern Gaul. Although some types of fibula which are common in the early Roman Period, particularly on military sites, are generally described as "Roman," the custom of wearing fibulae in the European provinces was a continuation of indigenous tradition, not a practice brought by the legions from Roman Italy. By the time that Rome was engaged in its expansion into temperate Europe, wearing fibulae was no longer the custom in Rome and in regions of Italy outside of the Celtic territories on the Po Plain. Yet fibulae were commonly worn among Roman troops north of the Alps from the start of the Roman presence there, and they are frequent both in Roman Period graves and on settlement sites.

Many fibulae found in Roman Period contexts are of types that clearly derive from indigenous Late Iron Age forms. Several varieties of simple wire fibulae of Middle and Late La Tène type continued to be manufactured and worn throughout the first century A.D. and into the second. The abundant *Aucissa*, thistle, and *Nertomarus* types were developed from Late La Tène forms. Because of a dearth of direct evidence for fibula manufacture—workshops on settlements that yield molds, scrap, and rejected pieces—we are poorly informed about exactly where the different types of fibula were produced and where new forms were developed. Large numbers of nearly identical fibulae indicate that some were mass-produced, while many unique specimens show that handcrafting by metalsmiths was also common.

Studies of Roman Period fibulae have demonstrated that some have distinctive regional distributions, while others occur more widely. Some types are particularly common in one Roman province and rare elsewhere. Some are common in the Roman territories, but unusual beyond the frontier. Others have very widespread distributions during the early

Roman Period, occurring abundantly both within the imperial provinces and in the unconquered lands.

At most large sites of the Late La Tène and the Roman Periods, a wide variety of fibula types are represented. In the smaller-scale societies of the Late Bronze Age and the Early Iron Age, fibula types were few in number, and types appear to have represented specific statuses in society. But in the larger, more complex societies based at the *oppida* of the Late Iron Age and then in the more cosmopolitan world of the early Roman Period, the number of types of fibula in use was vastly greater, as the enormous fibula spectrum from Manching indicates. The evidence suggests that fibulae no longer served as bearers of information about the wearer's identity in the same way that they had earlier; instead, personal choice was probably the determining factor in fibula selection, especially for people living in cosmopolitan settings, such as military bases and trading settlements. Strong supporting evidence for this idea comes from the recent discovery of the stock-in-store of a jeweler's shop in first-century A.D. Augsburg. The building was destroyed in a fire, perhaps associated with the uprisings in A.D. 69–70, and much of the material from the shop was deposited in a pit. Excavations in 1985 revealed at least six different types of fibula in the assemblage, suggesting that buyers could select any of the six types to purchase and wear. This is not to say that fibulae lost all significance as devices for communicating information, just that they acquired a wider range of possible meanings and that a greater degree of choice may have been involved in the individual's selection of the type to wear than had existed in the smaller communities of earlier times.

Clothing

Clothing is important in virtually all human societies for communicating information about the identity of the wearer and the values to which he or she subscribes. Prehistoric Iron Age traditions of clothing (see chapter 3) were actively maintained in the Rhineland and in the provinces along the Danube well into Roman times. Loose-fitting tunics and, in cold weather, cloaks, were worn by both men and women. Women sometimes wore shawls, men trousers. The evidence comes from two principal sources—grave goods representing fasteners and other surviving accoutrements of costume, and stone relief sculptures portraying both men and women and the garments they wore. Different kinds of bronze fibulae and other brooches indicate that women were more conservative

158

than men in retaining traditional dress customs, in many cases into the third century A.D. But even in men's dress modes, strong continuity from the La Tène Period is often evident in their clothing. The persistence of Iron Age clothing customs among the populations of the frontier provinces in Europe attests to the emphasis of indigenous values and ideology in the early Roman Period, much in the way that the reproduction of the traditional rural dwellings does. These patterns are apparent irrespective of the different kinds of garments required during the different seasons.

BURIAL PRACTICE

At the time of the Roman conquests, from the middle of the first century B.C. to the middle of the first century A.D., the dominant funerary ritual in Rome and in other parts of Roman Italy included cremation of the washed, anointed, and fully clothed body and burial of the cremated remains in an urn (Figure 20). A libation vessel of ceramic or glass, used for pouring an offering over the cremated remains, was typically set beside the urn in the grave. Additional grave goods were few, though there was some variation with wealth and status of the individual buried. Goods often included a ceramic lamp, believed to have served to guide the deceased into the next world, and a coin, perhaps intended as payment to the ferryman for transport across the River Styx. Sometimes jewelry and a drinking vessel were included in the grave. In contrast to burial practices in Iron Age temperate Europe (see chapter 2), men and women were not sharply distinguished in their graves, weapons were not placed in burials, and large sets of pottery, jewelry, or personal ornaments were rare.

During the early Roman Period, we find a wide variety of burial rites in the frontier zone of temperate Europe. Many graves show a continuation of Iron Age traditions; others reflect a mixing of practices from indigenous traditions and newly introduced ideas. Some show the adoption of practices much like those of Roman Italy. Graves constructed in the tradition of the indigenous Iron Age peoples surely represent individuals who wanted to emphasize their identities as native peoples in the face of the changes introduced by the Roman newcomers. For the other two categories, it is usually not clear whether the graves represent natives who adopted some or all of the Italic Roman practices, or Roman soldiers or civilians buried in traditions from their homeland.

159

Fig. 20. Reconstruction of a typical Roman Period burial ceremony. The mourners are placing a glass vessel, perhaps containing perfume or incense, into the urn that already contains the cremated remains of the deceased. Around the grave are incense burners. From Fasold 1992, fig. 9. Used by permission of Württembergisches Landesmuseum, Stuttgart.

I have discussed above the four rich graves at Goeblingen-Nospelt, from the four decades following the conquest of Gaul (see chapter 4). Those four reflect continuation of Late Iron Age burial practices, with weapons, horse-riding equipment, and large quantities of feasting utensils and personal ornaments. Yet borrowing from Roman practices is apparent—most of the feasting utensils were of Roman character, and the sets of dinnerware may indicate the adoption of Roman dining practices.

Like the four burials at Goeblingen-Nospelt from the very beginning of the Roman Period, many men's graves in regions west of the Rhine contain weapons in the local Late Iron Age fashion, throughout the first and second centuries and into the third century A.D. These graves are especially well represented in the Low Countries and west of the upper Rhine in Germany. The practice of including weapons in graves represents strong resistance to the new burial practices and powerful assertion of local traditions.

Numerous women's graves similarly illustrate the maintenance of indigenous traditions. At Rohrbach near Saarbrücken in western Germany, a richly outfitted woman's burial dating to the first half of the first century A.D. contained a set of nine ceramic vessels, six bronze fibulae, a glass perfume bottle, two bronze mirrors, a bronze pin, and iron shears. This large quantity of grave goods was characteristic of rich burials of the Late La Tène Period in this region, but very different from Roman practices. The four large thistle fibulae probably were worn to fasten the woman's outer garment, while the two small hinged fibulae served to secure undergarments.

The cemetery at Wederath in the middle Moselle Valley region presents exceptionally good evidence for the continuity of traditional practices and for the gradual changes that the community underwent during the Roman Period. The cemetery was used from the third century B.C. until the fourth century A.D., and there is no evidence to suggest a break in the continuity. A single community seems to have used the cemetery as its burial place throughout those centuries of the Late Iron Age and the early and middle Roman Period. A total of some two thousand graves have been excavated and studied, constituting an exceptionally rich and well-documented database for investigation of the questions we are addressing in this book.

Grave 2370 was situated in a part of the cemetery with other well-outfitted burials of the second half of the first century A.D. On the basis of the grave goods, most were identified by the excavators as women's graves. This was a cremation burial, like the majority from that period, and it contained four ceramic vessels and one glass vessel, five bronze fibulae, a bronze folding mirror, four Roman coins (one silver and three bronze), and a wooden box with metal fittings.

The pottery vessels and the glass bottle are Roman in style, though the gray wide-mouthed pot probably derives its shape from local traditional forms. The fibulae, coins, and mirror are all of types that were current in provincial Roman Europe at the time. But the constitution of the burial assemblage is indigenous in character, not Roman. In fact, the combination of multiple fibulae, mirror, coin, and containers is the same pattern that occurs in the grave at Dühren and others of the Late La Tène Period (see chapter 3), from about two hundred years earlier. This grave illustrates the persistence of a specific kind of native burial practice. This adherence to tradition indicates a strong assertion of native identity on the part of the woman buried here and of those who carried out the funeral ceremony.

At the Roman settlement of Cambodunum, modern Kempten in the Alpine foothills of southern Bavaria, the first century A.D. graves excavated at the Keckwiese cemetery resemble more closely Italic Roman practices, with cremation urns, small quantities of accompanying pottery, occasionally lamps and coins, and jewelry in the form of fibulae. But as the publication of the cemetery shows, many of the graves contain animal bones, probably the remains of food offerings placed in the graves. Pigs are best represented, then cattle, next sheep; wild animals are present in only a few instances. Much of the pottery is of indigenous Iron Age character, including both high jars with horizontal painted band decoration and coarser handmade cooking pots with incised comb ornament.

Many of the graves show variations from the standard Roman practice of the time (see also chapter 8). Amphorae are included in a number of the graves, a category of container that would be extremely unusual in burials in Roman Italy. Grave 131 contained an iron lancehead. Some graves had larger quantities and more diverse assemblages of goods than typical Roman burials. Grave 195 contained a bronze coin, a bronze fibula, a small bronze ring, two bronze beads, a small iron ring, an iron bracelet, four nails, a glass perfume bottle, a glass bowl, fragments of two other glass vessels, a perforated section from a red deer antler, a pot with horizontal painted bands, a thin-walled ceramic bowl, a conical cooking pot, and two jugs. The quantity and character of these goods is much more like the practices of the Late Iron Age than like Roman practices in Italy.

The first century A.D. cemetery at Bad Cannstatt near Stuttgart demonstrates a different variation on the adoption of Roman practices. The graves contained few items other than very small amounts of Roman-style pottery, ceramic lamps, and coins. The paucity of personal ornaments led investigators to conclude that the bodies were generally cremated without their usual clothing and jewelry. There are no apparent signs in this cemetery of individuals expressing their identity as members of indigenous groups. That says nothing about who they were, of course, only about who they, or those burying them, wanted to represent themselves as in this final stage of the funerary ritual.

As these examples illustrate, the burial evidence from the first two centuries of the Roman Period in temperate Europe indicates a variety of information concerning the ways people chose to represent themselves in this important ritual of expression. In many cases, individuals re-created the traditional practices of their Iron Age forebears, in others they combined indigenous elements with new ones adopted from Roman tradition, and in others they created new patterns without obvious reference to their native practices. The range of variation is vast, and every cemetery, every individual grave is different and needs to be examined and interpreted separately.

RITUAL

All human societies use ritual practices to create and communicate essential meanings about relationships between people and between people and the supernatural. Analysis of ritual provides insight into the values and attitudes of a community. There is strong evidence throughout the Roman frontier provinces for the continuation of traditional practices of ritual activity throughout the Roman Period. Ritual and religion are complex subjects in any archaeological context, and particularly so in situations in which different groups interact and borrow practices from one another. The exchange of ideas through contact played an important role in affecting ritual behavior, and the stress inherent in any contact situation such as the Roman conquest and occupation of temperate Europe itself created changes in religious expression. We cannot analyze sites in the Roman provinces with a simple dichotomy between indigenous prehistoric and Roman. Ritual behavior in the Late Iron Age in the region was diverse and complex. New ideas and practices introduced by Roman occupation were also highly variable, in large part because of the varied origins of the Roman soldiers. The coming together of these multifarious traditions and practices resulted in an extremely wide variety of practices that we interpret as ritual.

Here I use as examples four of the most common kinds of site illustrating continuing practice of prehistoric ritual during the Roman Period. These are rectangular enclosures, water deposits, burned offerings, and sanctuaries dedicated to pre-Roman deities.

A substantial proportion of the rectangular enclosures that have been excavated have yielded archaeological evidence of use during the Roman Period as well as in the Late La Tène Period. Excavations at the enclosures at Fellbach-Schmiden and at Riedlingen, both in southwest Germany (see chapter 3), recovered pottery and other materials that indicate that the sites were used for ritual activities into the Roman Period. The site of Empel in the Netherlands is a particularly illuminating exam-

163

ple of the continuation of Iron Age ritual practices after the Roman conquest.

Empel is situated on the south bank of the Maas River in the central part of the Netherlands, in the northern part of the Roman province of Germania Inferior. People used the site as a place to deposit objects as offerings, principally between 100 B.C. and A.D. 200. Among the more than 2,000 objects recovered in the course of excavations were over 1,000 coins, some Celtic but mostly Roman, nearly 500 fibulae, and over 100 pieces of Roman military equipment. During the Late Iron Age it was the site of an open-air sanctuary, without identifiable structures. The excavations recovered some 100 metal objects from this period, including coins, fibulae, belt hooks, and fragments of swords and axes. In the post-conquest period, probably after A.D. 70, a stone temple was erected on the site of the prehistoric sanctuary (Figure 21). People continued to deposit objects at the site, including many of the same categories that had been deposited in the Late Iron Age, such as coins, fibulae, finger-rings, weapons, horse harness equipment, and thousands of joints of meat, represented in the archaeological material by the surviving animal bones.

The Roman Period sanctuary provides information that is not available from the Iron Age site—an inscription confirming the function of the site and the deity to whom it was dedicated (Figure 22). A slab of silver-plated bronze bearing a votive inscription (Figure 23) indicates the worship of the deity Hercules Magusenus, a characteristic combination of names and attributes that linked indigenous and Roman identities. A small bronze statue of the Roman god Hercules (Figure 24) adds support to the identification of the sanctuary as one dedicated to that deity. The excavators note the preponderance of military articles among the offerings and the absence of objects regularly associated with women.

The special importance of Empel is in demonstrating the continued use of a site for ritual activities based in the indigenous prehistoric traditions. Similar categories of objects were deposited at the sanctuary in Iron Age and Roman times. The depositing of weapons and horse-riding equipment was a characteristic native practice, very different from typical Roman ritual. The inscription illustrates the combining of attributes of traditional native deities with gods newly introduced onto the scene by the Roman troops, an amalgamating of functions characteristic of the religious syncretism in the province of Germania Inferior.

Deposits of objects in water for ritual purposes are common throughout European prehistory and down to the modern day. Many sites show

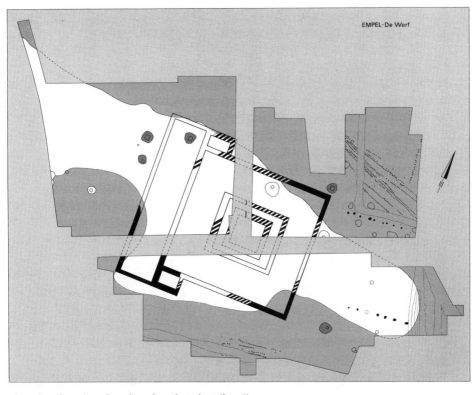

Fig. 21. Plan of the sanctuary at Empel in the Netherlands, showing the stone and mortar foundation from the Roman Period and many of the features dug into the subsoil. *(1–4)* Roman Period walls. *(5–7)* postholes. *(8)* Roman Period wells, in which many of the offerings were found. From Roymans and Derks 1994, p. 18, fig. 6. Plan courtesy of Nico Roymans, Vrije Universiteit, Amsterdam.

continued use from late prehistoric into Roman times, frequently with the same kinds of objects deposited throughout. At the source of the Seine in eastern France, wooden sculptures of humans and of human body parts, and a variety of metal objects, were deposited at the spring during the Late Iron Age. In Roman times, statuary dedicated to the goddess Sequana, a pre-Roman deity of the river, were placed in the spring or erected around it.

Many wells on Roman settlements have yielded objects that were deliberately dropped into them, apparently in the practice of ritual similar to

165

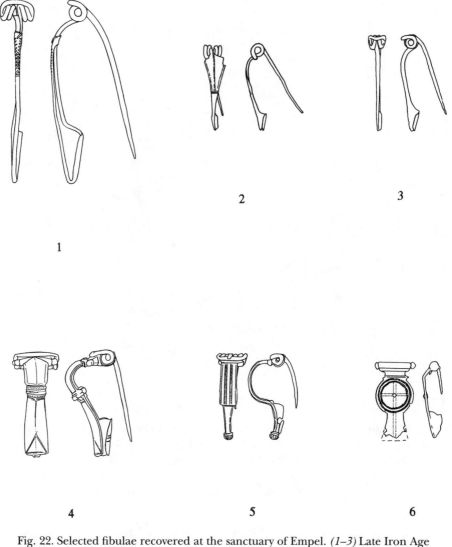

Fig. 22. Selected fibulae recovered at the sanctuary of Empel. *(1–3)* Late Iron Age fibulae. *(4–6)* Roman Period fibulae. All are shown at the same scale; *(1)* is about 3.75 in. (9.6 cm) long. From Roymans and Derks 1994, p. 15, fig. 3; p. 135, fig. 1; and p. 136, fig. 2. Reproduced by permission of Nico Roymans.

that of prehistoric times. Important examples are at the civilian settlement associated with the Roman fort at Buch in southwest Germany. In the course of excavations in 1978, two wells were found that contained objects deposited in them. Well 9 contained a nearly complete, but un-

Fig. 23. Silver-coated bronze plaque from Empel bearing votive
inscription to Hercules Magusenus, about 3 in. (7.8 cm) wide.
Photograph courtesy of Nico Roymans.

finished, Roman bronze infantry helmet, a chain mail shirt, and wooden
sculpture of a male figure believed by the excavators to represent a deity.
Well 13 yielded a large bronze cauldron, two bronze pails with iron handles, a bronze casserolle, a bronze pan, a canteen of sheet iron with
bronze parts, an iron balance, and an iron tripod. The assemblage in
Well 9 is reminiscent of many weapon deposits from the Late Iron Age,
such as those at Gournay-sur-Aronde in northern France and Tiefenau
in Switzerland (see chapter 3). The set of iron tools and bronze vessels
in Well 13 is like a large series of metal hoards that date to the Late La
Tène Period. The two well deposits at Buch date to the middle of the
third century A.D.

At Bregenz on the eastern end of Lake Constance in Austria, a deposit
of about 100 bronze and iron fibulae recovered near the site of a Roman
Period temple has been interpreted as a votive offering. About 80 of the
fibulae were of bronze, all of the same characteristic provincial Roman
type, made sometime around A.D. 50–70. Close analysis of the bronze
fibulae shows that they are very similar and were probably all made by
the same bronzesmith. Between 22 and 24 fibulae were of iron, of a common Late La Tène wire type. Offering deposits of fibulae are common

167

Fig. 24. Bronze statue of Hercules from Empel, about 3 in. (8.1 cm) high. Photograph courtesy of Nico Roymans.

from the Late La Tène Period in temperate Europe, and they occur during the early Roman Period, especially during the first half of the first century A.D. Another well-documented fibula desposit is at Nuits-Saint-Georges in the Côte-d'Or region of France.

"Burned offering places" (*Brandopferplätze*) constitute another significant category of ritual site from prehistoric times that continued to play an important role in the Roman Period. Besides ashes, charcoal, and burned animal bones, these sites often include quantities of weapons, horse gear, personal ornaments, metal vessels, and tools—much the same categories of objects that occur in Late Iron Age rich burials and in water-offerings. The distribution of known sites of this type from prehistoric and Roman times shows a remarkably similar pattern, strongly suggesting direct continuity among the communities practicing this particular ritual. A new site was recently discovered at Gauting in Upper Bavaria. Excavations yielded two areas of intense burning. One formed a circle of ash about 33 ft. (10 m) in diameter; below the circle was a 10 by 1 1/2 ft. (3.0 x 0.4 m) rectangular area full of charcoal, enclosed by a wall of cobbles. A short distance from the ash pile was an area about

108 sq. ft. (10 m²) in area that contained abundant burned animal bones and sherds of characteristic Late La Tène graphite-clay pottery with comb-incised decoration. Around both burned areas were numerous Late La Tène–type fibulae of iron, pottery, and fragments of glass bracelets, as well as scattered Roman Period fibulae, belt buckles, glass fragments, and broken iron tools. All of the objects show signs of fire. Coins on the site attest to its use as late as the third century A.D.

Many indigenous Iron Age deities were worshiped in the Roman Period. In fact only with the textual sources of Roman writers and the representations during the Roman Period of the anthropomorphized deities do we become familiar with the majority of the pre-Roman gods and goddesses. An example is the indigenous goddess Sirona, a deity linked to warm springs and healing. Inscriptions dedicated to this goddess are particularly common in eastern France, the Moselle region, and the upper Rhine, but she is represented as far west as Brittany and as far east as Hungary. She is usually shown in a long cloak and is regularly associated with particular attributes, including a branch or ear of grain, a snake, and a bowl containing three eggs. The branch or grain is thought to represent abundance, the snake rebirth (because snakes shed their skins), and the eggs fertility. In inscriptions and in representations Sirona is frequently associated with the Roman male god Apollo, or with the indigenous interpretation Apollo Grannus (see chapter 9). An important sanctuary dedicated to Sirona and Apollo was excavated at Hochscheid in the Moselle Valley region and found to date to the second half of the second century A.D. There at the site of a Gallo-Roman temple were found two stone altars, one dedicated to Apollo and Sirona, the other to Apollo alone. The figures are represented at almost life size. Sirona is shown with a snake wound around her right arm, and in her left hand she holds a bowl with three eggs in it.

Conclusion

The examples discussed in this chapter are intended to illustrate the point that many communities in the conquered lands in temperate Europe continued to produce their traditional material culture, and the behaviors and practices of which that material culture was a part. But I disagree with those investigators who suggest that such continuity in house types, pottery, fibulae, burial practices, and ritual activity indicates that communities were isolated, cut off from the changes introduced by Rome to the more urban areas. In the relatively densely inhabited landscape of late prehistoric and Roman Period temperate Europe, no communities were isolated to that extent. Research on communities in Hungary that persisted in making Late La Tène–style pottery and metal ornaments through the second century B.C. shows that excavated settlements nonetheless yield some Roman-style objects as well. The presence of such "imports" at otherwise native-style settlements underscores the connectedness of all communities during this period. I have no doubt as investigators in other parts of Roman Europe turn their attention increasingly to the rural areas and the small, native-style settlements, they will find similar patterns to those documented for Hungary.

We must regard the multifarious indications of the continued production of Iron Age–style pottery, La Tène–type fibulae, dedications of objects at Roman Period sanctuaries, and the rest, as expressions of conscious behavior on the part of the indigenous peoples. People continued to build traditional farmhouses, even if they incorporated some innovations suggested by newly introduced architectural ideas; to make traditional pottery and fibulae; and to deposit objects in ritual contexts as they had during the prehistoric Iron Age because these actions of production made statements for them about their relationship to their traditions on the one hand and to the changing circumstances on the other. These were active re-creations, not passive repetitions.

The reproduction of the traditional houses, pottery, fibulae, burial practices, and ritual behaviors can be understood in terms of what Paul Stoller calls "cultural resistance." As he shows through analysis of such behaviors in recent West Africa, such resistance can be a powerful factor in determining the course of interactions between colonizers and the colonized. Such widespread maintenance and reproduction of traditions in the face of powerful external cultural influences is a much more common phenomenon than armed rebellion, as James Scott demonstrates in his study of peasant resistance in Malaysia. In the early Roman Period armed rebellion occurred as well. The uprising of the Batavians in the lower Rhine region under Civilis in A.D. 69 is well documented historically, and destruction layers at many Roman centers, such as Augusta Vindelicum (Augsburg) at about this same time attest to those events. But the reproduction of indigenous Late Iron Age practices and objects was a much more pervasive and effectual form of resistance to the changes brought by the Roman occupation.

CHAPTER 8

Town, Country, and Change

New Towns and Cities in the Frontier Zone

COMPARED TO the urbanized coasts of the Mediterranean Sea in Italy, Greece, Dalmatia, and southern Spain, the number and size of new towns that were established in the frontier zone of temperate Europe were very small. But within the context of temperate Europe, the new foundations, with much in their organization and structure that reflected Mediterranean ideas and architectural materials, represented a departure from indigenous settlement forms. After the military forts, the towns were the principal places at which Roman values and lifestyle were transmitted to the indigenous peoples of the provinces.

Architects from the Mediterranean region introduced the geometric street grid pattern to temperate Europe, and some native peoples seem to have adopted it eagerly. They also brought stone architecture and Mediterranean-style urban centers. The standard complex of Roman town structure was transmitted to the new foundations north of the Alps, including stone walls with often massive gates, fora, baths, and amphitheaters. From one perspective, the urban centers constitute a profound transformation in the European landscape, the introduction of a wholly new set of features from the Mediterranean world. Modern artists' conceptions of Roman towns such as Colonia Claudia Ara Agrippinensium (Cologne), Augusta Treverorum (Trier), and Augusta Vindelicum (Augsburg) frequently show stone buildings with tile roofs, paved roads, and residents in togas very much as they looked in the towns of Roman Italy. But recently, new perspectives have suggested other ways of interpreting the evidence.

The Romans did not introduce urbanization *per se* to the provinces of temperate Europe, but instead built upon the urban tradition that had developed in the Late Iron Age in the *oppida*. It can be reasonably argued that the development of the *oppida* in the latter half of the second century B.C. was the first development of urbanism in temperate Europe, and that by the time the Romans arrived on the scene, some indigenous peoples had become accustomed to the idea of large centers inhabited by thousands of people and performing centralized functions of produc-

171

tion and commerce. In Gaul, some of the *oppida* remained occupied after the conquest and until the Roman establishment of provincial infrastructure. In the case of Bibracte, for example, it has been demonstrated that in the first decades A.D., two generations after the conquest of Gaul, a large part of the *oppidum* population moved from the hilltop settlement on Mont Beuvray to the newly established Roman settlement of Augustodunum (Autun) in the valley below.

Recent studies have argued that much of the public building in the new towns was sponsored not by the Roman state or the provincial government, but by members of the indigenous elite groups, as a way of demonstrating their wealth and power on the one hand, and their links with the cosmopolitan Roman fashions on the other. In this view, Roman architecture was employed for a purpose fully consistent with indigenous traditions of competition, previously expressed in construction of grandiose *oppidum* walls and outfitting of lavish burials.

While much of the urban architecture was sponsored by local elites in the towns, this fact does not allow us to state that the indigenous peoples as a whole embraced the Roman urban form. The stone buildings with dedicatory inscriptions provide vivid and lasting testimony to the wealth and power of the elite, and to their interest in re-creating their identities as cosmopolitan, "Romanized" natives. But only a tiny proportion of the whole populace is represented by public architecture and inscriptions. The great majority of the people are not so represented, and we cannot assume that they also eagerly embraced the new styles, forms, and values. In fact, nonelites are poorly represented in the urban settings, and we need to turn to the rural contexts to learn more about them and their reactions to the ongoing changes (see below).

The urban centers played active roles in the political functioning of the provinces. We can understand the Roman urban centers as complex instruments for the display of political imagery in the form of statues, triumphal arches, and stages on which power relations could be acted out publicly, as in the theater, the amphitheater, and the forum. The provincial cities were inhabited principally by local elites. The introduction of the *civitas* system to the provinces constituted a means for the centralized control of the countryside. While much urban architecture was sponsored by wealthy indigenous individuals, it is not clear at this stage whether the urban centers as a whole were primarily introduced by the authorities in Rome, or created on the Roman model by the local elites.

A few examples will illustrate the character of some of the early Roman cities established in the frontier provinces of Germania Inferior, Germania Superior, and Raetia. Most had their origins in military bases that attracted civilian settlement. All of the important early Roman towns continued to be occupied throughout the Roman Period, the Middle Ages, and into modern times. As a result of this continuous occupation and building activity over two thousand years, many finds from the early Roman establishments have come to light in the course of modern construction, but because of the presence of the modern cities it has not been possible to conduct extensive excavations.

Municipium Batavorum, later Ulpia Noviomagus, modern Nijmegen in the Netherlands, was established as a town on the lower Rhine in pre-Flavian times, before A.D. 69. Dutch archaeologists have interpreted the layout, architecture, pottery, and burial customs to show that its inhabitants were not indigenous people from the surrounding countryside, but Gauls who identified strongly with Roman society or persons of Mediterranean origin. This urban center thus grew from immigrants, not a native population base. Sometime just after A.D. 70, the new center of Ulpia Noviomagus was established. This was a large military base encompassing over 100 acres (40 ha) of land and serving as a major defense point on the river.

Colonia Claudia Ara Agrippinensium, modern Cologne in Germany, is a well-researched example of a large Roman city. It was founded as a military base sometime before the time of Christ. The location was already the site of a major settlement of the Ubii, a group indigenous to that part of the Rhineland. Sources tell us that the then governor of Gaul, Agrippa, invited the Ubii in 39–38 B.C. to settle at this place from across the Rhine (see chapter 4). After the Varus disaster, Rome developed the site as a major frontier base for the legions. The Rhine fleet was stationed just upstream. In A.D. 50 the settlement was officially designated as a Roman colonial city, and the Roman authorities encouraged the settlement of veterans at the site. About A.D. 85 it was selected as capital of the province of Germania Inferior. The city wall enclosed about 237 acres (96 ha) of land, and its population during the second and the first half of the third century is estimated at fifteen thousand, with another five thousand persons living just outside the walls. Besides being an important frontier point, the city became a major economic center of the Roman Rhineland. Throughout its history Roman Cologne is known to have had a very mixed population, made up of indigenous peoples, army veterans, military and civilian administrative personnel, and immigrant merchants and craftworkers.

The indigenous population at Roman Cologne is recognizable from the archaeological evidence, but not much represented in the textual sources. Through the first half of the first century A.D., pottery was still being made in forms and techniques characteristic of the pre-Roman peoples of the region. Some vessels are nearly identical to earlier ones, others reflect an adoption of newly introduced features of ceramics. Local traditions of fibula production were carried forth into the Roman Period. In the realm of religion and ritual, indigenous deities such as the Matronae and Epona were much represented on stone sculpture in the Roman city.

Augusta Treverorum, modern Trier in Germany, was probably first occupied by Roman troops around 30 B.C. when a garrison may have been established on the Petrisberg Hill on the eastern side of the city. There was no major Late Iron Age center at Trier, but numerous finds from the modern city indicate the presence of small-scale settlement on the site. The establishment of the Roman city took place sometime between 19 and 13 B.C. and is associated with the presence of Agrippa and the Emperor Augustus in Gaul. From early in its development as a Roman center, it was probably intended to be the capital of the Treveri region. The first major phase of construction was during the third quarter of the first century A.D., when the baths known as the Barbarathermen were constructed. Around A.D. 100 the amphitheater and circus were built. The city wall was constructed in the second third of the second century, and the major baths, the Kaiserthermen, and the imperial palace were constructed in the years A.D. 289–340.

In addition to the monumental architecture in stone, the excavations at Trier have revealed large numbers of small wooden structures built at the same time, though these have received less research attention. The contrast between Mediterranean-style buildings with walls bearing paintings, ornamental brick floors, mosaics, and tiled roofs, and wood-built houses with sunken floors and wattle-and-daub walls suggests that elite groups at the city identified strongly with the Roman world, while the majority continued to live with material culture linked closely to earlier indigenous traditions.

Mogontiacum, modern Mainz in Germany, was established as a base for two legions in about 13 B.C., specifically to support campaigns into Germanic territory across the Rhine. Later, it became a central point for provisioning troops stationed along the *limes*. The civilian city was constructed to the northeast of the legionary camp, but very little is known about it because of the lack of systematic excavations.

Augusta Vindelicum, modern Augsburg in Germany, probably began as a military base at Augsburg-Oberhausen. From the beginning of this century, gravel-quarrying operations near the confluence of the Wertach and Lech Rivers recovered large quantities of military weapons, tools, and pottery. A two-week excavation in August 1913 yielded about 10,000 objects from an area about 10 ft. (3 m) wide and 100 ft. (30 m) long on the edge of the gravel pit. These abundant artifacts indicate the presence of a military base of the early Roman Period close by, but systematic searching has failed to locate it. The chronology of the objects, in particular the 378 coins, allows the material to be dated in the period 8 B.C.–A.D. 17. After the abandonment of this elusive base, perhaps because of a flood, another was established about A.D. 15 on the high terrace between the Lech and the Wertach. This fort was abandoned sometime during the 70s or 80s. On the same site at the end of the first century the provincial capital of Raetia, Augusta Vindelicum, developed and grew rapidly. A city wall enclosing 161 acres (65 ha) of land was constructed between 170 and 180, perhaps in response to threats of attack during the period of the Marcomannic Wars. Because of extensive medieval and modern building in the city of Augsburg, archaeological research has been limited.

The Auerberg in Upper Bavaria (the Roman name is unknown) is an example of a small civilian settlement of the early Roman Period. It was occupied from about A.D. 10 to 40, by indigenous peoples of the area, Roman colonists, and soldiers. All of the architecture was of wood. Long rectangular houses were arranged on streets, as at the *vicus* of Regensburg-Kumpfmühl, and they measured roughly 82 by 26 ft. (25 x 8 m). The community carried out much manufacturing. Seven pottery kilns have been identified, bronze and iron working attested, and glass production is represented. Loom weights show that weaving was done on the site. Both local La Tène–style pottery and Roman wares are present, including imports from Italy and southern Gaul. Manufacturing evidence includes military equipment, indicating that this community produced goods for the army as well as for civilian use.

RURAL LANDSCAPES

Military bases and urban centers were the places where changes introduced by Rome were taken up most quickly and most thoroughly. Change in rural settings was both later and less pervasive. In rural parts of Raetia, evidence for the adoption of new features associated with the Roman presence does not appear until over half a century after the conquest. Similarly in northern Gaul, the influence of Rome was considerably less in rural districts than in towns. In Hungary, traditional Late Iron

Age patterns persisted in rural regions well into the Roman Period. Near the major Roman centers in the frontier zone, villas were introduced in the countryside. Even within regions, there can be considerable variation. For example, in the landscapes west of the lower Rhine, north of the loess soils in the Netherlands, Belgium, and Germany, traditional wood-built farmhouses persisted during the Roman Period. To the south in the loess zones, villas became numerous during the late first and second centuries A.D.

The villa was a distinctive new feature in the countryside, in both its physical and its organizational aspects. The most elaborate villas comprised complexes that included a luxurious stone-built dwelling, structures associated with farming, livestock-raising, and craft production, a system of baths with water of different temperatures, and a small temple for religious worship. In the Roman provinces, a wide variety of structures and institutions have been understood under this term, most of them much more modest than the few luxurious ones with bath complexes and mosaic floors. Essential features of the villa are that it existed in a rural setting, it was usually part of an agricultural system, and it usually comprised one dwelling, not a cluster of dwellings. Some investigators would add the qualification that the dwelling must be at least partly of stone to differentiate a villa from a typical indigenous structure. The villa building and the villa system of agricultural production and rural organization were essential elements of the rural landscape as it was transformed during the Roman Period.

Yet while the villa is a very characteristically "Roman" complex that was introduced into the provinces during the first century A.D., research over the past two decades has challenged the traditional view of the villa as a normative architectural entity imported from Roman Italy that was reproduced in its standard form throughout the provinces. In his aerial survey of Picardy in northern France, Roger Agache documented the presence of many villas, and in the process showed that considerable variability existed in the size and form of the structures. Few fit the standard model of large, complex buildings with luxury accoutrements such as elaborate bath systems and mosaic floors. The great majority were small and of very modest character. Agache's evidence suggests that most villas were built and owned by indigenous individuals, many of modest means and status in their communities. Similar patterns have been identified in the region of Trier and in Britain. There is little evidence to suggest that many villas were owned by individuals who had moved from Italy northward to the frontier provinces. All indications are that these rural complexes were built and owned by locals. Lavishly constructed and ornamented villas are rare in the frontier provinces compared to Italy, underscoring the point that wealthy Romans from the Mediterranean lands did not often invest in villas in the north.

Two examples illustrate the variety of forms and types. In some instances, it is possible to show that Roman Period villas were built as revisions of typical prehistoric buildings that stood on the same site. At Mayen in the Rhineland, for example, the earliest phase of a villa complex was a rectangular, post-built hut with wattle-and-daub walls, of typical Iron Age character. A later phase of architecture on the site, dated to early in the first century A.D., is characterized by a rectangular structure with stone foundation, but post-supported walls. In subsequent rebuildings, the structure was enlarged, with the addition of more rooms and a colonnade. This change over time may represent the progressive adoption on the part of the local residents of ideas and values from the cosmopolitan world of Rome. The multi-roomed structure made possible the spatial separation of different categories of persons living in the complex and the division of different activities into specialized spaces. The colonnade added a special touch that shows that the residents subscribed to the ornamental traditions of the Roman world.

A second example comes from a different region, the province of Raetia in what is now southern Bavaria. Around the middle of the first century A.D. a farmstead was established at Oberndorf on the opposite bank of the Lech River from a military base at Burghöfe. Total excavation in 1988 and 1989 revealed that in the first phase, buildings were of wood, with frames of large vertical posts sunk into the ground, the technology of Iron Age architecture. About ten wooden buildings, some very small, were erected. The excavator states that their arrangement shows no clear planning or pattern, and he thinks structures were added to the arrangement haphazardly. But he considers this complex, enclosed by a wattle fence, to be a villa—precursor to the stone-built villa that succeeds it.

Around the middle of the second century, the dwelling within this complex was rebuilt in stone in a villa format, and made considerably larger, though it remained small compared to other villas of the period. The enclosed area was increased from about 3 acres (1.2 ha) to about 10 acres (4 ha). The residence was oriented toward the south, and its entrance was enhanced by columns of local white limestone. The windows were outfitted with glass. A bath complex was added, with the standard warm, tepid, and cold baths, but it was unusually small.

Other excavation results show that this complex did not fit the model of the classic Roman villa. Three wood-lined wells, dendrochronologically dated at A.D. 138, 142, and 151, contained remains of expected cereals—barley, oats, and emmer and spelt wheats—together with flax, fennel, and strawberry. But they also preserved seeds of weeds that we might not expect within an enclosed villa complex—thistles, stinging nettle, and shepherd's purse. Peculiarities among the faunal remains— many fewer animal bones in the pits than usual on villa sites in the region, and of the bones present, an unusually high proportion of horse bones— probably relate to interaction with the fort across the river.

The Oberndorf complex illustrates continuity in settlement structure, from Iron Age–style wooden architecture to Mediterranean-fashion stone. The layout of postholes and fence ditches of the first phase is reminiscent of those at Late Iron Age settlements in the region. The stone buildings adhered to the plan established for the wooden architecture; many were erected directly above their predecessors. Nico Roymans refers to "farming as cultural construction" in reference to similar patterns of Roman Period continuity with indigenous Iron Age practice in the Netherlands. At Oberndorf we see aspects of the idea of the Roman villa adopted around the middle of the second century A.D., but the resulting farmstead is similar to its Iron Age predecessors in its arrangement.

Several important points emerge from studies of the villas in the frontier regions of temperate Europe. The adoption of some of the architectural forms of the "standard" Roman villas (i.e., in Roman Italy) on the part of indigenous peoples cannot be taken to indicate that the inhabitants transformed themselves into "Romans." The villa was only one of many elements that were adopted by some indigenous groups in temperate Europe, but transformed and modified to be useful in the indigenous cultural system; this subject will be treated further in chapter 9.

As noted above, the villa in the different regions of the frontier zone of temperate Europe was not a simple copy of the Italian form. Each of the thousands of villas that have been excavated in temperate Europe is unique. Regional patterns in form and structure can be identified. In the German provinces, for example, the most characteristic form was the small villa with a relatively large central room or hall serving as the principal organizing feature, and with a corridor linking different parts of the building. This hall space links the villas with prehistoric dwellings, and the large open gathering space probably served the same purpose in the Roman Period as it did in the Iron Age.

Rural settlement can inform us about the degree to which different groups in indigenous society adopted aspects of Roman culture. As noted above, the new urban centers were showplaces for the display of Roman power and of native elites' wealth and affiliation with the cosmopolitan culture of the empire. The rural landscapes, in contrast, show much less taking up of Roman ways, and it is in the rural settings that we can expect to find markedly differing degrees of adoption of and resistance to the new elements offered by Rome. Rural areas, from the lower Rhine region to southern Bavaria, show much less adoption of Roman architecture, material culture, and lifestyle; and when such evidence does appear, it is markedly later than in the urban centers.

Several investigators have conducted work recently on the connections between rural settlement and ideology. In investigations of rural contexts in the lower Rhine region of the Netherlands, researchers observe that in the northern part of Germania Inferior, where the soils are rich in sand and clay, farm buildings retained their traditional long rectangular form and vertical-timber architecture that goes back to the Late Bronze Age in the region. These buildings housed human occupants at one end and livestock, particularly cattle, at the other. Even though the farm-houses remained traditional in character, they do show changes during the early Roman Period, particularly in growing differences in size and in wealth of material culture. During the second century some farmhouses evince features derived from Roman architecture, such as wooden porticos and sometimes partial stone foundations and some painted walls, as at Rijswijk (see chapter 7). These were most likely houses of local elites.

While earlier investigators interpreted the limited adoption of Roman elements and their integration into essentially local architectural expressions in terms of the wealth available to the local elites who wanted to imitate the "classic" Roman villa, the maintenance of traditional farm-house architecture may be understood best in terms of ideology of agriculture and rural life. The house-barn combination developed during a long tradition from the Late Bronze Age through the prehistoric Iron Age, and the pattern of humans living in close contact with their livestock was, according to this view, an important element in the ideology of the people of this region. The local elites made conscious choices to reproduce the traditional farmhouse, and to add a limited number of Roman features, rather than to transform their dwellings and build more thoroughly "Roman" structures.

This argument can be supported with reference to evidence for ritual activities revolving around cattle, most evident in special deposits of cattle bones associated with settlements. Cattle became progressively more important in the local economy during the early Roman Period. Farm-houses became longer during this time, to accommodate more cattle, and the size of the animals increased during the first two centuries A.D., indicating selective breeding. The increasing importance of cattle to the local society and its economy can be understood in the context of the needs of the growing Roman urban centers, and especially the army, for large quantities of both meat and hides (see chapter 6).

INDIGENOUS RESPONSES TO CHANGE

The peoples that the Roman troops encountered in Gaul and south of the Danube were not completely homogeneous culturally or linguisti-cally, though many groups shared important features. The archaeologi-cal evidence of settlements and burials during the final two centuries B.C. makes clear that these lands were inhabited by communities with somewhat varied practices and material cultures that exhibit some re-gional variation. Communities that occupied *oppida* were different from those in small unfortified settlements. Material culture in central Gaul was similar, but not identical, to that in southern Bavaria, for example. The increased interaction between communities in these regions and groups in northern parts of the continent, to the east, and southward in the Alps, makes clear that they were open to a variety of influences that left their traces in the material evidence. The incoming Roman troops introduced yet more variety. Some were from Roman central Italy, some from regions of northern Italy, and some from other places. For exam-ple, some of the troops in Tiberius's army that invaded southern Bavaria in 15 B.C. had their origins in Gaul. Hence a richly varied cultural mix developed in the newly conquered provinces.

In order to understand the character of the frontier zone in Europe during the first century and a half of the Roman Empire, we need to abandon the mindset that classifies the populace as either "Romans" or "natives." Investigators agree that relatively few people moved from Roman Italy to settle in the provinces of temperate Europe. Even with considerable movement of individuals between provinces during the early empire, the vast majority of the population in all regions was indige-nous. Thus when we examine something as apparently "Roman" as a stone-built temple or a villa with painted interior walls, we are dealing in almost all instances with indigenous elites commissioning architects familiar with Mediterranean styles. As noted in the preceding sections, while many such structures are superficially Mediterranean in style, most show, on close examination, clear local features.

New Opportunities in the Frontier Provinces

Some individuals and communities appear to have gone to great lengths to maintain their traditional patterns of domestic architecture, pottery production, personal ornamentation, and ritual practice, but there are no cases in which we can assert that behavior and material culture were unaffected by the changes brought by incorporation into the Roman Empire. In Roman Britain it is apparent that the economic and social conditions established by the Roman conquest offered unprecedented opportunities for commercial development and for social advancement. The needs of the military bases and of the new urban centers created a sudden demand for foodstuffs, metals, building materials, and other goods. Those in a position to capitalize on these needs—to manage extractive industries, manufacturing, and commerce—could gain in wealth and status. Since economic matters were rarely recorded in the surviving texts, we know little about the individuals who played important roles in these activities, but occasionally evidence gives insight into specific cases. A tombstone found on the middle Danube informs us of a soldier who had served as a translator. After completion of his service, he went into business as a merchant trading across the frontier to the north. Another source tells about the owner of a brick factory in what is now southwestern Germany. It is likely that the majority of such individuals were members of the indigenous elites, but it is also quite possible that others were able to benefit from the great changes taking place to play a part in these commercial developments. Many young men chose, or were forced, to leave their native communities and agricultural activity to join the Roman army as auxiliary soldiers. For many, this was surely an attractive alternative—soldiers were paid cash wages, and after retirement they could expect substantial pensions and perhaps could afford to purchase villas of their own.

The point of these observations is that the conquest by Rome and the establishment of the administration and infrastructure of new provinces meant substantial changes for the indigenous peoples. Many individuals had strong motivations for connecting themselves with the Roman economy and Roman values, while others resisted the changes. In this light we can understand the variety of responses evident in the public architecture, private dwellings, ritual complexes, graves, pottery, ornaments, and other aspects of material culture, in terms of the variety of perceived opportunities and threats represented by the Roman administration. The burial evidence from this period provides useful information about the ways people integrated new elements with their traditional practices. I cite two examples, the cemetery on the Keckwiese at Kempten in southern Bavaria and a grave from a cemetery at Nijmegen in the Netherlands.

At Kempten, also discussed in chapter 7, archaeologists have excavated about four hundred graves, the great majority dating between about A.D. 15 and 85. The earliest traces of the Roman Period settlement at Kempten, the ancient town of Cambodunum, are wooden buildings beginning around A.D. 15; by the middle of the first century more substantial structures were being built of stone. This site thus conforms to the pattern of many in the frontier zone—a place newly established a generation after the conquest, with evidence of both indigenous and Mediterranean styles of architecture. The burials show the integration of new Roman elements with traditional ones. The dead were cremated, following practice common both in Roman Italy and in the lands north of the Alps. Many of the graves contained characteristically Mediterranean goods, such as perfume or incense bottles, ceramic lamps, mirrors, and coins; but mirrors and coins also occur often in indigenous Late Iron Age graves. Much of the pottery at Kempten consists of imports from Italy and southern Gaul, but there are also many vessels that closely resemble local Late Iron Age types (Figure 25). Fibulae are strikingly diverse, indicating that the inhabitants of Kempten had considerable choice in the form of ornaments they could purchase and wear. Many of the fibulae are types based on local Late Iron Age forms. Overall, the burials at Kempten look much more like those of local people adopting products readily available through the increased commercial networks than like newcomers bringing in foreign practices.

Nijmegen Grave 8 was situated in a large pit lined with wood, within an enclosure outlined with stones. It was part of a cemetery associated with a civilian settlement, and this grave is thought to date between A.D. 80 and 100. The cremated remains were placed in a glass urn which had been set in one corner of the chamber. The grave contained numerous grave goods, unburned by the cremation fire. A twenty-three-piece service of *terra sigillata* pottery from the southern Gallic production center at La Graufesenque was arranged in one corner and along one side. Other objects included plain everyday pottery, eight four-sided glass bottles and two other glass vessels, and a set of bronze vessels comprising

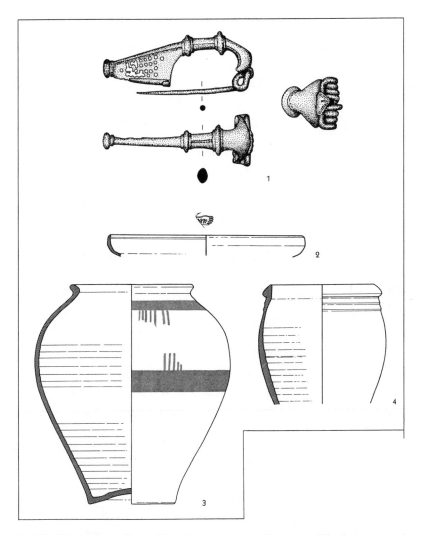

Fig. 25. Objects from Grave 49 in the cemetery at Kempten. The large ceramic vessel (3) is similar in form to many at the Late Iron Age *oppida*, and it bears painted decoration similar to that on many of the finer wares of that context. The fibula (1) is similar to those in the Heimstetten graves (see chapter 4). The vessel is about 10 in. (25.1 cm) high; the fibula is about 3.5 in. (8.8 cm) long. From Mackensen 1978, plate 14. Used by permission of Bayerisches Landesamt für Denkmalpflege, Munich.

two jugs, a basin, and an amphora. A washing set of silver—a jug and a handled bowl with niello decoration—were supplemented by four strigils (metal implements used to scrape the body after exercise) and an enamel-ornamented bronze vessel. A writing kit included an ink pot with silver lid, two iron styli, a knife, and a spatula. The burial assemblage further included three iron spearheads and remains of a shield.

The presence of weapons in the grave makes clear that this individual was being identified as a native who had not fully given up his identity to adopt a Roman one. The overall wealth of grave goods also is non-Roman. Yet unlike the most highly "Romanized" of the graves at Goeblingen-Nospelt, Grave B of around 25–15 B.C., Nijmegen 8 contained very few locally made objects—only the plain pottery and the weapons. The table service of *terra sigillata* suggests the adoption of Roman dining practices, while the bronze and silver vessels point to Roman customs of athletic activity, bathing, and personal toiletries. The writing equipment is particularly interesting, because it implies that this individual had learned to write, an important sign of the adoption of a specific Roman elite practice.

Integrated Ideologies: Native Deities in Roman Form

One of the clearest expressions of the changes that took place in the new Roman provinces of temperate Europe was the creation of new representations of indigenous deities that integrated Roman conceptions with local ones. The issue is complex, because in most instances we only learn of the identity and attributes of traditional deities after they have been named in inscriptions and represented in Roman-style sculpture. The indigenous Iron Age peoples generally did not portray their deities in human form, and, because these prehistoric peoples left no written record, no inscriptions inform us of their names or attributes. In order to study the character of the indigenous Celtic and Germanic deities, we must begin with their representations in the Roman media of stone and ceramic sculpture and Latin inscriptions. Then we need to remove from our examination those aspects of the deities that are distinctively Roman, in order to get at the non-Roman, indigenous elements. Here I cite three of the better-documented deities.

Epona was an indigenous Celtic horse goddess, first well known after the introduction of Roman stone sculptural traditions. The name is related to the Celtic word for "horse." Stone carvings and ceramic figurines of Epona, most often shown either riding side-saddle on a horse or posed between two horses, are abundant in Gaul and in the Rhineland, and they occur in the Danubian provinces, and as far afield as north Africa. She was protectoress of horses and of the people who worked with and depended upon them. Epona was revered especially by soldiers in cavalry units in the Roman army, especially those stationed along the Rhine and Danube frontiers. The attributes that accompany representations of the goddess frequently allude to fertility and to healing. She is often portrayed holding fruit or other forms of food. Epona was even celebrated among some in the city of Rome, one of very few deities that originated in temperate Europe to be so honored.

Evidence for the celebration of cults of mother goddesses during the early Roman Period is particularly abundant in the Rhineland, where carved stone sculptures and inscriptions dedicated to two main variants, the Matronae Aufaniae and the Matronae Vacallinehae, are common (Figure 26). The former are frequently portrayed as three seated women, often holding fruits and associated with other plants and with animals. The themes of fertility and growth are indicated by the attributes shown with these deities, most of which date to the second century A.D.

Nehalennia was a Celtic goddess revered in the lower Rhine region. Shrines to this deity have been discovered on the North Sea coast of the Netherlands at Domburg and Colijnsplaat. She was a goddess of seafarers, providing them with protection during their voyages. Inscriptions dedicated to Nehalennia indicate that some suppliants were Roman citizens; their personal names suggest that many were of Celtic background, others Germanic. Carved stones dedicated to her often bear marine symbolism and representations of sea creatures or of the Roman god Neptune. She is also linked to fertility—she often has a fruit basket in her lap and another next to her on the ground. The sides of her altars often bear cornucopias and trees.

Following the establishment of the imperial administration and infrastructure in the provinces along the Rhine and Danube Rivers, and the introduction of diverse new fashions, manufactured goods, ideas, and values, the first and second centuries A.D. were times of relative peace and great prosperity. Indigenous elites adopted many aspects of Roman civilization, and Mediterranean-style towns flourished along the major rivers of the frontier zone. But in the closing decades of the second century, conditions became more turbulent along the frontiers. The best documented disturbance was the Marcomannic Wars of A.D. 166–80, but they were only one of many signs that profound changes were occurring, not only beyond the frontiers but also within the Roman provinces.

Fig. 26. Sculpture dedicated to mother goddesses in the Rhineland, discovered beneath the cathedral in Bonn; now in the Rheinisches Landesmuseum, Bonn. Note the baskets of fruit the figures hold on their laps, a typical attribute of these deities. Width at base about 34 in. (87 cm). Photograph courtesy of Rheinisches Landesmuseum, Bonn.

CHAPTER 9

Transformation into New Societies

CREATING NEW SOCIETIES IN THE FRONTIER PROVINCES

IN CHAPTER 8 we examined the adoption by indigenous elites of many aspects of Roman civilization and the development of prosperous societies in the frontier provinces. The subject of the present chapter is the transformation of communities in these regions into new societies through complex processes of interaction between different indigenous groups and between those groups and representatives of Rome. Chapters 6, 7, and 8 concerned mainly the decades between the conquest and the middle of the second century A.D.; this chapter focuses on the second half of the second century and the first half of the third (Figure 27).

Earlier studies of this period have tended to frame the analysis in terms of progressively "Romanized" provincial populations and their interactions with ever-more threatening barbarian groups beyond the frontiers. My approach is different. I examine the changes in terms of interaction and negotiation between groups living within the provinces. The archaeological evidence makes clear that the peoples inhabiting the European frontier provinces became increasingly heterogeneous as they responded to the changes resulting from the Roman presence. Groups in different regions distinguished themselves by their material culture and burial practices, for example. Within communities status differences between individuals were significant, as we have seen already; elites were much more active in adopting the trappings of Roman civilization than were other groups. The changes that we observe in the archaeological evidence can best be explained by examining both internal dynamics within the provinces and effects of interactions with groups outside.

The majority of the inhabitants of the Roman provinces during the first, second, and third centuries were descendants of the local prehistoric peoples. Soldiers stationed in the region and persons who moved in from neighboring parts of Europe introduced new traditions and new ideas and contributed to the makeup of the provincial populations. There is no archaeological evidence for large-scale abandonment of any of the frontier regions before, during, or after the Roman conquests, nor is there indication of any mass immigration from outside. In the

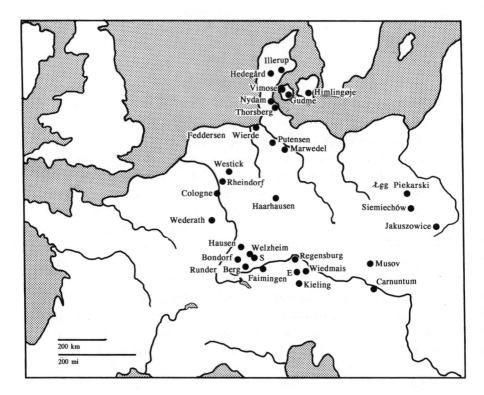

Fig. 27. Map showing the locations of places mentioned in chapters 9, 10,
and 11. E = Ergolding. S = Schirenhof.

architecture, burial practices, ritual behavior, pottery, and personal ornaments of the early Roman Period, we can identify elements that originated in the traditions of the indigenous Iron Age peoples. A recent
investigation of the genetic evidence for population movements in Europe supports the archaeological indications that there were no large-
scale migrations into the region at this time.

Cross-cultural analyses of frontier situations show that frontier zones
are highly dynamic places in which diverse groups interact and in the
process transform their identities. A variety of different changes typically
take place. In the competition for status and political power, groups and
individuals often manipulate their material culture to distinguish themselves from competitors. In the course of such competition, people are
likely to reproduce traditional forms of material culture in extreme expressions. Other times groups meld together, losing their distinctive

identities and creating new societies characterized by material signs different from those of any of the earlier traditions. These changes can take place very rapidly. Through comparison of the full range of material culture in frontier zones, we should be able to distinguish some groups that cling to their traditional practices and identities and others that participate in the creation of new amalgamated social units.

This chapter focuses on the ways in which the peoples of Roman-occupied temperate Europe constructed their lives, their communities, and their identities in terms of the wide variety of choices and challenges with which they were faced during this dynamic time. The Roman Empire of which these groups were part was cosmopolitan and multiethnic on a large scale. There existed no "pure" Roman culture, nor any common "provincial Roman" society, but instead a wide variety of amalgamations of different traditions, constantly shifting over time. Past approaches have tended to overemphasize standardization in the Roman provinces and to neglect the important evidence of local and even individual variation. In the frontier provinces, identities were always in a state of change, under negotiation and in competition. The character of regional, or "tribal," groups varied greatly, depending upon factors such as their traditional backgrounds, their experiences in late prehistoric times and during the conquest, interactions with their neighbors, and relations established with representatives of Rome. Different persons perceived their options differently and responded to changes around them in different ways. All of these levels of variability can be recognized in the archaeological evidence—no two settlements or cemeteries are exactly alike, and the similarities and differences can tell us much about the patterns of change.

DISRUPTIONS ON THE DANUBE FRONTIER: THE MARCOMANNIC WARS

The relative peace and prosperity of the European frontier provinces during the first century and the first half of the second century A.D. were disrupted by a series of invasions on the middle Danube known as the Marcomannic Wars, between A.D. 166 and 180, during the reign of the emperor Marcus Aurelius. The Marcomanni, first mentioned by Caesar, were regarded by the Roman authors as a major Germanic tribal group that inhabited regions north of the Danube and posed a long-term threat to Roman territories. Philologists inform us that the name means "inhabitants of a border land" (from old German *marka* = "border region," and *mann* = "person"), but the origin of the name is unclear as is the border to which it refers. Roman armies confronted them at various times, most significantly during the A.D. 160s and 170s.

The Marcomannic Wars actually involved many different groups north of the Danube. Roman writers named some twenty-five peoples, but the principal ones were the Marcomanni and the Quadi. The Roman writers indicated that the wars resulted from migrations of peoples, some southward from the North Sea and Baltic coasts, others within central Europe, but the actual reasons behind the outbreak of aggression against the Roman provinces at this time are unclear.

Roman literary sources about the wars are scanty and ambiguous. The course of the conflicts must be patched together from incomplete accounts, and modern investigators disagree on many aspects of the events. The first major attack apparently took place in 166, at a time when many Roman troops that had been stationed on the Danube were away fighting the Parthians on the eastern frontier of the empire. After defeating the Parthians in 166, the Roman army could turn its full attention to the events unfolding on the middle Danube.

As the result of battles along the Danube frontier between 166 and 168, Rome became concerned that the invaders might attack Italy via the east Alpine passes. A war party of Marcomanni and Quadi broke through the Roman defenses in Upper Pannonia, severely defeating the Roman forces there, twenty thousand of whom were recorded to have suffered casualties. The invaders pillaged the Roman province, crossed the eastern Alps into northeast Italy, and attacked the Roman base at Aquileia on the north coast of the Adriatic Sea. Finally Roman forces were able to drive them from Italy and back across the Danube. From 170 to 173 Rome launched a series of offensives northward from their base at Carnuntum on the Danube, now in Austria just east of Vienna.

Following a few years of peace, in 179–80 Roman forces again drove northward across the Danube, establishing temporary military camps in enemy territory, a number of which have been identified archaeologically. In March of 180 Marcus Aurelius died. His nineteen-year-old son Commodus carried on the war for a time, but the death of Marcus Aurelius effectively ended the Roman offensives across the middle Danube. As in the case of the earlier Roman campaigns across the Rhine toward the Elbe (see chapter 4), there is scholarly debate as to Rome's intentions on the middle Danube—whether Marcus Aurelius aimed at conquering new territory to incorporate into the empire, or only at destroying the potential of the Marcomanni and their allies to invade Roman lands.

One important result of the Marcomannic Wars was the destruction of both military bases and civilian settlements within the Roman frontier provinces. At many sites, such as Regensburg-Kumpfmühl (see chapter 6), archaeologists encounter extensive burned layers attesting to destruction by the invaders. After the end of the wars in 180, much effort was devoted to rebuilding in these regions.

Sources of Information about the Provincial Societies

The available written sources provide little information about the dynamics of establishing the new provincial administrations or about interactions between groups within the provinces. They deal with issues of most direct concern to the central Roman administration, and the character of the local peoples and the nature of the changes they were experiencing were not subjects about which Roman authors wrote. We lack detailed accounts of the ways in which Roman administrators negotiated with indigenous elites for the establishment of new systems of government and provisioning. Except for personal names, the written sources indicate little about the cultural and ethnic diversity of the populations in the provinces. From information about rebellions against the Roman administration (see chapter 6), we gain some insight into issues of identity and resistance on the part of native peoples, but the textual sources tell little about perceived cultural or ethnic boundaries, interrelationships between groups within the provinces, or means people used to maintain, reinforce, and re-create their identities under changing circumstances. The texts portray the provincial societies as essentially Roman in character. They were written by individuals from Rome or others who had fully adopted Roman literacy and worldview, and when they described indigenous peoples, writers tended to take account only of the elites. As we have seen in chapter 8, indigenous elites tended to eagerly adopt Roman material culture and lifestyles.

The archaeological evidence provides us with a different perspective. It shows a much more complex picture than the texts imply. House forms, pottery styles, personal ornaments, burial practices, and ritual behavior all indicate considerable regional, community, and individual variability. The elites who had access to and adopted Roman fashions are clearly visible, but the archaeological evidence also allows us to examine the great majority of people who did not embrace the new styles in the same way.

GLOBALIZATION AND THE ROMAN EMPIRE

In order to understand the nature of the changes among the peoples of temperate Europe during the early Roman Period, we need to consider two different and opposing processes that were operating at the same time. One was a strong trend toward uniformity in outlook, architecture, material culture, and lifestyle. Roman architecture—apparent in public buildings in the cities, temple structures, baths, military forts, and villas—and pottery, coins, and other portable items in the provinces of temperate Europe are similar, but not identical, to those in other parts of the Empire, such as in Spain, North Africa, Egypt, and the Near East. But it is important to bear in mind that this apparent homogeneity of material expression, lifestyle, and to some extent worldview was restricted to the elites in the different provinces. As indigenous elites acquired status in the imperial aristocracy, they may have come to identify themselves first as members of the Roman nobility, and second as members of their local societies. The transmission of Roman ideology—a particular vision of the world and of how societies should operate—was a powerful force in bringing about change in Europe and throughout the empire. Much of the material culture of the provincial Roman world can be understood in terms of this ideology, particularly in the urban centers where Roman architecture and statuary were prominently displayed.

The concept of globalization, adapted to the conditions of the Roman Period, is useful for examining these processes. The essence of the idea is that changes in one place have observable effects at distant locations. In the modern world the concept is especially applied to economies, but a more essential way to think about it is as the transmission of information over distances. While many popular models of globalization emphasize the development of homogeneous structures among participants, we need to consider global processes also in terms of variability. This is the situation we find in the archaeological evidence in the Roman frontier provinces. Societies entering global networks tend to experience similar changes, such as shifting from kin-based systems of social organization and traditional rules of behavior, toward more cosmopolitan and

heterogeneous attitudes and values. On the individual level, globalization processes result in changes in self-definition, as the person comes
to identify with a larger social network. But beyond such common processes, we need to ask how individuals of different status in their societies
are affected.

In all parts of the Roman frontier zone in temperate Europe, there
was an interval of time between the conquest and the beginning of the
organization of provincial administration and building of imperial infrastructure. In Raetia for example, there is practically no trace of Roman
influence in rural contexts before the middle of the first century A.D.
Thus it took about a century for "Romanization," as it is represented in
the material evidence, to take place. In the Rhineland, distinctively
Roman settlements were first constructed during the first century A.D.—
over half a century after Caesar's conquest of Gaul—in the new urban
centers. By the end of that century, substantial changes had taken place
in many rural environments, resulting from the need to generate sizable
surpluses of agricultural produce for provisioning the military forces stationed in the provinces.

Together with the effects of Roman policy in integrating elites into
the empire and the widespread, if not universal, desire among them to
participate in the Roman authority system and lifestyle, movements of
individuals between different parts of the empire also played a significant
role in creating common societies. The clearest evidence for the movement of individuals is in the form of inscriptions, especially on gravestones. They record especially movements of craftworkers and merchants, but other settlers are sometimes mentioned as well. All such
incoming individuals brought their beliefs, practices, and values, and
thus added to the diverse mix of peoples and traditions in the frontier
provinces. It is not clear whether such migration occurred more during
the Roman Period than before, or whether it is only more apparent to
us in Roman times because of the inscriptions. As we have seen in chapter
3, the circulation of fibulae, belthooks, pottery, and other goods
throughout temperate Europe during the Late Iron Age makes clear that
considerable interregional movement took place then.

RISE OF REGIONAL CONSCIOUSNESS

At the same time that they create some degree of uniformity over great
distances, processes of globalization also stimulate reactions that take the

form of often exaggerated expressions of regional identity and lead to nationalistic movements. Such reactions are apparent today in many places. Some are relatively peaceful, such as in Canada, Hawaii, and Scotland, while others are violent, as in the former Yugoslavia, Rwanda, Northern Ireland, and in the Basque country.

Such a trend toward regionalization is apparent in temperate Europe beginning late in the first century A.D. In contrast to the strong forces of homogenization represented by Roman urban centers, military bases and personnel, and the indigenous elites who in many respects transformed themselves into members of the imperial aristocracy, the archaeological evidence shows that many native peoples reacted against the trend toward uniformity by creating distinctive regional burial patterns, ritual practices, and pottery styles. The Roman policy of cultivating the indigenous elites with citizenship and special status in the provincial hierarchies tended to increase status differences between them and the rest of their communities. While the elites adopted empire-wide styles and identified themselves in their roles as new members of the imperial aristocracy, nonelites tended instead to reinforce their identities as members of traditional local groups. The result was a multiplicity of regionally and locally distinctive creations of material culture that combined elements of traditional native practice, newly adopted features of Roman style, and new expressions that peoples developed in the dynamic environments of the provinces. We can understand these new creations as active strategies aimed at asserting local identities and establishing boundaries between communities in the increasingly homogeneous society of the Roman Empire, similar to some of the nationalistic movements that are emerging today in response to the processes of globalization.

Siegmar von Schnurbein uses the second and early third century cemeteries of Welzheim and Schirenhof, both near Schwäbisch-Gmünd in southwestern Germany, to illustrate the divergence of local populations in their material culture. The two sites are only about 12 miles (20 km) apart, but they were located in different provinces during the Roman Period. Welzheim was in Germania Superior, Schirenhof in Raetia. In the Welzheim cemetery, 161 graves were excavated; at Schirenhof, 310. All were cremations, but the predominant practices in the two cemeteries differed. At Welzheim, the most common practice was the placement of the cremated bones and ashes on the base of the grave or in a small pit; at Schirenhof, most graves contained an urn that held the remains.

In Raetia during the second and third centuries, a whole series of ceramic types became common that differ markedly from those in neighboring provinces. Examples include three distinctive types of urn: the *diota*, with small semicircular handles; grape urns with relief ornament in the shape of a bunch of grapes (see Figure 29 [4]); and *Kolbenrandurnen*, with thickened inturned rims. No predecessor forms have been identified for these types, either in the region or elsewhere; thus it is apparent that local potters developed these new forms during the second century. Other objects distinctive of Raetia include the characteristic local pottery known as Raetian Ware (see below) and bracelets of the Wiggensbach type, with incised linear ornament along the exterior and at the two terminals.

Gravestones in Raetia and in Noricum frequently bear representations of the deceased; in Germania Superior this practice is rare. Representations of the goddess Epona, Gallo-Roman temples, and Jupiter-giant columns (see below), are all common in Germania Superior, but not in Raetia. These very apparent differences illustrate the point that the material culture in different regions, even in neighboring provinces such as Germania Superior and Raetia, became distinctive during the early part of the Roman Period. This pattern is particularly striking when we compare it with that of the Middle and Late La Tène Periods of the Iron Age. Cemeteries, *oppida*, and smaller settlements in these regions display a greater degree of homogeneity during the Late Iron Age than they do from the second half of the first century A.D. to the third century A.D. It is apparent that a process of differentiation between peoples of the different regions was underway during the early Roman Period that created more distinctive identities.

This process can be identified as early as the early first century A.D. in the Rhineland and in Gallia Belgica in the emergence of Belgic Ware ceramics (see below). Regionally distinctive developments become particularly clear after the middle of the second century A.D. In the middle and lower Rhineland, for example, major changes took place in artistic expression at this time that led to the creation of distinctive local traditions. Both mosaics and pottery show the increasing use of bright colors in their designs, and colorful decorations were applied to glass vessels. Ornate glass containers with thin strings of colored glass applied to the outside made in Cologne, and ceramic beakers with writing around the rims made in Trier, were local specialties that became very popular in the regions in which they were produced. These regionally distinctive fashions appeared at the same time as the rebirth of La Tène ornament in metalwork, a subject discussed in the next section.

NATIVE RESISTANCE AND THE RE-CREATION OF TRADITIONAL SYMBOLS

The issue of resistance on the part of conquered peoples, and its expression in various forms, has become a major theme of research in colonial studies. Edward Said, James Scott, and Gayatri Spivak have examined patterns of behavior of indigenous peoples in modern colonial and post-colonial contexts, and we can apply the ideas they have developed to the Roman Period. The essence of the problem is identifying and analyzing behaviors of indigenous, generally nonliterate peoples, in terms of expression of their resistance to the forces that controlled their lives. Recent ethnographic and historical studies, such as those by Scott and by Paul Stoller, show that peoples in colonial contexts express their resistance to the dominating imperial forces through a number of means besides outright armed rebellion. One is more or less subtle forms of noncooperation—arriving late for work projects, working slowly and perhaps sloppily, and creating uncomplimentary stories and songs about representatives of authority.

Another is re-creating aspects of traditional local culture, even those that have fallen out of use but remain in the popular memory, as expressions of the essence of the community's sense of itself and of its past. People use such expressions to create a needed sense of personal and group identity, even while in a larger sense they may feel they are under the domination of a foreign authority. Examples include language, songs, stories, religious rituals, textiles, pottery, and personal ornaments. Today Maya women in central America weave decorative textiles that they feel connect them directly with their ancestors' traditions before the time of the Spanish conquests. Similarly, Andean textiles produced during the Spanish colonial period embodied complex patterns of information about political, ethnic, and religious affiliations encoded in ways that were familiar to members of the indigenous societies but not understood or even recognized as a system of communication by the Spaniards.

In the frontier provinces of Roman Europe, many signs of such re-creation of local traditions appear during the second half of the second century. The most striking are personal ornaments such as bronze fibulae and belt attachments constructed in the La Tène style, but the same re-creation of indigenous forms is apparent in pottery, sculpture, domestic architecture, burial practice, ritual structures, even in religion and language. This phenomenon has long been known as the "Celtic Renaissance," but it has not been fully explained in terms of the social dynamics of the period.

In an important article in 1965, Ramsay MacMullen argued that the La Tène style and the practices of the prehistoric Iron Age survived in places where the effects of Rome were weak and in media that do not survive archaeologically. As we have seen in chapter 7, local-style handmade pottery is well represented throughout the first century A.D. and into the second at Roman sites. Recent studies of these traditional, often undecorated wares, makes clear that potters continued to make such vessels as cooking pots and for other everyday uses. Thus we may not have to look to the backwaters of early Roman Europe to find where the old traditions were maintained—the evidence might be there in the midst of Roman sites, simply largely ignored by most archaeologists because it does not fit the standard model of the Roman Period.

Why did people begin producing large numbers of bronze ornaments in the traditional style during the second half of the second century A.D., following a century and a half during which such objects were much less common? MacMullen suggests that the explanation lies in the breakdown of systems of production and circulation in Roman Europe resulting from the military invasions of the second half of the second century, notably the Marcomannic Wars and the conflicts associated with them. According to this view, large numbers of people fled the urban centers for rural environments where they came into contact with craftworkers employing the old styles.

But with the ever-increasing evidence for the persistence of indigenous crafts throughout the frontier provinces, there is no need to hypothesize backwaters where the La Tène style survived. The question is no longer where did people gain access to the old styles, but rather why did they choose to re-create and employ them in large quantities in the second half of the second century. As we have seen in chapter 7, the styles were continually re-created in pottery, metal ornaments, domestic architecture, and other media, and people preserved the connection between those styles and preconquest traditions in memory. Some individuals and groups adopted new Roman fashions more readily than others, and some maintained their connections to the earlier styles, as we see in burials, house forms, and other aspects of material culture. When the political and economic advantages of adoption and maintenance of Roman fashions began to wane in the second half of the second century A.D., with growing tensions along the borders and decline in the prosperity of the provinces, more individuals chose to rekindle or reemphasize their connections with their indigenous traditions.

The most striking examples of this re-creation are in metalwork ornaments that were worn in very visible places on people's bodies, such as fibulae on the shoulder or chest and belthooks at the waist. Many of these re-create very precisely the ornament of the La Tène style that had been dominant in these regions during the final five centuries before the conquests (Figure 28). Cast bronze fibulae in the so-called trumpet form are a common expression of this revival, and they have been recovered in particular abundance in the regions along the Rhine and Danube Rivers.

Bronze openwork ornaments, including belthooks, clothing fasteners, and scabbard decorations, are other examples of La Tène–style metalwork in this period. Military paraphernalia is abundantly represented at bases along the Rhine and Danube, but also found at distant locations to which soldiers apparently brought them from the frontier zones. The considerable range of variation in specific forms suggests that they were not the products of only a few workshops, but instead the reflection of a popular style produced in many different places. Striking examples include the decorative disk from Dormagen and the gilded belt ornament from Cologne, both on the lower Rhine, and seven cast openwork belthooks from the cemetery at Regensburg on the Danube. Workshop debris, including miscast and discarded pieces, confirms that the objects were made in many local shops in the frontier regions.

Enamel inlay in bronze ornaments such as neckrings, fibulae, weapons, and vessels, was a common decorative technique throughout the La Tène Period in temperate Europe. During the second half of the second century A.D. this style became popular again in the Roman provinces, particularly in northern Gaul and in the Rhineland, where there is evidence for workshops that produced enamel and fibulae at Cologne. Enamel was used particularly to decorate fibulae, but also appears on other objects, such as belt buckles, horse harness gear, and vessels.

NEW CREATIONS IN THE FRONTIER ZONE

As noted above, frontier zones are by their very nature exceptionally dynamic areas. The coming together of groups and individuals of diverse

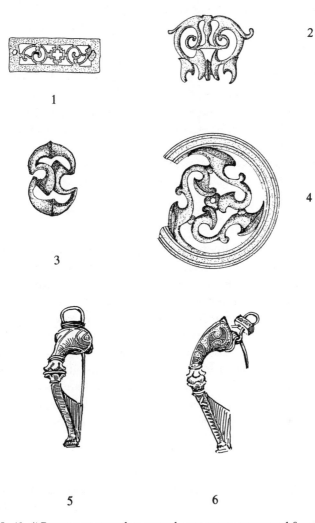

Fig. 28. *(1–4)* Bronze openwork personal ornaments recovered from Roman military bases in the frontier zone. *(2, 3, 4)* all display the trumpet form characteristic of La Tène ornament. *(1)* Osterburken. *(2)* Weissenburg. *(3)* Saalburg. *(4)* Zugmantel. All drawn to same scale; *(1)* is about 2 in. (4.95 cm) long. *(5, 6)* Trumpet fibulae. *(5)* Kassel. *(6)* Saalburg. *(1–4)* from Oldenstein 1976. Used by permission of Susanne Sievers, RGK. *(5, 6)* from Collingwood 1930, p. 50, fig. 7. Used courtesy of the Society of Antiquaries of London.

indigenous and outside traditions, the politically volatile situation on most frontiers, and the interactions between peoples of the frontier zone and groups in the hinterlands, all contribute to a situation conducive to complex patterns of sharing, borrowing, and adapting. The frontier zone of early Roman Period Europe was a region in which such diverse groups interacted, and the result was the formation of new societies that created new styles and practices out of elements of local groups and those adopted from fashions introduced by different peoples who moved into these regions. Development of new pottery varieties, forms of domestic architecture, burial practices, ritual behaviors, and symbols are among the kinds of evidence that illustrate these processes of change.

Pottery

A variety of different traditions of pottery production are represented in the frontier zone. Some ceramics preserve indigenous Iron Age techniques of manufacture, form, and decoration; these include both handmade coarse wares and wheelmade fine painted wares (see chapter 7). Others were imported, mostly from southern and central Gaul, but also from Italy. Some new pottery types reflect extensive borrowing from imported wares. In many cases, new kinds of pottery were developed in the provinces, without clear antecedents among either indigenous or imported wares. These are of particular interest here, because they reflect the creation of new patterns rather than the maintenance or adaptation of old ones. I mention just three examples of these regionally distinctive new ceramics.

BELGIC WARE

Belgic Ware is a term used to designate a variety of similar kinds of pottery manufactured in Germania Inferior between the time of Caesar and the middle of the third century A.D. The shapes derived from the local Late La Tène wares, but the potters adopted technical and formal ideas from newly introduced Roman practices. Thus these wares represent new creations, unlike either the indigenous prehistoric pottery or the imported Roman forms, but embodying elements from both.

In the same regions in which Belgic Ware was produced, local potters of the early Roman period adopted the general themes of Roman *terra sigillata*, but as early as the second decade of the first century A.D. they diverged from the detailed ornament of the Italic variety. Instead of ivy and grape leaves and tendrils, local potters decorated their vessels with oak and beech leaves. They chose not to portray scenes as on the Italic

200

ware, but frequently added rich geometrical themes to the patterns of floral ornament.

The pottery known as Raetian Ware was developed at the end of the first century A.D. It is a fine pottery characterized by a black polished exterior with stamped geometric ornament (Figure 29). The most common forms are thin-walled eating and drinking vessels. Some investigators suggest that because this style of pottery has no clear local precedents, it must have been introduced by immigrant potters from provinces to the west, but there are no clear prototypes there either. Raetian Ware apparently became extremely popular quickly, and it replaced fine pottery types that had been imported from workshops in Germania Superior and Gaul. The center of production was in western Raetia. Workshops have been identified at Straubing, Westerndorf, Schwabmünchen, Günzburg, Aislingen, Faimingen, and Mangolding-Mintraching. It was in use all over the province of Raetia, and some was exported to neighboring regions. The enormous popularity of Raetian Ware during the second century A.D. may reflect the eagerness with which consumers adopted this new sign of regional identity in place of the standard forms of provincial Roman pottery that had been brought in from outside.

While Raetian Ware was particularly popular in western parts of the province of Raetia during the second century A.D., in southeastern Raetia and Noricum a new type of plain earthenware developed, known as Norican Ware. Among the most common forms were large white-painted jars, which retained typical elements of Late La Tène form and decoration. At Kieling in southeastern Bavaria, archaeologists excavated a kiln used in the production of Norican Ware. The pottery, which was hard-fired and mostly wheel-made, shows characteristic coarse temper and rough surface texture. Norican Ware contrasts with the ornate pottery in use at the same time in urban contexts, and its development in the second century A.D. can be understood as the expression of identity by rural communities to set themselves off from the homogenizing influences of urbanized Roman culture.

Domestic Architecture

In earlier chapters, I discussed farmhouses at Rijswijk in the Netherlands and local versions of villas at Mayen in the Rhineland and Oberndorf in

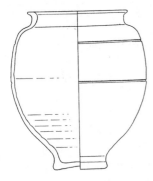

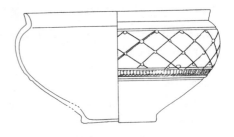

2

1

3

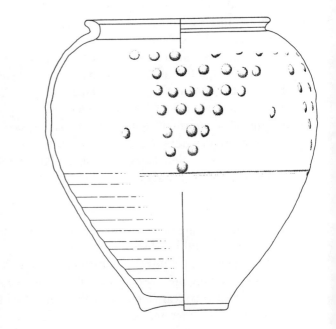

4

Fig. 29. *(1–3)* vessels of Raetian Ware from the cemetery at Ergolding in Bavaria, Germany. *(1)* beaker with red slip and two parallel rills around the body; height about 6.4 in. (16.2 cm). *(2)* bowl with pattern of incised crossing lines and raised points, and with shiny black slip; mouth diameter about 7.9 in. (20 cm). *(3)* beaker with incised pattern and added raised points and lunulae, and with remains of black slip on exterior; mouth diameter about 2.4 in. (6.1 cm). *(4)* "Grape urn," a type distinctive to Raetia, with five groups of about 22 hemispherical knobs on the body; height about 11.6 in. (29.5 cm). From Struck 1996, plates 43, A7; 78, 4; 83, 1; 86, 11. Used by permission of Bayerisches Landesamt für Denkmalpflege, Munich.

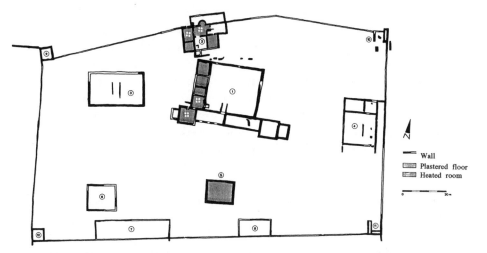

Fig. 30. Plan of the villa at Bondorf near Böblingen, southwest Germany. Dark lines indicate stone and mortar walls, shading shows plastered floors, and shaded areas with four white squares represent rooms with heating systems beneath them (hypocausts). From Planck 1976, p. 46, fig. 24. Used by permission of Jörg Biel, Landesdenkmalamt Baden-Württemberg, Stuttgart.

Bavaria. Other villas in the provinces reflect a more thorough adoption of Roman-style architecture and layout, while still maintaining features that distinguish them from the "classic Italian" villas. At Bondorf near Böblingen in Baden-Württemberg, a large villa was completely excavated in 1975. In the first phase of construction at the beginning of the second century A.D., the villa was built of wood. Around the middle of the second century, the villa was rebuilt in stone and enclosed by a stone and mortar wall within a rectangle measuring about 512 by 318 ft. (156 x 97 m) (Figure 30). The residence had an extensive, 197 ft. (60 m)–long facade and was 89 ft. (27 m) wide. Elegantly decorated pilasters and columns attest to the wealth of the owner and to that person's embrace of Roman fashions. Two rooms of the large residence were heated with a hypocaust system—the tile floor was supported by pillars built of stacked tiles, and hot air forced under the floor provided warmth to the rooms. Other buildings on the site housed workshops. One exceptionally finely built structure situated directly in front of the middle of the residence contained fragmentary statuary including remains of figures of Mercury and Victory and is thought to have been a small temple. The eleven buildings in the enclosure make up one of the largest villa complexes in the region.

Terra sigillata pottery was especially abundant on the site, and it included vessels made in southern Gaul and in the Rhineland. Glass vessels, spoons, needles, and spindle whorls are among the household wares recovered. Hoes, hammers, shovels, and part of a threshing machine represent the agricultural technology. The cellar of the residence contained large quantities of burned cereal grains, and numerous animal bones attest to the meat consumption of the inhabitants. The evidence from Bondorf indicates the enthusiastic adoption of the Roman villa idea by an individual who could afford to construct a grandiose complex that included all of the luxury features. But there is no clear indication of the identity of this individual—whether a veteran of Roman military service who was able to set himself up with this establishment with his veteran's pay, or a member of the indigenous elite using wealth accumulated through land rents or commercial enterprise. Whoever the person was, the intention of the villa complex is clear—to display wealth, status, and cosmopolitan fashion in the form of an elaborate monument to the Roman ideal of the rural estate and to create a striking contrast to the much more modest dwellings of people in the surrounding settlements.

Burial Practice

The integration of aspects of indigenous and Roman traditions is particularly evident in burial rites. The varied practices employed in the different regions of the frontier zone of Roman Europe illustrate the extent to which some local groups clung tenaciously to their traditional rituals, some adopted practices introduced by Roman troops and administrators that took up residence in their territories, and others developed new patterns that were neither much like the earlier indigenous practices nor like contemporary Italic Roman ones. Much research has assumed that the presence of objects deemed "Roman," such as *terra sigillata* pottery, glass vessels, and lamps, indicate that the buried individual identified himself or herself, or was identified by those conducting the funerary ceremony, as Roman. But the situation is more complex.

Many cemeteries have been investigated in the frontier zone. In some regions, such as the Netherlands, at the beginning of the Roman Period we can distinguish clearly between cemeteries of the indigenous peoples and those of the Roman troops, because of distinctive burial practices and grave goods. Those contrasts disappear by the second century as the groups became more alike through the sharing of territory and experiences, and through intermarriage (see chapter 6). In other places, the distinction between native and Roman military cemeteries is never clear. During the early Roman Period, cremation was the dominant burial practice, just as it had been in the Late La Tène Period and as it was in Italy at the time. There was considerable variation, both regional and individual, in the ways in which cremation burials were arranged. In Roman Italy, the most common practice was to include a few modest objects in the grave, such as one or two ceramic vessels, a lamp, a glass container of perfume, and occasionally one or two items of jewelry. In the frontier zone, we find a great variety in the composition of burial assemblages. Some cemeteries conform closely to Roman practices evident in Italy, while others are different. To illustrate the variety, I shall discuss examples from a major urban center in Germania Inferior (Cologne), a rural town in the Moselle Valley near Trier (Wederath), a military base on the Danube (Regensburg), and a villa in Raetia (Ergolding).

COLOGNE

Burial evidence at Roman Cologne is an example of practices at a major urban center in the provinces (on Cologne see also chapter 8). Five main cemeteries surround the city, and numerous smaller ones are scattered in the vicinity (Figure 31). A large cemetery with over twelve hundred graves, including both inhumations and cremations, is situated just northwest of the city walls. The other four are located along major roads leading from Cologne to other centers: Neuss to the north, Aachen to the west, Trier to the southwest, and Bonn to the south. Different cemeteries are thought to have been used by different groups within the city's population. In some cemeteries, elaborate grave monuments are common, in others they are rare.

Funerary rituals and burial practices in the Cologne cemeteries show tremendous variation, a typical situation in the cosmopolitan urban centers in which peoples of different backgrounds and traditions met, lived as neighbors, and intermarried. Above-ground monuments, sarcophagi, and as grave goods ceramic lamps, glass perfume bottles, and Roman pottery reflect Roman customs. Weapons in men's graves, elaborate sets of jewelry in women's, and the burial of horses in the northwest cemetery, show the practice of indigenous traditions.

Compared to Rome at the time, the graves at Cologne, like those elsewhere in Lower Germany, were substantially outfitted with goods. Much of the pottery was produced locally in styles and techniques that blended indigenous and newly introduced patterns, such as *terra nigra*, *firnis*, and various fine and coarse wares. But imported pottery was also common, including *terra sigillata* from Gaul and the upper Rhine region, as well as beakers with painted epigrams from Trier. Cologne became a major cen-

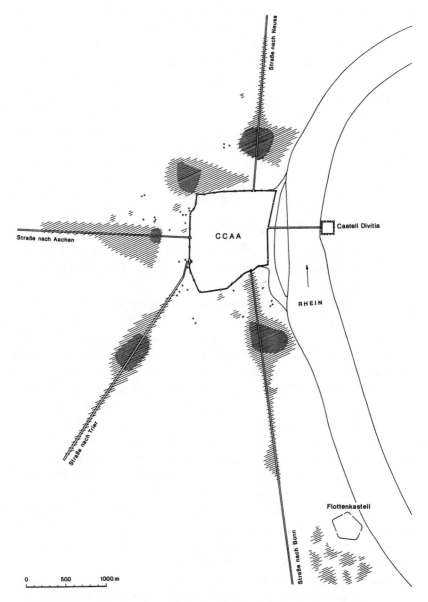

Fig. 31. Plan showing the walled city of Colonia Claudia Ara Agrippinen-
sium, now Cologne, and the roads leading to other important cities.
Hatched areas indicate major cemeteries. South of the city was the base of
the Rhine fleet (*Flottenkastell*). From Naumann-Steckner 1997, p. 10, fig. 3.
Used by permission of Friederike Naumann-Steckner,
Römisch-Germanisches Museum, Cologne.

ter of glass production, and glass vessels were more frequent grave goods here than elsewhere.

Besides pottery and glass vessels, women's graves characteristically contained personal ornaments, such as bone and jet hair pins, earrings and necklaces of gold and glass, and fingerrings and bracelets of bronze, bone, jet, silver, and gold. Cosmetics boxes made of wood, bone, or bronze are common. Men's graves often had razors or strigils. Wealthy graves of both sexes sometimes included writing equipment—wood and wax tablets, styli, and ink bottles. A few graves contained occupational implements, such as doctors' and barbers' tools.

A number of graves stand out as distinctly different. Some men's burials have weapons such as a sword, shield, and battle axe, along with shears and a whetstone. Associated women's graves contain neckrings, belt chains, and fibulae. Such graves occur together in particular cemeteries, for example along the road leading to Bonn. Some researchers interpret them as the burials of "Germans"—individuals from east of the Rhine frontier. But we cannot equate burial practice with ethnicity in this cosmopolitan milieu in which people borrowed fashions and symbols from a variety of traditions.

The practice of erecting monumental stones over graves was introduced by the incoming Romans. It was common in Rome but remained exceptional in the conquered regions. Tombstones carved and erected at Cologne display local features that distinguish them from those in Rome and elsewhere. The cosmopolitan atmosphere of Cologne is conveyed by the origins of individuals identified on gravestones. For example, in the cemetery at the base of the Rhine fleet, 1.8 miles (3 km) south of the city walls, have been recovered gravestones of an L. Octavius from Asia Minor (modern Turkey) and of an L. Valerius Verecundus, a member of the Iberian people known as the Ruteni.

WEDERATH

Wederath in the Moselle River region was the site of a Late Iron Age village and a Roman Period *vicus* called Belginum (see chapter 5). Between 1954 and 1985 the Rheinisches Landesmuseum in Trier excavated about twenty-five hundred graves dating from the third century B.C. to the fourth century A.D. Graves at Wederath first start to show signs of strong Roman influence around 20 B.C., about a generation after Caesar's conquest of the region. The most striking characteristic of the roughly two thousand graves that date to the Roman Period is the continuity with earlier traditions expressed in burial practice and grave goods. Burial was by cremation, and grave goods were burned along with the corpse.

Graves of the first and early second centuries include goods typical of the Late Iron Age, such as numerous pieces of jewelry, weapons, tools, and vessels of pottery, glass, and wood. Characteristically Roman objects in the graves include lamps, glass vessels containing perfume, mirrors, and medical implements. Men's and women's graves were often characterized by gender-specific sets of goods, similar to the situation in the Late Iron Age and different from Roman practice. Men's burials were marked by single fibulae, weapons, and tools; women's by multiple fibulae, beads, fingerrings, mirrors, cosmetics containers, toiletries, and terracotta figurines of deities.

Traditional handmade pottery is common in graves at Wederath into the second century A.D., but new kinds of Roman and Roman-inspired pottery were common from 20 B.C. on. Much of the Roman-style pottery was made by local potters, based on imported prototypes. Local potters also developed new forms, including Belgic Ware. While much of the character of the Roman Period graves at Wederath can be understood in terms of continuity of tradition from the La Tène Period, together with adoption of newly available Roman goods, important patterns of change are also apparent in the cemetery during the first two centuries A.D.

The excavator identifies several significant trends during these centuries. One is the gradual divergence from the traditional burial rules of the Late Iron Age during the first century A.D. Graves of this time are characterized by increasing variability in their contents, with a marked emphasis on individual identity with respect to particular occupations, not just sex or age categories. For example, two graves contained tongs associated with the practice of dentistry along with other medical implements. Another included tools used in pottery production. The changes set in motion by the incorporation of this region into the greater Roman world included the attribution of new significance to individuals' skills and abilities, particularly as they related to talents of economic value in the Roman provinces. Perhaps as individuals' skills led to new economic benefits, their personal identities became more directly represented by the material accoutrements of their professions, in their graves as well as in their everyday lives.

Another reflection of changes in traditional patterns of material culture and individual identity is in the wider distribution of objects that had been special emblems of high status—for example, coins and mirrors associated with women. In the Late Iron Age, both coins and mirrors were placed in women's graves that were otherwise distinguished by their burial wealth. In the early Roman Period at Wederath, coins and mirrors continue to occur in women's graves, but they are no longer restricted to the richer category of burials—they are found in a broad spectrum of graves. Their wider distribution in the social world of the community at Wederath during the Roman period probably reflects changes in both the availability of such goods and in the rules that governed who had access to them.

Between the end of the first century A.D. and the middle of the second, the graves at Wederath show a tendency toward simpler burials, with less variation between them and with fewer grave goods. This trend may represent a reaction to the greater availability of previously restricted goods, such that display of valued objects became less fashionable. At the same time that graves were becoming more alike in character and less well outfitted with goods, the practice of constructing stone monuments above them grew in popularity. But at Wederath only a small proportion of the excavated burials had such monuments. The evidence suggests that this new form of status display replaced the earlier practice of equipping graves with wealth. This Roman custom may have been adopted by the elites at Wederath, both because it was new and different, and because it required a greater outlay of wealth than did the deposition of goods in a grave. These above-ground stone monuments displayed information about the deceased, including the deceased's name, family, and often occupation. The monuments were thus a new medium in this region that communicated information about the identity of the individual and of his or her family in a form that remained plainly visible to the living, something that the goods placed in graves could not do.

REGENSBURG

A large cemetery comprising about three thousand cremation graves and about two thousand inhumations, all dating between A.D. 180 and 260, was excavated at the Roman military center of Castra Regina at modern Regensburg on the Danube. Most of the pottery is distinctive of Raetia and different from that of neighboring provinces. It includes Raetian Ware as well as the regionally characteristic urn forms mentioned above—the grape urns and *diota* urns. The Regensburg pottery is very different from that at the well-studied contemporaneous Roman cemetery at the military base at Bad Cannstatt near Stuttgart, 120 miles (200 km) to the west. The Regensburg cemetery is thus an important piece of evidence for the emergence of distinctive regional traditions during the second and third centuries.

Much of the material in the Regensburg graves shows strong links with prehistoric traditions in the area. Many of the ceramic vessels are similar to Late Iron Age pottery, especially the tall, thin pots used here as urns. Metal ornaments in these late second and third century graves are similar to those of the Late La Tène Period. Seven rectangular openwork bronze belthooks in the graves bear motifs that characterize La Tène design, including spirals, palmettes, and trumpet-shapes. Although the Regensburg graves contained some provincial Roman pottery imported from other regions, the predominant aspects of the cemetery are the distinctively Raetian forms and the connections with preconquest traditions in pottery and metalwork.

The cemetery at Ergolding near Landshut in Lower Bavaria was used by the occupants of a villa complex from about A.D. 150 to 250. All seventy-nine graves are cremations, mostly with the remains placed in a vessel and buried in a pit (Figure 32). The majority of the accompanying grave goods had been in the funeral pyre. The principal category of burial equipment was pottery, but fibulae and other personal ornaments were also present. Size of the cemetery and the length of time during which it was used suggest an average of about twenty-five adults in the community at any one time.

An analysis of the Ergolding cemetery interprets it as that of a community resident at a single villa, including members of the family of the owner and other persons who worked at the establishment. The arrival in A.D. 179 and 180 of a legion, the Third Italian Legion, at Castra Regina (Regensburg), 29 miles (48 km) to the north, is likely to have created a much increased demand for agricultural produce in the northeastern part of the province. The expansion of both the military establishment and associated civilian populations at Regensburg may help to account for the growth and flourishing of villas throughout northeast Raetia during this period.

Burial practice was closer to traditional Late La Tène ritual than to Roman practices in Italy. The Ergolding graves do not generally contain the kinds of objects that characterize contemporaneous burials in Italy, such as lamps, coins, incense burners, or special vessels for pouring offerings. Especially important is the presence of large quantities of handmade pottery characteristic of the indigenous ceramic traditions (Figure 33 [6, 7, 8]). The handmade pottery at Ergolding is very similar to that at the Late La Tène settlement at Hascherkeller, just 1.2 miles (2 km) to the west. This pottery makes clear that the community was largely, if not

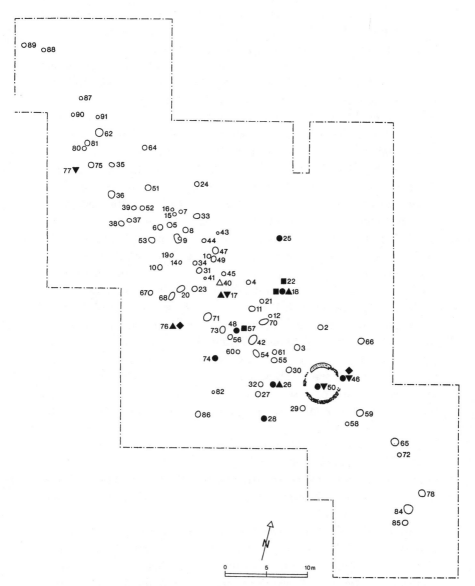

Fig. 32. Plan of the cemetery at Ergolding in Bavaria. Each grave is numbered. The broken line indicates the extent of the excavated area. Filled
shapes mark graves that Struck interprets as most Romanized on the basis of
grave goods, as follows: *circle:* coin; *downward triangle:* incense burner; *upward
triangle:* lamp; *square:* libation vessel; *diamond:* unburned perfume bottle.
From Struck 1996, p. 95, fig. 19. Used by permission of Bayerisches
Landesamt für Denkmalpflege, Munich.

exclusively, of local origin. The presence of imported *terra sigillata*, as well as other pottery forms introduced into the area, indicates that other kinds of pottery were available by the time the cemetery was in use, even though local styles continued to dominate the assemblages. Local potters could have chosen to produce imitations of the *terra sigillata* and other new fine wares, but instead they continued to make ceramics in the traditional forms. Fibulae and other personal ornaments in the cemetery show both a continuity with earlier metalworking traditions in the region and adoption of new styles from neighboring areas.

In the central area of the cemetery, many graves reflect a burial practice closer to the "standard" Roman one, and they contained personal ornaments of higher quality than elsewhere. Graves in this part of the cemetery had little handmade pottery, few animal bones, and more sherds bearing inscriptions than those in other parts. In graves to the northwest of this central area, the practice is more of native character and less Roman, fewer personal ornaments occur, they are of lower quality, more animal bones are in the graves, and there is more local handmade pottery. This pattern is consistent with our general observation that more elite individuals tended to adopt Roman practices and goods to a greater extent than did less elite ones. Elites had more options than others, and they used the material symbols of "Romanization" as means of expressing their status. These graves in the central part of the Ergolding cemetery may represent members of the families of the owners of the villa, while the other graves may represent families of workers on the estate.

Over time, there was a decline in special ornaments in the graves and an increase in adopted Roman practices. Among graves that contain larger assemblages of objects than average, those assemblages tend in the later phases to be dominated by pottery, especially *terra sigillata*, rather than metal ornaments.

Many of the grave goods, including some types of fibulae and imported pottery, attest to the openness of this community to the outside, whether in receiving immigrants from other regions with their personal goods or imports via trade with other communities. Some of the inscriptions may suggest the presence in this small community of immigrants from elsewhere in the empire. For example, the inscription SEQVANA on pottery in one grave might reflect the presence of an immigrant from the land of the Sequani in Gaul. But there is no compelling reason to think that the inscription necessarily names the individual in the grave or anyone else represented in the Ergolding cemetery. An inscribed vessel could find its way into a person's possession, and into a grave, through many

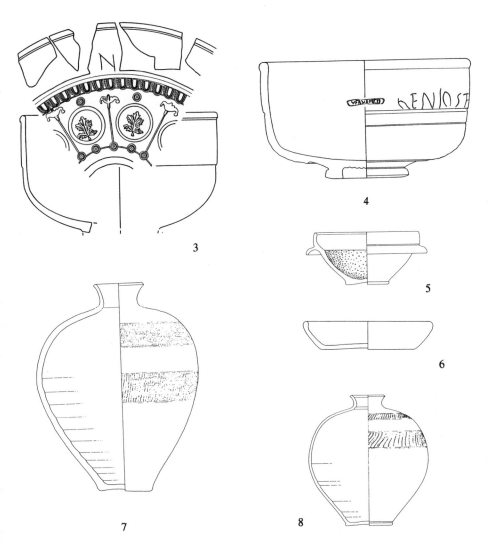

Fig. 33. Selection of objects from Grave 26 at Ergolding, showing a combination of indigenous and Roman material culture. *(1)* ceramic lamp, about 3.5 in. (8.8 cm) long. *(2)* fragmentary cast bronze horse fibula, about 1.25 in. (3.2 cm) long. *(3, 4)* terra sigillata pottery. *(3)* has a rim diameter of about 9.5 in. (24.2 cm), *(4)* of about 10.2 in. (25.9 cm). *(5)* food grater, about 7.4 in. (18.8 cm) in rim diameter. *(6)* low bowl with traces of red slip, diameter about 9.0 in. (22.9 cm). *(7, 8)* jars of orange-to-brownish red fabric, with dull black glaze and horizontal bands of ornament; heights about 14.5 in. (36.7 cm) and 9.1 in. (23.0 cm), respectively. Also in the grave were bones of two pigs and a chicken, and a coin minted during the reign of the emperor Antoninus Pius (A.D. 138–61). From Struck 1996, plates 35–38, 39. Used by permission of Bayerisches Landesamt für Denkmalpflege, Munich.

different mechanisms during this dynamic period. It could have been a gift from someone in Gaul, a trade item, or a souvenir acquired by someone from Raetia during a trip to Gaul.

Ritual Structures

In ritual practice, whether concerned with religious, political, or social purposes, important themes of a group's traditions and values are recreated for the benefit of the individuals in the group and for its cohesion. Ritual practice changes to adapt to changing circumstances. Thus examination of ritual activity, or of its material manifestations, can provide information about changing relationships between communities and between humans and their supernatural world.

GALLO-ROMAN TEMPLES

The best-documented category of ritual place in the Roman frontier zone is the so-called Gallo-Roman temple. This characteristic complex consisted of an interior rectangular building, the *cella*, and an outer structure around it. For both, the wall could be solid or it could be formed by a colonnade. In both cases, the purpose seems to have been to construct a passageway, closed off from the outside, around the central building. The *cella* was used as a place to arrange cult objects, such as statues of deities or altars. The whole structure was situated in a ritual area, or *temenos*, rectangular in shape and bounded by a wall. Horne and King's gazeteer lists 354 such temples on the continent, but many more have been reported since their publication of 1980. They are especially well represented in central France, Picardy, and the western middle Rhineland.

Since Klaus Schwarz's 1975 study of the Late La Tène enclosure at Holzhausen in Bavaria, his idea has been generally accepted that the Gallo-Roman temple of temperate Europe derived, at least in part, from the post-build structures evident in many of the excavated *Viereckschanzen* (see chapter 3). At Holzhausen, the remains of a substantial post-based building were discovered in the west corner of the enclosure. It had an inner structure about 20 by 26 ft. (6 x 8 m) in size represented by unusually large postholes and an outer rectangle of posts about 33 by 36 ft. (10 x 11 m). Archaeologists uncovered a similar structure, 33 by 33 ft. (10 x 10 m) in size, inside such an enclosure at Wiedmais, also in Bavaria. These foundations may indicate the presence of an ambulatory, or outer walkway, thus providing a direct link with the subsequent Gallo-Roman temple structures.

In his analysis of Gallo-Roman temples, Markus Trunk concurs that the form was of indigenous origin in the regions conquered by Rome in which the Late La Tène style of material had been predominant, and hence where the *Viereckschanzen* had been constructed. No precise parallels for these structures exist in the Classical world. The material used in the construction and the techniques of building were Roman in origin. Thus, this common ritual configuration represents an amalgamation of local ritual traditions with adopted architectural techniques. Every temple is unique, and each reflects a different combination of elements of form, style, and structure. Evidence indicates that temples were sponsored by indigenous elites and designed by architects from southern Gaul, working to the specifications of the local sponsors.

Investigations at Faimingen on the Danube in western Bavaria yield valuable information about the practice of different traditions in a ritual place. Shortly after A.D. 90 a small Roman fort was built on the site, and a *vicus* settlement developed next to it. Around A.D. 120 the fort was abandoned, probably because the river-crossing at which it was situated was no longer threatened, and it was destroyed about A.D. 140. Following the destruction and the filling of the defensive ditch—sometime between A.D. 140 and 155—an enclosure surrounded by a palisade was built along what had been the southern wall of the fort. Excavations uncovered two lines of postholes in a foundation trench, indicating posts some 16 ft. (5 m) in height packed tightly together. The lines are oriented exactly north-south and east-west, and they extend over 79 ft. (24 m) in each direction. Inside the enclosure the excavators found remains of a structure built of wood-and-daub, and associated quantities of pottery and twenty-one perforated astragali (knuckle bones of animals) that they interpret as offerings. Directly above this enclosure a stone temple of Roman style was built in about A.D. 160 (Figure 34). Six inscriptions found in the area indicate that the temple was dedicated to Apollo-Grannus, a deity of mixed Roman and indigenous features and associated with the healing powers of water.

The excavators argue that the enclosure of A.D. 140–60 was a re-created version of the late prehistoric rectangular enclosure common throughout Late Iron Age Europe. The shape and orientation are similar, and the palisade at Faimingen is very like that at the Iron Age enclosure at Holzhausen and distinctly different from Roman palisade fences.

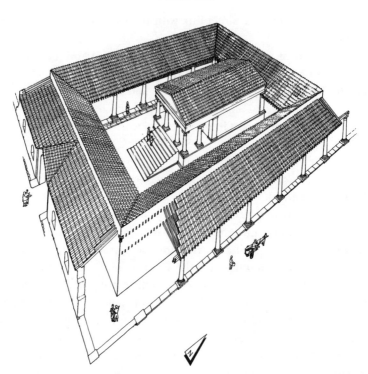

Fig. 34. Reconstruction drawing of the stone-built phase 3 of the Gallo-Roman temple at Faimingen. From Weber 1981, p. 125, fig. 4. Used by permission of Susanne Sievers, RGK.

The remains of the wood-and-daub building and of the objects interpreted as offerings also match finds from the prehistoric enclosures.

Faimingen shows the maintenance of tradition in sanctuary architecture and ritual behavior by indigenous peoples over a number of generations after the Roman arrival. The enclosure constructed around the middle of the second century A.D.—some 150 years after the conquest—was fundamentally different from Roman sanctuaries but shared important characteristics with enclosed ritual spaces of the Late Iron Age. It may have been constructed specifically on top of the disused fort as a symbolic means for the indigenous people to reappropriate the land following the Roman army's departure from the site. The Roman-style stone-built temple was then constructed on top of the enclosure. The final report of the excavation notes details of the architecture that vary from standard Italian practice. These may have resulted from disagreements between the architect and the sponsor. Most of these temples in Gaul and Germany were commissioned by individuals who identified themselves primarily as natives, not as Romans, while the design and supervision of the buildings were done by architects trained in southern Gaul. Such temples are best understood as expressions of the desire by powerful local individuals and groups to sponsor grandiose architecture in the new cosmopolitan style to demonstrate both their status and their association with the new fashions.

A RITUAL COMPLEX AT AN URBAN CENTER

Similar patterns indicating complex integration of traditional indigenous ritual practice and new themes introduced during the early Roman Period are apparent at urban sanctuaries. One of the largest and most complex is at Trier in the Altbachtal part of the city. Twelve acres (5 ha) of land are occupied by about seventy buildings believed to have had ritual significance. Excavations reveal pits and postholes of Late Iron Age date, suggesting that the place was important ritually then too. The first Roman Period temple was constructed of wood during the Augustan Period, and only after the middle of the first century did stone architecture appear. It is very difficult to sort out which aspects of the place are of indigenous, preconquest character; which are Gallo-Roman (i.e., local tradition mixed with influences introduced by Rome); and which are more purely Roman. This difficulty points up the extent to which elements from these different traditions became integrated in the development of the provincial societies. Evidence from inscriptions shows that the temple of Lenus Mars was a major site of public ritual activity once Trier had been established as a Roman colony by the time of the Emperor Claudius (A.D. 41–54).

The deities worshiped at Trier-Altbachtal appear to have been for the most part indigenous ones, but linked to Roman imperial gods, as in the case of Lenus Mars. As usual, representations of local deities in statuary show them in the Roman conception, since the prehistoric peoples of temperate Europe did not usually portray their deities in anthropomorphic form. An important status distinction in ritual practice is apparent at Trier that is likely to have existed at many ritual sites of this period. Indigenous elites adopted ideas and practices from Roman traditions, and integrated their local gods and their attributes with those of the Roman pantheon. Nonelites probably had less to do with the official Roman deities and practiced traditional forms of what we might call folk religion.

The complex mixing of traditions is further apparent in evidence for ritual practices. For example, excavators found animal bones in pits between buildings 18 and 19 at Altbachtal, apparently remains of sacrifices.

217

Represented are an old male goat that had been skinned, several young female goats, young pigs, chickens, and a cow. Such deposition of un-burned animal bones is reminiscent of the Late Iron Age ritual complex at Gournay-sur-Aronde in northern France (see chapter 3), while skin-ning an animal in sacrificial ritual was a Mediterranean practice. Thus even in the details of conducting rituals, we have indication of the com-bining of elements of indigenous and Roman traditions to create new amalgamations.

JUPITER-GIANT COLUMNS

Like Gallo-Roman temples, Jupiter-giant columns are a feature of the landscapes that had been occupied during the Late Iron Age by groups whose material culture was in the Late La Tène style. About 150 are known, and fragments are frequently discovered that attest to newly iden-tified ones. The principal concentrations are in the Rhineland and in regions just to the west, with exceptionally large numbers around Mainz, in the Moselle Valley, and in the lower Neckar region. The earliest col-umns, dated by inscriptions on them, were erected around A.D. 60, the latest around A.D. 260.

These columns are usually made of local stone, typically limestone or sandstone (Figure 35). They were carved in segments of separate blocks arranged on top of one another to a height of up to 49 ft. (15 m). At the bottom is a four-sided block, each side bearing the representation of a deity, most often the Roman gods Juno, Minerva, Mercury, and Hercules, identified by attributes that accompany them. Above this block is a col-umn ending in an ornate Corinthian capital.

On the top of the column is typically a statue of a horse-riding figure in human form, usually riding over a fallen creature whose upper half is human and whose lower half consists of two snakes. There is consider-able variation in the position and detailed features of the underlying figure, and some variation in the rider above. In two cases, the rider is accompanied by metal lightning bolts, once of iron and once of bronze, in other instances the figure has a hole through his raised right hand, indicating where some object, perhaps a lightning bolt, was originally placed. In some cases, the rider holds a wheel, most often in the left hand.

Some of these monuments are located near sanctuaries, some near villas, others near towns. Often the stones from columns are found built into other structures, for example in Christian church foundations and even in church walls where the relief figures are in plain view. Christianity first became a significant religious movement in the European frontier

Fig. 35. Restored Jupiter-giant column at Hausen an der Zaber in southwest Germany. Height about 24 ft. (7.35 m). Photograph courtesy of Jörg Biel, Landesdenkmalamt Baden-Württemberg, Stuttgart.

provinces during the third and fourth centuries, particularly in urban areas. The reuse of early Roman Period ritual structural elements in Christian churches raises important questions about continuity in religious belief from pre-Christian into Christian times, but that subject lies beyond the scope of our topic here. Sometimes they are found in deposits in water, such as in wells, in some cases with other objects that indicate special ritual deposition. In at least two instances, for example, deer bones and antlers were found associated with fragments of columns in shafts that may have been wells originally.

Some elements of these columns connect them with Roman tradition, some with indigenous, but the structures as a whole are unique creations in this provincial context. Most, but not all, of the deities represented

219

on the four-sided blocks at the base of the monuments are of Roman origin, but all are well represented in contexts that combine Roman and native religious beliefs and practices. On some representations, deities bear attributes of distinctly non-Roman, indigenous character. For example, the Roman god Vulcan is sometimes portrayed with attributes of the indigenous Celtic god Sucellus, and a deity that looks like Venus is shown with attributes suggesting fertility.

Columns were an important element in architecture in the Mediterranean world, and single monumental columns dedicated to deities stood in Rome. Carved stones set upright were a significant La Tène tradition in temperate Europe, as the surviving examples from Pfalzfeld in the Rhineland and Holzgerlingen in Württemberg attest. Trees were an important symbolic element in indigenous European mythology and iconography. Representations of trees occur on the Gundestrup cauldron, and a bronze and gold model of a tree has been recovered on the settlement at Manching. The Jupiter-giant column at Hausen in Württemberg (Figure 35) is decorated with oak leaves and acorns, suggesting a link between these columns and tree imagery. The oak was sacred to both Roman Jupiter and the indigenous Celtic sky god.

No close prototype for the rider and giant has been identified, but the theme has been compared with portrayals of Roman emperors. But the figures on top of the columns are not in Roman style; they are local adaptations of that theme. Celtic and Germanic peoples held the horse in special regard and often represented it in iconography, in burial contexts, and in mythology. The theme of horse-born attacker trampling an enemy has been compared with the representation on the Early La Tène bronze scabbard from the cemetery at Hallstatt in Austria. The scene is similar, but there is a gap of four centuries between the scabbard and these columns, and not many related representations are known from that interval. It may be significant that both the rider in the Hallstatt scabbard scene and many of the horseback riders on the columns are associated with representations of wheels.

Wheels are portrayed prominently on many objects believed to have been of ritual importance in Iron Age Europe. Examples include the "sun chariot" from Trundholm in Denmark from the Bronze Age, the Hallstatt scabbard, and the Gundestrup cauldron. Wealthy burials of the Late Bronze and Early Iron Ages often contained wheeled vehicles, and in the Late Iron Age, small bronze representations of wheels are common in votive deposits. In prehistoric Europe, a wheel-god is recognized, regularly associated with this object. Scholars relate the wheel to sun symbolism both in Celtic iconography and in Scandinavia. A connection might then be made with the Roman sun and sky deity, Jupiter, and with the indigenous sky god and wheel god.

One view suggests that the wide distribution of these monuments in the western provinces of the Roman frontier zone attests to successful Roman propaganda in spreading images of their chief god Jupiter into the countryside as well as in the cities. But as the discussion above indicates, these structures are much more complex in their significance than simply representations of Jupiter. The principal importance of these columns is that they embody meaningful elements from indigenous tradition and from Roman ritual and belief, reworked into a complex new form. They stood as highly visible, tangible expressions, for all to see, of an ideology advocated by elites (who sponsored the construction of the columns) in the new societies, created through the manipulation of elements of both local and foreign traditions.

Conclusion

As the examples presented above show, the changes that took place among the peoples of Rome's frontier provinces were diverse. There was no typical response to the opportunities offered, nor restrictions imposed, by the new circumstances. Except for a small proportion of individuals of elite status, such as the persons who constructed and rebuilt the villa complex at Bondorf, the evidence suggests not a wholesale adoption of Roman fashions to the exclusion of local practices, but instead creative amalgamations of indigenous traditions and new ideas. The societies that developed during the first three centuries after Christ in the frontier zone were different in important ways both from the earlier indigenous societies and from groups in Roman territories elsewhere.

Historians, working from the written documents, tend to portray this time as one of increasing tension and uncertainty in the Roman border provinces. Beginning with the events known as the Marcomannic Wars that started in A.D. 166 and continuing with the incursions across the frontier by Alamanni, Franks, Goths, and others in the third century, historians represent this period in terms of the disintegration of the Roman border defenses as the result of invasions by large and formidable barbarian armies. The archaeological evidence, on the other hand, allows us to see this as a time of dynamic creativity in the frontier provinces, as people constructed their worlds and their identities from complex combinations of elements from their indigenous traditions and from practices and motives introduced by Roman troops, administrators, and others. Cross-cultural analyses of frontier situations help us to understand the mechanisms of change. Especially important is the point that in these dynamic contexts, new communities emerge that create forms of material culture quite different from those of their predecessors. Many archaeologists have interpreted such new forms as evidence for immigration from elsewhere, but they can be better understood in terms of the dynamics of the frontier societies, as I have outlined above.

These two models are not mutually exclusive, they simply represent the state of affairs from the perspectives of different participants. The ancient writers represented the official Roman perspective, and that was concerned primarily with maintaining order and defending the frontier borders. The populace of the provinces who built houses, made pottery, ordered fibulae from local bronzesmiths, buried their dead, and practiced rituals at the sacred sites were constructing their lives and their material cultures in ways that helped them to adapt to the changing circumstances around them. These adaptations were complex and they were different for every region, community, and individual. We need to understand the societies that formed under these circumstances in terms of varied responses to the spread of Roman influence and power, including selective adoption of elements of the Roman lifestyle, especially by native elites, and also reaction to those influences, especially on the part of individuals who had no direct access to the social and political benefits of close affiliation with the Roman authority structure.

In addition to the historical and the archaeological perspectives, we should also mention the contributions made by paleobotanists to understanding the character of the changes in the Roman provinces during these centuries. Hansjörg Küster is a paleoethnobotanist who studies the ways that people in the past utilized plant resources and the ways that human activities impacted the plant environment. In his investigations of pollen cores from bogs and seed samples from settlement sites he has found that the evidence from the natural environment and from patterns of food production during the first three centuries A.D. indicates strong patterns of continuity. While the large numbers of soldiers stationed along the Rhine and Danube frontiers created a new level of demand for food resources, the basic ingredients of the diet—spelt wheat and barley—remained the same from the prehistoric Iron Age through the early Roman Period (though spelt had not been known in Roman Italy). During the third century, when many aspects of the imperial system weakened, cities declined, and many villas were abandoned, the resulting pattern of settlement and of resource exploitation came to resemble circumstances that existed in the Late Iron Age, before the Roman conquests.

Impact across the Frontier

I n 1986, workmen digging a channel for a new drainage pipe on the shore of the Store Baelt on the southeast coast of the Danish island of Fyn encountered thick deposits of pottery and metal objects, including Roman silver coins. Archaeologists from the National Museum in Copenhagen were called in, and they quickly realized that the workers had uncovered a trade port from the Roman Period. Systematic excavations revealed a densely occupied settlement extending about 3,000 ft. (900 m) along the shore, with rich cultural deposits attesting to the importation of Roman goods and intensive craft production on the site. The importance of this discovery was immediately apparent to the archaeologists. Just 3 miles (5 km) inland from the coast was the site of Gudme, a place where extraordinary quantities of gold ornaments and unusually large numbers of Roman luxury goods had been found since early in the nineteenth century. Subsequent excavations at the ancient port of Lundeborg and ongoing research at Gudme have revealed a complex of sites that were closely linked to the Roman world through trade and were themselves growing centers of political power during the second and third centuries. As a result of these investigations on the island of Fyn and other research on contemporaneous sites elsewhere in Denmark and Sweden, we are developing a new understanding of the unexpectedly strong impact of the Roman provinces on these peoples of northern Europe. The new findings make it apparent that the first trade ports and the first urban centers of northern Europe were created in the context of interaction with Rome.

All of this new knowledge about political centralization, urbanization, and commercial networks on the coasts of Scandinavia during the Roman Period is based solely on the archaeological evidence—historical texts tell us nothing about any of it. Viewed in the context of all of the lands east and north of the Roman frontier in Europe, these developments in the north are just a portion of complex and varied patterns of change among peoples who established and maintained contacts with the Roman Empire. Investigation of these relationships between indigenous peoples in the unconquered lands and the Roman provinces tells us important things about all of the parties involved.

CROSS-FRONTIER INTERACTIONS AND THE ROMAN PROVINCES

Interactions with peoples beyond the frontier were critically important for the Roman provinces in temperate Europe. Without the foodstuffs, leather supplies, iron, and other goods that were produced by communities in the unconquered lands and traded to the military bases and growing urban centers along the frontiers, Rome would not have been able to maintain its armed forces or administrative superstructure in the provinces. And without the friendly relations the provinces were able to establish with chiefs and kings beyond the borders, the imperial lands would have been subject to much more frequent and concerted incursions from outside.

The cross-frontier interactions resulted in important changes for all parties involved. These changes are particularly apparent in the archaeological evidence among the peoples in the unconquered lands. Many were eager to receive Roman manufactured goods and to integrate them into their everyday lives and their rituals, as Roman objects found in settlement debris and in burials indicate. The patterns in some of the most richly outfitted graves show that the deceased individuals were familiar with Roman customs, especially banqueting, and practiced versions of those customs in their own communities. Many communities adapted their economic systems in order to produce surplus goods for trade to the Roman provinces. Some grew in size as a result. In some instances, we can identify increases in social status among individuals who played organizational roles in the expanding trade systems. At some sites far from the frontier, interactions with the Roman world played a major role in the creation of new political units.

The most profound effect of the interactions was to spread Roman goods, practices, and values beyond the provinces out to regions far removed from the territories conquered by Rome. When auxiliary soldiers returned home to regions such as Denmark or Poland, they brought with them not only their weapons and perhaps Roman bronze vessels and ornate pottery, but also personal familiarity with large-scale political organization, cities, writing, and all of the myriad other features that distinguished Roman civilization from the cultures of the peoples of northern Europe. At the same time, the service of northern Europeans in the auxiliary forces of the Roman provinces introduced into the Empire cultural influences very different from those of the Mediterranean world and even from those of Roman Gaul. The Germanic societies of the north became more Roman, and the Roman provinces became more Germanic. Through these interactions, the pattern was set for the emergence of the Germanic kingdoms of the early Middle Ages, with their complex intermixing of features from Roman and indigenous societies.

In the preceding chapters, we have seen how the Roman conquest and administration of the provinces were much more a matter of negotiation and compromise than they were out-and-out power politics. In this chapter, I challenge another long-held belief—that the boundaries of the Roman Empire were fixed and closed and that the provincial Romans and the barbarians outside did not mix much. As we shall see, interactions between peoples on the two sides of the frontier were important for all involved, and both the provincial Romans and the unconquered groups outside developed strong dependencies on one another.

For over two hundred years the boundaries of the empire survived intact. Then around the middle of the third century A.D.—a time of crisis throughout the Roman world, Rome bowed to increasingly frequent incursions across the *limes* and pulled back its defenses to the upper Rhine–upper Danube lines. As we have seen, the first and second centuries A.D. were a time of great growth and prosperity in the Rhineland and in the provinces south of the Danube. The need for provisioning the 110,000 troops stationed on these borders with food and supplies played a major role in economic changes both within the provinces and across the imperial frontier. The cities that developed and flourished in the Rhine and Danube regions (see chapter 8), as well as numerous smaller towns throughout the provinces, also required vast supplies from rural regions. It is particularly against this background of population increase in the frontier zones of the empire, especially by communities that depended upon others for food and raw materials, that we need to examine the questions of interaction across the frontier.

THE EVIDENCE

Both archaeological and textual evidence attest to interactions between the provinces and peoples outside. The archaeological evidence is much more abundant, but the textual sources provide some specific information lacking from the archaeological record.

Archaeology

The principal archaeological evidence for interactions is thousands of objects made in Italy and in the Roman provinces that are recovered in archaeological contexts in the unconquered territories. These are commonly called "Roman imports," but the term is imprecise. Many such objects originated not in Rome, but in the provinces, and it is not clear that the makers would necessarily have identified themselves as "Roman." "Import" implies trade, but other mechanisms were also involved in the transmission of goods from the imperial lands across the frontier.

Roman, or provincial Roman, objects in central Europe and Scandinavia were recognized as foreign products already during the nineteenth century when the discipline of archaeology was developing as a systematic body of knowledge and methods. Archaeologists of this period were fascinated with all of the evidence for interaction with the Roman world, and many studies from the late nineteenth and early twentieth centuries concerned these Roman objects. Hansjürgen Eggers's pathbreaking study *Der römische Import im freien Germanien*, published in 1951, presented all of the information known about them up to that time. He included a catalogue of 2,257 contexts in which Roman objects had been found beyond the frontiers. The principal categories were bronze vessels, fine pottery, glassware, silver vessels, statuettes, and weapons. He divided the objects chronologically into Late Iron Age, Early Roman Period, and Late Roman Period, and discussed trade routes and literary references to trade, but did not dwell on questions concerning the roles the objects played in the indigenous societies. Now, as the result of over forty years of intensive research throughout Europe, we can say a great deal more about these objects and their meaning than Eggers could. The total number of Roman objects discovered has increased greatly since Eggers's study, and, more importantly, archaeologists are devoting much more attention to questions of context—where the objects are found and what other items are found with them. We can now say more about the significance of these objects and of the interactions of which they were an integral part.

Texts

Roman writers such as Tacitus provide some contemporaneous information about interactions across the frontier. He informs us about the active commerce in the frontier zone, between the Roman provinces and peoples to the east. He noted the giving of gifts by provincial Roman authorities to leaders among Germanic groups in the unconquered territories. We learn about the free passage of Roman merchants in the unconquered lands, and of merchants from some allied groups beyond the frontier who were welcomed into the provinces. It is apparent from Tacitus and other Roman writers that regular movement of persons and goods took place across the frontier. But as is always the case with written sources, we need to ask how representative of actual conditions Tacitus's remarks were. The archaeological evidence provides a broader view into cross-frontier interactions.

The textual sources mention a number of goods that the Roman provinces obtained through trade from peoples beyond the frontier. These include livestock, in particular oxen and horses. Specific products from livestock are mentioned, especially ox hides. The commerce also involved humans—slaves and prisoners of war are noted, though details of the status of such persons are unclear. Grain is mentioned in the context of payment of tribute. A number of different authors mention amber, a substance prized by Romans for use as jewelry, as medicine, and for the aroma it emits when burned. At least one account cites weapons among the products sought by the Roman provinces. Specifically for the lower Rhine region, textual sources mention geese, feathers, down, salted pork, soap, and women's hair. Unfortunately all of these products are mentioned in rather incidental ways; we do not have any systematic discussions in the Roman sources of the goods that the Roman world obtained from the unconquered lands. In this respect the sources are very different from those of another much-studied context of cross-frontier interaction, the North American fur trade. In that instance a primary source of information is the extensive inventories of trade goods that French fur traders carried to exchange for beaver pelts. Such information about specific goods, their quantities, and their places of origin are generally lacking from the Roman sources, because those subjects were not of particular interest to the writers. The chance find at Tolsum, in West Friesland in the Netherlands, of an inscribed tablet that documents the sale of an ox to two Roman centurions provides an unusual glimpse into a commercial transaction on the northwest coast of Europe.

In a few instances, textual and epigraphic sources yield interesting details about specific Romans who were engaged in trade across the frontier. One concerns a Roman of equestrian status who, during the time of Nero's reign (A.D. 54–68), traveled from the Roman center of Carnuntum on the Danube (just east of Vienna) to the Baltic coast in order to trade for amber. According to Pliny's account, he was very successful and returned with great quantities of the fossil resin. In another case a gravestone of the first century A.D. commemorates one Q. Atilius Primus, who served in the Roman army in the role of translator at a Danube frontier post. After completion of his military service, he took advantage of his special knowledge of groups across the frontier and began a career as a merchant.

Besides trade, two other mechanisms of interaction are described in the written sources. One is mercenary service, the other, payment of subsidies. Throughout its provinces, Rome hired auxiliary troops to supplement the regular legions (see chapter 6). Many were recruited from the conquered territories, but Rome also hired soldiers from the unconquered lands. This practice went back at least as far as Caesar; in his account of the Gallic Wars he mentions Germanic cavalry troops in his service. From then on, Germanic troops were frequently mentioned in the texts. Their status ranged from individuals hired for specific military crises to regular units of auxiliary troops in Roman army service. Arminius, who led the forces that defeated Varus and his legions, may have gained his knowledge of Roman military tactics from his service as an officer in the Roman army (see below). We are not well informed about Germanic auxiliaries after the completion of their service. While some are likely to have remained in the Roman provinces in which they served, the majority probably returned to their homelands.

Roman policy included a number of strategies for maintaining peace along the frontiers. One was to establish mutually beneficial alliances with groups near the imperial boundary, setting up relations with "client kings." Another was paying subsidies to leaders of groups beyond the frontier to buy peace. Tacitus mentions this tactic at the end of the first century A.D., and subsequent writers refer to the practice as well. The aim was to maintain good relations with the peoples who inhabited the regions bordering on the frontiers, often in the hope that they would help to protect Rome's frontiers from other, hostile groups. The payment of subsidies resulted in the circulation of Roman wealth, largely in the form of silver and gold coins, across the frontier, and in the cultivation of close relations between provincial administrators and potentates in lands outside the imperial borders.

INTERPRETATION

Approaches to questions of interaction between the Roman provinces and the regions across the frontier are changing, largely because archaeologists and historians are becoming more familiar with anthropological data from other, comparable, contexts and thus are examining these processes of contact and interaction between societies with a broader perspective. We are accustomed to regard boundaries as fixed political frontiers, like the borders of modern nation-states. Roman written accounts of provincial boundaries can create this impression, since they tend to describe the state of affairs at the time of writing and not mention changes over time. Modern maps showing the provinces reinforce this notion of solid and unyielding borders. But the situation was much more fluid, as recent studies of both the textual and the archaeological evidence demonstrate. Perhaps the changes over the past decade in the political geography of Europe—reunification of Germany, breakup of Yugoslavia, and independence of former Soviet republics—provide a useful corrective to our usual assumption that boundaries are fixed and immutable.

Provincial boundaries shifted over time, with new conquests by Roman armies and with barbarian incursions that resulted in loss of provincial territories. The maps that we examine today showing locations and boundaries of Roman provinces represent specific moments in time, not the full sweep of Rome's five centuries in temperate Europe.

Earlier studies of interactions between the Roman provinces and the peoples across the frontiers, such as Eggers's work of 1951, interpreted the archaeological finds largely in terms of the written sources left by writers such as Tacitus and Cassius Dio. Based on those authors, investigators suggested a number of mechanisms to explain how objects from the Roman world came to the unconquered regions. These included barter trade, gift exchange, political or diplomatic gift-giving, and plunder. The focus of these studies was on the objects and on the Roman side of the interactions. But the situation is changing, as some researchers are thinking more about cultural dynamics in cross-cultural interactions and about the roles that the Roman objects played in the native societies.

Arminius

Before we turn to the archaeological evidence, it will be useful to consider a well-documented historical example of a person who exemplifies the complex patterns of interaction between Romans and natives. Arminius was a native of the region east of the Rhine, a member of the group called the Cherusci by Roman writers. His main role in history was as leader of the indigenous forces that attacked and defeated the army of the Roman general Varus in September of the year A.D. 9, destroying three legions and associated troops, totaling some 15,000–20,000 men (see chapter 1). His specific circumstances make him a valuable source of insight into relations between the different groups on either side of the frontier, and by considering his case we can get some idea of the effects of interactions on the thousands of others whose names and life stories we do not know.

According to Roman authors, Arminius was a member of the elite of the Cherusci people. He was born in either 18 or 16 B.C. and died in A.D. 21. He acquired Roman citizenship and even status as a Roman equestrian. One theory regarding how he gained these honors is that he served as the commander of an auxiliary unit in the Roman army. Another idea is that he had been brought to Rome by the Emperor Augustus for schooling and there acquired citizenship and equestrian status. There is some evidence that as a military leader he may have served in the suppression of the Pannonian uprising in A.D. 7–8. It has been suggested that after that uprising, he led his troops back to Germania, and that the attack on Varus's troops began as an uprising there. For that action, Arminius enlisted the cooperation of a number of different groups besides the Cherusci. He probably drew on his experience in the Roman army and his knowledge about organization of large military units that enabled him to command such a substantial body of troops, much larger than usual among the peoples east of the Rhine. Since Arminius had served for an extended time in the Roman military, he had won the trust of the Roman officers, including Varus.

Arminius's father-in-law, Segestes, was a strong ally of Rome who had aided Roman designs on the lands east of the Rhine and had been made a Roman citizen by the Emperor Augustus. According to textual sources, Segestes opposed Arminius's plan to attack the Roman armies and even tried to warn Varus of the intentions, but to no avail.

In the attack on Varus's forces, Arminius could apply all he had learned about Roman tactics and specifically what he had experienced in the Pannonian crisis. The recent discovery and ongoing excavation of the battle site indicate that Arminius selected a place for the attack in which the Roman troops would be at great disadvantage, hemmed in by a swamp on one side and a steep hill on the other.

The textual sources thus show that Arminius belonged to both his native Germanic culture and to that of the Roman world. His position in both of these contexts indicates what we need to expect as we consider the extensive archaeological evidence for interactions across the frontier. In A.D. 21 Arminius was murdered by a member of his own group, the Cherusci, perhaps because of his continuing ambitions for power.

Segestes provides us with an instructive counterexample to Arminius. Also linked to both his native Germanic society and to the Romans, he sided ultimately with Rome. In A.D. 15 he settled within Roman territory, in Gaul, together with his daughter, Arminius's wife. In what could be seen as an ultimate irony, Arminius's son was raised in Italy. These complex family interconnections with the Roman and the Germanic worlds provide a useful view into the intercultural relations in which individuals could be involved. Other indigenous leaders who adopted aspects of Roman culture provide similiar insights on the processes of cross-cultural interaction. Well-documented individuals include Civilis of the Batavians on the lower Rhine and Marbod of the Marcomanni in the region of Bohemia and Moravia. These are among the few that happened to be named and described by Roman authors; innumerable others played similar roles, but they are represented only by the archaeological evidence.

Phases of Interaction: Archaeology and Historical Dates

The thousands of Roman objects that have been found in the unconquered regions present a complex array of data about the interactions and about the ways the recipients used the imports. The chronological patterns of the imports in relation to developments in the Roman Empire help us to see changing patterns of interaction over time, and the spatial patterning illustrates the differences in interactions for peoples in different regions of the lands beyond the frontiers. Siegmar von Schnurbein has identified four main phases in the cross-frontier interactions, each defined by historically documented events and each reflected in the patterns of Roman imports in contexts beyond the imperial boundaries. The first is before 12 B.C. Roman trade and travel in central and northern Europe are apparent already in the second century B.C., for example in the Roman wine amphorae at the *oppidum* of Manching (see chapter 3). Roman luxury objects sometimes were placed in especially wealthy burials. The rich woman's grave at Dühren in Baden, dated at around 125 B.C., included a Roman bronze jug and pan (see chapter 3), and a warrior's grave at Kelheim in Bavaria from about 100 B.C. contained a Roman bronze wine jug. These are among the relatively few Roman goods that were brought into temperate Europe, probably through trade, before the Roman conquests began.

The second phase is from 12 B.C. to A.D. 16, during which time Rome carried out campaigns across the lower and middle Rhine, reaching as far as the Elbe River, with both land troops and naval forces. Rome's policy toward the peoples and territories east of the Rhine changed substantially during these years. Initially, it was to defend Roman territory along the Rhine and contain the unfriendly groups east of the river. In 11 or 10 B.C. a series of major offensive campaigns under the command of Drusus penetrated into the lands east of the Rhine as far as the Elbe and succeeded in defeating several major Germanic groups. But then after the Varus disaster in the Teutoburg Forest in A.D. 9, and especially after Tiberius recalled Germanicus to Rome in A.D. 16, Rome gave up serious attempts at conquering additional territory in that region. As outlined in chapter 4, during this phase, Roman forces built a series of forts along the Lippe River in northern Germany, at Rödgen and Marktbreit in central Germany, and at Dangstetten on the upper Rhine. Some were used only a few years, others a couple of decades. But by the time of the Teutoburg Forest catastrophe, most had been either destroyed or abandoned.

During the prehistoric Iron Age, the lands east of the middle and lower Rhine had been occupied by peoples in small communities, and there is no evidence of interregional political organization (see chapter 3). But in reaction to Roman campaigns across the river in Gaul and Roman incursions across the Rhine, communities banded together to raise forces to counter the threat of invasion. Roman texts indicate that these groups chose leaders in times of war to coordinate the efforts of fighters from diverse groups. We may see an archaeological expression of this process in the richly outfitted burials of this period (see below). The result of such organization was to amass sizable armies to meet the Roman threat. This process culminated in the defeat of the three legions in the Teutoburg Forest in A.D. 9.

Even though they were occupied only a few years, these forts were important in bringing indigenous peoples of those regions into direct contact with representatives of the Roman world—the soldiers based at the forts. From what we know about the supplying of the army along the frontier (see chapter 6), it is likely that the troops at the forts obtained foodstuffs, manufactured goods, and raw materials from the surrounding populations, and considerable interaction probably took place between individuals. While these forts were not occupied for a long period relative to the duration of the Roman Empire, the couple of decades of their existence surely had a profound effect on the peoples who lived in their vicinities. Excavated forts reveal aspects of Roman lifestyle with which the indigenous peoples would have become familiar, including pottery of different types and origins; metal weapons and other military equipment, tools, and personal ornaments; and coins. Exotic foods imported from the Mediterranean region are represented at the forts. Excavations at Oberaden have revealed olives, figs, wine grapes, even pepper, along with the usual wine amphorae.

The third phase dates from A.D. 16, when Rome ceased its serious campaigns east of the lower Rhine, following Tiberius's recall of Germanicus to Rome, to the Marcomannic Wars of A.D. 166–80. This was the time of greatest interaction between the provincial Roman world and peoples beyond the frontier, as demonstrated by great masses of Roman imports found throughout central, eastern, and northern Europe. It was also the period of greatest prosperity of the Rhineland, one of the richest parts of the Roman Empire.

Terra sigillata continued to be relatively scarce in lands along the frontier throughout the first century A.D., but from the end of that century, it was brought to many regions to the north and east, such as to Feddersen Wierde and other settlements on the North Sea coast, central regions of Germany, particularly modern Thuringia, and further east to the region of Jakuszowice in modern Poland. It first began to appear in quantity along the frontier east of the Rhine around the middle of the second century A.D., when settlements such as Westick were established. Some burials richest in Roman goods in the unconquered lands were outfitted late in the first and during the first part of the second century A.D., including the rich grave at Mušov in Moravia and those at Marwedel on the lower Elbe.

The fourth phase dates from the end of the Marcomannic Wars to the crises of the middle of the third century A.D., when Germanic groups overwhelmed the frontiers, and Rome redrew its imperial boundary to the upper Rhine and upper Danube. Toward the end of the second century A.D. a decline is apparent in Roman objects reaching communities in the unconquered lands, probably related to the disruptions associated with the Marcomannic Wars. Analysis of the archaeological evidence shows that Roman coins, *terra sigillata*, and bronze vessels all declined in quantity beyond the frontier during this period. But one category of Roman imports increased—weapons. It is likely that many northern Europeans participated in the Marcomannic Wars of A.D. 166–80, either fighting as mercenaries of the Romans or on the side of their foes. When they returned home, they brought their weapons, and perhaps others captured from their enemies, with them. The large quantities of Roman swords and other weapons deposited in lakes and bogs in Denmark and neighboring regions at the end of the second and start of the third century attest to major changes in the political configurations of northern Europe during this period (see below).

Geography of Interaction

The most common of the imports—thousands of bronze, ceramic, and glass vessels, and coins—are not mentioned as trade goods in the Roman textual sources. This discrepancy is an important indication of the disparity between the written and archaeological indicators of the interactions.

In the 1970s Lotte Hedeager called attention to patterns among the Roman imports that varied with distance from the frontier. In the lands closest to the provinces, most Roman imports are of everyday character—goods that Romans of average means might use in their households. Further away from the imperial borders, Roman goods of better quality occurred. The most exotic Roman products are found at the greatest distances from the frontier. Subsequent research has shown that the situation is more complex than this outline suggests, but the model provides a useful approach to the material.

FRONTIER ZONE

In the landscapes within 60 miles (100 km) of the Rhine and Danube, exceptionally large concentrations of Roman imports have been recovered in two areas—in the region of the Lippe and Ruhr Rivers east of the lower Rhine, and north of the middle Danube. The settlement of Westick in the Ruhr region of Germany is characteristic of many indigenous sites east of the Rhine. The earliest materials date to the beginning of the second century A.D., at the height of prosperity of the Roman Rhineland. Archaeologists found an unusually high proportion of Roman goods—about one-third of all pottery and metal objects on the site were of Roman origin. Roman-made bronze ornaments include a buckle, a decorative bust from an ornate table, and a fragment of a statuette. The abundant everyday Roman pottery and bronze ornaments at Westick were fully integrated with the material culture of the indigenous inhabitants. This evidence suggests that the frontier-zone populations of these regions engaged in regular trade with the provinces. Such commerce in everyday Roman goods need not have been highly organized or regulated, and it may have been carried on by individual merchants or farmers traveling across the border to trade at border posts or at military sites or civilian settlements within the provinces. It is clear from the occurrence of these Roman products that the indigenous peoples living near the frontier favored provincial Roman products and went to some effort, in terms of producing exchange goods and investing the time required for trade, in order to acquire them.

Only a few cemeteries in these regions include graves with Roman bronze and glass vessels. In the cemetery of some 250 cremation graves at Rheindorf, near Düsseldorf, almost all contained some Roman objects, mostly pottery, but including thirty-six bronze vessels and seven glass vessels. Similarly, in the lands north of the middle Danube, Roman bronze and glass vessels were placed in some wealthy burials.

The Roman luxury objects in the graves in these two regions can best be understood in terms of both cross-frontier trade and political relations. As noted above, we know from written sources that Roman troops relied on goods imported across the frontier, including grain, meat, and raw materials such as leather and iron. It is likely that communities such as Westick were engaged in such production and trade, and elite persons who managed the commercial systems were able to acquire the luxury products that we find in graves such as those at Rheindorf.

The richly outfitted burial at Mušov in Moravia in the middle Danube region shows how client kings allied with Rome displayed their status (see description in chapter 5). The grave contained an extraordinary set of Roman banqueting finery together with local signs of elite male status in these regions beyond the imperial frontier (Figure 36). This combination of Roman and indigenous prestige goods suggests that the deceased individual was a chief or king courted by Roman authorities to maintain the peace along this part of the frontier. Like Arminius, he may have served at some stage as leader of a contingent of auxiliary troops in the Roman army.

The lack of such burials east of the lower Rhine may be the result of the political circumstances there. Since the Roman campaigns east of the Rhine between 12 B.C. and A.D. 16, particularly since the Varus debacle of A.D. 9, relations between the inhabitants of those landscapes and the Roman authorities were tense, according to the historical sources. It is likely that there were no local leaders among the indigenous groups who had both the power over their own people and the trust of the Romans to merit the kind of Roman attention suggested by the rich grave at Mušov.

FRONTIER ZONE TO THE ELBE

In a zone between 60 and 240 miles (100–400 km) from the provincial borders, large numbers of Roman objects have been found. While these

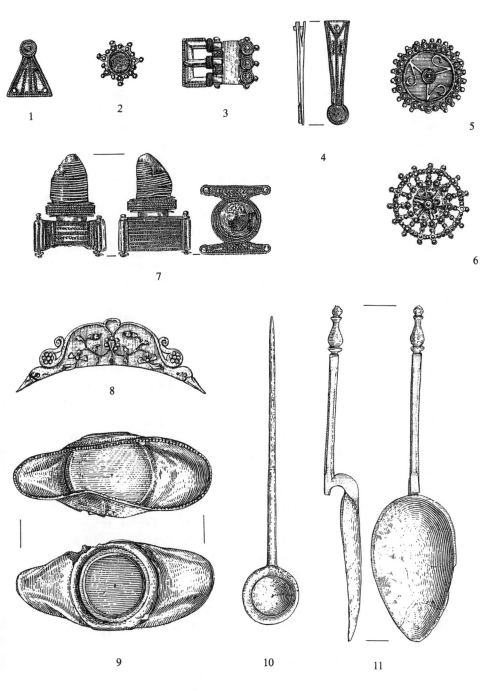

Fig. 36. Selected objects from the rich burial at Mušov in the Czech Republic.
(1–4) gilded silver attachments for a belt. *(5, 6)* gold pendants. *(7)* gilded silver
spur with inlaid prong. *(8)* handle for a silver vessel. *(9)* silver plate. *(10, 11)* silver
spoons. All objects shown at the same scale; *(1)* is about 1.1 in. (2.85 cm) long.
From Tejral 1992, p. 435, fig. 37 and p. 453, fig. 46. Used by permission of
Susanne Sievers, RGK.

occur widely distributed across the landscape, certain regional concentrations are apparent. Notable concentrations are in the Saale region south of the middle Elbe (modern Thuringia in Germany), around the tributaries of the upper Elbe (Bohemia in the Czech Republic), along the southern part of the lower Elbe (Lower Saxony, Germany), along the middle and lower Weser (Lower Saxony), and on the North Sea coast in the Dutch province of Friesland. The great majority of contexts in which Roman objects occur are burials.

Among a variety of mechanisms that were probably responsible for the transmission of Roman-made objects into these regions, two stand out as especially important for explaining the patterns in the archaeological evidence. One is the return of auxiliary troops to their homelands, bringing with them goods from the provinces in which they had served. The other is the development of production systems to generate goods to supply to the Roman provinces in exchange for desired objects of Roman manufacture.

Many individual men from beyond the frontier served as mercenary troops in the Roman army, sometimes as regular auxiliaries for periods of up to twenty or twenty-five years, sometimes just for special emergencies (see chapter 6). Roman military service by men from central and northern Europe was probably a much more important factor in cultural change than has been thought. Any individual who served in the Roman army for a period of years would have been exposed to the Latin language, to a substantial portion of Roman material culture, and to Roman practices of custom and organization. Many earned Roman citizenship through their military service. When they returned home to their native regions—which the majority probably did—they brought with them their familiarity with the Roman political system and probably a taste for many aspects of the Roman way of life, including ornate bronze and glass vessels and likely also wine and exotic foods. The vast numbers of Roman objects that have been found all over central and northern Europe probably result largely from soldiers' returning home, bringing with them things they acquired. One of the many motivations for the establishment of the trade centers discussed below may have been to supply former Roman soldiers with luxuries to which they had become accustomed or that they were eager to acquire.

The impact of the experience of auxiliary service is apparent in burial practices in the lands beyond the frontier. The practice of including weapons in some men's graves in northern Europe began to grow about the same time the first auxiliary soldiers would have been returning to their homelands. Some burials contain weapons made in provincial Roman workshops, while others include both weapons and sets of Roman metal vessels of types used in feasting rituals.

It is significant that the expansion of the practice of including weapons in burials in northern Europe happened at the same time that the Roman armies were campaigning east of the Rhine. This phenomenon is observable throughout the landscapes east and northeast of the Rhine, from Denmark to Bohemia and beyond. There are two ways of thinking about the meaning of this change, and they are not mutually exclusive. The explanation may be that with the onset of serious Roman efforts to conquer the lands between the Rhine and the Elbe, men's status as warriors assumed greater importance than it had, hence their weaponry became a component of the burial assemblage as part of the representation of their identity. Another possibility is that as larger numbers of men went to the provinces to earn wages as auxiliary soldiers, the practice of serving in the Roman army became a marker of status. Whether any specific man had served in the auxiliary forces or not, it was the practice of such service by some that raised the significance of the symbols of warfare for all men.

For the most part, the weapons buried in graves beyond the frontier were local products. But during the latter half of the second century and during the third, many Roman-made weapons, especially swords, were placed in burials. In many cemeteries in the lower Elbe region, such as Putensen, Roman swords are well represented among the burial goods. In some graves, even more elaborate Roman weaponry occurs, suggesting that those individuals may have not only served in auxiliary units of the Roman army, but also achieved considerable status in that role. Some of the most striking finds of Roman military gear in men's graves occur far from the frontier. Grave A4103 at Hedegård in Denmark had a highly ornate legionary soldier's dagger, together with other weapons (see below). A richly outfitted warrior's grave at Siemiechów in Poland contained a complete Roman legionary's helmet, an iron sword, lance point, shield, two knives, numerous metal ornaments, and many local ceramic vessels.

At Putensen, south of the Elbe River near Hamburg, archaeologists excavated 988 graves, most of them cremations placed in urns. The vast majority of the urns were local handmade pottery, but seven were bronze vessels of Roman or central European manufacture. The Putensen graves contained large numbers of iron weapons, including swords, lance and spear points, axes, shields, and chain mail, as well as pottery, tools, spurs, personal ornaments, and gaming pieces. Grave 150 exemplifies the rich burials at this cemetery and others in the lower Elbe region. It contained the cremated remains of a man about thirty years old, placed in a bronze cauldron. Grave goods included two Roman bronze casserolles and attachments from two drinking horns, a two-edged sword with iron sheath, a shield, an iron lancehead, and a knife. Three pairs of spurs were present, rein ornaments, and a buckle. Personal ornaments included six silver fibulae, a bronze fibula, an iron fibula, and a silver pin. This unusually richly outfitted grave, containing local symbols of elite status, signs of warfare and of cavalry activity, and Roman feasting gear, represents a new configuration of themes in this region, linked to interaction with the Roman world. The presence of this grave in the large cemetery emphasizes the connection between the individual buried here and the larger community of which he was a member—he presumably possessed special status.

We encounter a different situation in a series of richly outfitted graves that are not part of large cemeteries, but stand by themselves. Two exceptionally rich graves were found at Marwedel on the west bank of the Elbe, both dating to the first half of the second century A.D. In Grave 1, the deceased was buried, uncremated, in a coffin carved from a treetrunk, with grave goods placed on the body and at the head and feet (Figure 37). At the head end was a set of feasting equipment, including a bucket, basin, dipper, and sieve, all bronze and all of Roman manufacture (Figure 38). A Roman bronze casserolle was also present. In the basin were two drinking horns of local manufacture, consisting of cow horns with ends and attachments of bronze. Two finely made local ceramic bowls completed the feasting assemblage. Weapons were represented by a knob from an iron sword that had apparently rusted away, a bronze knife, and a silver-coated bronze buckle from a belt to which weapons had been attached. An ornate spur attests to the individual's horseback riding. A silver fibula and an ornate bronze fibula were part of the personal ornamentation (Figure 39). The fibulae, silver belt attachments, and attachments for the drinking horns display exquisite workmanship and attest to the patronage of highly specialized craftworkers by the warrior-elites of this period. Grave 2 was also an inhumation, and it contained Roman bronze vessels arranged at the foot end of the grave, including a pail, large casserolle, dipper, and sieve. A pair of drinking horns had terminals in the form of bulls' heads. Two ornate silver casserolles and two highly decorated silver beakers are unusually fine Roman imports. Fragments of two green glass beakers were also recovered. Other objects in the grave included a pair of ornate silver spurs attached to leather shoes, a gold fingerring, a bronze fibula with silver overlay, five small bronze ring fibu-

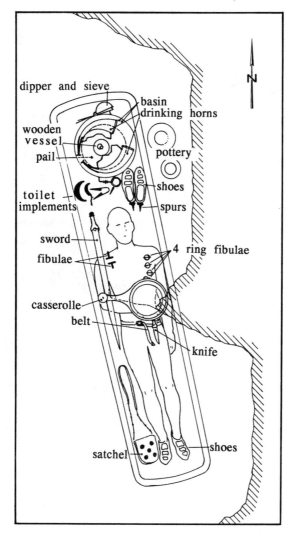

Fig. 37. Reconstruction of Grave 1 at Marwedel, showing
positions of objects in the grave. From Laux 1992, p. 319, fig. 3B.
Used by permission of Susanne Sievers, RGK.

lae, and a bag with silver buttons. Unlike Grave 1, this one contained no
evidence of weapons, but the presence of the ornate spurs suggests that
weapons may have been present originally but rusted away.

In both of the Marwedel graves, the imports included whole sets of
vessels—mostly bronze but also silver and glass—designed specifically for
feasting rituals, and in each case the Roman vessels were combined with

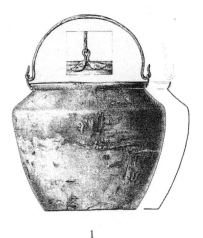

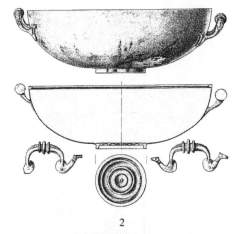

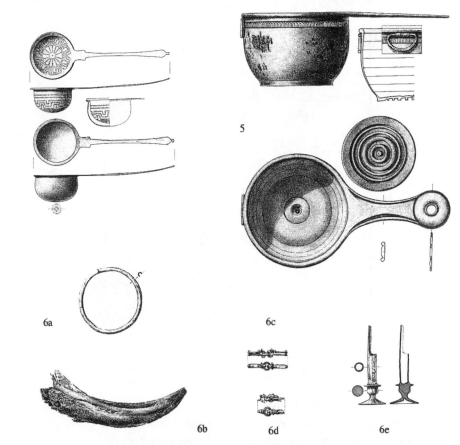

Fig. 38. Vessels from Marwedel Grave 1. *(1–5)* are Roman bronze vessels.
(1) cauldron. *(2)* basin. *(3)* sieve. *(4)* dipper. *(5)* casserolle. *(6a–e)* are parts of one of
the two drinking horns in the grave. *(6a)* bronze rim. *(6b)* horn. *(6c, 6d)* attachments for a strap or chain. *(6e)* bronze terminal. *(1–5)* are shown at the same scale;
(1) is about 10 in. (26.0 cm) high. *(6a–e)* are shown at the same scale;
the external diameter of *(6a)* is about 2.7 in. (6.9 cm). From Laux 1992.
Used by permission of Susanne Sievers, RGK.

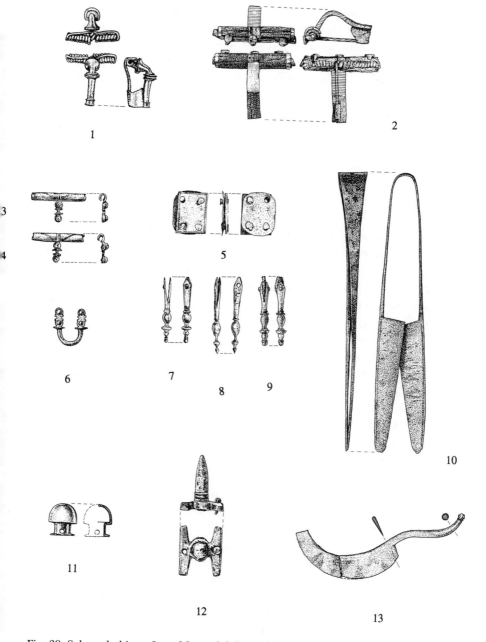

Fig. 39. Selected objects from Marwedel Grave 1. *(1, 2)* silver fibulae. *(3–9)* silver belt attachments. *(10)* bronze shears. *(11)* silver knob from the hilt of a sword. *(12)* bronze spur. *(13)* bronze razor. All shown at same scale; *(10)* is about 6.5 in. (16.4 cm) long. From Laux 1992. Used by permission of Susanne Sievers, RGK.

indigenous drinking horns. The weapons and spur in Grave 1 and the spurs in Grave 2 suggest service in the cavalry auxiliary of the Roman army. The precious metals—gold and silver ornaments—indicate exceptionally high status and wealth in the local society. The topographical situation—separate from the rest of the community rather than part of a large cemetery like Putensen—suggests that status differences between elites and others were increasing over time.

In many regions across the frontier there were communities that changed their economies in order to produce goods for trade to the Roman provinces. Particularly good evidence of this process is apparent at the settlement of Feddersen Wierde, situated on the North Sea coast of Lower Saxony, just north of Bremerhaven, 150 miles (250 km) from the nearest point on the frontier. This settlement was established in the decades before the time of Christ and was occupied until the fifth century A.D. The site was completely excavated and it provides exceptionally good information about changes in the indigenous community that accompanied growth in interaction with the Roman world. In its earliest phase, the settlement comprised five farmsteads of equal size, each consisting of a long building divided into living quarters for the human occupants at one end and stalls for livestock at the other. The buildings of the first phase contained a total of ninety-eight stalls for livestock. Several interrelated changes are evident over time—a gradual growth in quantities of Roman imports, growth in the population of the settlement and in the stall capacity, and increase in differentiation in status between families inhabiting different buildings. At its peak, the stall capacity of the settlement was 443. We have abundant textual evidence for trade in livestock and in animal products such as meats and hides from this part of Europe to the Roman provinces. From the end of the first century A.D. on, one dwelling and production unit on the settlement stood out from the others, with a more substantial hall, a special craft production area where bronze and iron were worked, a palisade separating it from the rest of the community, and a concentration of Roman imports. The Roman imports on the site include ornate *terra sigillata* pottery, decorative fibulae and other kinds of pins, beads, glassware, coins, basalt grindstones, and exotic objects such as a fan with an ivory handle.

The evidence of increasing livestock-raising capacity together with active importation of Roman goods at Feddersen Wierde suggests that the community was engaged in the trade of cattle and cattle products to the Roman Rhineland. The changes in the character of the buildings, especially the emergence of a single architectural unit that dominated in size, economic productive capacity, and consumption of Roman goods, suggests that growth of trade with the Roman world, intensification of production of surpluses, and social differentiation were interrelated processes.

Feddersen Wierde exemplifies changes among communities that were directly the result of production of supplies for the Roman provinces, but changes also took place at other sites that were not as directly linked with the needs of the provinces. A recently excavated settlement at Warburg-Daseburg, about 120 miles (200 km) east of the lower Rhine near the upper Weser River, dates to the first half of the first century A.D. The occupants of this small farming settlement manufactured fine metal jewelry, working in iron, bronze, lead, and even silver. Particularly well represented in the workshop debris is the process of making bronze fibulae. Bronze and silver were imported from the Roman provinces to the west. The craftworkers manufactured fibulae that borrowed stylistic themes from provincial Roman ornaments, but they transformed them into distinctive local products. There was no trace of any elite organization apparent, such as a large central settlement or rich graves nearby, suggesting that members of the basically agricultural community worked part-time to produce the high-quality personal ornaments for trade. This site shows that some production, even in bronze and silver, was not concentrated in large centers but dispersed in small communities throughout the countryside. Even for the manufacture of personal ornaments of bronze and silver for local consumption, these small producers were dependent upon raw materials from the provincial industries on the other side of the Rhine.

BEYOND THE ELBE

At distances greater than 240 miles (400 km) from the frontier, we find different patterns in the imports and their contexts. The majority of the most spectacular Roman imports—those displaying the most exquisite craftsmanship and comprising the largest quantities of precious metals—are found at these distant locations. In association with them we find the largest and most complex commercial centers that developed for supplying goods to the Roman provinces. Well-documented examples are in Poland to the east and in Denmark to the north.

The settlement of Jakuszowice in southern Poland was intensively occupied from the second century B.C. to the fifth century A.D. Recent excavations have yielded many Roman imports including fibulae and other jewelry, some with gold and silver ornament; glass fingerrings and beads; glass gaming pieces; bronze mirrors; wheelmade pottery, some inscribed with Latin letters; and forty-four silver coins from the late first to the early third centuries. A fragment of a fibula known as an "onion-head" fibula (because of onion-shaped knobs at the two ends of the spring) suggests personal contacts between members of the community and the Roman world. Such fibulae were insignia of high rank in the Roman Empire, and they were sometimes presented by Roman officials to counterparts in allied societies. This fibula suggests that an elite family resided at Jakuszowice, and richly equipped graves nearby support that interpretation. Among the many crafts represented in the settlement deposits is the working of gold and silver, probably specifically to serve the needs of the local elites.

Other industrial activities represented on the settlement include iron production, bronze working, and the processing of tin and lead. Carving debris shows that amber was worked on the site. Jakuszowice is near the Holy Cross Mountains (Góry Swietokrzyskie), where extensive mining of high-grade iron ore was carried out from the late prehistoric Iron Age throughout the Roman Period. The community at Jakuszowice may have been involved in shipping iron and amber westward to the Roman provinces in exchange for the goods represented on the settlement.

In south-central Poland, four richly outfitted inhumation graves at Łęg Piekarski, all dating between about A.D. 70 and 150, are united in containing silver vessels of Roman manufacture, unusual objects that only occur in contexts also distinguished by lavish local products. Grave 2, for example, contained the skeleton of a man placed inside a wooden chamber under a stone cairn covered by a tumulus of soil. With him were two silver cups, a silver bucket, eight bronze vessels, bronze attachments from two drinking horns, a silver fibula, a gold fingerring, bronze horse-riding equipment, iron remains of a shield, four bone dice, and twenty-nine stone gaming pieces. The other graves contained comparable objects, and attest to the consistency throughout many of the lands beyond the frontier of this common pattern of elite burial, with lavish Roman feasting equipment, weaponry, precious metal ornaments, and horse-riding equipment. As in the case of the Marwedel graves, these at Łęg Piekarski may represent former auxiliary troops. They might reflect the development of a set of elite symbols around service in the Roman army and the associated material paraphernalia.

In Denmark we find similar patterns. At the site of Hedegård on the Jutland peninsula, two hundred graves excavated in a large cemetery date to the end of the final century B.C. and the first century A.D. They proved to be more richly outfitted than most in northern Europe, with exceptional quantities of gold and silver ornaments and of weapons. At least four graves contained Roman imports, principally finely crafted bronze vessels. Grave A4103, dated to the first half of the first century A.D., contained a highly ornate Roman soldier's dagger and sheath, together with two Roman bronze vessels, a lancehead, a knife, and shears, apparently the burial equipment of a man who had served as an auxiliary soldier on the Roman frontier (Figures 40, 41).

The most spectacular complex of sites in northern Europe linked to the Roman world are at Gudme and Lundeborg in the southeastern part of the Danish island of Fyn. The fame of Gudme began in 1833, when a farmer plowed up a hoard of forty-nine gold objects, including rings, pendants, and other ornaments, weighing nearly 9 pounds (4 kg). Late in the nineteenth century the local landowner began excavations at the associated cemetery of Møllegårdsmarken. Among some 2,000 graves that have been excavated there to date, archaeologists have found over 130 sizable Roman objects, including bronze vessels, glass vessels, and *terra sigillata*, along with smaller items such as Roman coins and glass beads.

Recent discoveries made through systematic excavations at the settlement complex of Gudme and at the harbor site of Lundeborg have profoundly changed our understanding of northern Europe during the Roman Period. The settlement excavations at Gudme have recovered substantial quantities of *terra sigillata* pottery, Roman silver tableware, a Roman bronze helmet, and a silver head from a statuette. Fragments of a Roman bronze statue that stood nearly 4 ft. (1.15 m) tall may represent an almost-lifesize sculpture brought to this northern community, or they could be scrap metal intended for the local production of bronze ornaments. Many ornate bronze fibulae and pendants have been recovered, silver fibulae with gold decoration on them, 210 Roman silver coins from the first through the third centuries, and over 300 from the fourth and fifth centuries. A fragment of a crucible with a small piece of gold adhering to the interior shows that gold was cast on the site.

Along with these large quantities of Roman imports 270 miles (450 km) from the Roman frontier, archaeologists were stunned in the spring of 1993 when, during the clearing of land in the modern village of Gudme for the construction of a new sports complex, they identified the remains of the largest building known in northern Europe from this period. The floor plan of the structure was apparent from the immense postholes in which vertical timbers had once rested to support the walls

Fig. 40. Roman legionary dagger, ornate scabbard, spearhead, knife, and shears as they were found in Grave A4103 at Hedegård, Denmark. Photograph courtesy of Orla Madsen, Haderslev.

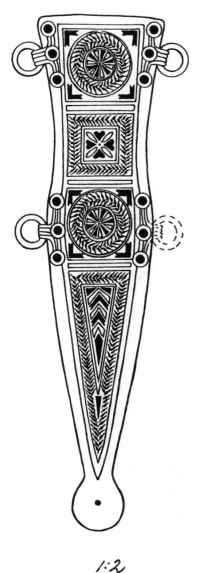

1:2

Fig. 41. Reconstruction drawing of the
ornate scabbard in fig. 40. Courtesy of
Orla Madsen.

and roof (Figure 42). The building was 154 ft. (47 m) long and 33 ft. (10 m)
wide, and it was dubbed the "king's hall" for its immense dimensions. In
association with this enormous building, the excavators recovered 114
Roman silver coins, a fragmentary silver statuette, and numerous pieces
of gold jewelry. These objects apparently were lost in and around the

249

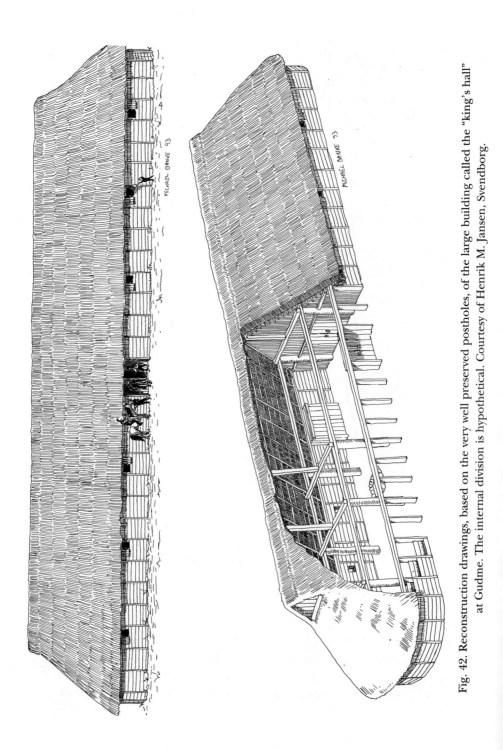

Fig. 42. Reconstruction drawings, based on the very well preserved postholes, of the large building called the "king's hall" at Gudme. The internal division is hypothetical. Courtesy of Henrik M. Jansen, Svendborg.

building; it is hard to imagine the quantities of wealth that must have been in the building when it was in use.

It is clear from the abundant precious metals and Roman luxury goods at the settlement of Gudme and in the graves of the neighboring Mølle-gårdsmarken cemetery that this was a special place. Gudme was a center of wealth, commerce, and power from the middle of the second century A.D. on, though already in the late prehistoric Iron Age some richly out-fitted graves indicate that the site was significant. The new discovery of the "king's hall" adds another dimension to our ideas about the role Gudme played in the process of political centralization that was under-way in Denmark at that time.

The discovery in 1986 of the port settlement of Lundeborg, 3 miles (5 km) east of Gudme on the coast (see above), shed further light on the nature of this economic and political center far from the Roman frontier. The Lundeborg excavations have recovered evidence indicating how the Roman goods arrived at Gudme, and also showing highly active craft production. This site had been selected because it was ideal for landing the boats of the period. Fragments of glass vessels, glass beads, and *terra sigillata* pottery show that Roman goods were unloaded from ships here for transport inland to Gudme. Objects that broke—glass and pottery—are represented by pieces that became deposited at the trade settlement. Those that survived intact—some glass and pottery and espe-cially bronze vessels, metal statuary, and coins—were brought on to Gudme. Yet 140 Roman silver denar coins have been recovered in the Lundeborg excavations, most of them minted between A.D. 138 and 192. The buildings in evidence at Lundeborg were not like the solid structures of the inland settlements, but were small, temporary huts, about 215 sq. ft. (20 m²) in internal area, probably used only during the warm months when shipping would have been particularly active.

Besides serving as the port of entry for substantial quantities of Roman goods destined for Gudme and probably elsewhere as well, the Lunde-borg settlement was also a site of considerable manufacturing activity. Crafts represented in the archaeological deposits include the working of gold, silver, bronze, bone, antler, amber, glass, and leather.

Imports are often well documented archaeologically, as they are here at Gudme and Lundeborg, but exports are much more difficult to ascer-tain. The Lundeborg traders may well have exported amber, a substance much favored by the Roman world and readily available on the Danish shores. Based on what we know about the goods the Roman world needed, and on exports from the same region in the Middle Ages, dried meat, dried fish, hides, cattle, and horses probably were other goods that commercial centers in the Scandinavian lands traded to the provinces.

In the east of Denmark, on the island of Zealand, excavation results show the development of a major regional political center that based its power in part on links with the Roman Empire. The principal evidence is in the burials. During the latter half of the second century A.D., a series of richly outfitted men's graves were established at Himlingøje, characterized by Roman imports, iron weapons, and riding equipment. These individuals who established the political dynasty on Zealand may have participated in the Marcomannic Wars and thereby gained their status and wealth. These graves are very similar in important respects to those believed to represent client kings near the frontier, such as the rich burial at Mušov (see above). During the first half of the third century, this political dynasty is represented by both men's and women's graves of exceptional wealth. By this time, weapons no longer characterized the rich men's graves, perhaps a sign that the political ascendency of the elites here was firmly established and did not need military symbolism to bolster it. Richly outfitted women's graves demonstrate through the buried goods strong links with other parts of Denmark and with continental Europe.

In this new political configuration, Roman luxury imports came to play a vital role in the expression and transference of power. The highest quality imports were retained by the political leaders in Denmark who controlled the interactions with the Roman provinces, and those individuals passed along to persons at lower levels in the status hierarchy Roman objects of lesser quality. The graves at Himlingøje reflect the elite's consumption of exceptional imports and also show how they expressed their status through local fine craft products.

Grave 1949–2, for example, contained the inhumed skeleton of a woman about forty-five years of age, equipped with Roman imports and with lavish locally made ornaments. The Roman goods included a bronze bucket, basin, and dipper-sieve set; 2 glass beakers; and a silver denar coin. Local objects included a huge silver fibula with a runic inscription (Figure 43), 4 other silver fibulae, a bronze fibula, a silver hair pin with sheet gold ornament, a gold bead and gold ornament, more than 66 glass beads, and some 43 amber beads, 2 gilded silver pendants, 2 gold bracelets, 2 gold fingerrings, 5 ceramic vessels, and some animal bones. The grave has been dated to the first half of the third century A.D. The bronze feasting set indicates connections to the Roman world; similar sets occur in other graves at Himlingøje. These northern elites apparently were closely familiar with Roman practices and values, probably as

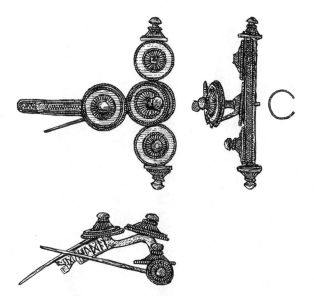

Fig. 43. Silver rosette fibula, with sheet gold ornament, from Grave 1949–2 at Himlingøje, Denmark. The catch-plate bears the runic inscription WIDUHUDAR, believed to be a man's name. Length of spring, including knobs on both ends, about 4.6 in. (11.6 cm). From Hansen 1995, plate 22. Used by permission of the Royal Society of Northern Antiquaries, Copenhagen.

a result of person-to-person interactions with their counterparts in the Roman provinces. The fibulae and other ornaments are all types that are common in rich women's burials in Denmark and neighboring regions, suggesting close family connections between elites in the different lands. The runic inscription on the large fibula is a special feature of wealthy women's burials (see below).

Important information about transformations in social and political organization in northern Europe in the context of interaction with the Roman world comes from the great weapon deposits in lakes and bogs of Denmark, southern Sweden, and northern Germany, particularly during the third century (see chapter 1). These enormous assemblages of weapons and ornaments came to scholarly attention in the middle of the nineteenth century with Conrad Engelhardt's studies of the now famous sites of Kragehul, Nydam, Vimose, and Thorsbjerg (Figure 44). Today, about thirty such sites are known. The tradition was an old one in the north, going back at least to the Hjortspring bog find of the mid-fourth century B.C. In the third century A.D. group of concern to us here,

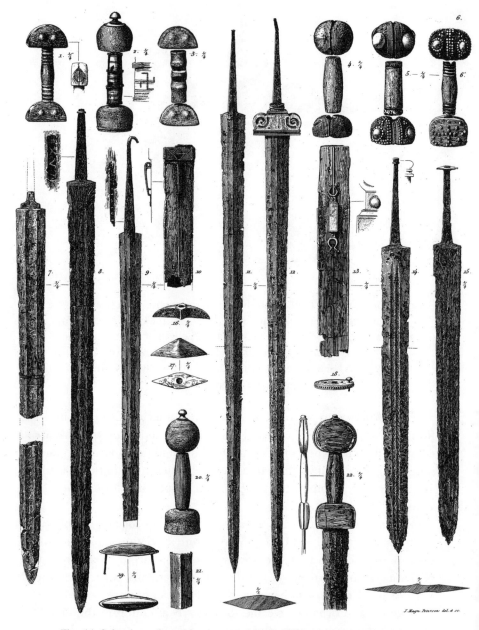

Fig. 44. Selection of swords recovered in the Vimose weapon deposit.
Note the Latin inscriptions on the two in the upper left. The wet and acidic
environment of the site resulted in the unusual preservation of the
wooden hilts. From Engelhardt 1869, plate 6.

hundreds of swords, spears, and shields were intentionally deposited in lakes and bogs, together with shirts of chain mail, clothing, personal ornaments, tools, bronze vessels, horse harness fittings, Roman coins, and even a pair of ships, the larger of which was 75 ft. (23 m) long, at the site of Nydam. There has never been any serious doubt that these objects were all deposited on purpose, but the nineteenth-century finds published by Engelhardt had been recovered in conditions different from modern scientific excavations, and interpreting the precise nature of the deposits has always been difficult. The recent research at Illerup makes clear that there, at least, a large number of objects were deposited in a single event, perhaps a ceremony marking a military victory (see chapter 1).

SIGNIFICANCE OF THE CROSS-FRONTIER INTERACTIONS

The interactions across the Roman frontier had major effects on the Roman provinces and on the groups outside, many of which had lasting impact.

Effects beyond the Frontiers

The most immediate impact of the interactions was economic. Communities in the frontier regions, such as Westick, exchanged quantities of surplus goods for everyday Roman pottery and bronze ornaments. They were stimulated to produce larger surpluses in order to participate in this trade, and the replacement of much of their native material culture by Roman objects had an effect on local pottery and metalworking industries. At Feddersen Wierde the effects of commerce with the Roman provinces is visible in the growth of the livestock-raising capacity of the settlement at the same time that Roman imports increased in quantity. All of the centers of production mentioned above, including Warburg-Daseburg, Jakuszowice, and Gudme/Lundeborg, reflect the economic impact of their interactions with the Roman world.

Important political changes also resulted. When auxiliary veterans returned to their homes in Germany, Poland, and Denmark, they brought with them not only their weapons and other accoutrements from the Roman provinces, their Roman citizenship, and knowledge of at least some Latin, but also new ideas about systems of social and military organization and about political processes. In the present state of research, it is difficult to judge to what extent the political centralization evident at Gudme and Himlingøje during the third century was the result of indigenous processes and to what extent it was stimulated by ideas brought by returning veterans. Surely many different factors were involved.

The weapon deposits in Denmark, southern Sweden, and northern Germany provide important evidence to show that much larger-scale military units were being deployed than are represented at any earlier time. The sizable military force represented by the weapons deposited at Illerup (see chapter 1) could only have been drawn from many communities in a large, politically unified region. The army represented at Illerup would have required a minimum of twelve boats the size of the Nydam ship to bring it to the coast of Jutland.

At the same time that new political centers were emerging and larger landscapes were becoming unified politically, there are other indicators of the creation of new identities among the peoples of northern Europe. The style of decoration known as Germanic art developed in this context of interaction. While some researchers trace its origins back to around the time of Christ, most agree that it emerged as a full-blown style during the second and third centuries. Early Germanic art is best represented in decorative metalwork, and it is characterized by the application of delicate gold filigree, granulation, and fine wires, and, during the third century, by garnet and glass inlay on metal ornaments. Some of the elements of the new style derive from the arts of the Roman provinces, others from the traditions of the indigenous peoples in the north.

Runes were developed in northern Europe as an indigenous form of writing sometime during the first or second century A.D. The majority of known early inscriptions are from Denmark, and the origin of this script probably lies in that region. Runologists believe that the script was consciously created by individuals intent to devise a system of writing comparable to the Latin alphabet, and that it emerged at this time because of personal contacts with members of Roman literate society. The earliest inscriptions occur on two main categories of objects—ornate fibulae in richly outfitted women's graves (see Figure 43), and weapons in the weapon deposits. Runes, like the Germanic style of decoration, can be understood in terms of the creation of distinctive modes of communication among the elites in the new political entities of northern Europe and, like the art, their origins lie in the interaction between indigenous and Roman traditions.

Effects on the Roman Provinces

The Roman provinces could not have existed as they did, with tens of thousands of troops stationed in the frontier zone and major urban centers in the Rhineland and along the Danube, without the constant supply of foodstuffs and raw materials from across the frontier. Without those sources of goods, Rome could have mounted only a much more modest effort in temperate Europe. As we have noted, from the time of Caesar on, the Roman military relied upon auxiliary troops hired from beyond the frontier as well as within the conquered territories. Rome's entire enterprise in Europe was possible only because it could draw on the resources provided by the native peoples on both sides of the frontier.

The presence of large numbers of auxiliary troops from outside the empire, as well as of merchants and other visitors, surely had an effect on provincial Roman ideology and attitudes, but very little work has been done on this topic. Most investigators have followed the Roman writers in assuming that Rome had a major impact on the barbarians, but that the barbarians had little effect on Rome. In the latter half of the third and in the fourth and fifth centuries, the barbarian impact becomes obvious, as non-Roman commanders assumed ever-more important roles in the imperial army. But future research will surely discern signs of influences from the earliest phases of Roman imperial activity in temperate Europe.

CONCLUSION

The interactions described in this chapter had two large-scale results for temperate Europe. One was the gradual breakdown of differences between the societies in the Roman provinces and the peoples in the lands east and north of the frontiers. The adoption by the indigenous elites in what are now Germany, Poland, and Denmark of Roman luxury goods, customs, and values, represented the beginning of a process that was to involve all members of their communities in subsequent centuries. Contacts between foreign auxiliary soldiers and provincial populations within the imperial borders resulted in changes in the provinces that made them gradually less different from the lands across the frontier.

The other major effect of the interactions was the formation, during the third century, of large tribal confederations among the peoples beyond the frontier, political units much greater than the tribal groups described by Caesar and Tacitus. The political configurations indicated by the great weapon deposits of the third century are part of the development that led to the emergence of the confederations known to us through historical sources as the Franks, Alamanni, and Goths, all of whom were first mentioned during this dynamic third century.

The interplay between these two processes—the increasing homogeneity of peoples within and outside of the Roman provinces, and the emergence of new and larger political entities among the Germanic groups beyond the frontier—will be a topic of the next, and final, chapter.

CHAPTER 11

Conclusion

THE CRISES OF THE THIRD CENTURY

THE THIRD CENTURY A.D. is regarded as a period of crisis throughout the Roman world that included intense political struggles in Rome, the decline in the power of the Roman Senate over the affairs of the empire, and a rise in the role of the army in internal as well as external matters. Written documents of the period make clear that the power of Rome and its central administration waned, and incursions by barbarians increased in scale and frequency on many of the empire's frontiers. Germanic peoples threatened the frontiers in the west and overran them several times after A.D. 259. On the eastern frontiers, the Goths disrupted the peace in the provinces along the lower Danube, while the Persians created unstable conditions further east. Archaeological evidence also indicates important changes during this time, but it provides a different perspective from the texts left by the Roman writers.

In many regions in Roman Europe, urban centers declined in size and in importance during the third century. Archaeologically, we can see an end to major building programs and often a reduction in the inhabited and fortified portions of the towns. Few new villas were established in the countryside, and many existing ones were abandoned. Settlement systems in rural areas returned to patterns that had been characteristic during the prehistoric Iron Age.

In the frontier zone in temperate Europe, textual sources describe attacks on the *limes* boundary and incursions across the border by a group called the Alamanni, first mentioned in A.D. 231. According to these written documents, in the years 259 and 260 the Alamanni attacked with such force that they effectively destroyed the imperial boundary, causing Rome to give up the Agri Decumates (roughly what is now the southwest German state of Baden-Württemberg) and to re-create the earlier imperial border along the upper Rhine and upper Danube Rivers. This view of the Alamanni destroying the Roman *limes* in massive attacks of the mid-third century has dominated thinking by historians and by many archaeologists, and the collapse of the imperial border in southwest Germany is often portrayed as an archetypal example of the barbarian overwhelming of Roman frontiers.

But the results of extensive recent archaeological research in southwest Germany show a different situation. Although the written sources portray the fall of the *limes* as a rather sudden event caused by increased attacks by the Alamanni around the middle of the third century, the archaeology shows that the Roman forsaking of the Agri Decumates was the result of a long process of cross-border interaction and migration and of frequent small-scale incursions by different groups over an extended period of time, probably many decades. Numerous excavated settlements and cemeteries west of the frontier attest to the immigration of peoples from outside, probably to take advantage of the opportunities offered by the thriving economy in the Roman provinces and to enjoy the attractions of the provincial lifestyle. Archaeological investigation of many frontier watchtowers along the *limes* has failed to produce evidence for widespread burning and destruction at the time of the supposed collapse of the frontier defenses. Thus the evidence now suggests a long and gradual process of change from a landscape dominated by the Roman military and administrative apparatus to one transformed through interaction with and migration by peoples from across the frontier.

These changes were happening at the same time that we witness a resurgence of the La Tène style (see chapter 7) and can best be understood in terms of varied expressions of reaction to, or rebellion against, Roman administration and ideology. In fact, actual immigration of peoples from east of the frontier may have been on a relatively small scale, despite the assertions of Roman observers, alarmed at the changes taking place around them. The ongoing interaction between peoples in the Agri Decumates and others outside, discussed in chapter 10, provided adequate means for the transmission of goods and styles that appear on the settlements and in the cemeteries during this time.

Similar processes are apparent elsewhere in the imperial frontier regions. On the lower Danube, the Goths appear in the historical record in A.D. 238, and in the lower Rhine region, the Franks are first mentioned in written sources in A.D. 257. During the 270s they, like the Alamanni to the south, are portrayed raiding across the Rhine into Roman territory on the west bank. In A.D. 286 we read of the Saxons, east and north of the Franks, also engaging in expanded military activities that threaten the Roman world.

New Confederations in Temperate Europe

The naming of these new groups—Alamanni, Goths, Franks, and Saxons, as well as Burgundians, Langobards, and others—by Roman authors during the third century indicates important changes that were taking place along and beyond the frontiers (Figure 45). The ways that these indigenous peoples were represented by third-century authors is very different from the ways such groups had been portrayed by Caesar in the first century B.C. and by Tacitus around A.D. 100. Those earlier writers described small tribal peoples inhabiting local landscapes throughout western and central Europe (chapter 5). The third-century groups are portrayed as much larger and better organized entities—tribal confederations—with considerably more ability to confront the Roman power structure. Ironically, these changes came about in large part as the result of the interactions between the small-scale communities beyond the frontiers and the Roman army and other inhabitants of the provinces.

In chapter 10 I described several processes that led to increased wealth and community size, and to greater social and political complexity, among the peoples east of the Roman frontier. These included the service of young men as auxiliaries in the Roman army, the Roman policy of supporting client kings in the regions across the border, and the growth of centers that produced goods for trade with the Roman provinces. These processes brought indigenous peoples into frequent and consequential contact with the Roman world. They resulted in the transfer of wealth from the empire to peoples outside the provinces, and they had the effect of creating larger communities and, as at Jakuszowice, Gudme, and Himlingøje, political centers that unified ever-larger regional populations. It can be argued that through its policy of hiring Germanic auxiliary troops, Rome effectively trained its future enemies in military organization and tactics. Early on in its campaigns in temperate Europe, Rome experienced the potentially catastrophic results of this policy, in the case of Arminius and his annihilation of Varus's legions in A.D. 9. Throughout the centuries of Rome's presence in temperate Europe, the provinces of the empire exerted a powerful attraction on peoples beyond the frontiers, as they were lured by Roman wine and luxury foods, baths, architecture, and other amenities of the cosmopolitan civilization.

The results of the inevitable clashes between these expanding indigenous confederations and the weakening Roman military in the frontier

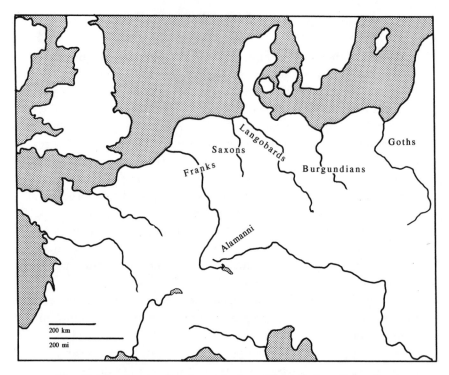

Fig. 45. Map showing locations of a few of the tribal confederations
mentioned in written sources of the third century A.D.

provinces are well represented at the Runder Berg, a hilltop settlement
established late in the third century in the former Agri Decumates, just
a few decades after the Roman administration gave up the *limes* boundary
and reestablished its border to the south. The Runder Berg is the most
thoroughly studied of over fifty such hillforts known in southwest Germany from this time. Excavations reveal a fortified settlement that included elite individuals in the early post-Roman society in the region.
Archaeologists have interpreted the material remains to indicate the
presence of an Alamannic king and his followers. Workshops on the settlement produced bronze and gold ornaments as well as weapons. Most
striking is the abundance of late Roman pottery and glassware, imported
from Gaul west of the Rhine, at least 90 miles (150 km) away. Apparently
after establishing this settlement following the expulsion of the Roman
military and civilian infrastructure from the region, the inhabitants organized trade systems to assure that they could have access to the Roman
luxury goods that they found so attractive.

During the third, fourth, and fifth centuries both textual and archaeological sources of information show complex and widely varied patterns of intermixing of features and practices of traditional indigenous groups, provincial Romans, and Germanic peoples from beyond the frontiers. Analyses of cemetery evidence from Late Roman Gaul show how burial practices were so complex and varied that it is virtually impossible to distinguish an individual's origin from tomb structures and grave goods during this time of profound change. Also outside of the Late Roman provinces, the archaeological evidence attests to complex patterns of mixing. For example, excavations at Haarhausen in Thuringia, 120 miles (200 km) east of the frontier, have uncovered three provincial Roman-type pottery kilns, constructed in the same way that kilns were built in Gaul and used for making the same kinds of provincial Roman pottery. They were clearly constructed and operated by individuals trained in Roman Gaul, but we cannot say who those potters were. They may have been individuals who had moved from Gaul eastward to practice their craft in a new market, or locals who had gone to Gaul to learn how to make the much-favored provincial pottery.

The Alamanni, Franks, Goths, and other groups emerged in this context of interaction during the late second and third centuries. In every case, they represented combinations of indigenous traits among the peoples of the unconquered lands and elements of provincial Roman society. The Franks on the lower Rhine were to form the basis of the Merovingian kingdoms of the post-Roman early Middle Ages, and of Charlemagne's new empire of the late eighth and early ninth centuries. But those developments are beyond the scope of this book.

NATIVES AND ROMANS IN WORLD ANTHROPOLOGICAL CONTEXT

The case examined in this book—the actions and experiences of indigenous peoples in the frontier zone of the Roman Empire in Europe—offers useful perspectives for broader considerations of interactions between imperial societies and peoples inhabiting the lands they conquer. In the Roman instance, we can examine patterns of change over several centuries, and the archaeological database in temperate Europe is exceptionally rich. The Roman written sources provide a useful historical framework for understanding the progression of conquest and important details about imperial strategy and organization, but, as we have seen, they must be used with critical caution with regard to what they say about the indigenous peoples. In many respects, the Roman conquest and administration of temperate Europe were similar to other instances of imperial expansion in world history. For example, many important similarities can be identified between Roman intentions and interactions in temperate Europe and Spanish activity both in Mexico and in South America. These New World contexts are subjects of much recent research by archaeologists, historians, and art historians, and they are identifying many patterns similar to those in Roman Europe discussed in this book. In this final section, I shall briefly note a few points that emerge from this study to situate it in the broader field of imperial interaction and frontier studies.

We need to be critically aware of the nature of entrenched categories in any study of interactions between expansionary states and indigenous peoples. As I have tried to show, when we examine the material evidence closely, categories such as "Roman," "provincial Roman," "native," "Celt," and "German" do not stand up to critical scrutiny. Instead, we see patterns of infinite variability—every settlement and every cemetery is unique. From the time of the conquests on, there were no purely "Roman" nor purely "indigenous" sites—all show some degree of integration of features from different traditions. In order to understand the ways that people were responding to the changes they were experiencing, we need to analyze the evidence on the level of individual variation.

As I have shown throughout this book, elite individuals among the indigenous peoples tended to adopt what they wanted from the newly introduced Roman traditions, and to transform it to suit their purposes. These processes of choosing and of transforming on the part of the natives explain why *terra sigillata* pottery produced in the Rhineland was different from that made in Italy and southern Gaul, why Gallo-Roman temples were different from Classical temples on the Mediterranean shores, and why the majority of representations of deities in temperate Europe are not just like figures of the same deities in Roman sculpture in Italy.

The material evidence indicates that indigenous peoples in the Roman provinces and others outside were engaged in similar processes of selecting, borrowing, and transforming elements of Roman culture. In examining Roman imports throughout central, northern, and eastern Europe, if we shift our focus from the places of origin of the objects, and ask instead, what role did they play in the indigenous societies that received and consumed them, we can learn important things about cultural dynamics among the peoples beyond the frontier. A recent study of import trade of luxury goods into Latin America during the nine-teenth and twentieth centuries shows how much information we can gain by focusing on the role the imports played in local patterns of consumption, display, and interaction, rather than viewing them principally from the perspective of the exporting European societies.

In the provinces and in lands hundreds of miles away from imperial Roman territory, the attraction of the material objects associated with the cosmopolitan lifestyle of the Mediterranean world was a powerful force for the elites of indigenous societies. The patterns of consumption of Roman-style goods, including not only the fine pottery, bronze vessels, and silver tableware, but also villas, baths, and temples, examined in the preceding chapters, raise interesting questions about the ways in which the peoples of temperate Europe identified with the Mediterranean civilization that introduced these luxuries. One cannot help but pose the question, who was more "Roman"—a farmer in the Isar Valley of Raetia who produced surplus wheat for the Roman troops stationed at Regensburg, but whose housewares included principally traditionally made goods such as Iron Age–style pottery; or a chief at Gudme in Denmark, hundreds of miles from the frontier who drank imported wine from Roman bronze vessels in his enormous hall whose interior was decorated with Roman bronze and silver sculptures? The question is of course moot, but it points up the great variability among groups and individuals in the degree to which they participated in adopting the cosmopolitan way of life exemplified by the Roman world.

Amid all of the variability in responses to the choices presented by the Roman presence, we can recognize significant patterns, and they may represent common features in all situations of interaction between expanding complex societies and indigenous groups. Especially striking is initial eager adoption of Roman luxury goods and lifestyle by the urban elites in the conquered territories, while rural areas and others in the society maintained the traditional Iron Age material culture. Over the course of a few generations, rural communities also began to adopt new patterns, but after another few generations, signs of re-creation, or re-newal, of old traditions appeared, perhaps as forms of resistance to pro-vincial Roman material culture and society. Over time, new traditions developed, adapting elements of both indigenous and introduced prac-tices and styles to create patterns different from any of the antecedents.

In the unconquered regions, the patterns are different but related. The elites embraced many aspects of the imperial lifestyle that they con-sumed and displayed privately, such as ornate feasting paraphernalia,

statuary, personal ornaments, and coins, but they did not adopt the public expressions of their affiliation with the cosmopolitan society—the
dwellings, baths, or temples of the Roman provinces. Except near the
frontiers, as at the site of Westick, the nonelite members of the societies
beyond the frontier did not adopt the new cosmopolitan styles, probably
because they had no direct access to the required goods. Beyond the
frontier we see no clear resurgence of long-dormant styles, as in the case
of the La Tène style in the provinces. When elements of the cosmopolitan
lifestyle were integrated with those of local tradition, such as in the emergence of the confederations of the Alamanni and the Franks, that development was driven more exclusively by the elites than was the case in the
Roman provinces.

The result was the creation of dynamic new societies, variously embodying elements of indigenous traditions and of the Roman world. New
archaeological discoveries, new ways of understanding the archaeological evidence, and new approaches to the textual sources, are helping us
to develop this view of the creation of the societies of Late Roman and
early medieval times in terms of the dynamics of interaction among dis-
parate groups on both sides of the imperial frontier.

The approach developed here can be applied productively to other
cases of imperialistic expansion and interaction with indigenous peoples,
such as, to cite just three examples, the Sumerian colonization of northern Mesopotamia, the Spanish conquest of Peru, and the creation of the
British Empire in India. The model might even offer some instructive
points of comparison with changes accompanying globalization today, as
some parts of the world enter quickly into the global system and begin
to adopt numerous aspects of cosmopolitan values and lifestyles, while
others remain on the peripheries, interacting only in limited ways with
the expanding markets and ideologies. The Roman case suggests that in
all instances of interaction between larger and more complex systems
and smaller less complex ones, we cannot assume that the larger will
dominate by force of political, economic, or military power. Indigenous
societies have diverse and often little-understood resources that enable
them to play determining roles in the outcomes of all such interactions.

✳ *Glossary* ✳

SOME TERMS I use in the text may not be familiar to readers. Here I provide a brief definition to indicate how each is used.

barbarian   As used by Greek and Roman writers, "other peoples" or "foreigners," usually with negative connotations.

elite   Individuals in a society with greater access to wealth and power than the majority of members possess.

farmstead   A farming unit including dwelling, outbuildings, and land.

fibula   A pin made of bronze or iron (more rarely silver or gold), similar in principle to a modern safety pin, used during the Late Bronze and Iron Ages and the Roman Period to fasten garments. Fibulae were often ornate, and their form and decoration were specific to particular times and places. Thus they can provide important information to the archaeologist about the date of a site and about contacts with other regions.

limes   The boundary, or limit, of the Roman Empire; specifically, the wall that connected the Rhine and Danube frontiers.

oppidum   *(plural oppida)* The term used by Caesar to designate the hilltop fortified settlements of Late Iron Age Gaul; now applied by archaeologists to all large fortified settlements of Late Iron Age temperate Europe.

runes   Letters that formed the first script of the Germanic peoples of central and northern Europe, developed sometime during the first or second century A.D. by groups familiar with the Latin alphabet.

temperate Europe   The part of Europe between the lands bordering the north shore of the Mediterranean Sea and the sub-Arctic regions.

terra sigillata   A variety of fine pottery used for tableware in the Roman world, red in color and with a smooth polished surface, often bearing relief ornament. It was manufactured in large quantities in the Roman provinces as well as in Italy.

vicus (plural vici)   A civilian settlement often associated with a Roman military base, whose inhabitants provided goods and services to the soldiers.

villa   In the Roman world, a rural residence together with a farming complex that included an often elaborate dwelling, workshops, and sometimes a bath system and a temple. There was great variety in the size and complexity of villas in the Roman provinces.

* Greek and Roman Authors *

I CITE a number of Greek and Roman authors in the text. Caesar and Tacitus I discuss in some detail, others I mention only in passing. Here I indicate when each author lived and in which language he wrote. All are represented in the Loeb Classical Library series of Greek and Latin texts with translations, published by Harvard University Press.

Julius Caesar   Lived from 100 to 44 B.C., Latin.
Cassius Dio   Lived from A.D. 155 to about 235, Greek.
Diodorus Siculus   Died sometime after 21 B.C., Greek.
Dionysius of Halicarnassus   Active late in the first century B.C., Greek.
Hecataeus   Active in late sixth and early fifth centuries B.C., Greek.
Herodotus   Lived from about 484 to about 425 B.C., Greek.
Josephus   Lived from A.D. 37 or 38 to about 100, Greek.
Livy   Lived from 59 B.C. to A.D. 17, Latin.
Pliny (the Elder)   Lived from A.D. 23 or 24 to 79, Latin.
Polybius   Lived from about 200 to about 120 B.C., Greek.
Posidonius   Lived from about 135 to about 51 B.C., Greek.
Strabo   Born about 64 B.C., died sometime after A.D. 21, Greek.
Tacitus   Lived from about A.D. 56 to about 117, Latin.

* Bibliographic Essay *

THE LITERATURE on the subjects discussed in this book is vast. I can mention only a portion here. The sources I cite in this section will lead the interested reader to the larger bibliographies. Complete citations for all books and articles mentioned here are in the bibliography in the next section.

CHAPTER 1: NATIVES AND ROMANS

Roman Disaster in the Teutoburg Forest

Reports on recent excavations: Schlüter 1992, 1995, 1997a and b. (For further discussion, see chapter 10.) Papers in Wiegels and Woesler 1995 examine many different aspects of the event and of the excavation results.

The Weapon Deposit at Illerup

Ilkjaer and Lønstrup 1983 and Ilkjaer 1997 present materials from the excavations. Broad examination of the north European weapon deposits: Fabech 1991 and 1996.

The Setting

Geography: Among many useful geographies of this region are Mutton 1968, Malmstrom 1971, and Unwin 1998. The *Diercke Weltatlas*, edited by Dornbusch and Kämmer (1996), contains excellent topographical and soil maps. Tichy 1990 reviews the geographical and climatological patterns.

Changes since the Roman Period: The best current overview is Küster's *Geschichte der Landschaft in Mitteleuropa* (1995). See also Pounds 1990.

The Cultural Landscape: Champion et al. 1984 and Cunliffe 1994 are useful syntheses of European prehistory. On the Paleolithic (Old Stone Age): Gamble 1986; on the Neolithic (New Stone Age): Whittle 1996. Bronze Age: Coles and Harding 1979.

Demography: Informative on estimating population sizes is McEvedy and Jones 1978. Vittinghoff 1990 and Lo Cascio in biblio 1994 are important recent discussions focusing on the Roman Period.

Origins and Growth of the Roman Empire

Overviews include Cary and Scullard 1975, C. Wells 1992, Crawford 1993, Scarre 1995, Burton 1996, Cornell 1996. Augustus's program of public architecture: Zanker 1990.

Why the Roman Empire Matters Today

Good starting points for the general reader interested in Rome are C. Wells's *The Roman Empire* (1992) and Scarre's *Historical Atlas of Ancient Rome* (1995). Awakening of interest in the Roman world during the Renaissance is treated in Kühn 1976, Hudson 1981, Sklenář 1983, Daniel and Renfrew 1988, Schnapp 1997.

Empires in World Perspective

Sinopoli's "The Archaeology of Empires" (1994) provides an excellent overview of empires as universal phenomena in human experience. Uruk expansion: Algaze 1993. Recent report about Hacinebi in Turkey: Stein et al. 1996. Akkadian Empire: Westerholz 1979, Assyrian: Larsen 1976, Mongol: Allsen 1987, Mogul: Richards 1993. In the New World, Aztec Empire: Smith 1996, Inca: D'Altroy 1992. Modern European empires: Pagden 1995 is a useful recent overview. Examples of postcolonial studies: Williams and Chrisman 1994, Prakash 1995, Cooper and Stoler 1997.

Different Ways of Knowing the Past

Texts and History: Introductions to critical theory: Dirks, Eley, and Ortner 1994; Calhoun 1995. Critical approaches to analysis of texts concerning indigenous peoples: Todorov 1984, Clifford and Marcus 1986, Said 1989, Mason 1990, Galloway 1992, Pratt 1992, Mignolo 1993 and 1994, Boone 1994, Schwartz 1994, Whitehead 1995, Hill (ed.) 1996. Applications of these ideas to the Roman Empire are to be found in Dyson 1975, van Es 1983, Timpe 1986 and 1989a, Dobesch 1989a and b, Christ 1995.

What Archaeology Can Tell Us: Many good textbooks in anthropological archaeology include Renfrew and Bahn 1996 and Sharer and Ashmore 1993. Integration of historical and archaeological sources: Feinman 1997. Some recent discussions of issues in interpretation of burial evidence: Chapman, Kinnes, and Randsborg 1981; Morris 1992; Struck 1993; Beck 1995; Jensen and Nielsen 1997. Role of personal ornaments and clothing in communicating information: Bogatyrev 1971, Kaiser 1990, Davis 1992, Chapman 1995, Eicher 1995, Sørensen 1997.

Analogy in Interpreting the Past: Pinker 1997 discusses the essential unity of human behaviors and responses, upon which the use of analogy in interpreting the past depends. Examples of analogy in historical and archaeological interpretation: Syme 1958, Wells 1974, Gruzinski and Rouveret 1976, Dyson 1985a and 1993, Bloemers 1991, Kopytoff 1993.

CHAPTER 2: EUROPE BEFORE THE ROMAN CONQUESTS

Discovery of a Prehistoric City

History of the Manching excavations: Krämer 1957, 1958, 1993.

New Perspectives on Indigenous Europeans

On Greek and Roman descriptions of Iron Age Europeans: Champion 1985 and 1995, Dobesch 1989a and b, Timpe 1989a, Rankin 1987 and 1995. Evidence for incipient writing in Late Iron Age communities: Jacobi 1974a, Krämer 1982, Laubenheimer 1987, Egg 1996.

Complex Societies of Late Prehistory

Overviews in English of the Late Bronze and Iron Ages: Champion et al. 1984, Pauli 1984, Wells 1984, Cunliffe 1994 and 1997, Collis 1997; many of the sites discussed in this section are treated in those works. Late Bronze Age settlement of Hascherkeller: Wells 1983. Grave at Hart an der Alz: Müller-Karpe 1955. Links between specific forms of jewelry and categories of persons: Pauli 1972. Communication of information about individual identity through belt plates, sword hilts, and pottery: Wells 1985, 1989, 1998a. Berlin-Lichterfelde: von Müller 1964. Torbrügge 1971 is a comprehensive study of water deposits, especially in European rivers, from prehistoric and historical times. Hallstatt: Kromer 1963. Mont Lassois: Joffroy 1960. Heuneburg: Kimmig 1983. Závist: Motyková, Drda, and Rybová 1988. Vix: Joffroy 1962. Hochdorf: Biel 1985a. Early Iron Age social structure: Arnold 1995, Dietler 1995. Feasting rituals represented by vessels in wealthy burials: Kossack 1970, Dietler 1990, Krausse 1996. Different perspectives on the interactions between temperate Europe and Mediterranean societies: Frankenstein and Rowlands 1978, Wells 1980, Bintliff 1984, Arafat and Morgan 1994, Sherratt 1995. Archaeology of the North European Plain: Herrmann 1989, Hässler 1991.

La Tène Style and Celts

Development of La Tène style and connection with peoples known as "Celts": Jacobsthal 1944; Pauli 1980; Frey 1991 and 1995a; Megaw and Megaw 1989, 1990, and 1995; Joachim 1995; Fitzpatrick 1996. Metalworking tools in La Gorge Meillet grave: Pauli 1978:458–60. Organization of craft production: P. Wells 1996. Jastorf and other traditions on the North European Plain: Müller 1985; Seyer 1985; Keiling 1989; Hässler 1988 and 1991; Hingst, Hummel, and Schutkowski 1990.

Migration and Interaction

Decline of Early Iron Age centers: see literature on the centers and trade with the Mediterranean, above. Flat-grave cemeteries of the succeeding period: Krämer 1964, Hodson 1968, Waldhauser 1978 and 1987. "Celtic migrations" of fourth and third centuries B.C.: Lorenz 1978, Pare 1991, Bujna and Szabó 1991, Kruta 1991a, Szabó 1991a, Vitali 1991, Frey 1995b, Jerem 1995. Anthony 1990 provides a valuable discussion of migration as a universal phenomenon; also Kaul and Martens 1995. Celtic mercenaries in Greek and other Mediterranean armies: Griffith 1935, Szabó 1991b.

CHAPTER 3: IRON AGE URBANIZATION

Urbanization and Complexity

Rankin 1987 provides a comprehensive overview of Classical texts concerning the indigenous Europeans called "Celts"; see also notes for chapter 2, above. Romans in southern Gaul, establishment of Gallia Narbonensis: Rivet 1988,

273

Dietler 1997. Warry 1995 discusses Roman confrontations with the invaders. Impact of invasions on Roman thinking: Timpe 1989a.

Late Iron Age Centers: The Oppida

Collis 1984 is the standard synthesis in English on the *oppida*. Other overviews: Cunliffe and Rowley 1976, Maier 1991, Woolf 1993a, Collis 1995, Drda and Rybová 1997. Dehn 1951 examines Caesar's descriptions of the *oppida* in Gaul. Manching is the most thoroughly investigated *oppidum*. A series of well-illustrated volumes present different categories of finds from the excavations there, including Jacobi 1974b on iron tools, van Endert 1991 on bronze objects, Gebhard 1989 on glass ornaments and 1991 on fibulae, Maier 1970 on painted pottery, Stöckli 1979 on plain and imported wares. Tarodunum: Weber 1989. Rectangular enclosures, or *Viereckschanzen*: Bittel, Schiek, and Müller 1990; *Archäologie in Deutschland*, vol. 4, 1995—see especially articles by Reichenberger and Krause. Schwarz 1975 on excavations at Holzhausen is a major study of these sites. More recent discussions include Reichenberger and Schaich 1996, Lehmann 1997.

Growth of Complex Economies

Introduction to Iron Age coinage: Allen and Nash 1980. Greek models for first Iron Age coinages: Mannsperger 1981. Steuer 1987 and Kellner 1990 argue that a money economy developed at the *oppida*. Meduna 1980 and Gebhard 1989 identify a fundamental shift in manufacturing, from a largely domestic-based pattern to one centered around specialized workshop production. Typology and distribution of Nauheim fibulae: Werner 1955. Drescher 1955 and Furger-Gunti 1977 report on experiments carried out to determine the complexity of the manufacturing process and the amount of time required to produce a Nauheim fibula. Rathje 1975 discusses the disproportionately larger need for energy for information processing in more complex societies; Haselgrove 1988 applies this idea to the Late Iron Age. Intensifying interactions between central and northern Europe: Klindt-Jensen 1950, Kaul 1991, Wells 1994. Blue glass bracelets in the Netherlands: Roymans and van Rooijen 1993. Hodde excavations: Hvass 1985. Borremose: Martens 1994. Møllegårdsmarken cemetery at Gudme: Thrane 1988.

Society and Everyday Life

On Caesar's remarks about Gallic society compared to the archaeology: Crumley 1974. Celtic society in general: Duval 1991. We learn about everyday life primarily from excavations of settlement sites. Overviews of the evidence: James 1993, Lloyd-Morgan 1995, Green (ed.) 1995. Textile production and clothing: Hald 1980. Religion: Pauli 1986 and 1992, Green 1995a, Webster 1995a. Gournay-sur-Aronde: Brunaux, Meniel, and Rapin 1980; Brunaux 1988. Druids: Ross 1995, Green 1997. Grave at Dühren: Fischer 1981, Polenz 1982. Reinheim: Keller 1965. Wederath 1216: Haffner 1989.

Interaction and Identity

Features of the "international warrior style" are discussed by Frey 1986 and Völling 1992. Homogeneity of fibulae in northern and southern temperate Europe: Müller 1994, Rieckhoff 1995.

CHAPTER 4: THE ROMAN CONQUESTS

Roman Conquests in Perspective

Good recent overviews are Badian 1968, Dyson 1985b, C. Wells 1992, Whittaker 1994. Julius Caesar's *The Gallic War* provides a firsthand account by the Roman general of his conquests in France and the other parts of ancient Gaul. The Edwards translation includes the original Latin on each left page, English on the right. The Wiseman translation contains many illustrations of relevant archaeological materials, as well as a helpful introduction.

Sources of Information

Colin Wells's (1995a) section on the Roman Empire in the recent *Guide to Historical Literature* of the American Historical Society provides an annotated bibliography of relevant works concerning especially the textual sources. Overview of both historical and archaeological sources: Duval 1994. Marcus Caelius stone: Busch 1995. Military diplomas: Dietz 1984, Mann and Roxan 1988, Eck and Roxan 1998. Regensburg inscription: Dietz and Fischer 1996, p. 113. Reddé et al. 1995 reports recent results of excavations at Alesia; Sievers 1995 discusses the weapons. Discoveries near Oberammergau of direct evidence from battles between Roman troops and native defenders: Zanier 1994a and b and 1997. Marktbreit: Pietsch, Timpe, and Wamser 1991; Pietsch 1995. Waldgirmes: von Schnurbein, Wigg, and Wigg 1995.

Conquest of Gaul: Historical Accounts

Useful recent discussions of Caesar's account: Drinkwater 1983, Polenz 1985, Dobesch 1989a and b, Timpe 1989a, Goudineau 1990, Christ 1995. My text is based largely on these works.

Rome in Southern Gaul: Rivet 1988 and Dietler 1997 synthesize the evidence.

Caesar's Campaigns, 58–51 B.C.: Suebi and Ariovistus: Peschel 1978a. Warry 1995 discusses Caesar's troop strength and tactics.

Caesar's Army: Discussions of the Roman army at the time of Caesar include Watson 1969, Grant 1974, Keppie 1984, Dixon and Southern 1992, Goldsworthy 1996.

Recent Critiques: Luttwak 1976 and Isaac 1990 (1992) provide different perspectives on the question of Rome's grand strategy. Importance of military ideology to the Roman elite: Harris 1979, Millett 1990a, Woolf 1993b.

Native Societies East of the Rhine

Although there has been no systematic study of groups east of the Rhine and their relations with the Roman world during and after Caesar's conquest of Gaul, there is abundant archaeological evidence. Syntheses in English: Todd 1975, 1992. Others: Capelle 1976, Jankuhn 1976, Motyková 1976, Pescheck 1978, Peschel 1978b, Seyer 1988, Hässler 1991, Joachim 1991, Lenz-Bernhard and Bernhard 1992, Becker 1996. Farriss's 1984 study of Yucatan and Hill's 1996 work on the Caribbean region offer useful models for comparison with the Roman case.

Framing the Question: See notes for chapter 5.

End of the *Oppida*: Evidence for decline and abandonment of the *oppida*: von Schnurbein 1993, Rieckhoff 1995, Wieland 1996. Recent excavations at Kelheim: Wells 1993. Anthropological studies of the decline of complex societies, providing potential models for the *oppida*: Tainter 1988, Yoffee and Cowgill 1988. Post-*oppidum* period graves in southern Bavaria: Krämer 1985, Rieckhoff 1995. In northern Bavaria, Altendorf: Pescheck 1978, Aubstadt: Völling 1995. Regensburg-Harting: Rieckhoff 1995. Examples of the complexity of burial practices: Chapman, Kinnes, and Randsborg 1981; Schultze 1992. Iron objects from Manching: Jacobi 1974b. Change in burial practice at the time of the *oppida*: Krämer 1985. Skeletal remains from the settlement deposits at Manching: Lange 1983, Hahn 1992, Schröter 1997.

Linking of post-*oppidum* graves and settlements in southern Bavaria with "Germans": Glüsing 1965 and 1989; Rieckhoff-Pauli 1983; Rieckhoff 1992, 1993, 1995. Völling 1994a examines several important types of fibula, 1994b belthooks. Argument that the post-*oppidum* finds represent mainly indigenous people, not immigrants: P. Wells 1995a and b. Problems linking historically documented migrations with archaeological evidence: Kaul and Martens 1995. Smaller late occupations at the *oppida*: Gebhard 1993, Wieland 1993. Diversity of pottery on post-*oppidum* settlements: Fischer 1988, Rieckhoff 1995. Eching: Winghart 1986. Auerberg: Ulbert 1975, 1995. Kempten: Mackensen 1978. Cologne: Carroll-Spillecke 1995.

Conquests East of the Rhine

In addition to works already cited, useful summaries of the historical background as it pertains to the lands along the Rhine and Danube are Timpe 1978, Kunow 1987, Bernhard 1990, Dietz 1995a.

South of the Danube: Schön 1986. Döttenbichl near Oberammergau: Zanier 1994a and b and 1997. Christlein 1982 and Fischer 1990 interpret the evidence to indicate sparse population in southern Bavaria at the time of the conquest. Heiligmann 1991 and 1995 and Wieland 1993 argue against this idea. Von Schnurbein 1985 and 1993 discuss reasons for the paucity of indigenous sites known from the period of the conquest. Küster 1986 and 1995 present results of his analyses of the plant remains.

Roman Military Activity across the Middle and Lower Rhine: Debate concerning Rome's intentions east of the lower Rhine: Timpe 1971 and 1995, Christ 1977, Welwei 1986, Kühlborn 1988, Wolters 1990a, Lehmann 1991 and 1995, Hanson 1997. Isaac 1990 critically examines evidence for planning and motivation on the part of the Roman military leaders; also Mann 1986. The military history of this region is reviewed by Schönberger 1985. Tongeren: Vanderhoeven 1996. Metzler's 1995 study of the Titelberg is a rich source of information. There is good reason to think that the small scale and relative lack of complexity of the peoples east of the Rhine prevented the Roman armies from successfully conquering those regions: see Willems 1986:383. Build-up of the Rhine defensive network: Gechter 1987, Bechert and Willems 1995. Industries in Rhineland: Horn 1987. Lippe Valley bases: von Schnurbein 1981, Asskamp 1989, Kühlborn 1989a and b and 1991. Bases east of Mainz: Schönberger and Simon 1976. Campaigns and Roman forts north of middle Danube: Bálek and Šedo 1996; Bálek, Droberjar, and Šedo 1994, Friesinger and Krinzinger 1997. Economic stimulation of Roman troops on the frontiers: Groenman-van Waateringe 1980, Roymans 1983, Drinkwater 1990, Millett 1990b. On *vici*: see notes for chapter 6.

Incorporating Indigenous Peoples into the Empire

Timpe 1989b and 1992a and b explore the changes in Roman relations with the peoples north of the Alps. Barrett, Fitzpatrick, and Macinnes 1989 is an important collection of papers on interactions between the Roman administration and the native peoples. Braund 1984 and 1989 and Pitts 1989 address political relationships with potentates outside of the empire. Roman commerce with central Europe before the conquest: Werner 1978, Fitzpatrick 1985, Svobodová 1985, Will 1987, Feugère and Rolley 1991, Woolf 1993b and c. Indigenous peoples as decision-making agents: Bell 1992, Cowgill 1993. Goeblingen-Nospelt graves: Haffner 1974, Metzler 1984, Böhme-Schönberger 1993. Openwork ornament on the scabbards: Werner 1977. Heimstetten graves: Keller 1984. Reinecke 1957 and Krämer 1962 place them in the developmental sequence of the Late La Tène tradition, while Menke 1974 and Mackensen 1978 view them as representative of outsiders who moved into Bavaria.

CHAPTER 5: IDENTITIES AND PERCEPTIONS

Roman Perceptions of Indigenous Europeans

Texts: Useful recent discussions of imperial literature concerning indigenous peoples include Hartog 1988, Said 1989 and 1993, Ferguson and Whitehead 1992, Friedman 1992 and 1994, Schwartz 1994, Lightfoot 1995, Whitehead 1995, Hill 1996 and 1998, Pels 1997, Stoler and Cooper 1997. Such works provide a good cross-cultural context in which we can view the specific case of Romans and native Europeans. Background concerning Greek and Roman perceptions of other peoples: Müller 1972. On portrayals by Classical writers of native Europeans: Thompson 1965, Evans 1981, Timpe 1986, Rankin 1987, Dobesch 1991, Champion 1995, Koch and Carey 1995. More specialized treatments: Walser 1956 and 1995, Wenskus 1961 and 1986, Zeitler 1986, Bringmann 1989, Dobesch 1989a and b, Flach 1995.

Pictorial Representations: European barbarians in the arts of Greece and Rome: Andreae 1991, Ferris 1994 and 1997, De Caro 1996. Trajan's column: Rossi 1971, Richmond 1982, Packer 1997. Marcus Aurelius's column: Zwikker 1941, Caprino et al. 1955. Coins as instruments of Roman propaganda about barbarian peoples: Levi 1952, Overbeck 1993.

Celts and Germans: Linguistic Evidence

Language and ethnicity: Eriksen 1992 and 1993. Language and early peoples of Europe: Schmidt 1979; Markey 1986; Untermann 1989 and 1993; Hines 1995, 1996, 1998; Evans 1995. Earliest datable evidence for languages of temperate Europe: Kruta 1991b. Inscribed sherds from Manching: Krämer 1982. Sword from Port: Wyss 1954. Coin inscriptions: Allen and Nash 1980. Negau helmet: Reinecke 1942. Meldorf fibula: Düwel and Gebühr 1981. Inscriptions in Germanic languages from northern Europe: Neumann 1983 and 1986, Antonsen 1986, Page 1987, Stoklund 1995 and 1996. Distribution of Celtic place names: Rix 1954. Complex language situation of region: Meid 1986.

Archaeological Evidence

Celts: Many books about the Iron Age Celts have appeared recently. Accessible works in English include Roymans 1990, Moscati et al. 1991, James 1993, Green (ed.) 1995, C. Wells 1995b, and Cunliffe 1997. Chapman 1992 is critical about the reality of the groups known to us as Celts. Wells 1998b includes a summary discussion of some of these issues.

Germans: There are fewer general works in English about the ancient Germans; Todd 1992 is the most accessible. Walser 1956 is fundamental for questions of linking Caesar's descriptions with archaeological evidence. Beck 1986 and Krüger 1988 contain important papers, and Wolfram 1995 is a good summary. Central and eastern Europe: von Uslar 1938, Shchukin 1989. On problems of distinguishing between Celts and Germans, and on the significance of that distinction: Hachmann, Kossack, and Kuhn 1962; Pescheck 1969 and 1977; Birkhan 1970; Rosenstock 1985 and 1986; Peschel 1988 and 1989; Schlette 1988; Rosenstock and Wamser 1989; Steidl 1991; Stöckli 1993; P. Wells 1995a and b and 1998a.

Dynamics of Identity and the Roman Conquests

A few works on cultural identity and ethnicity that are particularly pertinent to issues of Celts, Germans, Romans, and the changes that Europeans experienced are Barth 1969; Patterson 1975; Hastrup 1982; Geary 1983; O'Brien 1986; Wallman 1986; Urla 1993; Wilson 1993; A. P. Cohen 1994; R. Cohen 1994; Modood, Beishon, and Virdee 1994; Romanucci-Ross and DeVos 1995. On the relationships between material culture and identity: Hodder 1982, Shennan 1989, Kobylinski 1991, Hides 1996, Jones 1996 and 1997, Dongoske et al. 1997.

Tribalization and Rome: On tribes as universal phenomena on the peripheries of state societies: Fried 1967, Whitehead 1992. Hill 1996 traces the process of tribalization in North America during the nineteenth century, illustrating mechanisms that might shed light on the Roman Period European context. Also relevant are papers in Ferguson and Whitehead 1992. Roman involvement in southern Gaul from the third century B.C.: Rivet 1988, Dietler 1997. Ament 1984 and 1986 propose models for the formation of Germanic groups at the time of Roman presence in Gaul. Flögeln settlement: Schmid and Zimmermann 1976. Harsefeld cemetery: Wegewitz 1937, Hässler 1977.

Indigenous Responses to Roman Categories: Native response to Roman categories: Meid 1986, Woolf 1997. Start of weapon burial in graves at this time: Schultze 1986 and 1988. Wederath: Haffner 1989. Völling 1992 and 1993 are important studies of spurs in burials and their role in marking high-status men, both within and outside the imperial borders. Braund 1984 and 1989 explores the concept of the "friendly king" outside the Roman imperial borders. Mušov grave: Böhme 1991, Tejral 1992.

CHAPTER 6: DEVELOPMENT OF THE FRONTIER ZONE

The Roman Frontier in Europe

Important recent studies of the Roman frontier include C. Wells 1972, 1976, and 1996; Mann 1975a and b; Mócsy 1978; Dyson 1985a and b and 1995; Willems 1986; Maxfield 1987; Maxfield and Dobson 1991; Whittaker 1989 and 1994; Bowman 1994a; Brun, van der Leeuw, and Whittaker 1993; Webster 1994; Elton 1996; Groenman–van Waateringe et al. 1997. Recent discussions of implications and complications of the concept "Romanization" include Freeman 1993, 1996, 1997a; Barrett 1997a and b; Whittaker 1997.

New Approaches to the Frontier

Development of Roman studies in the late nineteenth century and the largely uncritical acceptance of ancient texts: Kühn 1976, Marchand 1996, Freeman 1997b, Schnapp 1997.

Rome and the Provincial Populace

Concept of elites: Marvick 1996. Roman policy of co-opting indigenous elites: Brunt 1976, Flaig 1995. Spread of Roman ideology: Woolf 1995 and 1996.

The Army and Indigenous Peoples

The Army on the Frontiers: Good discussions of the Roman army on the European frontiers include Davies 1974 and 1989, Gechter 1987, Kunow 1987, Keppie 1991, Bowman 1994a and b, Campbell 1994, von Schnurbein 1997. Alföldy 1968 and Holder 1980 deal specifically with the auxiliary units. Induction of men from conquered regions into the army: Willems 1986, Dietz 1995a. Heterogeneous nature and indigenous culture of auxiliary troops: Haynes 1993. Behavior of Roman troops indicating indigenous origins: van Enckevort and Willems 1994. Firmus gravestone: Gechter 1987. Finds at frontier forts that suggest soldiers from across the frontier: von Uslar 1934 and 1980, Schönberger and Simon 1980, Kühlborn and Reichmann 1992, Beckmann 1995. Germans in Roman service: Bang 1906, Waas 1965, Gechter and Kunow 1983. Titelberg: Metzler 1995. Petrisberg at Trier: Gilles 1992, Metzler 1995:550.

Rebellions: Dyson 1975 is an important study of native rebellions in the Roman provinces. Batavian revolt: Willems 1986:401, Schmitt 1993.

Forts and Natives: Placement of forts in the landscape: Kunow 1987, Bechert and Willems 1995. Relations between military bases and communities around them: Bloemers 1983, Sommer 1988a, Pfahl and Reuter 1996. Marktbreit: Pietsch 1995. Waldgirmes: von Schnurbein, Wigg, and Wigg 1995. Regensburg-Kumpfmühl: Faber 1994.

Vici: General discussions in Sommer 1988a and b and 1991. Lahr-Dillingen: Struck 1983.

Soldiers and Native Women: Useful discussions in Watson 1969:133–42, Campbell 1978, Roxan 1991.

Supplying the Troops: Economy of the European provinces: Greene 1986, Wacher 1987 parts 7 and 8, Pleket 1990, Frézouls 1990, Wells 1999. Supply of foodstuffs to military bases: Peacock and Williams 1986, Whittaker 1994. Of manufactured goods: Oldenstein 1976 and 1985, Sommer 1988a, Bishop and Coulston 1993, Gschwind 1997. Garbsch 1982 provides a good overview of *terra sigillata* production and circulation; also on pottery: Czysz 1985 and 1987. Changes in indigenous economic systems brought by troop demands: Groenman-van Waateringe 1980, Birley 1981, Roymans 1983, Bloemers 1994, Crumley 1994. Iron-producing sites across the frontier: Jażdżewski 1965:153–54, Grünert 1988, Leube 1989, Henning 1991. Schwabegg kilns: Czysz 1987.

Supply, Production, and Identity: Interpreting persistence of native styles of production in terms of resistance: Hingley 1997; see also chapters 7 and 9. Idea that the objects people use affect their identity and worldview: Douglas and Isherwood 1979, Csikszentimahaly and Rochberg-Halton 1981, Barrett 1994, Thomas 1996. Heterogeneity of material culture in the frontier zone: Seidel 1996.

CHAPTER 7: PERSISTENCE OF TRADITION

Post-Conquest Continuities

Presence of Iron Age–type pottery on virtually all early Roman sites: von Schnurbein 1985, Fischer 1988, Planck 1988. Continuity of settlement from prehistoric into Roman times: Wightman 1970 and 1985, Heger 1980, Heiligmann 1995.

Settlement Architecture

Significance of houses in expression of cultural values: Samson 1991, Blanton 1994, Colloredo-Mansfield 1994, Grinker 1996. Rijswijk: Bloemers 1978. Roymans 1995 explores the farmhouse architecture of the early Roman Period in the Netherlands. Late Iron Age–style settlements in Roman Period in Hungary: Gabler 1991 and 1994. Continuities in indigenous architecture: Wieland 1993, Lenz 1995. The case of the Amish is presented in Schwieder and Schwieder 1975, Hostetler 1993. Berching-Pollanten: Fischer, Rieckhoff-Pauli, and Spindler 1984. Use of Late La Tène style materials well into the Roman Period: Maier 1983a. Sequence in the Isar valley of Bavaria: Fischer 1985; Struck 1992, 1995, 1996. Straubing: Prammer 1989.

Manufactured Goods

Pottery: Ethnographic studies of pottery that provide useful perspectives include David, Sterner, and Gavua 1988; Braun 1991; Dietler and Herbich 1994; Gosselain 1992; Crown 1994, MacEachern 1998. Comparison of Late Iron Age–style pottery from prehistoric and Roman contexts: von Schnurbein 1993:246–47. Wieland 1993 and Flügel 1996 are important recent studies of such pottery in Roman contexts. Gradual replacement of native ceramics by Roman styles: Willis 1996.

Fibulae: Böhme-Schönberger 1994 is an excellent recent discussion of the use of fibulae in the Roman Period; also Rieckhoff 1975, Völling 1994a. Fibulae from Manching: Gebhard 1991. First-century A.D. jewelry shop at Augsburg: Bakker 1985.

Clothing: Eicher 1995 and Hendrickson 1996 are useful collections of papers about clothing and identity. Clothing of the northwestern Roman provinces: Böhme 1985, Wild 1985.

Burial Practice

Funerary and burial rituals in Rome and in the Roman provinces: Jones 1987a and 1993, Haffner 1989, Fasold 1992 and 1993. Weapon graves in the provinces: De Laet and van Doorselaer 1962, Engels 1972. Rohrbach grave: Böhme 1978. Wederath cemetery: Haffner 1989, Grave 2370: Abegg 1989. Kempten cemetery: Mackensen 1978. Bad Cannstatt: Nierhaus 1959.

Ritual

Discussion of archaeology and ritual: papers in Garwood et al. 1991. Haselgrove 1995 and 1996a and b explore questions of continuity of settlement and ritual activity from the Iron Age into the Roman Period, particularly in northern Gaul; also Goudineau, Fauduet and Coulon 1994. Empel: Roymans and Derks 1994. Water deposits: Torbrügge 1971. Seine Source: Deyts 1983. Well at Buch: Planck 1978. Tiefenau: Müller 1990. Iron hoards from the Late Iron Age: Rybová and Motyková 1983. Fibula hoard from Bregenz: Konrad 1994. Nuits-Saint-Georges: Fauduet and Pommeret 1985. Burned offering places: Maier 1985a and 1985b.

Gauting: Egger 1984. Goddess Sirona: Fischer 1991:35–36, Green 1995b, and Faust et al. 1996:171–73.

Conclusion

On the concept of cultural resistance: Stoller 1995. Scott 1985 and 1990 explore resistance in modern colonial contexts. Other examples of resistance and its archaeological indicators: Guamán Poma de Ayala 1978; Le Gall 1983; Adorno 1986; Stern 1987; Miller, Rowlands, and Tilley 1989; Knaut 1995; Alcock 1997; Stoler and Cooper 1997.

CHAPTER 8: TOWN, COUNTRY, AND CHANGE

New Towns and Cities in the Frontier Zone

The map of Roman urban centers in Alcock 1993:130, fig. 45, shows the sparseness of such places in the European provinces compared to the Mediterranean regions. Growth of towns: Frere 1977, Poulter 1987, Bloemers 1990, Vermeulen 1995. Eager adoption by indigenous elites north of the Alps of Mediterranean-style architecture: Drinkwater 1987, Jones 1987b, King 1990:66–67, Trunk 1991. Such architecture largely restricted to elite contexts: Hingley 1997; and to urban sites: Whittaker 1997. Nijmegen: Willems 1990, Roymans 1995. Cologne: Hellenkemper 1987, Carroll-Spillecke 1995. Settlements of the Ubii at Cologne: Gechter 1990 and 1991. Trier: Cüppers 1984, 1990, Gilles 1992. Mainz: Decker and Selzer 1976, Rupprecht 1990. Augsburg: von Schnurbein 1985. Auerberg: Ulbert 1975, 1995.

Rural Landscapes

Villas: Percival 1976 and 1987, Agache 1978, Smith 1978 and 1997, Todd (ed.) 1978, Wightman 1978 and 1985, Gaubatz-Sattler 1994, Slofstra 1995, Haselgrove 1996a and b. New approaches to rural landscapes: Ferdière 1988, Hingley 1989. Mayen: Percival 1976:36–38. Oberndorf: Czysz 1989. Roymans 1995 and 1996 are important studies of rural sites in the Netherlands. Rural economy during the Roman Period: Haversath 1984, Rupp 1991, papers in Bender and Wolff 1994.

Indigenous Responses to Change

New Opportunities in the Frontier Provinces: New economic opportunities presented by the establishment of Roman infrastructure: Todd 1978. Tombstone of a Roman soldier-turned-merchant: Kolník 1978. Owner of brick factory in southwest Germany: Kuhnen 1994. Kempten cemetery: Mackensen 1978. Nijmegen Grave 8: Koster 1993.

Integrated Ideologies: Native Deities in Roman Form: These goddesses are discussed in Green 1992 and 1995b. Specialized studies—Epona: Euskirchen 1993. Mother goddesses: von Petrikovits 1987. Nehalennia: Hondius-Crone 1955.

CHAPTER 9: TRANSFORMATION INTO NEW SOCIETIES

Creating New Societies in the Frontier Provinces

On the new societies comprised of native peoples and newcomers to the provinces, in addition to works already cited, see Hassall 1987, Goudineau 1991, Burnham 1995. Cavalli-Sforza, Menozzi, and Piazza 1994 argue from their genetic studies that the populations of Europe show little evidence for large-scale migrations. Lightfoot and Martinez 1995 provide a useful general model for the study of frontier zones.

Disruption on the Danube Frontier: The Marcomannic Wars

On the Marcomannic Wars: Franke 1930, Dietz 1995b:138–54, Dietz and Fischer 1996:74–83. Roman military bases north of the middle Danube: Droberjar 1993 and 1994, Tejral 1992 and 1997.

Sources of Information about the Provincial Societies

Evidence of personal names is discussed by Neumann 1986 and Untermann 1989. Dietz and Weber 1982 show the limited kinds of information available about identity, diversity, and migration in the provinces in southern Germany.

Globalization and the Roman Empire

See general works cited for chapter 4 on Roman expansion. In several studies, Woolf has examined critically the spread of influence and ideology: 1990 and 1996. Friedman 1992 and 1994 and Appadurai 1996 offer views on globalization that can be useful for examining the Roman Empire. Emergence of a uniform civilization after the mid-first century A.D.: Czysz 1995:184. Movement by individuals between provinces: Dietz and Weber 1982, Wierschowski 1995.

Rise of Regional Consciousness

Von Schnurbein 1982 examines regional differences between peoples in neighboring provinces. Horn 1987 discusses distinctive developments in the Roman Rhineland.

Native Resistance and the Re-Creation of Traditional Symbols

On topic of resistance, see also chapter 7. Said 1993, Scott 1985, Spivak 1988, and Ortner 1995 deal with resistance among indigenous peoples in modern colonial and postcolonial contexts. Maya resistance to the Spanish conquerors: Jones 1989. Stoller 1995 examines patterns of resistance in modern Africa. Cummins 1994 shows how native textiles in South America contained messages unknown to the Spanish. Mattingly 1997 examines the subject of resistance in the context of the Roman Empire. Hingley 1997 and Webster 1997a and b address this theme in Roman Britain. Key studies of the "Celtic Renaissance," or the resurgence of the La Tène style, during the late second and third centuries A.D., are MacMullen

1965 and Schleiermacher 1965. For related syntheses, see Horn 1987 and Czysz 1995. Wieland 1993 and Flügel 1996 examine ceramic evidence pertaining to this phenomenon (see chapter 7). Related developments in ornamental metalwork: Böhme 1972, Werner 1977, Böhme-Schönberger 1994. Connection between resistance and religion: Webster 1995b.

New Creations in the Frontier Zone

Pottery: Belgic Ware: Willems 1986, Horn 1987. Raetian Ware: Czysz 1995, Struck 1996. Norican Ware: Maier 1983b.

Domestic Architecture: Bondorf villa: Planck 1975, Gaubatz-Sattler 1994.

Burial Practice: Netherlands cemeteries: Willems 1986. Burials at Cologne: Naumann-Steckner 1997. Wederath: Haffner 1989. Regensburg: von Schnurbein 1977. Ergolding: Struck 1992, 1995, 1996.

Ritual Structures: Late Iron Age rectangular enclosures: see notes for chapter 3. Trunk 1991 is an extensive analysis of Roman Period temples and of their links with the prehistoric structures. Faimingen: Weber 1981; Eingartner, Eschbaumer, and Weber 1993. Altbachtal ritual complex: Kyll 1966, Scheid 1995, Gilles 1996. Jupiter-giant columns: Bauchhenss and Noelke 1981, Bauchhenss 1984, Green 1986, Fischer 1991, Faust et al. 1996:202–10. Davidson 1988 examines some of the motifs associated with these columns. Early Christianity in the frontier provinces: Merrifield 1987, chapter 4; James 1988, chapter 4; King 1990, chapter 9. Iron Age carved standing stones, and Gundestrup cauldron: Megaw and Megaw 1989. Bronze and gold tree at Manching: Maier 1990.

Conclusion

Formation of larger tribal confederations during the third century: see chapter 11. Küster 1986 and 1995 document evidence in the vegetation record for continuity of land use practices from Late Iron Age to Roman times.

CHAPTER 10: IMPACT ACROSS THE FRONTIER

Cross-Frontier Interactions and the Roman Provinces

On supplies that the Roman provinces obtained from across the frontier, see chapter 6. Hedeager 1992 discusses the importance of the knowledge of the provincial Roman world that returning auxiliaries brought home with them.

The Evidence

Archaeology: First comprehensive study of Roman imports beyond the frontier: Eggers 1951. Among the most useful subsequent investigations are Schmid 1982; Kunow 1983, 1985, and 1986; Godłowski 1985; Hansen 1987 and 1995; Wolters 1990b, 1991, 1995, and 1997; Stupperich 1991 and 1995; von Schnurbein and Erdrich 1992; Musil 1994; von Schnurbein 1995; Erdrich 1995; Franzius 1995;

Roman Reflections 1996; Heiligmann 1997. Many of these studies include consideration of the Roman textual sources.

Texts: Goods from beyond the frontier imported by the provinces: Hansen 1987, Tausend 1987, Whittaker 1994. Amber trade: Bohnsack and Follmann 1976. North American fur trade: Saum 1965. Tolsum tablet: Boeles 1951:129–30. Merchants in the frontier provinces: Schlippschuh 1974. Gravestone of Q. Atilius Primus: Kolník 1978. Service by "Germans" (peoples from regions east of the frontier) in the Roman army: Bang 1906, Waas 1965, Alföldy 1968. Importance of military service in relations across the frontier: Mann 1986. Client or "friendly" kings: Braund 1984 and 1989, Pitts 1989, Wolters 1990c, Kehne 1997 (see chapter 5). Diplomatic relations and treaties: Stahl 1989.

Interpretation

Recent work by Dyson 1993, Isaac 1993, Kopytoff 1993, Roymans 1993, Whittaker 1993, and C. Wells 1996 has been instrumental in changing our views of the Roman frontier. Von Schnurbein 1995 notes the role played by the division of Germany during the Cold War on the thinking of European scholars about the Roman frontier.

Arminius: Arminius has been the subject of numerous studies, from highly romanticized and nationalistic views in the eighteenth and nineteenth centuries, to more balanced and critical ones in recent years. Important discussions: Timpe 1970 and 1995, Callies 1973, Lehmann 1989 and 1995, Demandt 1995, Maurach 1995, van Wickevoort Crommelin 1995, Wiegels and Woesler 1995.

Phases of Interaction: Archaeology and Historical Dates: Archaeology of the regions across the frontier that were importing Roman goods: Reichmann 1979, Keiling 1989, Leube 1989, Schmidt and Nitzsche 1989, von Uslar 1990, Schwarz 1991, Steuer 1994, Frank 1997. The phases of importation are defined by Erdrich 1995 and von Schnurbein 1995.

Geography of Interaction: Hedeager 1978 developed the model for quality of imports and distance from the frontier; P. Wells 1992 builds on her scheme. Frontier zone—Westick: Schoppa 1970. Similar patterns across the frontier and in the provinces: Wigg and Wigg 1994. Rheindorf cemetery: Eggers 1951, Waugh 1993. Mušov grave: Böhme 1991, Tejral 1992. Frontier zone to the Elbe—Weapon graves east of the frontier: Weski 1982, Schultze 1986. Putensen cemetery: Wegewitz 1972, Roggenbuck 1983. Siemiechów: Jażdżewska 1986 and 1992. Marwedel graves: Laux 1992. Feddersen Wierde: Haarnagel 1975, 1979, Haarnagel and Schmid 1984, Schmid 1994. Warburg-Daseburg: Günther 1990. Beyond the Elbe—Jakuszowice: Godłowski 1991. Iron production in Poland: Piaskowski 1985. Łęg Piekarski: Wielowiejski 1989. Hedegård: Madsen 1995a and b and 1997. The literature on Gudme and Lundeborg is growing rapidly: Thrane 1988 and 1993; Thomsen, Blaesild, Hardt, and Michaelsen 1993; Michaelsen and Sørensen 1993 and 1996; Michaelsen 1994; Nielsen, Randsborg, and Thrane 1994; Thomsen 1997. Rise of political center at Himlingøje on Zealand: Hansen 1995.

Weapon deposits in Denmark and neighboring countries: Engelhardt 1863–69, 1866, 1867; Ilkjaer and Lønstrup 1983; Ilkjaer 1997; Fabech 1991 and 1996; see also chapter 1.

Significance of the Cross-Frontier Interactions

Effects beyond the Frontiers: Economic prosperity generated by Roman demand for goods: *Roman Reflections in Scandinavia* 1996. Studies of the effects of cross-cultural imports in other contexts, with implications for understanding our case: Rogers 1990, Thomas 1991, Helms 1994, Orlove 1997. Importance of acquiring Roman imports to the emerging social system in Denmark: Hansen 1996. Development of early Germanic art: Haseloff 1981. Amalgamation of indigenous and provincial Roman techniques and styles: von Carnap-Bornheim 1997. Origin and development of runes: Antonsen 1986, Page 1987, Odenstedt 1990, Stoklund 1995 and 1996, Rausig 1996, Düwel 1997.

Effects on the Roman Provinces: see chapter 6 on supplies acquired by the provinces from the lands beyond the frontier. Information Rome had about peoples of northern Europe: Kehne 1995.

Chapter 11: Conclusion

The Crises of the Third Century

Crises of the third century in the Roman world: see histories of Rome cited in chapter 1; King and Henig 1981. Overwhelming of the *limes*: Nuber 1990, Kuhnen 1992.

New Confederations in Temperate Europe

Formation of new tribal confederations during the third century and later: Geary 1988, Demandt 1993, Hedeager 1993. Origins of the Alamanni: Christlein 1979, Geuenich 1997, Nuber 1997. Of the Franks: Périn and Feffer 1987, James 1988. Of the Goths: Bierbrauer 1994, Heather 1996. Runder Berg: *Der Runde Berg bei Urach*, 1974–84. Haarhausen kilns and transfer of ceramic technology: Dušek 1992, Stoll 1993, Bücker 1997.

Natives and Romans in World Anthropological Context

Studies of other contexts that compare in significant ways with the Roman-native interactions in temperate Europe: Cooper 1994, Lockhart 1994, Fane 1996, Cooper and Stoler 1997, Kepecs 1997.

* Bibliography of Works Cited *

Abegg, A. 1989. Grab 2370: Eine wohlhabende Frau aus Belginum. In Haffner, pp. 299–316.

Adorno, R. 1986. *Guaman Poma: Writing and Resistance in Colonial Peru*. Austin: University of Texas Press.

Agache, R. 1978. *La Somme pré-romaine et romaine*. Amiens: Société des antiquaires de Picardie.

Alcock, S. E. 1993. *Graecia Capta: The Landscapes of Roman Greece*. Cambridge: Cambridge University Press.

———. 1997. Greece: A Landscape of Resistance? In Mattingly, pp. 103–15.

Alföldy, G. 1968. *Die Hilfstruppen der römischen Provinz Germania Inferior*. Düsseldorf: Rheinland-Verlag.

Algaze, G. 1993. *The Uruk World System: The Dynamics of Expansion of Early Mesopotamian Civilization*. Chicago: University of Chicago Press.

Allen, D. F., and D. Nash. 1980. *The Coins of the Ancient Celts*. Edinburgh: Edinburgh University Press.

Allsen, T. T. 1987. *Mongol Imperialism*. Berkeley: University of California Press.

Ament, H. 1984. Der Rhein und die Ethnogenese der Germanen. *Praehistorische Zeitschrift* 59:37–47.

———. 1986. Die Ethnogenese der Germanen aus der Sicht der Vor- und Frühgeschichte. In W. Bernhard and A. Kandler-Pálsson, eds., *Ethnogenese europäischer Völker*, pp. 247–56. Stuttgart: Gustav Fischer.

Andreae, B. 1991. The Image of the Celts in Etruscan, Greek and Roman Art. In Moscati et al., pp. 61–69.

Anthony, D. W. 1990. Migration in Archeology. *American Anthropologist* 92:895–914.

Antonsen, E. H. 1986. Die ältesten Runeninschriften. In Beck, pp. 321–43.

Appadurai, A. 1996. *Modernity at Large: Cultural Dimensions of Globalization*. Minneapolis: University of Minnesota Press.

Arafat, K., and C. Morgan. 1994. Athens, Etruria and the Heuneburg. In I. Morris, ed., *Classical Greece: Ancient Histories and Modern Archaeologies*, pp. 108–34. Cambridge: Cambridge University Press.

Arnold, B. 1995. The Material Culture of Social Structure: Rank and Status in Early Iron Age Europe. In Arnold and Gibson, pp. 43–52.

Arnold, B., and D. B. Gibson, eds., 1995. *Celtic Chiefdom, Celtic State*. Cambridge: Cambridge University Press.

Asskamp, R. 1989. Haltern. In Asskamp, pp. 21–43.

———, ed. 1989. *2000 Jahre Römer in Westfalen*. Mainz: Philipp von Zabern.

Badian, E. 1968. *Roman Imperialism*. Oxford: Blackwell.

Bakker, L. 1985. Ausgrabungen an der Kornhausgasse in der Provinzhauptstadt Augusta Vindelicum-Augsburg. *Das archäologische Jahr in Bayern 1985*:101–4.

Bálek, M., E. Droberjar, and O. Šedo. 1994. Die römischen Feldlager in Mähren. *Památky Archeologické* 85:59–74.

Bálek, M., and O. Šedo. 1996. Das frühkaiserzeitliche Lager bei Mušov: Zeugnis eines augusteischen Feldzugs ins Marchgebiet? *Germania* 74:399–414.

Bang, M. 1906. *Die Germanen im römischen Dienst bis zum Regierungsanstritt Constantins I.* Berlin: Weidmannsche Buchhandlung.

Barrett, J. C. 1994. *Fragments from Antiquity.* Cambridge, MA: Blackwell.

———. 1997a. Romanization: A Critical Comment. In Mattingly, pp. 51–66.

———. 1997b. Theorising Roman Archaeology. In Meadows, Lemke, and Heron, pp. 1–7.

Barrett, J. C., A. P. Fitzpatrick, and L. Macinnes, eds. 1989. *Barbarians and Romans in North-West Europe.* Oxford: British Archaeological Reports, International Series 471.

Barth, F., ed. 1969. *Ethnic Groups and Boundaries.* London: Allen and Unwin.

Bauchhenss, G. 1984. *Denkmäler des Juppiterkultes aus Mainz und Umgebung.* Bonn: Habelt.

Bauchhenss, G., and P. Noelke. 1981. *Die Jupitersäulen in den germanischen Provinzen.* Cologne: Rheinland-Verlag.

Bechert, T., and W.J.H. Willems. 1995. *Die römische Reichsgrenze zwischen Mosel und Nordseeküste.* Stuttgart: Konrad Theiss.

Beck, H., ed. 1986. *Germanenprobleme in heutiger Sicht.* Berlin: Walter de Gruyter.

Beck, L., ed. 1995. *Regional Approaches to Mortuary Analysis.* New York: Plenum.

Becker, M. 1996. *Untersuchungen zur römischen Kaiserzeit zwischen südlichem Harzrand, Thüringer Becken und Weisser Elster.* Halle: Landesamt für Denkmalpflege Sachsen-Anhalt.

Beckmann, B. 1995. Die germanischen Funde in den Kastellen des Taunuslimes und ihre Beziehungen zum Fundgut in der Germania libera. In Hansen, pp. 410–13.

Bell, J. 1992. On Capturing Agency in Theories about Prehistory. In Gardin and Peebles, pp. 30–55.

Bellot, J., W. Czysz, and G. Krahe, eds. 1985. *Forschungen zur provinzialrömischen Archäologie in Bayerisch-Schwaben.* Augsburg: Historischer Verein für Schwaben.

Bender, H., and H. Wolff, eds. 1994. *Ländliche Besiedlung und Landwirtschaft in den Rhein-Donau-Provinzen des Römischen Reiches.* Espelkamp: Marie L. Leidorf.

Bernhard, H. 1990. Die römische Geschichte in Rheinland-Pfalz. In Cüppers, pp. 39–168.

Biel, J. 1985a. *Der Keltenfürst von Hochdorf.* Stuttgart: Konrad Theiss.

———. 1985b. Die Ausstattung des Toten. In D. Planck, J. Biel, G. Süsskind, and A. Wais, eds., *Der Keltenfürst von Hochdorf*, pp. 78–105. Stuttgart: Landesdenkmalamt Baden-Württembergs.

Bierbrauer, V. 1994. Archäologie und Geschichte der Goten vom 1.–7. Jahrhundert. *Frühmittelalterliche Studien* 28:51–171.

Bintliff, J. 1984. Iron Age Europe in the Context of Social Evolution from the Bronze Age to Historic Times. In J. Bintliff, ed., *European Social Evolution: Archaeological Perspectives*, pp. 157–226. Bradford: University of Bradford Press.

Birkhan, H. 1970. *Germanen und Kelten bis zum Ausgang der Römerzeit*. Vienna: Österreichische Akademie der Wissenschaften, Phil.-Hist. Klasse, Sitzungsbericht 272.

Birley, A. R. 1981. The Economic Effects of Roman Frontier Policy. In King and Henig, pp. 39–53.

Bishop, M. C., and J.C.N. Coulston. 1993. *Roman Military Equipment*. London: Batsford.

Bittel, K., W. Kimmig, and S. Schiek, eds. 1981. *Die Kelten in Baden-Württemberg*. Stuttgart: Konrad Theiss.

Bittel, K., S. Schiek, and D. Müller. 1990. *Die keltischen Viereckschanzen*. Stuttgart: Atlas archäologischer Geländedenkmäler in Baden-Württemberg.

Blagg, T., and M. Millett, eds. 1990. *The Early Roman Empire in the West*. Oxford: Oxbow.

Blanton, R. E. 1994. *Houses and Households: A Comparative Study*. New York: Plenum.

Bloemers, J.H.F. 1978. *Rijswijk (Z.H.) 'De Bult': Eine Siedlung der Canenefaten*. Amersfoort.

———. 1983. Acculturation in the Rhine/Meuse Basin in the Roman Period: A Preliminary Survey. In Brandt and Slofstra, pp. 159–210.

———. 1990. Lower Germany: *plura consilio quam vi*: Proto-urban Settlement Developments and the Integration of Native Society. In Blagg and Millett, pp. 72–86.

———. 1991. Relations Between Romans and Natives: Concepts of Comparative Studies. In Maxfield and Dobson, pp. 451–54.

———. 1994. Die sozial-ökonomischen Aspekte der ländlichen Besiedlung an Niederrhein und Niedermaas in Germania Inferior und das Limesvorfeld von Christi Geburt bis zum 5. Jahrhundert nach Christi. In Bender and Wolff, pp. 123–39.

Boeles P. 1951. *Friesland tot de Elfde Eeuw (Frisia to the Eleventh Century)*. 's Gravenhage: Martinus Nijhoff.

Bogatyrev, P. 1971. *The Functions of Folk Costume in Moravian Slovakia*. Trans. R. G. Crum. The Hague: Mouton.

Böhme, A. 1972. Die Fibeln der Kastelle Saalburg und Zugmantel. *Saalburg Jahrbuch* 29.

———. 1978. Das frühkaiserzeitliche Brandgrab von Rohrbach als Zeugnis der keltischen "Menimane"-Tracht. *Archäologisches Korrespondenzblatt* 8:209–13.

Böhme, A. 1985. Tracht- und Bestattungssitten in den germanischen Provinzen und der Belgica. In H. Temporini, ed., *Aufstieg und Niedergang der römischen Welt* II, 12, 3, pp. 423–55. Berlin: Walter de Gruyter.

Böhme, H. W. 1991. Ausgewählte Funde aus dem germanischen Königsgrab von Mušov (Südmähren/ČSFR) anlässlich der Restaurierung. *Archäologisches Korrespondenzblatt* 21:291–304.

Böhme-Schönberger, A. 1993. Die reichen Gräber von Goeblingen-Nospelt als Zeichen der Romanisierung der einheimischen Bevölkerung. In Struck, pp. 337–43.

———. 1994. Fibeln und Fibeltracht: Römische Kaiserzeit im Provinzialrömischen Gebiet und Beziehungen zur Germania magna. In *Reallexikon der germanischen Altertumskunde*, vol. 8, pp. 511–23.

Bohnsack, D., and A. B. Follmann. 1976. Bernstein und Bernsteinhandel. In *Reallexikon der germanischen Altertumskunde*, vol. 2, pp. 288–98.

Boone, E. 1994. Writing and Recording Knowledge. In Boone and Mignolo, pp. 3–26.

Boone, E. H., and W. D. Mignolo, eds. 1994. *Writing Without Words: Alternative Literacies in Mesoamerica and the Andes*. Durham: Duke University Press.

Bowman, A. K. 1994a. *Life and Letters on the Roman Frontier: Vindolanda and Its People*. London: British Museum Press.

———. 1994b. The Roman Imperial Army: Letters and Literacy on the Northern Frontier. In A. K. Bowman and G. Woolf, eds., *Literacy and Power in the Ancient World*, pp. 109–25. Cambridge: Cambridge University Press.

Brandt, R., and J. Slofstra, eds. 1983. *Roman and Native in the Low Countries: Spheres of Interaction*. Oxford: British Archaeological Reports, International Series 184.

Braun, D. P. 1991. Why Decorate a Pot? Midwestern Household Pottery, 200 B.C.– A.D. 600. *Journal of Anthropological Archaeology* 10: 360–97.

Braund, D. 1984. *Rome and the Friendly King: The Character of the Client Kingship*. London: Croom Helm.

———. 1989. Ideology, Subsidies and Trade: The King on the Northern Frontier Revisited. In Barrett, Fitzpatrick, and Macinnes, pp. 14–26.

Bringmann, K. 1989. Topoi in der taciteischen Germania. In Jankuhn and Timpe, pp. 59–78.

Brun, P., S. van der Leeuw, and C. R. Whittaker, eds. 1993. *Frontières d'empire: Nature et signification des frontières romaines*. Nemours: Mémoires du Musée de Préhistore d'Ile-de-France.

Brunaux, J.-L. 1988. *The Celtic Gauls: Gods, Rites and Sanctuaries*. Trans. D. Nash. London: Seaby.

Brunaux, J.-L., P. Meniel, and A. Rapin. 1980. Un sanctuaire gaulois à Gournay-sur-Aronde (Oise). *Gallia* 38:1–25.

Brunt, P. A. 1976. The Romanization of the Local Ruling Classes in the Roman Empire. In Pippidi, pp. 161–74.

Bücker, C. 1997. Römischer Lebensstil im freien Germanien. In Fuchs et al., pp. 135–41.

Bujna, J., and M. Szabó. 1991. The Carpathian Basin. In Moscati et al., pp. 277–85.

Burnham, B. C. 1995. Celts and Romans: Towards a Romano-Celtic Society. In Green, pp. 121–41.

Burton, G. P. 1996. Rome (History): From Augustus to the Antonines (31 B.C.–A.D. 192). In *Oxford Classical Dictionary*, 3d ed. pp. 1327–31.

Busch, R. 1995. Kenotaph des Marcus Caelius. In Busch, pp. 156–57.

———, ed. 1995. *Rom an der Niederelbe*. Neumünster: Wachholtz.

Caesar, J. *The Battle for Gaul*. Trans. A. and P. Wiseman, 1980. Boston: David R. Godine.

———. *The Gallic War*. Trans. H. J. Edwards, 1986. Cambridge, MA: Harvard University Press.

Calhoun, C. 1995. *Critical Social Theory*. Oxford: Blackwell.

Callies, H. 1973. Arminius. In *Reallexikon der germanischen Altertumskunde*, vol. 1, pp. 417–20.

Campbell, B. 1978. The Marriage of Soldiers Under the Empire. *Journal of Roman Studies* 68:153–66.

———. 1994. *The Roman Army, 31 BC–AD 337*. London: Routledge.

Capelle, T. 1976. Zur archäologischen Gliederung und Siedlungsgeschichte der Elbgermanen in der älteren römischen Kaiserzeit. In H. Temporini, ed., *Aufstieg und Niedergang der römischen Welt* II, 5, 1, pp. 127–42.

Caprino, C., A. M. Colini, G. Gatti, M. Pallottino, and P. Romanelli. 1955. *La Colonna di Marco Aurelio*. Rome: "L'Erma" di Bretschneider.

von Carnap-Bornheim, C. 1997. Neue Forschungen zu den beiden Zierscheiben aus dem Thorsberger Moorfund. *Germania* 75:69–99.

Carroll-Spillecke, M. 1995. Neue vorkoloniezeitliche Siedlungsspuren in Köln. *Archäologische Informationen* 18/2:143–52.

Cary, M., and H. H. Scullard. 1975. *A History of Rome Down to the Reign of Constantine*. 3d ed. New York: St. Martin's.

Cavalli-Sforza, L. L., P. Menozzi, and A. Piazza. 1994. *The History and Geography of Human Genes*. Princeton: Princeton University Press.

Champion, T. C. 1985. Written Sources and the Study of the European Iron Age. In T. C. Champion and J.V.S. Megaw, eds., *Settlement and Society: Aspects of West European Prehistory in the First Millennium B.C.*, pp. 9–22. Leicester: Leicester University Press.

———. 1995. Power, Politics and Status. In Green, pp. 85–94.

Champion, T., C. Gamble, S. Shennan, and A. Whittle. 1984. *Prehistoric Europe*. New York: Academic Press.

Chapman, M. 1992. *The Celts: The Construction of a Myth*. New York: St. Martin's.

———. 1995. "Freezing the Frame": Dress and Ethnicity in Brittany and Gaelic Scotland. In Eicher, pp. 7–28.

Chapman, R., I. Kinnes, and K. Randsborg, eds. 1981. *The Archaeology of Death.* Cambridge: Cambridge University Press.

Christ, K. 1977. Zur augusteischen Germanienpolitik. *Chiron* 7:149–205.

———. 1995. Caesar und die Geschichte. In M. Weinmann-Walser, pp. 9–22.

Christlein, R. 1979. *Die Alamannen.* Stuttgart: Konrad Theiss.

———. 1982. Zu den jüngsten keltischen Funden Südbayerns. *Bayerische Vorgeschichtsblätter* 47:275–92.

Chropovský, B., ed. 1977. *Ausklang der Latène-Zivilisation und Anfänge der germanischen Besiedlung im mittleren Donaugebiet.* Bratislava: Vydavatel'stvo Slovenskej Akadémie Vied.

Clifford, J., and G. E. Marcus. 1986. *Writing Culture: The Poetics and Politics of Ethnography.* Berkeley: University of California Press.

Cohen, A. P. 1994. *Self Consciousness: An Alternative Anthropology of Identity.* London: Routledge.

Cohen, R. 1994. *Frontiers of Identity: The British and the Others.* London: Longman.

Coles, J. M., and A. F. Harding. 1979. *The Bronze Age in Europe.* New York: St. Martin's.

Collingwood, R. G. 1930. Romano-Celtic Art in Northumbria. *Archaeologia* 80:37–58.

Collis, J. 1984. *Oppida: Earliest Towns North of the Alps.* Sheffield: Department of Prehistory and Archaeology.

———. 1995. The First Towns. In Green, pp. 159–75.

———. 1997. *The European Iron Age.* London: Routledge.

Colloredo-Mansfield, R. 1994. Architectural Conspicuous Consumption and Economic Change in the Andes. *American Anthropologist* 96:845–65.

Cooper, F. 1994. Conflict and Connection: Rethinking Colonial African History. *American Historical Review* 99:1516–45.

Cooper, F., and A. L. Stoler, eds. 1997. *Tensions of Empire: Colonial Cultures in a Bourgeois World.* Berkeley: University of California Press.

Cornell, T. J. 1996. Rome (History): From the Origins to 31 B.C. In *Oxford Classical Dictionary,* 3d ed., pp. 1322–27.

Cottam, S., D. Dungworth, S. Scott, and J. Taylor, eds., 1994. *TRAC 94: Proceedings of the Fourth Annual Theoretical Roman Archaeology Conference.* Oxford: Oxbow.

Cowgill, G. 1993. Beyond Criticizing New Archaeology. *American Anthropologist* 95:551–73.

Crawford, M. 1993. *The Roman Republic.* 2d ed. Cambridge, MA: Harvard University Press.

Crown, P. L. 1994. *Ceramics and Ideology: Salado Polychrome Pottery.* Albuquerque: University of New Mexico Press.

Crumley, C. L. 1974. *Celtic Social Structures.* Ann Arbor: University of Michigan.

———. 1994. The Ecology of Conquest. In C. L. Crumley, ed., *Historical Ecology,* pp. 183–201. Santa Fe: School of American Research.

Csikszentimahaly, M., and E. Rochberg-Halton. 1981. *The Meaning of Things: Domestic Symbols and the Self.* Cambridge: Cambridge University Press.

Cummins, T. 1994. Representation in the Sixteenth Century and the Colonial Image of the Inca. In Boone and Mignolo, pp. 188–219.

Cunliffe, B. 1997. *The Ancient Celts.* Oxford: Oxford University Press.

———, ed. 1994. *The Oxford Illustrated Prehistory of Europe.* Oxford: Oxford University Press.

Cunliffe, B., and T. Rowley, eds. 1976. *Oppida: The Beginnings of Urbanisation in Barbarian Europe.* Oxford: British Archaeological Reports, Supplementary Series 11.

Cüppers, H. 1990. Trier. In Cüppers, pp. 577–616.

———, ed. 1984. *Trier: Augustusstadt der Treverer.* Mainz: Philipp von Zabern.

———, ed. 1990. *Die Römer in Rheinland-Pfalz.* Stuttgart: Konrad Theiss.

Czysz, W. 1985. Töpfer, Ziegler und Geschirrhändler. In Petzet, pp. 158–61.

———. 1987. Das römische Töpferdorf Rapis und die Terra-sigillata-Manufaktur bei Schwabegg. *Das archäologische Jahr in Bayern 1987*:123–32.

———. 1989. Ausgrabungen in einem römischen Gutshof bei Oberndorf a. Lech. *Das archäologische Jahr in Bayern 1989*:133–40.

———. 1995. Das zivile Leben in der Provinz. In Czysz et al., pp. 177–308.

Czysz, W., K. Dietz, T. Fischer, and H.-J. Kellner, eds. 1995. *Die Römer in Bayern.* Stuttgart: Konrad Theiss.

D'Altroy, T. N. 1992. *Provincial Power in the Inka Empire.* Washington: Smithsonian Institution.

Daniel, G., and C. Renfrew. 1988. *The Idea of Prehistory.* Edinburgh: Edinburgh University Press.

Dannheimer, H., and R. Gebhard, eds., 1993. *Das keltische Jahrtausend.* Mainz: Philipp von Zabern.

David, N., J. Sterner, and K. Gavua. 1988. Why Pots Are Decorated. *Current Anthropology* 29:365–89.

Davidson, H.R.E. 1988. *Myths and Symbols in Pagan Europe: Early Scandinavian and Celtic Religions.* Syracuse: Syracuse University Press.

Davies, R. W. 1974. The Daily Life of the Roman Soldier. In H. Temporini, ed., *Aufstieg und Niedergang der römischen Welt* II, 1, pp. 299–338. Berlin: Walter de Gruyter.

———. 1989. *Service in the Roman Army.* Edinburgh: Edinburgh University Press.

Davis, F. 1992. *Fashion, Culture, and Identity.* Chicago: University of Chicago Press.

De Caro, S. 1996. The Northern Barbarians as Seen by Rome. In *Roman Reflections in Scandinavia,* pp. 25–29.

Decker, K. V., and W. Selzer. 1976. Mogontiacum: Mainz von der Zeit des Augustus bis zum Ende der römischen Herrschaft. In H. Temporini, ed., *Aufstieg und Niedergang der römischen Welt* II, 5, 1, pp. 457–559. Berlin: Walter de Gruyter.

Dehn, W. 1951. Die gallischen 'Oppida' bei Cäsar. *Saalburg Jahrbuch* 10:36–49.

De Laet, S., and A. Van Doorselaer. 1962. Gräber der römischen Kaiserzeit mit Waffenbeigaben aus Belgien, den Niederlanden und dem Grossherzogtum Luxemburg. *Saalburg Jahrbuch* 20:54–61.

Demandt, A. 1993. Die westgermanischen Stammesbünde. *Klio* 75:387–406.

———. 1995. Arminius und die frühgermanische Staatenbildung. In Wiegels and Woesler, pp. 185–96.

Deyts, S. 1983. *Les bois sculptés des Sources de la Seine.* Paris: Gallia Supplément.

Dietler, M. 1990. Driven by Drink: The Role of Drinking in the Political Economy and the Case of Early Iron Age France. *Journal of Anthropological Archaeology* 9:352–406.

———. 1995. Early "Celtic" Socio-Political Relations: Ideological Representation and Social Competition in Dynamic Comparative Perspective. In Arnold and Gibson, pp. 64–73.

———. 1997. The Iron Age in Mediterranean France: Colonial Encounters, Entanglements, and Transformations. *Journal of World Prehistory* 11:269–358.

Dietler, M., and I. Herbich. 1994. Ceramics and Ethnic Identity. In *Terre cuite et société*, pp. 459–72. Juan-les-Pins: Éditions APDCA.

Dietz, K. 1984. Das älteste Militärdiplom für die Provinz Pannonia Superior. *Bericht der Römisch-Germanischen Kommission* 65:159–268.

———. 1995a. Okkupation und Frühzeit. In Czysz et al., pp. 18–99.

———. 1995b. Die Blütezeit des römischen Bayern. In Czysz et al., pp. 100–176.

Dietz, K., and T. Fischer. 1996. *Die Römer in Regensburg.* Regensburg: Friedrich Pustet.

Dietz, K., and G. Weber. 1982. Fremde in Rätien. *Chiron* 12:409–43.

Dirks, N. B., G. Eley, and S. B. Ortner, eds. 1994. *Culture, Power, History: A Reader in Contemporary Social Theory.* Princeton: Princeton University Press.

Dixon, K. R., and P. Southern. 1992. *Roman Cavalry.* London: Batsford.

Dobesch, G. 1989a. Caesar als Ethnograph. *Wiener Humanistische Blätter* 31:18–51.

———. 1989b. Europa in der Reichskonzeption bei Caesar, Augustus und Tiberius. *Acta Archaeologica Academiae Scientiarum Hungaricae* 41:53–59.

———. 1991. Ancient Literary Sources. In Moscati et al., pp. 35–41.

Dongoske, K. E., M. Yeatts, R. Anyon, T. J. Ferguson. 1997. Archaeological Cultures and Cultural Affiliation: Hopi and Zuni Perspectives in the American Southwest. *American Antiquity* 62:600–608.

Dornbusch, J., and H.-J. Kämmer, eds. 1996. *Diercke Weltatlas.* Braunschweig: Westermann.

Douglas, M., and B. Isherwood. 1979. *The World of Goods.* New York: Basic Books.

Drda, P., and A. Rybová. 1997. Keltská oppida v centru Boiohaema—Die keltischen Oppida im Zentrum Boiohaemums. *Památky Archeologické* 88:65–123.

Drescher, H. 1955. Die Herstellung von Fibelspiralen. *Germania* 33:340–49.

Drinkwater, J. F. 1983. *Roman Gaul.* Ithaca, NY: Cornell University Press.

———. 1987. Urbanization in Italy and the Western Empire. In Wacher, vol. 1, pp. 345–87.

———. 1990. For Better or Worse? Towards an Assessment of the Economic and Social Consequences of the Roman Conquest of Gaul. In Blagg and Millett, pp. 210–19.

Droberjar, E. 1993. Die römische Keramik vom Burgstall bei Mušov, Mähren. *Archaeologia Austriaca* 77:39–103.

———. 1994. Objekt 63 in der römischen Höhenbefestigung Mušov-Burgstall (Tschechische Republik). *Archäologisches Korrespondenzblatt* 24:73–79.

Dušek, S. 1992. *Römische Handwerker im germanischen Thüringen.* Stuttgart: Konrad Theiss.

Duval, A. 1991. Celtic Society in the First Century B.C. In Moscati et al., pp. 485–90.

———, ed. 1994. *Vercingétorix et Alésia.* Paris: Réunion des Musées Nationaux.

Düwel, K. 1997. Germanische Runen, lateinische Inschriften. In Fuchs et al., pp. 491–98.

Düwel, K., and M. Gebühr. 1981. Die Fibel von Meldorf und die Anfänge der Runenschrift. *Zeitschrift für Deutsches Altertum und Deutsche Literatur* 110, 3:159–75.

Düwel, K., H. Jankuhn, H. Siems, and D. Timpe, eds. 1985. *Untersuchungen zum Handel und Verkehr der vor- und frühgeschichtlichen Zeit in Mittel- und Nordeuropa.* Göttingen: Vandenhoeck und Ruprecht.

Dyson, S. L. 1975. Native Revolt Patterns in the Roman Empire. In H. Temporini, ed. *Aufstieg und Niedergang der römischen Welt* II, 3, pp. 138–75. Berlin: Walter de Gruyter.

———. 1985a. Introduction. In S. L. Dyson, ed., *Comparative Studies in the Archaeology of Colonialism,* pp. 1–7. Oxford: British Archaeological Reports, International Series 233.

———. 1985b. *The Creation of the Roman Frontier.* Princeton: Princeton University Press.

———. 1993. The Roman Frontier in Comparative Perspective: The View from North America. In Brun, van der Leeuw, and Whittaker, pp. 149–57.

———. 1995. Is There a Text in this Site? In D. B. Small, ed., *Methods in the Mediterranean: Historical and Archaeological Views on Texts and Archaeology,* pp. 25–44. Leiden: E. J. Brill.

Eck, W., and M. M. Roxan. 1998. Zwei Entlassungsurkunden—*tabulae honestae missionis*—für Soldaten der römischen Auxilien. *Archäologisches Korrespondenzblatt* 28:95–112.

Egg, M. 1996. *Das hallstattzeitliche Fürstengrab von Strettweg bei Judenburg in der Oststeiermark.* Mainz: Römisch-Germanisches Zentralmuseum.

Egger, M. 1984. Ein keltisch-römischer Kultplatz in Gauting. *Das archäologische Jahr in Bayern 1984*:90–92.

Eggers, H. J. 1951. *Der römische Import im freien Germanien*. Hamburg: Museum für Völkerkunde und Vorgeschichte.

Eicher, J. B., ed. 1995. *Dress and Ethnicity*. Oxford: Berg.

Eingartner, J., P. Eschbaumer, and G. Weber. 1993. *Der römische Tempelbezirk in Faimingen-Phoebiana*. Mainz: Philipp von Zabern.

Elton, H. 1996. *Frontiers of the Roman Empire*. Bloomington: Indiana University Press.

van Enckevort, H., and W.J.H. Willems. 1994. Roman Cavalry Helmets in Ritual Hoards from the Kops Plateau at Nijmegen, The Netherlands. *Journal of Roman Military Equipment Studies* 5:126–37.

van Endert, D. 1991. *Die Bronzefunde aus dem Oppidum von Manching*. Stuttgart: Franz Steiner.

Engelhardt, C. 1863–1869. *Mosefund*. Copenhagen: G.E.C. Gad.

———. 1866. *Denmark in the Early Iron Age, Illustrated by Recent Discoveries in the Peat Mosses of Sleswig*. London: Williams and Norgate.

———. 1867. *Om Vimose-fundet*. Copenhagen: Thieles bogtrykkeri.

Engels, H.-J. 1972. Frührömische Waffengräber aus dem pfälzischen Rheintal. *Archäologisches Korrespondenzblatt* 2:183–89.

Erdrich, M. 1995. Rom und die germanischen Stämme in Niedersachsen. In Busch, pp. 47–70.

Eriksen, T. H. 1992. *Us and Them in Modern Societies: Ethnicity and Nationalism in Mauritius, Trinidad and Beyond*. Oslo: Scandinavian University Press.

———. 1993. *Ethnicity and Nationalism: Anthropological Perspectives*. London: Pluto Press.

van Es, W. A. 1983. Introduction. In Brandt and Slofstra, pp. 1–10.

Euskirchen, M. 1993. Epona. *Bericht der Römisch-Germanischen Kommission* 74:607–838.

Evans, D. E. 1981. Celts and Germans. *Bulletin of the Board of Celtic Studies* 29:230–55.

———. 1995. The Early Celts: The Evidence of Language. In Green, pp. 8–20.

Fabech, C. 1991. Booty Sacrifices in Southern Scandinavia: A Reassessment. In Garwood et al., pp. 88–99.

———. 1996. Booty Sacrifices in Southern Scandinavia. In *Roman Reflections in Scandinavia*, pp. 135–38.

Faber, A. 1994. *Das römische Auxiliarkastell und der Vicus von Regensburg-Kumpfmühl*. Munich: C. H. Beck.

Fane, D., ed. 1996. *Converging Cultures: Art and Identity in Spanish America*. New York: Brooklyn Museum.

Farriss, N. M. 1984. *Maya Society under Colonial Rule*. Princeton: Princeton University Press.

Fasold, P. 1992. *Römischer Grabbrauch in Süddeutschland*. Aalen: Limesmuseum.

———. 1993. Romanisierung und Grabbrauch: Überlegungen zum frührömischen Totenkult in Rätien. In Struck, pp. 381–95.

Fauduet, I., and C. Pommeret. 1985. Les fibules du sanctuaire des Bolards à Nuits-Saint-Georges (Côte-d'Or). *Revue archéologique de l'Est et du Centre-Est* 36:61–116.

Faust, S., K.-J. Gilles, K. Goethert, K.-P. Goethert, J. Hupe, S. Klementa, L. Schwinden, and F. Unruh. 1996. Katalog. In Kuhnen, pp. 89–270.

Feinman, G. M. 1997. Thoughts on New Approaches to Combining the Archaeological and Historical Records. *Journal of Archaeological Method and Theory* 4:367–77.

Ferdière, A. 1988. *Les campagnes en Gaule romaine*, vol. 1: *Les hommes et l'environnement en Gaule rurale (52 av. J.-C.–486 ap. J.-C.)*. Paris: Editions Errance.

Ferguson, R. B., and N. L. Whitehead, eds. 1992. *War in the Tribal Zone: Expanding States and Indigenous Warfare.* Sante Fe: School of American Research.

Ferris, I. 1994. Insignificant Others: Images of Barbarians on Military Art from Roman Britain. In Cottam et al., pp. 24–31.

———. 1997. The Enemy Without, The Enemy Within: More Thoughts on Images of Barbarians in Greek and Roman Art. In Meadows, Lemke, and Heron, pp. 22–28.

Feugère, M., and C. Rolley. 1991. *La Vaiselle tonds-républicaine bronze.* Dijon: Université de Bourgogne.

Fischer, F. 1981. Sinsheim-Dühren. In Bittel, Kimmig, and Schiek, pp. 471–72.

———. 1988. Südwestdeutschland im letzten Jahrhundert vor Christi Geburt. In Planck, pp. 235–50.

———. 1991. Schicksale antiker Kultdenkmäler in Obergermanien und Raetien. In *4. Heidenheimer Archäologie-Colloquium*, pp. 29–45. Heidenheim: Heimat- und Altertumsverein.

Fischer, T. 1985. Eine Grabung im Gewerbegebiet des römischen Gutshofes (Villa rustica) von Eugenbach, Gde. Altdorf, Lkr. Landshut. In B. Engelhardt, ed., *Archäologische Denkmalpflege in Niederbayern*, pp. 156–73. Munich: Bayerisches Landesamt für Denkmalpflege.

———. 1990. *Das Umland des römischen Regensburg.* Munich: C. H. Beck.

Fischer, T., S. Rieckhoff-Pauli, and K. Spindler. 1984. Grabungen in der spätkeltischen Siedlung im Sulztal bei Berching-Pollanten. *Germania* 62:311–72.

Fitzpatrick, A. 1985. The Distribution of Dressel 1 Amphorae in Northwestern Europe. *Oxford Journal of Archaeology* 4:305–40.

———. 1996. 'Celtic' Iron Age Europe: The Theoretical Basis. In Graves-Brown, Jones, and Gamble, pp. 238–55.

Flach, D. 1995. Der taciteische Zugang zu der Welt der Germanen. In Wiegels and Woesler, pp. 143–66.

Flaig, E. 1995. Römer werden um jeden Preis? Integrationskapazität und Integrationswilligkeit am Beispiel des Bataveraufstandes. In Weinmann-Walser, pp. 45–60.

Flügel, C. 1996. Handgemachte Grobkeramik aus *Arae Flaviae*-Rottweil. *Fundberichte aus Baden-Württemberg* 21:315–400.

Frank, K. 1997. Germanen im Taubergebiet vor und nach der Aufgabe des Limes. In Fuchs et al., pp. 69–72.

Franke, A. 1930. Marcomanni. In *Paulys Realencyclopädie der classischen Altertumswissenschaft*, vol. 28, cols. 1609–37. Stuttgart: Alfred Druckenmüller.

Frankenstein, S., and M. J. Rowlands. 1978. The Internal Structure and Regional Context of Early Iron Age Society in Southwestern Germany. *Institute of Archaeology Bulletin* 15:73–112.

Franzius, G., ed. 1995. *Aspekte römisch-germanischer Beziehungen in der frühen Kaiserzeit*. Espelkamp: Marie L. Leidorf.

Freeman, P.W.M. 1993. 'Romanisation' and Roman Material Culture: review of Millett, *The Romanization of Britain*. *Journal of Roman Archaeology* 6:438–45.

———. 1996. Roman Frontier Studies: What's New? *Britannia* 27:465–70.

———. 1997a. 'Romanization'—'Imperialism': What Are We Talking About? In Meadows, Lemke, and Heron, pp. 8–14.

———. 1997b. Mommsen Through to Haverfield: The Origins of Romanization Studies in Late 19th-c. Britain. In Mattingly, pp. 27–50.

Frere, S. S. 1977. Town Planning in the Western Provinces. *Bericht der Römisch-Germanischen Kommission* 58, *Beiheft*, pp. 87–103.

Frey, O.-H. 1986. Einige überlegungen zu den Beziehungen zwischen Kelten und Germanen in der Spätlatènezeit. *Marburger Studien zur Vor- und Frühgeschichte* 7:45–79.

———. 1991. The Formation of the La Tène Culture. In Moscati et al., pp. 127–46.

———. 1995a. Das Grab von Waldalgesheim: Eine Stilphase des keltischen Kunsthandwerks. In Joachim, pp. 159–206.

———. 1995b. The Celts in Italy. In Green, pp. 515–32.

Frézouls, E. 1990. Gallien und römisches Germanien. In Vittinghoff, pp. 429–509.

Fried, M. H. 1967. *The Evolution of Political Society*. New York: Random House.

Friedman, J. 1992. The Past in the Future: History and the Politics of Identity. *American Anthropologist* 94:837–59.

———. 1994. *Cultural Identity and Global Process*. London: Sage.

Friesinger, H., and F. Krinzinger, eds. 1997. *Der römische Limes in Österreich*. Vienna: Österreichische Akademie der Wissenschaften.

Fuchs, K., M. Kempa, R. Redies, B. Theune-Grosskopf, and A. Wais, eds. 1997. *Die Alamannen*. Stuttgart: Archäologisches Landesmuseum Baden-Württemberg.

Furger-Gunti, A. 1977. Zur Herstellungstechnik der Nauheimer-Fibeln. In *Festschrift Elisabeth Schmid*, pp. 73–84. Basel: Geographisch-Ethnologische Gesellschaft.

Gabler, D. 1991. The Survival of Late La Tène Settlements in the Roman Period. In Maxfield and Dobson, pp. 424–31.

———. 1994. Die ländliche Besiedlung Oberpannoniens. In Bender and Wolff, pp. 377–419.

Galloway, P. 1992. The Unexamined Habitus: Direct Historical Analogy and the Archaeology of the Text. In Gardin and Peebles, p. 178–95.

Gamble, C. 1986. *The Palaeolithic Settlement of Europe.* Cambridge: Cambridge University Press.

Garbsch, J. 1982. *Terra Sigillata: Ein Weltreich im Spiegel seines Luxusgeschirrs.* Munich: Prähistorische Staatssammlung.

Gardin, J.-C., and C. S. Peebles, eds. 1992. *Representations in Archaeology.* Bloomington: Indiana University Press.

Garwood, P., D. Jennings, R. Skeates, and J. Toms, eds. 1991. *Sacred and Profane: Proceedings of a Conference on Archaeology, Ritual and Religion.* Oxford: Oxford University Committee on Archaeology.

Gaubatz-Sattler, A. 1994. *Die Villa rustica von Bondorf (Lkr. Böblingen).* Stuttgart: Konrad Theiss.

Geary, P. 1983. Ethnic Identity as a Situational Construct in the Early Middle Ages. *Mitteilungen der Anthropologischen Gesellschaft in Wien* 113:15–26.

———. 1988. *Before France and Germany: The Creation and Transformation of the Medieval World.* New York: Oxford University Press.

Gebhard, R. 1989. *Der Glasschmuck aus dem Oppidum von Manching.* Stuttgart: Franz Steiner.

———. 1991. *Die Fibeln aus dem Oppidum von Manching.* Stuttgart: Franz Steiner.

———. 1993. Ergebnisse der Ausgrabungen in Manching. In Dannheimer and Gebhard, pp. 113–19.

Gechter, M. 1987. Das römische Heer in der Provinz Niedergermanien. In Horn, pp. 110–38.

———. 1990. Early Roman Military Installations and Ubian Settlements in the Lower Rhine. In Blagg and Millett, pp. 97–102.

———. 1991. Die frühe ubische Landnahme am Niederrhein. In Maxfield and Dobson, pp. 439–41.

Gechter, M., and J. Kunow. 1983. Der frühkaiserzeitliche Grabfund von Mehrum: Ein Beitrag zur Frage von Germanen in römischen Diensten. *Bonner Jahrbücher* 183:449–68.

Geuenich, D. 1997. Herkunft und "Landnahme" der Alamannen. In Fuchs et al., pp. 73–78.

Gibbon, E. 1776–1788. *The History of the Decline and Fall of the Roman Empire.* London: Penguin, 1994 ed., 3 vols.

Gilles, K.-J. 1992. Neue Funde und Beobachtungen zu den Anfängen Triers. *Trierer Zeitschrift* 55:193–232.

———. 1996. Tempelbezirke im Trierer Land. In Kuhnen, pp. 72–87.

Glüsing, P. 1965. Frühe Germanen südlich der Donau. *Offa* 21–22:7–20.

Glüsing, P. 1989. Die Germanen im Spannungsfeld der römischen Okkupation. In Asskamp, pp. 70–80.

Godłowski, K. 1985. Der römische Handel in die Germania libera aufgrund der archäologischen Quellen. In Düwel et al., pp. 337–66.

———. 1991. Jakuszowice: A Multi-Period Settlement in Southern Poland. *Antiquity* 65:662–75.

Goldsworthy, A. K. 1996. *The Roman Army at War: 100 BC–AD 200.* Oxford: Clarendon.

Gosselain, O. P. 1992. Technology and Style: Potters and Pottery Among the Bafia of Cameroon. *Man* 27:559–86.

Goudineau, C. 1990. *Cesar et la Gaule.* Paris: Editions Errance.

———. 1991. The Romanization of Gaul. In Moscati et al., pp. 509–14.

Goudineau, C., I. Fauduet, and G. Coulon, eds. 1994. *Les sanctuaires de tradition indigène en Gaule romaine.* Paris: Editions Errance.

Grant, M. 1974. *The Army of the Caesars.* London: Weidenfeld and Nicholson.

Graves-Brown, P., S. Jones, and C. Gamble, eds. 1996. *Cultural Identity and Archaeology.* London: Routledge.

Green, M. J. 1986. Jupiter, Taranis and the Solar Wheel. In Henig and King, pp. 65–76.

———. 1992. *Dictionary of Celtic Myth and Legend.* New York: Thames and Hudson.

———. 1995a. The Gods and the Supernatural. In Green, pp. 465–88.

———. 1995b. *Celtic Goddesses.* London: British Museum.

———. 1997. *The World of the Druids.* London: Thames and Hudson.

———, ed., 1995. *The Celtic World.* London: Routledge.

Greene, K. 1986. *The Archaeology of the Roman Economy.* Berkeley: University of California Press.

Griffith, G. T. 1935. *The Mercenaries of the Hellenistic World.* Cambridge: Cambridge University Press.

Grinker, R. R. 1996. Reconstructing the House in Anthropology. *American Anthropologist* 98:856–58.

Groenman-van Waateringe, W. 1980. Die verhängnisvolle Auswirkung der römischen Herrschaft auf die Wirtschaft an der Grenze des Reiches. *Offa* 37:366–71.

Groenman-van Waateringe, W., B. L. van Beek, W.J.H. Willems, and S. L. Wynia, eds. 1997. *Roman Frontier Studies 1995.* Oxford: Oxbow Books.

Grünert, H. 1988. Eisenproduktion und Eisenverarbeitung. In Krüger, pp. 473–87.

Gruzinski, S., and A. Rouveret. 1976. Histoire et acculturation dans le Mexique colonial et l'Italie méridionale avant la romanisation. *Mélanges de l'École Française de Rome, Antiquité* 88:61–219.

Gschwind, M. 1997. Bronzegiesser am raetischen Limes: Zur Versorgung mittelkaiserzeitlicher Auxiliareinheiten mit militärischen Ausrüstungsgegenständen. *Germania* 75:607–38.

Guamán Poma de Ayala, F. 1978. *Letter to a King: A Peruvian Chief's Account of Life Under the Incas and Under Spanish Rule.* ed. C. Dilke, New York: Dutton.

Günther, K. 1990. *Siedlung und Werkstätten von Feinschmieden der älteren Römischen Kaiserzeit bei Warburg-Daseburg.* Münster: Aschendorff.

Haarnagel, W. 1975. Die Wurtensiedlung Feddersen Wierde im Nordsee-Küstengebiet. In *Ausgrabungen in Deutschland,* vol. 2, pp. 10–29. Mainz: Römisch-Germanisches Zentralmuseum.

———. 1979. *Die Grabung Feddersen Wierde.* Wiesbaden: Franz Steiner.

Haarnagel, W., and P. Schmid. 1984. Siedlungen. In G. Kossack, K.-E. Behre, and P. Schmid, eds., *Archäologische und naturwissenschaftliche Untersuchungen an ländlichen und frühstädtischen Siedlungen im deutschen Küstengebiet vom 5. Jahrhundert v.Chr. bis zum 11. Jahrhundert n. Chr.,* vol. 1, pp. 167–244. Weinheim: Acta Humaniora.

Hachmann, R., G. Kossack, and H. Kuhn. 1962. *Völker zwischen Germanen und Kelten.* Neumünster: Wachholtz.

Haffner, A. 1974. Zum Ende der Latènezeit im Mittelrhein. *Archäologisches Korrespondenzblatt* 4:59–72.

———. 1989. *Zum Totenbrauchtum der Kelten und Römer am Beispiel des Treverer-Gräberfeldes Wederath-Belginum.* Mainz: Philipp von Zabern.

Hahn, E. 1992. Die menschlichen Skelettreste. In F. Maier, U. Geilenbrügge, E. Hahn, H.-J. Köhler, and S. Sievers, eds., *Ergebnisse der Ausgrabungen 1984–1987 in Manching,* pp. 214–34. Stuttgart: Franz Steiner.

Hald, M. 1980. *Ancient Danish Textiles from Bogs and Burials: A Comparative Study of Costume and Iron Age Textiles.* Copenhagen: National Museum.

Hansen, U. L. 1987. *Römischer Import im Norden.* Copenhagen: Det Kongelige Nordiske Oldskriftsselskab.

———. 1995. *Himlingøje-Seeland-Europa: Ein Gräberfeld der jüngeren römischen Kaiserzeit auf Seeland, seine Bedeutung und internationalen Beziehungen.* Copenhagen: Det Kongelige Nordiske Oldskriftsselskab.

———. 1996. Trade and Contact Between Scandinavia and the Roman Empire in the First to Fourth Centuries A.D. In *Roman Reflections in Scandinavia,* pp. 101–3.

Hanson, W. S. 1997. Forces of Change and Methods of Control. In Mattingly, pp. 67–80.

Harris, W. V. 1979. *War and Imperialism in Republican Rome, 327–70 B.C.* New York: Oxford University Press.

Hartog, F. 1988. *The Mirror of Herodotus: The Representation of the Other in Historical Writing.* Trans. J. Lloyd. Berkeley: University of California Press.

Haselgrove, C. 1988. Coinage and Complexity: Archaeological Analysis of Socio-Political Change in Britain and Non-Mediterranean Gaul During the Late Iron Age. In D. B. Gibson and M. N. Geselowitz, eds., *Tribe and Polity in Late Prehistoric Europe,* pp. 69–96. New York: Plenum.

———. 1995. Social and Symbolic Order in the Origins and Layout of Roman Villas in Northern Gaul. In Metzler et al., pp. 65–76.

Haselgrove, C. 1996a. Roman Impact on Rural Settlement and Society in Southern Picardy. In Roymans, pp. 127–87.

———. 1996b. La romanisation de l'habitat rural dans la vallée de l'Aisne d'après les prospections de surface et les fouilles récentes. *Revue archéologique de Picardie*, special no. 11:109–20.

Haseloff, G. 1981. *Die germanische Tierornamentik in der Völkerwanderungszeit.* Berlin: Walter de Gruyter.

Hassall, M. 1987. Romans and non-Romans. In Wacher, vol. 2, pp. 685–700.

Hässler, H.-J. 1977. *Zur inneren Gliederung und Verbreitung der vorrömischen Eisenzeit im südlichen Niederelbegebiet.* Materialhefte zur Ur- und Frühgeschichte Niedersachsens 11.

———. 1988. Zur Nienburger Kultur während der vorrömischen Eisenzeit in Nordwestdeutschland. In Horst and Schlette, pp. 307–41.

———. 1991. Vorrömische Eisenzeit. In Hässler, pp. 193–237.

———, ed. 1991. *Ur- und Frühgeschichte in Niedersachsen.* Stuttgart: Konrad Theiss.

Hastrup, K. 1982. Establishing an Ethnicity: The Emergence of the "Icelanders" in the Early Middle Ages. In D. Parkin, ed., *Semantic Anthropology,* pp. 145–60. New York: Academic Press.

Haversath, J.-B. 1984. *Die Agrarlandschaft im römischen Deutschland der Kaiserzeit (1.-4. Jh. n. Chr.).* Passau: Passavia Universitätsverlag.

Haynes, I. P. 1993. The Romanisation of Religion in the *Auxilia* of the Roman Imperial Army from Augustus to Septimius Severus. *Britannia* 24:141–57.

Heather, P. 1996. *The Goths.* Oxford: Blackwell.

Hedeager, L. 1978. A Quantitative Analysis of Roman Imports in Europe North of the Limes and the Question of Roman-Germanic Exchange. In K. Kristiansen and C. Paludan-Müller, eds., *New Directions in Scandinavian Archaeology,* pp. 191–216. Copenhagen: National Museum.

———. 1992. *Iron-Age Societies.* Oxford: Blackwell.

———. 1993. The Creation of Germanic Identity: A European Origin-Myth. In Brun, van der Leeuw, and Whittaker, pp. 121–31.

Heger, N. 1980. Das Weiterleben keltischen Volkstums und keltischer Kulturelemente in der römischen Kaiserzeit. In Pauli, pp. 48–50.

Heiligmann, J. 1991. Zur Bevölkerung des Limesgebietes östlich des Rheins und nördlich der Donau. In W. Haase, ed., *Aufstieg und Niedergang der römischen Welt* II, 33, 3, pp. 2226–42. Berlin: Walter de Gruyter.

———. 1995. Die Bevölkerung im süddeutschen Raum in augusteischer und frühtiberischer Zeit. In Wiegels and Woesler, pp. 29–39.

———. 1997. Rom und seine germanischen Nachbarn. In Fuchs et al., pp. 54–58.

Hellenkemper, H. 1987. Colonia Claudia Ara Agrippinensium. In Horn, pp. 459–72.

Helms, M. W. 1994. Essay on Objects: Interpretations of Distance Made Tangible. In Schwartz, pp. 355–77.

Hendrickson, H., ed. 1996. *Clothing and Difference: Embodied Identities in Colonial and Post-Colonial Africa.* Durham: Duke University Press.

Henig, M., and A. King, eds. 1986. *Pagan Gods and Shrines of the Roman Empire.* Oxford: Oxford University Committee for Archaeology.

Henning, J. 1991. Schmiedegräber nördlich der Alpen. *Saalburg Jahrbuch* 46:65–82.

Herrmann, J., ed., 1989. *Archäologie in der Deutschen Demokratischen Republik.* 2 vols. Stuttgart: Konrad Theiss.

Hides, S. 1996. The Genealogy of Material Culture and Cultural Identity. In Graves-Brown, Jones, and Gamble, pp. 25–47.

Hill, J. D. 1996. Introduction: Ethnogenesis in the Americas, 1492–1992. In Hill, pp. 1–19.

———. 1998. Violent Encounters: Ethnogenesis and Ethnocide in Long-Term Contact Situations. In J. G. Cusick, ed., *Studies in Culture Contact: Interaction, Culture Change, and Archaeology,* pp. 146–71. Carbondale, IL: Center for Archaeological Investigations.

———, ed. 1996. *History, Power, and Identity: Ethnogenesis in the Americas, 1492–1992.* Iowa City: University of Iowa Press.

Hines, J. 1995. Cultural Change and Social Organisation in Early Anglo-Saxon England. In G. Ausenda, ed., *After Empire: Towards an Ethnology of Europe's Barbarians,* pp. 75–88. Woodbridge: Boydell.

———. 1996. Britain after Rome: Between Multiculturalism and Monoculturalism. In Graves-Brown, Jones, and Gamble, pp. 256–70.

———. 1998. Demography, Ethnography, and the Stages of Archaeolinguistics: The Celtic and Germanic Languages from a Protohistorical Perspective. Manuscript.

Hingley, R. 1989. *Rural Settlement in Roman Britain.* London: Seaby.

———. 1997. Resistance and Domination: Social Change in Roman Britain. In Mattingly, pp. 81–102.

Hingst, H., S. Hummel, and H. Schutkowski. 1990. Urnenfriedhöfe aus Schleswig-Holstein. *Germania* 68:167–222.

Hodder, I. 1982. *Symbols in Action.* Cambridge: Cambridge University Press.

Hodson, F. R. 1968. *The La Tène Cemetery at Münsingen-Rain.* Bern: Stämpfli.

Holder, P. A. 1980. *Studies in the Auxilia of the Roman Army from Augustus to Trajan.* Oxford: British Archaeological Reports, International Series 80.

Hondius-Crone, A. 1955. *The Temple of Nehalennia at Domburg.* Amsterdam: J. M. Meulenhoff.

Horn, H. G. 1987. Das Leben im römischen Rheinland. In Horn, pp. 139–317.

———, ed. 1987. *Die Römer in Nordrhein-Westfalen.* Stuttgart: Konrad Theiss.

Horst, F., and B. Krüger, eds. 1985. *Produktivkräfte und Produktionsverhältnisse in ur- und frühgeschichtlicher Zeit.* Berlin: Akademie-Verlag.

Horst, F., and F. Schlette, eds. 1988. *Frühe Völker in Mitteleuropa.* Berlin: Akademie-Verlag.

Hostetler, J. A. 1993. *Amish Society.* 4th ed. Baltimore: Johns Hopkins University Press.

Hudson, K. 1981. *A Social History of Archaeology.* London: Macmillan.

Hvass, S. 1985. *Hodde: Et vestjysk landsbysamfund fra aeldre jernalder.* Copenhagen: Universitetsforlaget.

Ilkjaer, J. 1997. Gegner und Verbündete in Nordeuropa während des 1. bis 4. Jahrhunderts. In Jørgensen and Clausen, pp. 55–64.

Ilkjaer, J., and J. Lønstrup. 1983. Der Moorfund im Tal der Illerup-Å bei Skanderborg in Ostjütland. *Germania* 61:95–116.

Isaac, B. 1990. *The Limits of Empire: The Roman Army in the East.* Oxford: Clarendon Press. (2d ed., 1992).

———. 1993. An Open Frontier. In Brun, van der Leeuw, and Whittaker, pp. 105–14.

Jacobi, G. 1974a. Zum Schriftgebrauch in keltischen Oppida nördlich der Alpen. *Hamburger Beiträge zur Archäologie* 4:171–81.

———. 1974b. *Werkzeug und Gerät aus dem Oppidum von Manching.* Wiesbaden: Franz Steiner.

Jacobsthal, P. 1944. *Early Celtic Art.* Oxford: Clarendon.

James, E. 1988. *The Franks.* Oxford: Blackwell.

James, S. 1993. *The World of the Celts.* London: Thames and Hudson.

Jankuhn, H. 1976. Siedlung, Wirtschaft und Gesellschaftsordnung der germanischen Stämme in der Zeit der römischen Angriffskriege. In H. Temporini, ed., *Aufstieg und Niedergang der römischen Welt* II, 5, 1, pp. 65–126. Berlin: Walter de Gruyter.

Jankuhn, H., and D. Timpe, eds. 1989. *Beiträge zum Verständnis der Germania des Tacitus* part 1. Göttingen: Vandenhoeck und Ruprecht.

Jażdżewska, M. 1986. Ein römischer Legionärshelm aus Polen. *Germania* 64:61–73.

———. 1992. Cimetière de La Tène III et de la période romaine à Siemiechów. *Inventaria Archaeologica: Pologne,* fascicule 64, pls. 386–92. Warsaw: Wydawnictwo Naukowe Pwn.

Jażdżewski, K. 1965. *Poland.* London: Thames and Hudson.

Jensen, C. K., and K. H. Nielsen, eds. 1997. *Burial and Society.* Aarhus: Aarhus University Press.

Jerem, E. 1995. Celts of Eastern Europe. In Green, pp. 581–602.

Joachim, H.-E. 1991. Jüngereisenzeitliche Siedlungsprobleme am Niederrhein. *Marburger Kolloquium 1989,* pp. 29–48. Marburg: Vorgeschichtliches Seminar.

———. 1995. *Waldalgesheim: Das Grab einer keltischen Fürstin.* Cologne: Rheinland-Verlag.

Joffroy, R. 1960. *L'Oppidum de Vix et la civilisation hallstattienne finale dans l'Est de la France.* Dijon: Bernigaud.

———. 1962. *Le trésor de Vix: Histoire et portée d'une grande découverte.* Paris: Fayard.

Jones, G. D. 1989. *Maya Resistance to Spanish Rule: Time and History on a Colonial Frontier.* Albuquerque: University of New Mexico Press.

Jones, R. 1987a. Burial Customs of Rome and the Provinces. In Wacher, vol. 2, pp. 812–37.

———. 1987b. A False Start? The Roman Urbanisation of Western Europe. *World Archaeology* 19:47–57.

———. 1993. Rules for the Living and the Dead: Funerary Practices and Social Organisation. In Struck, pp. 247–54.

Jones, S. 1996. Discourses of Identity in the Interpretation of the Past. In Graves-Brown, Jones, and Gamble, pp. 62–80.

———. 1997. *The Archaeology of Ethnicity: Constructing Identities in the Past and Present.* London: Routledge.

Jørgensen, A. N., and B. L. Clausen, eds. 1997. *Military Aspects of Scandinavian Society in a European Perspective, AD 1–1300.* Copenhagen: National Museum.

Kaiser, S. B. 1990. *The Social Psychology of Clothing and Personal Adornment.* New York: Macmillan.

Kaul, F. 1991. The Dejbjerg Carts. In Moscati et al., pp. 536–37.

Kaul, F., and J. Martens. 1995. Southeast European Influences in the Early Iron Age of Southern Scandinavia: Gundestrup and the Cimbri. *Acta Archaeologica* 66:111–61.

Kehne, P. 1995. Geographische und ethnographische Informationen über das nördliche Germanien und die Elberegion. In Busch, pp. 25–34.

———. 1997. Die Eroberung Galliens, die zeitweilige Unterwerfung Germaniens, die Grenzen des *Imperium Romanum* und seine Beziehungen zu germanischen *gentes* im letzten Jahrzehnt der Forschung. *Germania* 75:265–84.

Keiling, H. 1989. Jastorfkultur und Germanen. In Herrmann, vol. 1, pp. 147–55.

Keller, E. 1984. *Die frühkaiserzeitlichen Körpergräber von Heimstetten bei München und die verwandten Funde aus Südbayern.* Munich: C. H. Beck.

Keller, J. 1965. *Das keltische Fürstengrab von Reinheim.* Mainz: Römisch-Germanisches Zentralmuseum.

Kellner, H.-J. 1990. *Die Münzfunde von Manching und die keltischen Fundmünzen aus Südbayern.* Stuttgart: Franz Steiner.

Kepecs, S. 1997. Native Yucatán and Spanish Influence: The Archaeology and History of Chikinchel. *Journal of Archaeological Method and Theory* 4, 3:307–30.

Keppie, L.J.F. 1984. *The Making of the Roman Army.* Totowa, NJ: Barnes and Noble.

———. 1991. Armies on Frontiers: Myth and Realities. In Maxfield and Dobson, pp. 455–57.

Kimmig, W. 1983. *Die Heuneburg an der oberen Donau.* Stuttgart: Konrad Theiss.

King, A. 1990. *Roman Gaul and Germany.* Berkeley: University of California Press.

King, A., and M. Henig, eds. 1981. *The Roman West in the Third Century.* Oxford: British Archaeological Reports, International Series 109.

Klindt-Jensen, O. 1950. *Foreign Influences in Denmark's Early Iron Age.* Copenhagen: Munksgaard.

Knaut, A. L. 1995. *The Pueblo Revolt of 1680: Conquest and Resistance in Seventeenth-Century New Mexico.* Norman: University of Oklahoma.

Kobylinski, Z., ed. 1991. *Ethnicity in Archaeology. Archaeologia Polona* 29.

Koch, J. T., and J. Carey. 1995. *The Celtic Heroic Age: Literary Sources for Ancient Celtic Europe and Early Ireland and Wales.* Malden, MA: Celtic Studies Publications.

Kolník, T. 1978. Q. Atilius Primus-Interprex Centurio und Negotiator: Eine bedeutende Grabinschrift aus dem 1. Jh. u. Z. im quadischen Limes-Vorland. *Acta Archaeologica Academiae Scientarum Hungaricae* 30:61–75.

Konrad, M. 1994. Ein Fibel-Depotfund aus Bregenz (Brigantium): Weihefund in einem Tempel? *Germania* 72:217–29.

Kopytoff, I. 1993. The Roman Frontier and the Uses of Comparison. In Brun, van der Leeuw, and Whittaker, pp. 143–48.

Kossack, G. 1970. *Gräberfelder der Hallstattzeit an Main und Fränkischer Saale.* Kallmünz: Michael Lassleben.

Koster, A. 1993. Ein reich ausgestattetes Waffengrab des 1. Jahrhunderts n. Chr. aus Nijmegen. In Struck, pp. 293–96.

Krämer, W. 1957. Zu den Ausgrabungen in dem keltischen Oppidum von Manching. *Germania* 35:32–44.

———. 1958. Manching, ein vindelikisches Oppidum an der Donau. In W. Krämer, ed., *Neue Ausgrabungen in Deutschland*, pp. 175–202. Berlin: Gebr. Mann.

———. 1962. Manching II: Zu den Ausgrabungen in den Jahren 1957 bis 1961. *Germania* 40:293–317.

———. 1964. *Das keltische Gräberfeld von Nebringen (Kreis Böblingen).* Stuttgart: Silberburg.

———. 1982. Graffiti auf Spätlatènekeramik aus Manching. *Germania* 60:489–99.

———. 1985. *Die Grabfunde von Manching und die latènezeitlichen Flachgräber in Südbayern.* Stuttgart: Franz Steiner.

———. 1993. Das Oppidum von Manching: Erforschungsgeschichte. In Dannheimer and Gebhard, pp. 107–111.

Krause, R. 1995. Viereckschanze mit 'zentralörtlicher Funktion.' *Archäologie in Deutschland* 4:30–33.

Krausse, D. 1996. *Hochdorf III: Das Trink- und Speiseservice aus dem späthallstattzeitlichen Fürstengrab von Eberdingen-Hochdorf (Kr. Ludwigsburg).* Stuttgart: Konrad Theiss.

Kromer, K. 1963. *Hallstatt: Die Salzhandelsmetropole des ersten Jahrtausends vor Christus in den Alpen.* Vienna: Naturhistorisches Museum.

Krüger, B., ed., 1988. *Die Germanen*. Berlin: Akademie-Verlag.

Kruta, V. 1991a. The First Celtic Expansion. In Moscati et al., pp. 195–213.

———. 1991b. Celtic Writing. In Moscati et al., pp. 491–97.

Kühlborn, J.-S. 1988. Die Zeit der augusteischen Angriffe gegen die rechtsrheinischen Germanenstämme. In *Kaiser Augustus und die verlorene Republik*, pp. 530–40. Berlin: Antikenmuseum.

———. 1989a. Zur Geschichte der augusteischen Militärlager in Westfalen. In Asskamp, pp. 9–17.

———. 1989b. Oberaden. In Asskamp, pp. 44–51.

———. 1991. Die Lagerzentren der römischen Militärlager von Oberaden und Anreppen. In Trier, pp. 129–40.

Kühlborn, J.-S., and C. Reichmann. 1992. Zum Befund der Grube 80/1 an der nordöstlichen Lagereck und ihren einheimischen Keramikfunden. In J.-S. Kühlborn and S. von Schnurbein, *Das Römerlager in Oberaden III*, pp. 86–88. Münster: Aschendorff.

Kühn, H. 1976. *Geschichte der Vorgeschichtsforschung*. Berlin: Walter de Gruyter.

Kuhnen, H.-P. 1994. Die Privatziegelei des Gaius Longinius Speratus in Grossbottwar, Kreis Ludwigsburg: Handel und Wandel im römischen Südwestdeutschland. *Fundberichte aus Baden-Württemberg* 19/1:255–64.

———, ed. 1992. *Gestürmt-Geräumt-Vergessen? Der Limesfall und das Ende der Römerherrschaft in Südwestdeutschland*. Stuttgart: Württembergisches Landesmuseum.

———, ed. 1996. *Religio Romana: Wege zu den Göttern im antiken Trier.* Trier: Rheinisches Landesmuseum.

Kunow, J. 1983. *Der römische Import in der Germania libera*. Neumünster: Wachholtz.

———. 1985. Zum Handel mit römischen Importen in der Germania libera. In Düwel et al., pp. 430–50.

———. 1986. Bemerkungen zum Export römischer Waffen in das Barbarikum. In C. Unz and A. Wais, eds., *Studien zu den Militärgrenzen Roms III*, pp. 740–46. Stuttgart: Konrad Theiss.

———. 1987. Die Militärgeschichte Niedergermaniens. In Horn, pp. 27–109.

Küster, H. 1986. Werden und Wandel der Kulturlandschaft im Alpenvorland: Pollenanalytische Aussagen zur Siedlungsgeschichte am Auerberg in Südbayern. *Germania* 64:533–59.

———. 1995. *Geschichte der Landschaft in Mitteleuropa*. Munich: C. H. Beck.

Kyll, N. 1966. Heidnische Weihe- und Votivgaben aus der Römerzeit des Trierer Landes. *Trierer Zeitschrift* 29:5–113.

Lange, G. 1983. *Die menschlichen Skelettreste aus dem Oppidum von Manching*. Wiesbaden: Franz Steiner.

Larsen, M. T. 1976. *The Old Assyrian City-State and Its Colonies*. Copenhagen: Akademisk Forlag.

Laubenheimer, F. 1987. De l'usage populaire de l'écriture grecque dans la Gaule du Centre-Est. *Revue archéologique de l'Est et du Centre-Est* 38:53–74.

Laux, F. 1992. Überlegungen zu den germanischen Fürstengräbern bei Marwedel, Gde. Hitzacker, Kr. Lückow-Dannenberg. *Bericht der Römisch-Germanischen Kommission* 73:315–76.

Le Gall, J. 1983. Témoignages monétaires d'un esprit de resistance à Alesia un siècle aprés Vercingetorix. In *La Patrie gauloise d'Agrippa au VIème siècle*, pp. 15–18. Lyon: L'Hermès.

Lehmann, G. A. 1989. Die Varus-Katastrophe aus der Sicht des Historikers. In Asskamp, pp. 85–95.

———. 1991. Zum Problem des römischen "Verzichtes" auf die Okkupation Germaniens. In Trier, pp. 217–28.

———. 1995. Das Ende der römischen Herrschaft über das "westelbische" Germanien. In Wiegels and Woesler, pp. 123–41.

Lehmann, H.-D. 1997. Stätten der Mantik: Ein Vorschlag zur Deutung der Funktion keltischer "Viereckschanzen" Süddeutschlands. *Archäologisches Korrespondenzblatt* 27:127–35.

Lenz, K. H. 1995. Germanische Siedlungen der Spätlatènezeit und der Römischen Kaiserzeit im rheinischen Braunkohlenrevier. *Archäologische Informationen* 18/2:157–62.

Lenz-Bernhard, G., and H. Bernhard. 1992. *Das Oberrheingebiet zwischen Caesars gallischem Krieg und der flavischen Okkupation (58 v.-73 n. Chr.): Eine siedlungsgeschichtliche Studie*. Speyer: Mitteilungen des Historischen Vereins der Pfalz, 89.

Leube, A. 1989. Germanische Stämme und Kulturen des 1. und 2. Jh. In Herrmann, vol. 1, pp. 156–65.

Levi, A. C. 1952. *Barbarians on Roman Imperial Coins and Sculpture*. New York: American Numismatic Society.

Lightfoot, K. G. 1995. Culture Contact Studies: Defining the Relationship between Prehistoric and Historic Archaeology. *American Antiquity* 60:199–217.

Lightfoot, K. G., and A. Martinez. 1995. Frontiers and Boundaries in Archaeological Perspective. *Annual Review of Anthropology* 24:471–92.

Lloyd-Morgan, G. 1995. Appearance, Life, and Leisure. In Green, pp. 95–120.

Lo Cascio, E. 1994. The Size of the Roman Population. *Journal of Roman Studies* 84:23–40.

Lockhart, J. 1994. Sightings: Initial Nahua Reactions to Spanish Culture. In Schwartz, pp. 218–48.

Lorenz, H. 1978. Totenbrauchtum und Tracht: Untersuchungen zur regionalen Gliederung in der frühen Latènezeit. *Bericht der Römisch-Germanischen Kommission* 59:1–380.

Luttwak, E. 1976. *The Grand Strategy of the Roman Empire from the First Century A.D. to the Third*. Baltimore: Johns Hopkins University Press.

MacEachern, S. 1998. Style, Scale and Cultural Variation: Technological Traditions in the Northern Mandara Mountains. In M. Stark, ed., *The Archaeology of Social Boundaries*, pp. 107–31. Washington: Smithsonian Institution Press.

Mackensen, M. 1978. *Das römische Gräberfeld auf der Keckwiese in Kempten.* Kallmünz: Michael Lassleben.

MacMullen, R. 1965. The Celtic Renaissance. *Historia* 14:93–104.

Madsen, O. 1995a. Hedegård: Et center fra sen førromersk jernalder i Midtjylland. *Archäologie in Schleswig* 4:20–36.

———. 1995b. Produktion, bebyggelse og samfundorganisation i sen førromersk og aeldre romersk jernalder. In *Produksjon og samfunn*, pp. 183–203. Oslo: Universitetets Oldsaksamling.

———. 1997. Pragtvåben. *Skalk* 2:3–9.

Maier, F. 1970. *Die bemalte Spätlatène-Keramik von Manching.* Wiesbaden: Franz Steiner.

———. 1986. Vorbericht über die Ausgrabung 1985 in dem spätkeltischen Oppidum von Manching. *Germania* 64:1–43.

———. 1990. Das Kultbäumchen von Manching. *Germania* 68:129–65.

———. 1991. The *Oppida* of the Second and First Centuries B.C. In Moscati et al., pp. 411–25.

Maier, R. A. 1983a. Volkstümliche Hirschterrakotten aus römischen Gräberfeldern bei Nassenfels und Pförring-Forchheim, Oberbayern. *Germania* 61:593–96.

———. 1983b. Römerzeitliche Töpferofen für "Norisches Bauerngeschirr" bei Kieling. *Das archäologische Jahr in Bayern 1983*:113–16.

———. 1985a. Römerzeitliche Brandopferplätze: Zeugnisse alpenrätischer Volksreligion. In Petzet, pp. 219–22.

———. 1985b. Ein römerzeitlicher Brandopferplatz bei Schwangau und andere Zeugnisse einheimischer Religion in der Provinz Rätien. In Bellot, Czysz, and Krahe, pp. 231–56.

Mallory, J. R. 1989. *In Search of the Indo-Europeans.* London: Thames and Hudson.

Malmstrom, V. H. 1971. *Geography of Europe.* Englewood Cliffs: Prentice-Hall.

Mann, J. C. 1975a. The Frontiers of the Principate. In H. Temporini, ed., *Aufstieg und Niedergang der römischen Welt* II, 1, pp. 508–33. Berlin: Walter de Gruyter.

———. 1975b. Power, Force and the Frontiers of the Empire. *Journal of Roman Studies* 69:175–83.

Mann, J. C., and M. M. Roxan. 1988. Discharge Certificates of the Roman Army. *Britannia* 19:341–47.

Mann, M. 1986. *A History of Power from the Beginning to A.D. 1760.* Cambridge: Cambridge University Press.

Mannsperger, D. 1981. Münzen und Münzfunde. In Bittel, Kimmig, and Schiek, pp. 228–47.

Marchand, S. L. 1996. *Down from Olympus: Archaeology and Philhellenism in Germany, 1750–1970.* Princeton: Princeton University Press.

Markey, T. L. 1986. Social Spheres and National Groups in Germania. In Beck, pp. 248–66.

Martens, J. 1994. Refuge-Fortified Settlement-Central Place? *Ethnographisch-Ar-chäologische Zeitschrift* 35:241–76.

Marvick, D. 1996. Elites. In A. Kuper and J. Kuper, eds., *The Social Science Encyclope-dia*, 2d ed., pp. 237–39. New York: Routledge.

Mason, P. 1990. *Deconstructing America: Representations of the Other.* London: Routledge.

Mattingly, D. J. 1997. Dialogues of Power and Experience in the Roman Empire. In Mattingly, pp. 7–26.

———, ed. 1997. *Dialogues in Roman Imperialism: Power, Discourse, and Discrepant Experience in the Roman Empire.* Journal of Roman Archaeology, Supplemen-tary Series, no. 23.

Maurach, G. 1995. Die literarische Form des Arminiusschlacht-Berichts. In Wie-gels and Woesler, pp. 167–73.

Maxfield, V. A. 1987. The Frontiers: Mainland Europe. In Wacher, vol. 1, pp. 139–93.

Maxfield, V. A., and M. J. Dobson, eds. 1991. *Roman Frontier Studies 1989.* Exeter: University of Exeter Press.

McEvedy, C., and R. Jones. 1978. *Atlas of World Population History.* Harmonds-worth: Penguin.

Meadows, K., C. Lemke, and J. Heron, eds. 1997. *TRAC 96: Proceedings of the Sixth Annual Theoretical Roman Archaeology Conference.* Oxford: Oxbow.

Meduna, J. 1980. *Die latènezeitlichen Siedlungen in Mähren.* Brno: Ceskoslovenská Akademie Ved.

Megaw, J.V.S., and M. R. Megaw 1990. *The Basse Yutz Find: Masterpieces of Celtic Art.* London: Society of Antiquaries.

Megaw, R., and V. Megaw. 1989. *Celtic Art.* London: Thames and Hudson.

———. 1995. The Nature and Function of Celtic Art. In Green, pp. 345–75.

Meid, W. 1986. Hans Kuhns 'Nordwestblock'-Hypothese: Zur Problematik der 'Völker zwischen Germanen und Kelten.' In Beck, pp. 183–212.

Menke, M. 1974. "Rätische" Siedlungen und Bestattungsplätze der frührö-mischen Kaiserzeit im Voralpenland. In G. Kossack and G. Ulbert, eds., *Stu-dien zur vor- und frühgeschichtlichen Archäologie*, vol. 1, pp. 141–59. Munich: C. H. Beck.

Merrifield, R. 1987. *The Archaeology of Ritual and Magic.* New York: Amsterdam Books.

Metzler, J. 1984. Treverische Reitergräber von Goeblingen-Nospelt. In Cüppers, pp. 87–99.

———. 1995. *Das treverische Oppidum auf dem Titelberg: Zur Kontinuität zwischen der spätkeltischen und der frührömischen Zeit in Nord-Gallien.* Luxembourg: Musée National d'Histoire et d'Art.

Metzler, J., M. Millett, N. Roymans, and J. Slofstra, eds. 1995. *Integration in the Early Roman West.* Luxembourg: Musée National d'Histoire et d'Art.

310

Metzler, J., R. Waringo, R. Bis, and N. Metzler-Zens. 1991. *Clemency et les tombes de l'aristocratie en Gaule Belgique.* Luxembourg: Musée National d'Histoire et d'Art.

Michaelsen, K. K. 1994. Godt skrot: en romersk statue i Gudme. *Årbog for Svendborg & Omegns Museum 1994*:8–15.

Michaelsen, K. K., and P. Ø. Sørensen. 1993. En kongsgård fra jernalderen. *Årbog for Svendborg & Omegns Museum 1993*:24–35.

———. 1996. Tusindvis af stolpehuller: uafbrudt bebyggelse i Gudme fra 3. årh. e. Kr. til vikingetid. *Årbog for Svendborg & Omegns Museum 1996*:8–20.

Mignolo, W. D. 1993. Misunderstanding and Colonization: The Reconfiguration of Memory and Space. *South Atlantic Quarterly* 92, 2:209–60.

———. 1994. Writing and Recorded Knowledge in Colonial and Post-Colonial Situations. In Boone and Mignolo, pp. 293–313.

Miller, D., M. Rowlands, C. Tilley, eds. 1989. *Domination and Resistance.* London: Allen and Unwin.

Millett, M. 1990a. *The Romanization of Britain.* Cambridge: Cambridge University Press.

———. 1990b. Romanization: Historical Issues and Archaeological Interpretation. In Blagg and Millett, pp. 35–44.

Mócsy, A. 1978. *Zur Entstehung und Eigenart der Nordgrenzen Roms.* Opladen: Westdeutscher Verlag.

Modood, T., S. Beishon, and S. Virdee. 1994. *Changing Ethnic Identities.* London: Policy Studies Institute.

Morris, I. 1992. *Death-Ritual and Social Structure in Classical Antiquity.* Cambridge: Cambridge University Press.

Moscati, S., O.-H. Frey, V. Kruta, B. Raftery, and M. Szabó, eds. 1991. *The Celts.* New York: Rizzoli.

Motyková, K. 1976. Die ältere römische Kaiserzeit in Böhmen im Lichte der neueren historisch-archäologischen Forschung. In H. Temporini, ed., *Aufstieg und Niedergang der römischen Welt* II, 5, 1, pp. 143–99. Berlin: Walter de Gruyter.

Motyková, K., P. Drda, and A. Rybová. 1988. Die bauliche Gestalt der Akropolis auf dem Burgwall Závist in der Späthallstatt- und Frühlatènezeit. *Germania* 66:391–436.

von Müller, A. 1964. *Die jungbronzezeitliche Siedlung von Berlin-Lichterfelde.* Berlin: Hessling.

Müller, F. 1990. *Der Massenfund von der Tiefenau bei Bern: Zur Deutung latènezeitlicher Sammelfunde mit Waffen.* Basel: Schweizerische Gesellschaft für Ur- und Frühgeschichte.

Müller, K. E. 1972. *Geschichte der antiken Ethnographie und ethnologischen Theoriebildung* 1. Wiesbaden: Franz Steiner.

Müller, R. 1985. *Die Grabfunde der Jastorf- und Latènezeit an unterer Saale und Mittelelbe.* Berlin: Deutscher Verlag der Wissenschaften.

Müller, R. 1994. Fibel und Fibeltracht: Latène-Fibeln. In *Reallexikon der germanischen Altertumskunde*, vol. 8, pp. 471–77.

Müller-Karpe, H. 1955. Das urnenfelderzeitliche Wagengrab von Hart a. d. Alz, Oberbayern. *Bayerische Vorgeschichtsblätter* 21:46–75.

Musil, J. 1994. Römische Waffen und Rüstung aus Böhmen. *Památky Archeologické* 85:5–14.

Mutton, A.F.A. 1968. *Central Europe*. 2d ed. London: Longmans.

Naumann-Steckner, F. 1997. *Tod am Rhein: Begräbnisse im frühen Köln*. Cologne: Römisch-Germanisches Museum.

Neumann, G. 1983. Die Sprachverhältnisse in den germanischen Provinzen des römischen Reiches. In W. Haase, ed., *Aufstieg und Niedergang der römischen Welt* II, 29, 2, pp. 1061–88. Berlin: Walter de Gruyter.

———. 1986. Germani cisrhenani—die Aussage der Namen. In Beck, pp. 107–30.

Neumann, G., and H. Seemann, eds. 1992. *Beiträge zum Verständnis der Germania des Tacitus*, part 2. Göttingen: Vandenhoeck und Ruprecht.

Nielsen, P. O., K. Randsborg, and H. Thrane, eds. 1994. *The Archaeology of Gudme and Lundeborg*. Copenhagen: Akademisk Forlag.

Nierhaus, R. 1959. *Das römische Brand- und Körpergräberfeld "Auf der Stieg" in Stuttgart-Bad Cannstatt*. Stuttgart: Silberburg.

Nuber, H. U. 1990. Das Ende des Obergermanisch-Rätischen Limes: Eine Forschungsaufgabe. In H. U. Nuber, K. Schmid, H. Steuer, and T. Zotz, eds., *Archäologie und Geschichte des ersten Jahrtausends in Südwestdeutschland*, pp. 51–68. Sigmaringen: Jan Thorbecke.

———. 1997. Rom und die Alamannen. In Fuchs et al., pp. 59–68.

O'Brien, J. 1986. Toward a Reconstitution of Ethnicity: Capitalist Expansion and Cultural Dynamics in Sudan. *American Anthropologist* 88:898–907.

Odenstedt, B. 1990. *On the Origin and Early History of the Runic Script*. Uppsala: Acta Academiae Regiae Gustavi Adolphi LIX.

Oldenstein, J. 1976. Zur Ausrüstung römischer Auxiliareinheiten: Studien zu Beschlägen und Zierat an der Ausrüstung der römischen Auxiliareinheiten des obergermanisch-raetischen Limesgebietes aus dem zweiten und dritten Jahrhundert n. Chr. *Bericht der Römisch-Germanischen Kommission* 57:49–284.

———. 1985. Manufacture and Supply of the Roman Army with Bronze Fittings. In M. C. Bishop, ed., *The Production and Distribution of Roman Military Equipment*, pp. 82–94. Oxford: British Archaeological Reports, International Series 275.

Orlove, B., ed. 1997. *The Allure of the Foreign: Imported Goods in Postcolonial Latin America*. Ann Arbor: University of Michigan Press.

Ortner, S. B. 1995. Resistance and the Problem of Ethnographic Refusal. *Comparative Studies in Society and History* 37:173–93.

Overbeck, B. 1993. Die Kelten im Spiegel der römischen Münzprägung. In Dannheimer and Gebhard, pp. 228–30.

Overbeck, B., and P. S. Wells. 1991. Vier neue keltische Münzen vom Kelheimer Mitterfeld. *Bayerische Vorgeschichtsblätter* 56:163–68.

The Oxford Classical Dictionary. 3d ed., 1996. Edited by S. Hornblower and A. Spawforth. Oxford: Oxford University Press.

Packer, J. 1997. *The Forum of Trajan in Rome.* Berkeley: University of California Press.

Pagden, A. 1995. *Lords of All the World: Ideologies of Empire in Spain, Britain and France c. 1500–c. 1800.* New Haven: Yale University Press.

Page, R. I. 1987. *Runes.* London: British Museum.

Pare, C. 1991. *Fürstensitze,* Celts and the Mediterranean World: Developments in the West Hallstatt Culture in the 6th and 5th Centuries B.C. *Proceedings of the Prehistoric Society* 57:183–202.

Patterson, O. 1975. Context and Choice in Ethnic Allegiance: A Theoretical Framework and Caribbean Case Study. In N. Glazer and D. P. Moynihan, eds., *Ethnicity: Theory and Experience,* pp. 305–49. Cambridge, MA: Harvard University Press.

Pauli, L. 1972. *Untersuchungen zur Späthallstattzeit in Nordwürttemberg.* Hamburg: Helmut Buske.

———. 1978. *Der Dürrnberg bei Hallein III.* Munich: C. H. Beck.

———. 1980. Die Herkunft der Kelten: Sinn und Unsinn einer alten Frage. In Pauli, pp. 16–24.

———. 1984. *The Alps: Archaeology and Early History.* Trans. E. Peters. London: Thames and Hudson.

———. 1986. Einheimische Götter und Opferbräuche im Alpenraum. In W. Haase, ed., *Aufstieg und Niedergang der römischen Welt* II, 18, 1, pp. 816–71. Berlin: Walter de Gruyter.

———. 1992. Quellen zur keltischen Religionsgeschichte. In H. Beck, D. Ellmers, and K. Schier, eds., *Germanische Religionsgeschichte,* pp. 118–44. Berlin: Walter de Gruyter.

———, ed. 1980. *Die Kelten in Mitteleuropa.* Salzburg: Landesregierung.

Peacock, D.P.S., and D. F. Williams. 1986. *Amphorae and the Roman Economy.* London: Longman.

Pels, P. 1997. The Anthropology of Colonialism: Culture, History, and the Emergence of Western Governmentality. *Annual Review of Anthropology* 26:163–83.

Percival, J. 1976. *The Roman Villa.* Berkeley: University of California Press.

———. 1987. The Villa in Italy and the Provinces. In Wacher, vol. 2, pp. 527–47.

Périn, P., and L.-C. Feffer. 1987. *Les Francs 1: A la conquête de la Gaule.* Paris: Armand Colin.

Pescheck, C. 1969. Zum Bevölkerungswechsel von Kelten und Germanen in Unterfranken. *Bayerische Vorgeschichtsblätter* 25:75–99.

———. 1977. Ausklang der Latène-Zivilisation und Anfänge der germanischen Besiedlung in Nordbayern. In Chropovský, pp. 249–59.

Pescheck, C. 1978. *Die germanischen Bodenfunde der römischen Kaiserzeit in Mainfranken.* Munich: C. H. Beck.

Peschel, K. 1978a. Die Sueben in Ethnographie und Archäologie. *Klio* 60: 259–309.

———. 1978b. *Anfänge germanischer Besiedlung im Mittelgebirgsraum.* Berlin: Deutscher Verlag der Wissenschaften.

———. 1988. Kelten und Germanen während der jüngeren Eisenzeit (2.-1. Jh. v. u. Z.). In Horst and Schlette, pp. 167–200.

———. 1989. Keltische Latènekultur und deren Randgruppen im Mittelgebirgsraum. In Herrmann, vol. 1, pp. 130–39.

von Petrikovits, H., ed. 1987. *Matronen und verwandte Gottheiten.* Cologne: Rheinland-Verlag.

Petzet, M., ed., 1985. *Die Römer in Schwaben.* Munich: Bayerisches Landesamt für Denkmalpflege.

Pfahl, S. F., and M. Reuter. 1996. Waffen aus römischen Einzelsiedlungen rechts des Rheins: Ein Beitrag zum Verhältnis von Militär und Zivilbevölkerung im Limeshinterland. *Germania* 74:119–67.

Piaskowski, J. 1985. Bemerkungen zu den Eisenverhüttungszentren auf polnischem Gebiet in ur- und frühgeschichtlicher Zeit. In Horst and Krüger, pp. 231–43.

Pietsch, M. 1995. Das augusteische Legionslager Marktbreit: Aktuelles zum Forschungsstand. In Wiegels and Woesler, pp. 41–66.

Pietsch, M., D. Timpe, and L. Wamser. 1991. Die augusteischen Truppenlager Marktbreit: Bisherige archäologische Befunde und historische Erwägungen. *Bericht der Römisch-Germanischen Kommission* 72:263–324.

Pinker, S. 1997. *How the Mind Works.* New York: W. W. Norton.

Pippidi, D. M., ed. 1976. *Assimilation et résistance à la culture gréco-romaine dans le monde ancien.* Paris: Société d'Édition "des Belles Lettres."

Pitts, L. F. 1989. Relations between Rome and the German 'Kings' on the Middle Danube in the First to Fourth Centuries A.D. *Journal of Roman Studies* 79:45–58.

Planck, D. 1975. Die Villa rustica bei Bondorf, Kreis Böblingen. *Archäologische Ausgrabungen 1975*:43–51.

———. 1978. Untersuchungen im Bereich des Kastelldorfes Buch, Gemeinde Rainau, Ostalbkreis. *Archäologische Ausgrabungen 1978*:52–60.

———. 1988. Der obergermanisch-rätische Limes in Südwestdeutschland und seine Vorläufer. In Planck, pp. 251–80.

———, ed., 1988. *Archäologie in Baden-Württemberg.* Stuttgart: Konrad Theiss.

Pleket, H. W. 1990. Wirtschaft. In Vittinghoff, pp. 25–160.

Polenz, H. 1982. Münzen in latènezeitlichen Gräbern Mitteleuropas aus der Zeit zwischen 300 und 50 vor Christi Geburt. *Bayerische Vorgeschichtsblätter* 47:27–222.

————. 1985. *Römer und Germanen in Westfalen.* Münster: Westfälisches Museum für Archäologie.

Poulter, A. 1987. Townships and Villages. In Wacher, vol. 1, pp. 388–411.

Pounds, N.J.G. 1990. *An Historical Geography of Europe.* Cambridge: Cambridge University Press.

Prakash, G., ed. 1995. *After Colonialism: Imperial Histories and Postcolonial Displacements.* Princeton: Princeton University Press.

Prammer, J. 1989. *Das römische Straubing.* Munich: Schnell and Steiner.

Pratt, M. L. 1992. *Imperial Eyes: Travel Writing and Transculturation.* London: Routledge.

Rankin, H. D. 1987. *Celts and the Classical World.* London: Croom Helm.

————. 1995. The Celts Through Classical Eyes. In Green, pp. 21–33.

Rathje, W. L. 1975. The Last Tango in Mayapán: A Tentative Trajectory of Production-Distribution Systems. In J. A. Sabloff and C. C. Lamberg-Karlovsky, eds., *Ancient Civilization and Trade,* pp. 409–48. Albuquerque: School of American Research.

Rausig, G. 1996. Roman Reflections. In *Roman Reflections in Scandinavia,* pp. 21–24.

Reallexikon der germanischen Altertumskunde, edited by H. Beck, H. Jankuhn, H. Kuhn, K. Ranke, and R. Wenskus. 1973 and later. Berlin: Walter de Gruyter.

Reddé, M., S. von Schnurbein, P. Barral, J. Bénard, V. Brouquier-Reddé, R. Goguey, H. Joly, H.-J. Köhler, and C. Petit. 1995. Fouilles et recherches nouvelles sur les travaux de César devant Alésia (1991–1994). *Bericht der Römisch-Germanischen Kommission* 76:73–158.

Reichenberger, A. 1995. Tempel und Brandopferstätten in Niederbayern. *Archäologie in Deutschland* 4:18–21.

Reichenberger, A., and M. Schaich. 1996. Vorbericht zur Ausgrabung der Viereckschanze von Plattling-Pankofen, Lkr. Deggendorf. *Vorträge des 14. Niederbayerischen Archäologentages,* pp. 83–153.

Reichmann, C. 1979. *Zur Besiedlungsgeschichte des Lippemündungsgebietes während der jüngeren vorrömischen Eisenzeit und der ältesten römischen Kaiserzeit.* Wesel: Hans Dambeck.

Reinecke, P. 1942. Der Negauer Helmfund. *Bericht der Römisch-Germanischen Kommission* 32:117–98.

————. 1957. Skelettgräber der frühen Kaiserzeit in Raetien. *Bayerische Vorgeschichtsblätter* 22:36–59.

Renfrew, C., and P. Bahn. 1996. *Archaeology: Theory, Methods, and Practice.* 2d ed. London: Thames and Hudson.

Richards, J. F. 1993. *The Mughal Empire.* Cambridge: Cambridge University Press.

Richmond, I. 1982. *Trajan's Army on Trajan's Column.* London: British School at Rome.

Rieckhoff, S. 1975. Münzen und Fibeln aus dem Vicus des Kastells Hüfingen (Schwarzwald-Baar-Kreis). *Saalburg Jahrbuch* 32.

Rieckhoff, S. 1992. Überlegungen zur Chronologie der Spätlatènezeit im süd-lichen Mitteleuropa. *Bayerische Vorgeschichtsblätter* 57:103–21.

———. 1993. Frühe Germanen in Südbayern. In Dannheimer and Gebhard, pp. 237–42.

———. 1995. *Süddeutschland im Spannungsfeld von Kelten, Germanen und Römern.* Trier: Rheinisches Landesmuseum.

Rieckhoff-Pauli, S. 1983. Spätkeltische und frühgermanische Funde aus Regens-burg. *Bayerische Vorgeschichtsblätter* 48:63–128.

Rivet, A.L.F. 1988. *Gallia Narbonensis: Southern France in Roman Times.* London: Batsford.

Rix, H. 1954. Zur Verbreitung und Chronologie einiger keltischer Ortsnamenty-pen. In *Festschrift für Peter Goessler,* pp. 99–107. Stuttgart: W. Kohlhammer.

Rogers, J. D. 1990. *Objects of Change: The Archaeology and History of Arikara Contact with Europeans.* Washington: Smithsonian Institution.

Roggenbuck, P. 1983. Das Grab 150 von Putensen, Kr. Harburg. *Hammaburg* 6:133–41.

Roman Reflections in Scandinavia. 1996. Rome: "L'Erma" di Bretschneider.

Romanucci-Ross, L., and G. DeVos, eds. 1995. *Ethnic Identity: Creation, Conflict, and Accommodation.* 3d ed. Walnut Creek, CA: Sage.

Rosenstock, D. 1985. Die ersten Grab- und Siedlungsfunde der Grossromstedter Kultur aus dem Landkreis Rhön-Grabfeld. *Das archäologische Jahr in Bayern 1985*:95–99.

———. 1986. Ein reicher Keramikkomplex der Grossromstedter Kultur aus Ober-streu, Landkreis Rhön-Grabfeld: Ein Beitrag zur frühgermanischen Besied-lung in Mainfranken. In *Aus Frankens Frühzeit: Festgabe für Peter Endrich,* pp. 113–32. Würzburg: Freunde Mainfränkischer Kunst und Geschichte.

Rosenstock, D., and L. Wamser. 1989. Von der germanischen Landnahme bis zur Einbeziehung in das fränkische Reich. In P. Kolb and E.-G. Krenig, eds., *Unterfränkische Geschichte,* vol. 1, pp. 15–89. Würzburg: Echter Verlag.

Ross, A. 1995. Ritual and the Druids. In Green, pp. 423–44.

Rossi, L. 1971. *Trajan's Column and the Dacian Wars.* Trans. J.M.C. Toynbee. Ithaca, NY: Cornell University Press.

Roxan, M. M. 1991. Women on the Frontiers. In Maxfield and Dobson, pp. 462–67.

Roymans, N. 1983. The North Belgic Tribes in the 1st Century B.C.: A Historical-Anthropological Perspective. In Brandt and Slofstra, pp. 43–69.

———. 1990. *Tribal Societies in Northern Gaul: An Anthropological Perspective.* Am-sterdam: Cingula.

———. 1993. Romanisation and the Transformation of a Martial Elite-Ideology in a Frontier Province. In Brun, van der Leeuw, and Whittaker, pp. 33–50.

———. 1995. Romanization, Cultural Identity and the Ethnic Discussion: The Integration of Lower Rhine Populations in the Roman Empire. In Metzler et al., pp. 47–64.

————. 1996. The Sword or the Plough: Regional Dynamics in the Romanisation of Belgic Gaul and the Rhineland Area. In Roymans, pp. 9–126.

————, ed. 1996. *From the Sword to the Plough.* Amsterdam: Amsterdam University Press.

Roymans, N., and T. van Rooijen. 1993. De voorromeinse glazen armbandproduktie in het Nederrijnse gebied en haar culturele betekenis. *Vormen uit vuur* 1993/3:2–10, 56–57.

Roymans, N., and T. Derks, eds. 1994. *De Tempel van Empel: Een Hercules-Heiligdom in het Woongebied van de Bataven.* 's-Hertogenbosch: Brabantse Regionale Geschiedbeoefening.

Der Runde Berg bei Urach, vols. 1–5. 1974–84. Heidelberg: Heidelberger Akademie der Wissenschaften, Kommission für Alamannische Altertumsforschung.

Rupp, V. 1991. Römische Landwirtschaft in der Wetterau. In Rupp, pp. 249–58.

————, ed. 1991. *Archäologie der Wetterau.* Friedberg: Bindernagel Buchhandlung.

Rupprecht, G. 1990. Mainz. In Cüppers, pp. 458–69.

Rybová, A., and K. Motyková. 1983. Der Eisendepotfund der Latènezeit von Kolín. *Památky Archeologické* 74:96–174.

Said, E. W. 1989. Representing the Colonized: Anthropology's Interlocutors. *Critical Inquiry* 15:205–25.

————. 1993. *Culture and Imperialism.* New York: Knopf.

Samson, R., ed. 1991. *The Social Archaeology of Houses.* Glasgow: Cruithne Press.

Saum, L. O. 1965. *The Fur Trader and the Indian.* Seattle: University of Washington Press.

Scarre, C. 1995. *The Penguin Historical Atlas of Ancient Rome.* London: Penguin.

Scheid, J. 1995. Der Tempelbezirk im Altbachtal zu Trier: Ein "Nationalheiligtum"? In Metzler et al., pp. 101–10.

Schleiermacher, W. 1965. Zum Fortleben von Latènetraditionen im Kunsthandwerk der römischen Kaiserzeit. *Gymnasium Beiheft* 5: 43–48.

Schlette, F. 1988. Frühe Völker in Mitteleuropa: Archäologische Kulturen und ethnische Gemeinschaften des 1. Jahrtausends v. u. Z. In Horst and Schlette, pp. 9–23.

Schlippschuh, O. 1974. *Die Händler im römischen Kaiserreich in Gallien, Germanien und den Donauprovinzen Raetien, Noricum und Pannonien.* Amsterdam: Hakkert.

Schlüter, W. 1992. Archäologische Zeugnisse zur Varusschlacht: Die Untersuchungen in der Kalkrieser-Niewedder Senke bei Osnabrück. *Germania* 70:307–402.

————. 1995. Neue archäologische Forschungen zur Örtlichkeit der clades Variana: Die spätaugusteischen Ausgrabungen in Kalkriese, Ldkr. Osnabrück. In Busch, pp. 35–46.

————. 1997a. Archäologische Forschungen zur Varusschlacht in der Kalkrieser-Niewedder Senke im Osnabrücker Land. In Seibt, Borsdorf, and Grütter, pp. 88–94.

Schlüter, W. 1997b. Archäologische Forschungen zur Örtlichkeit der Varusschlacht. In Jørgensen and Clausen, pp. 65–75.

Schmid, P. 1982. Zum Handel im niedersächsischen Küstengebiet während der ersten Jahrhunderte nach Christi Geburt. *Jahrbuch der Männer vom Morgenstern* 61:79–109.

———. 1994. Feddersen Wierde. In *Reallexikon der germanischen Altertumskunde*, vol. 8, pp. 249–66.

Schmid, P., and H. Zimmermann. 1976. Flögeln: Zur Struktur einer Siedlung des 1. bis 5. Jhs. n. Chr. im Küstengebiet des südlichen Nordsee. *Probleme der Küstenforschung im südlichen Nordseegebiet* 11:1–77.

Schmidt, B., and W. Nitzschke. 1989. *Ein Gräberfeld der Spätlatènezeit und der frührömischen Kaiserzeit bei Schkopau, Kr. Merseburg.* Berlin: Deutscher Verlag der Wissenschaften.

Schmidt, K. H. 1979. On the Celtic Languages of Continental Europe. *Bulletin of the Board of Celtic Studies* 28:189–205.

Schmitt, O. 1993. Anmerkungen zum Bataveraufstand. *Bonner Jahrbücher* 193:141–60.

Schnapp, A. 1997. *The Discovery of the Past.* Trans. I. Kinnes and G. Varndell. New York: Harry N. Abrams.

von Schnurbein, S. 1977. *Das römische Gräberfeld von Regensburg.* Kallmünz: Lassleben.

———. 1981. Untersuchungen zur Geschichte der römischen Militärlager an der Lippe. *Bericht der Römisch-Germanischen Kommission* 62:5–101.

———. 1982. Die kulturgeschichtliche Stellung des nördlichen Rätien. *Bericht der Römisch-Germanischen Kommission* 63:5–16.

———. 1985. Die Funde von Augsburg-Oberhausen und die Besetzung des Alpenvorlandes durch die Römer. In Bellot, Czysz, and Krahe, pp. 15–43.

———. 1993. Nachleben in römischer Zeit? In Dannheimer and Gebhard, pp. 244–48.

———. 1995. *Vom Einfluss Roms auf die Germanen.* Opladen: Westdeutscher Verlag.

———. 1997. Die Organisation des Römischen Heeres und die Struktur des Limes in Germanien. In Jørgensen and Clausen, eds., pp. 11–18.

von Schnurbein, S., and M. Erdrich. 1992. Das Projekt: Römische Funde im mitteleuropäischen Barbaricum, dargestellt am Beispiel Niedersachsen. *Bericht der Römisch-Germanischen Kommission* 73:5–27.

von Schnurbein, S., A. Wigg, and D. G. Wigg. 1995. Ein spätaugusteisches Militärlager in Lahnau-Waldgirmes (Hessen). *Germania* 73:337–67.

Schön, F. 1986. *Der Beginn der römischen Herrschaft in Rätien.* Sigmaringen: Thorbecke.

Schönberger, H. 1985. Die römischen Truppenlager der frühen und mittleren Kaiserzeit zwischen Nordsee und Inn. *Bericht der Römisch-Germanischen Kommission* 66:321–497.

Schönberger, H., and H.-G. Simon. 1976. *Römerlager Rödgen*. Berlin: Gebr. Mann.

———. 1980. *Das Kastell Okarben und die Besetzung der Wetterau seit Vespasian*. Berlin: Gebr. Mann.

Schoppa, H. 1970. Funde aus der germanischen Siedlung Westick bei Kamen, Kreis Unna: Das römische Fundgut. In H. Beck, ed., *Spätkaiserzeitliche Funde in Westfalen*, pp. 222–49. Münster: Aschendorfsche Verlagsbuchhandlung.

Schröter, P. 1997. Review of G. Lange, *Die menschlichen Skelettreste aus dem Oppidum von Manching* (1983). *Bayerische Vorgeschichtsblätter* 62:290–94.

Schultze, E. 1986. Zur Verbreitung von Waffenbeigaben bei den germanischen Stämmen um den Beginn unserer Zeitrechnung. *Jahrbuch der Bodendenkmalpflege in Mecklenburg* 1986:93–117.

———. 1988. Bemerkungen zu den spätlatènezeitlichen Waffengräbern des mitteleuropäischen Raumes. In Horst and Schlette, pp. 111–20.

———. 1992. Zu den Grab- und Bestattungssitten in Mitteleuropa während der ersten Jahrhunderte n. Chr. *Praehistorische Zeitschrift* 67:201–19.

Schwartz, S. B., ed. 1994. *Implicit Understandings: Observing, Reporting, and Reflecting on the Encounters Between Europeans and Other Peoples in the Early Modern Era*. Cambridge: Cambridge University Press.

Schwarz, K. 1975. Die Geschichte eines keltischen Temenos im nördlichen Alpenvorland. In *Ausgrabungen in Deutschland*, vol. 1, pp. 324–58. Mainz: Römisch-Germanisches Zentralmuseum.

Schwarz, W. 1991. Römische Kaiserzeit. In Hässler, pp. 193–237.

Schwieder, E., and D. Schwieder. 1975. *A Peculiar People: Iowa's Old Order Amish*. Ames: Iowa State University Press.

Scott, J. C. 1985. *Weapons of the Weak: Everyday Forms of Peasant Resistance*. New Haven: Yale University Press.

———. 1990. *Domination and the Arts of Resistance*. New Haven: Yale University Press.

Seibt, F., U. Borsdorf, and H. T. Grütter, eds. 1997. *Transit Brügge-Novgorod: Eine Strasse durch die europäische Geschichte*. Essen: Pomp.

Seidel, M. 1996. Frühe Germanen am unteren Main: Bemerkungen zu neuen Zeugnissen der Przeworsk-Kultur aus Oberhessen. *Germania* 74:238–47.

Seyer, H. 1985. Zum Stand der Produktivkräfte während der vorrömischen Eisenzeit im Jastorfbereich. In Horst and Krüger, pp. 217–25.

Seyer, R. 1988. Siedlungs- und Stammesgebiete in den Jahrzehnten um den Beginn unserer Zeitrechnung. In Krüger, pp. 203–25.

Sharer, R. J., and W. Ashmore. 1993. *Archaeology: Discovering Our Past*. 2d ed. Mountain View, CA: Mayfield.

Shchukin, M. B. 1989. *Rome and the Barbarians in Central and Eastern Europe*. 2 vols. Oxford: British Archaeological Reports, International Series 542.

Shennan, S., ed. 1989. *Archaeological Approaches to Cultural Identity*. London: Unwin Hyman.

Sherratt, A. 1995. *Fata morgana:* Illusion and Reality in 'Greek-Barbarian Relations.' *Cambridge Archaeological Journal* 5, 1:139–56.

Sievers, S. 1995. Die Waffen. In Reddé et al., pp. 135–57.

Sinopoli, C. M. 1994. The Archaeology of Empires. *Annual Review of Anthropology* 23:159–80.

Sklenář, K. 1983. *Archaeology in Central Europe: The First 500 Years.* Trans. I. Lewitová. New York: St. Martin's.

Slofstra, J. 1995. The Villa in the Roman West: Space, Decoration and Ideology. In Metzler et al., pp. 77–90.

Smith, J. T. 1978. Villas as a Key to Social Structure. In Todd, pp. 149–86.

———. 1997. *Roman Villas.* New York: Routledge.

Smith, M. E. 1996. *The Aztecs.* Cambridge, MA: Blackwell.

Sommer, C. S. 1988a. Kastellvicus und Kastell. *Fundberichte aus Baden-Württemberg* 13:457–707.

———. 1988b. Die römischen Zivilsiedlungen in Südwestdeutschland. In Planck, pp. 281–310.

———. 1991. Life Beyond the Ditches: Housing and Planning of the Military Vici in Upper Germany and Raetia. In Maxfield and Dobson, pp. 472–76.

Sørensen, M.L.S. 1997. Reading Dress: The Construction of Social Categories and Identities in Bronze Age Europe. *Journal of European Archaeology* 5:93–114.

Spivak, G. C. 1988. Can the Subaltern Speak? In Williams and Chrisman, pp. 66–111.

Stahl, M. 1989. Zwischen Abgrenzung und Integration: Die Verträge der Kaiser Mark Aurel und Commodus mit den Völkern jenseits der Donau. *Chiron* 19:289–317.

Steidl, B. 1991. Frühkaiserzeitliche germanische Besiedlung in der Wetterau. In Rupp, pp. 217–33.

Stein, G. J., R. Bernbeck, C. Coursey, A. McMahon, N. F. Miller, A. Misir, J. Nicola, H. Pittman, S. Pollock, and H. Wright. 1996. Uruk Colonies and Anatolian Communities: An Interim Report on the 1992–1993 Excavations at Hacinebi, Turkey. *American Journal of Archaeology* 100:205–60.

Stern, S. J., ed. 1987. *Resistance, Rebellion, and Consciousness in the Andean Peasant World, 18th to 20th Centuries.* Madison: University of Wisconsin Press.

Steuer, H. 1987. Gewichtgeldwirtschaften im frühgeschichtlichen Europa. In K. Düwel, H. Jankuhn, H. Siems, and D. Timpe, eds., *Untersuchungen zu Handel und Verkehr der vor- und frühgeschichtlichen Zeit in Mittel- und Nordeuropa* part 4: *Der Handel der Karolinger- und Wikingerzeit,* pp. 405–527. Göttingen: Vandenhoeck und Ruprecht.

———. 1994. Archäologie und germanische Sozialgeschichte. In K. Düwel, ed., *Runische Schriftkultur in kontinental-skandinavischer und -angelsächsischer Wechselbeziehung,* pp. 10–55. Berlin: Walter de Gruyter.

Stöckli, W. E. 1979. *Die Grob- und Importkeramik von Manching.* Wiesbaden: Franz Steiner.

———. 1993. Römer, Kelten und Germanen: Probleme von Kontinuität und Diskontinuität zur Zeit von Caesar und Augustus zwischen Hochrhein und Rheinmündung. *Bonner Jahrbücher* 193:121–40.

Stoklund, M. 1995. Die Runen der römischen Kaiserzeit. In Hansen, pp. 317–46.

———. 1996. Runes. In *Roman Reflections in Scandinavia*, pp. 112–14.

Stoler, A., and F. Cooper. 1997. Between Metropole and Colony: Rethinking a Research Agenda. In Cooper and Stoler, pp. 1–56.

Stoll, O. 1993. Der Transfer von Technologie in der römischen Antike. *Münsterische Beiträge zur antiken Handelsgeschichte* 12, 2:93–118.

Stoller, P. 1995. *Embodying Colonial Memories: Spirit Possession, Power and the Hauka in West Africa.* New York: Routledge.

Struck, M. 1992. Römerzeitliche Siedlungen und Bestattungsplätze im unteren Isartal: Zur Besiedlung Nordosträtiens. *Archäologisches Korrespondenzblatt* 22:243–54.

———. 1995. Analysis of Social and Cultural Diversity on Rural Burial Sites in North-Eastern Raetia. In P. Rush, ed., *Theoretical Roman Archaeology: Second Conference Proceedings*, pp. 70–80. Aldershot: Avebury.

———. 1996. *Römische Grabfunde und Siedlungen im Isartal bei Ergolding, Landkreis Landshut.* Kallmünz: Michael Lassleben.

———, ed., 1993. *Römerzeitliche Gräber als Quellen zu Religion, Bevölkerungsstruktur und Sozialgeschichte.* Mainz: Johannes Gutenberg Universität.

Struck, W. 1983. Neue Ausgrabungen im römischen Vicus von Lahr-Dinglingen, Ortenaukreis. *Archäologische Ausgrabungen in Baden-Württemberg 1983*:135–37.

Stupperich, R. 1991. Frühkaiserzeitliche figürliche Bronzen im nordwestlichen Germanien. In Trier, pp. 167–84.

———. 1995. Bemerkungen zum römischen Import im sogenannten Freien Germanien. In Franzius, pp. 45–98.

Svobodová, H. 1985. Antické importy z keltskych oppid v Cechách a na Morave (Antike Importe aus den keltischen Oppida in Böhmen und Mähren). *Archeologické rozhledy* 37:653–68.

Syme, R. 1958. *Colonial Elites: Rome, Spain, and the Americas.* New York: Oxford University Press.

Szabó, M. 1991a. The Celts and Their Movements in the Third Century B.C. In Moscati et al., pp. 303–19.

———. 1991b. Mercenary Activity. In Moscati et al., pp. 333–36.

Tacitus. *The Annals.* Trans. J. Jackson. 5 vols., 1969–81. Cambridge, MA: Harvard University Press.

———. *Germania.* Trans. M. Hutton, 1980. Cambridge, MA: Harvard University Press.

Tainter, J. A. 1988. *The Collapse of Complex Societies.* Cambridge: Cambridge University Press.

Tausend, K. 1987. Die Bedeutung des Importes aus Germanien für den römischen Markt. *Tyche* 2:217–27.

Tejral, J. 1992. Die Probleme der römisch-germanischen Beziehungen unter Berücksichtigung der neuen Forschungsergebnisse im niederösterreichisch-südmährischen Thayaflussgebiet. *Bericht der Römisch-Germanischen Kommission* 73:377–468.

———. 1997. Mušov—Burgstall, Bez. Breclav: Römische Station. In Friesinger and Krinzinger, pp. 287–93.

Thomas, J. 1996. *Time, Culture and Identity: An Interpretative Archaeology.* New York: Routledge.

Thomas, N. 1991. *Entangled Objects: Exchange, Material Culture, and Colonialism in the Pacific.* Cambridge, MA: Harvard University Press.

Thompson, E. A. 1965. *The Early Germans.* Oxford: Clarendon.

Thomsen, P. O. 1997. Jernbarrer fra Lundeborg: indikationer på germansk handel med råvarer. *Årbog for Svendborg & Omegns Museum* 1997:8–18.

Thomsen, P. O., B. Blaesild, N. Hardt, and K. K. Michaelsen. 1993. *Lundeborg— en handelsplads fra jernalderen.* Svendborg: Svendborg & Omegns Museum.

Thrane, H. 1988. Import, Affluence and Cult. In B. Hårdh, L. Larsson, D. Olausson, and R. Petré, eds. *Trade and Exchange in Prehistory,* pp. 187–96. Lund: Lunds Universitets Historiska Museum.

———. 1993. *Guld, guder og godtfolk.* Copenhagen: National Museum.

Tichy, F. 1990. Geographisch-klimatologische Bedingungen der gesamten europäischen Geschichte. In Vittinghoff, pp. 1–19.

Timpe, D. 1970. *Arminius-Studien.* Heidelberg: C. Winter.

———. 1971. Der römische Verzicht auf die Okkupation Germaniens. *Chiron* 1:267–84.

———. 1978. Die Siedlungsverhältnisse Mainfrankens in caesarisch-augusteischer Zeit nach den literarischen Quellen. In Pescheck, pp. 119–29.

———. 1986. Ethnologische Begriffsbildung in der Antike. In Beck, pp. 22–40.

———. 1989a. Entdeckungsgeschichte. In *Reallexikon der germanischen Altertumskunde,* vol. 7, pp. 337–89.

———. 1989b. Die Absicht der Germania. In Jankuhn and Timpe, pp. 106–27.

———. 1992a. Der Sueben-Begriff bei Tacitus. In Neumann and Seemann, pp. 278–310.

———. 1992b. Die Landesnatur der Germania des Tacitus. In Neumann and Seemann, pp. 258–77.

———. 1995. Geographische Faktoren und politische Entscheidungen in der Geschichte der Varuszeit. In Wiegels and Woesler, pp. 14–27.

Todd, M. 1975. *The Northern Barbarians, 100 B.C.–A.D. 300.* London: Hutchinson University Library.

———. 1978. Villas and Romano-British Society. In Todd, pp. 197–208.

———. 1992. *The Early Germans.* Oxford: Blackwell.

————, ed. 1978. *Studies in the Romano-British Villa.* Leicester: Leicester University Press.

Todorov, T. 1984. *The Conquest of America: The Question of the Other.* Trans. R. Howard. New York: Harper and Row.

Torbrügge, W. 1971. Vor- und frühgeschichtliche Flussfunde. *Bericht der Römisch-Germanischen Kommission* 51–52:1–146.

Trier, B., ed. 1991. *Die römische Okkupation nördlich der Alpen zur Zeit des Augustus.* Münster: Aschendorff.

Trunk, M. 1991. *Römische Tempel in den Rhein- und westlichen Donauprovinzen.* Augst: Forschungen in Augst.

Ulbert, G. 1975. Der Auerberg. In *Ausgrabungen in Deutschland,* vol. 1, pp. 409–33. Mainz: Römisch-Germanisches Zentralmuseum.

————. 1995. Auerberg. In Czysz et al., pp. 417–19.

Untermann, J. 1989. Sprachvergleichung und Sprachidentität: methodische Fragen im Zwischenfeld von Keltisch und Germanisch. In H. Beck, ed., *Germanische Rest- und Trümmersprachen,* pp. 211–39. Berlin: Walter de Gruyter.

————. 1993. Sprachliche Zeugnisse der Kelten in Süddeutschland. In Dannheimer and Gebhard, pp. 23–27.

Unwin, P.T.H. 1998. *A European Geography.* Harlow: Longman.

Urla, J. 1993. Cultural Politics in an Age of Statistics: Numbers, Nations, and the Making of Basque Identity. *American Ethnologist* 20:818–43.

von Uslar, R. 1934. Die germanische Keramik in den Kastellen Zugmantel und Saalburg. *Saalburg Jahrbuch* 8:61–96.

————. 1938. *Westgermanische Bodenfunde des ersten bis dritten Jahrhunderts nach Christus aus Mittel- und Westdeutschland.* Berlin: Walter de Gruyter.

————. 1980. Germanische Keramik aus Steinkastell und vicus in Heddernheim und aus dem Osthafen in Frankfurt: Zur Entstehung der rhein-wesergermanischen Keramik. *Fundberichte aus Hessen* 19/20:697–724.

————. 1990. Die Germanen. In Vittinghoff, pp. 657–751.

Vanderhoeven, A. 1996. The Earliest Urbanisation in Northern Gaul: Some Implications of Recent Research in Tongres. In Roymans, pp. 189–260.

Vermeulen, F. 1995. The Role of Local Centres in the Romanization of Northern Belgica. In Metzler et al., pp. 183–98.

Vitali, D. 1991. The Celts in Italy. In Moscati et al., pp. 220–35.

Vittinghoff, F. 1990. Demographische Rahmenbedingungen. In Vittinghoff, pp. 20–24.

————, ed. 1990. *Europäische Wirtschafts- und Sozialgeschichte der römischen Kaiserzeit.* Stuttgart: Klett-Cotta.

Völling, T. 1992. Dreikreisplattensporen: Anmerkungen zu einem Spornfund aus Hopferstadt, Ldkr. Würzburg. *Archäologisches Korrespondenzblatt* 22:393–402.

————. 1993. Sporen aus Ringelsdorf, Niederösterreich. *Archaeologia Austriaca* 77:105–11.

Völling, T. 1994a. Studien zu Fibelformen der jüngeren vorrömischen Eisenzeit und ältesten römischen Kaiserzeit. *Bericht der Römisch-Germanischen Kommission* 75:147–282.

———. 1994b. Bemerkungen zu einem Lochgürtelhaken aus Alzey. *Germania* 72:291–97.

———. 1995. *Frühgermanische Gräber von Aubstadt im Grabfeldgau (Unterfranken).* Kallmünz: Michael Lassleben.

Waas, M. 1965. *Germanen im römischen Dienst im 4. Jahrhundert nach Christus.* Bonn: Rheinische Friedrich-Wilhelms-Universität.

Wacher, J., ed., 1987. *The Roman World.* 2 vols. London: Routledge and Kegan Paul.

Wachtel, N. 1977. *The Vision of the Vanquished: The Spanish Conquest of Peru Through Indian Eyes, 1530–70.* Trans. B. and S. Reynolds. New York: Harper and Row.

Waldhauser, J. 1987. Keltische Gräberfelder in Böhmen. *Bericht der Römisch-Germanischen Kommission* 68:25–179.

———, ed. 1978. *Das keltische Gräberfeld bei Jenišův Újezd in Böhmen.* Teplice: Krajské Muzeum.

Wallman, S. 1986. Ethnicity and the Boundary Process in Context. In J. Rex and D. Mason, eds., *Theories of Race and Ethnic Relations*, pp. 226–45. Cambridge: Cambridge University Press.

Walser, G. 1956. *Caesar und die Germanen: Studien zur politischen Tendenz römischer Feldzugsberichte.* Wiesbaden: Franz Steiner.

———. 1995. Zu Caesars Tendenz in der geographischen Beschreibung Galliens. *Klio* 77:217–23.

Warry, J. 1995. *Warfare in the Classical World.* Norman: University of Oklahoma Press.

Watson, G. R. 1969. *The Roman Soldier.* Ithaca, NY: Cornell University Press.

Waugh, K. E. 1993. The Germanic Cemetery at Rheindorf: Problems with the Identification of Gender and Status. In Struck, pp. 297–304.

Weber, G. 1981. Neue Ausgrabungen am "Apollo-Grannus-Heiligtum" in Faimingen. *Bericht der Römisch-Germanischen Kommission* 62:103–217.

Weber, G. 1989. Neues zur Befestigung des Oppidums Tarodunum, Gde. Kirchzarten, Kreis Breisgau-Hochschwarzwald. *Fundberichte aus Baden-Württemberg* 14:273–88.

Webster, J. 1994. The Just War: Graeco-Roman Texts as Colonial Discourse. In Cottam et al., pp. 1–10.

———. 1995a. Sanctuaries and Sacred Places. In Green, pp. 445–64.

———. 1995b. *Interpretatio:* Roman Word Power and the Celtic Gods. *Britannia* 26:153–61.

———. 1997a. A Negotiated Syncretism: Readings on the Development of Romano-Celtic Religion. In Mattingly, pp. 165–84.

———. 1997b. Necessary Comparisons: A Post-Colonial Approach to Religious Syncretism in the Roman Provinces. *World Archaeology* 28:324–38.

Wegewitz, W. 1937. *Die langobardische Kultur im Gau Moswidi (Niederelbe).* Hildesheim: August Lax.

———. 1972. *Das langobardische Brandgräberfeld von Putensen, Kreis Harburg.* Hildesheim: August Lax.

Weinmann-Walser, M., ed. 1995. *Historische Interpretationen.* Stuttgart: Franz Steiner.

Wells, C. M. 1972. *The German Policy of Augustus.* Oxford: Oxford University Press.

———. 1974. The Ethnography of the Celts and of the Algonkian-Iroquoian Tribes. In J.A.S. Evans, ed., *Polis and Imperium,* pp. 265–78. Toronto: Hakkert.

———. 1976. The Impact of the Augustan Campaigns on Germany. In Pippidi, pp. 421–32.

———. 1992. *The Roman Empire,* 2d ed. Cambridge, MA: Harvard University Press.

———. 1995a. Early Western Europe, Pre-Roman North Africa, and Rome. In M. E. Norton and P. Gerardi, eds., *The American Historical Association's Guide to Historical Literature,* 3d ed., vol. 1, pp. 192–230. New York: Oxford University Press.

———. 1995b. Celts and Germans in the Rhineland. In Green, pp. 603–20.

———. 1996. *Profuit invitis te dominate capi*: Social and Economic Considerations on the Roman Frontiers. *Journal of Roman Archaeology* 9:436–46.

Wells, P. S. 1980. *Culture Contact and Culture Change: Early Iron Age Central Europe and the Mediterranean World.* Cambridge: Cambridge University Press.

———. 1983. *Rural Economy in the Early Iron Age: Excavations at Hascherkeller in Bavaria, 1978–1981.* Cambridge, MA: Peabody Museum.

———. 1984. *Farms, Villages, and Cities: Commerce and Urban Origins in Late Prehistoric Europe.* Ithaca, NY: Cornell University Press.

———. 1985. Material Symbols and the Interpretation of Cultural Change. *Oxford Journal of Archaeology* 4:9–17.

———. 1989. Intensification, Entrepreneurship, and Cognitive Change in the Bronze-Iron Age Transition. In M.L.S. Sørensen and R. Thomas, eds., *The Bronze Age-Iron Age Transition in Europe,* pp. 173–83. Oxford: British Archaeological Reports, International Series 483.

———. 1992. Tradition, Identity, and Change Beyond the Roman Frontier. In E. M. Schortman and P. A. Urban, eds., *Resources, Power, and Interregional Interaction,* pp. 175–88. New York: Plenum.

———. 1993. *Settlement, Economy, and Cultural Change at the End of the European Iron Age: Excavations at Kelheim in Bavaria, 1987–1991.* Ann Arbor: International Monographs in Prehistory.

———. 1994. Interactions between Denmark and Central Europe in the Late Prehistoric Iron Age: The Prelude to Gudme and Lundeborg. In Nielsen, Randsborg, and Thrane, pp. 151–59.

———. 1995a. Identities, Material Culture, and Change: "Celts" and "Germans" in Late Iron Age Europe. *Journal of European Archaeology* 3:169–85.

Wells, P. S. 1995b. Manufactured Objects and the Construction of Identities in Late La Tène Europe. *EIRENE* 31:129–50.

———. 1996. Location, Organization, and Specialization of Craft Production in Late Prehistoric Central Europe. In B. Wailes, ed., *Craft Specialization and Social Evolution*, pp. 85–98. Philadelphia: University Museum.

———. 1998a. Identity and Material Culture in the Later Prehistory of Central Europe. *Journal of Archaeological Research* 6:239–98.

———. 1998b. Who, Where, and What Were the Celts? *American Journal of Archaeology* 102:814–16.

———. 1999. Production within and beyond Imperial Boundaries: Goods, Exchange, and Power in Roman Europe. In P. N. Kardulias, ed., *World Systems Theory in Practice: Leadership, Production, and Exchange*, pp. 85–101. New York: Rowman and Littlefield.

Welwei, K.-W. 1986. Römische Weltherrschaftsideologie und augusteische Germanienpolitik. *Gymnasium* 93:118–37.

Wenskus, R. 1961. *Stammesbildung und Verfassung.* Cologne: Böhlau.

———. 1986. Über die Möglichkeit eines allgemeinen interdisziplinären Germanenbegriffs. In Beck, pp. 1–21.

Werner, J. 1955. Die Nauheimer Fibel. *Jahrbuch des Römisch-Germanischen Zentralmuseums* 2:170–86.

———. 1977. Spätlatène-Schwerter norischer Herkunft. In Chropovský, pp. 367–96.

———. 1978. Zur Bronzekanne von Kelheim. *Bayerische Vorgeschichtsblätter* 43:1–18.

Weski, T. 1982. *Waffen in germanischen Gräbern der älteren römischen Kaiserzeit südlich der Ostsee.* Oxford: British Archaeological Reports, International Series 147.

Westerholz, A. 1979. The Old Akkadian Empire in Contemporary Opinion. In M. T. Larsen, ed., *Power and Propaganda: A Symposium on Ancient Empires*, pp. 107–24. Copenhagen: Akademisk Forlag.

Whitehead, N. L. 1992. Tribes Make States and States Make Tribes: Warfare and the Creation of Colonial Tribes and States in Northeastern South America. In Ferguson and Whitehead, pp.127–50.

———. 1995. The Historical Anthropology of Text: The Interpretation of Ralegh's *Discoverie of Guiana. Current Anthropology* 36:53–74.

Whittaker, C. R. 1989. Supplying the System: Frontiers and Beyond. In Barrett, Fitzpatrick, and Macinnes, pp. 64–80.

———. 1993. What Happens When Frontiers Come to an End? In Brun, van der Leeuw, and Whittaker, pp. 133–42.

———. 1994. *Frontiers of the Roman Empire.* Baltimore: Johns Hopkins University Press.

———. 1997. Imperialism and Culture: The Roman Initiative. In Mattingly, pp. 143–64.

Whittle, A.W.R. 1996. *Europe in the Neolithic*. Cambridge: Cambridge University Press.

van Wickevoort Crommelin, B. R. 1995. *Quintili Vare, legiones redde!* Die politische und ideologische Verarbeitung einer traumatischen Niederlage. In Franzius, pp. 1–43.

Wiegels, R., and W. Woesler, eds., 1995. *Arminius und die Varusschlacht*. Paderborn: Ferdinand Schöningh.

Wieland, G. 1993. Spätkeltische Traditionen in Form und Verzierung römischer Grobkeramik. *Fundberichte aus Baden-Württemberg* 18:61–70.

———. 1996. *Die Spätlatènezeit in Württemberg*. Stuttgart: Konrad Theiss.

Wielowiejski, J. 1989. Die römerzeitlichen Silbergefässe in Polen: Importe und Nachahmungen. *Bericht der Römisch-Germanischen Kommission* 70:191–241.

Wierschowski, L. 1995. *Die regionale Mobilität in Gallien nach den Inschriften des 1. bis 3. Jahrhunderts n. Chr.* Stuttgart: Franz Steiner.

Wigg, A., and D. G. Wigg. 1994. Ein römischer Münzschatzfund aus dem Lahntal bei Wetzlar. *Germania* 72:298–313.

Wightman, E. M. 1970. *Roman Trier and the Treveri*. New York: Praeger.

———. 1978. The Pattern of Rural Settlement in Roman Gaul. In H. Temporini, ed., *Aufstieg und Niedergang der römischen Welt* II, 2, 4, pp. 584–657. Berlin: Walter de Gruyter.

———. 1985. *Gallia Belgica*. Berkeley: University of California Press.

Wild, J. P. 1985. The Clothing of Britannia, Gallia belgica and Germania inferior. In H. Temporini, ed., *Aufstieg und Niedergang der römischen Welt* II, 12, 3, pp. 362–422. Berlin: Walter de Gruyter.

Will, E. L. 1987. The Roman Amphoras from Manching. *Bayerische Vorgeschichtsblätter* 52:21–36.

Willems, W.J.H. 1986. *Romans and Batavians: A Regional Study in the Dutch Eastern River Area*. Amsterdam: University of Amsterdam.

———. 1990. *Romeins Nijmegen: Vier Eeuwen Stad en Centrum aan de Waal*. Den Haag: Matrijs.

Williams, P., and L. Chrisman, eds. 1994. *Colonial Discourse and Post-Colonial Theory: A Reader*. New York: Columbia University Press.

Willis, S. 1996. The Romanization of Pottery Assemblages in the East and North-East of England during the First Century A.D. *Britannia* 27:179–219.

Wilson, R. 1993. Anchored Communities: Identity and History of the ät Maya-Q'eqchi'. *Man* 28:121–38.

Winghart, S. 1986. Spätkeltische und frührömische Siedlungsfunde aus Eching, Lkr. Freising, Obb. *Ausgrabungen und Funde in Altbayern* 1985–1986:59–62.

Wolf, E. R. 1982. *Europe and the People Without History*. Berkeley: University of California Press.

Wolfram, H. 1995. *Die Germanen*. 2d ed. Munich: C. H. Beck.

Wolters, R. 1990a. Der Germanicus-Dupondius, die Tabula Siarensis und der römische Verzicht auf die Okkupation Germaniens. *Numismatische Zeitschrift* 101:7–16.

———. 1990b. Der Waren- und Dienstleistungsaustausch zwischen dem Römischen Reich und dem Freien Germanien in der Zeit des Prinzipats. *Münsterische Beiträge zur antiken Handelsgeschichte* 9:14–44.

———. 1990c. *Römische Eroberung und Herrschaftsorganisation in Gallien und Germanien: Zur Entstehung und Bedeutung der sogenannten Klientel-Randstaaten.* Bochum: Universitätsverlag Dr. N. Brockmeyer.

———. 1991. Der Waren- und Dienstleistungsaustausch zwischen dem Römischen Reich und dem Freien Germanien in der Zeit des Prinzipats. *Münsterische Beiträge zur antiken Handelsgeschichte* 10:78–132.

———. 1995. Römische Funde in der *Germania magna* und das Problem römisch-germanischer Handelsbeziehungen in der Zeit des Prinzipats. In Franzius, pp. 99–117.

———. 1997. Rom und das rechtsrheinische Germanien nach der Okkupationsphase: Wirtschaftliche und politische Beziehungen. In Seibt, Borsdorf, and Grütter, pp. 95–103.

Woolf, G. 1990. World-Systems Analysis and the Roman Empire. *Journal of Roman Archaeology* 3:44–58.

———. 1993a. Rethinking the Oppida. *Oxford Journal of Archaeology* 12:223–34.

———. 1993b. European Social Development and Roman Imperialism. In Brun, van der Leeuw, and Whittaker, pp. 13–20.

———. 1993c. The Social Significance of Trade in Late Iron Age Europe. In C. Scarre and F. Healy, eds., *Trade and Exchange in Prehistoric Europe*, pp. 211–18. Oxford: Oxbow.

———. 1995. The Formation of Roman Provincial Cultures. In Metzler et al., pp. 9–18.

———. 1996. Monumental Writing and the Expansion of Roman Society in the Early Empire. *Journal of Roman Studies* 86:22–39.

———. 1997. Beyond Romans and Natives. *World Archaeology* 28, 3: 339–50.

Wyss, R. 1954. Das Schwert des Korisios. *Jahrbuch des Bernischen Historischen Museums* 34:201–22.

Yoffee, N., and G. L. Cowgill, eds. 1988. *The Collapse of Ancient States and Civilizations.* Tucson: University of Arizona Press.

Zanier, W. 1994a. Eine römische Katapultpfeilspitze der 19. Legion aus Oberammergau: Neues zum Alpenfeldzug des Drusus im Jahr 15 v. Chr. *Germania* 72:587–96.

———. 1994b. Eine Oberammergauer Passion im Jahre 15 v. Chr.? *Das archäologische Jahr in Bayern 1994*:97–100.

———. 1997. Ein einheimischer Opferplatz mit römischen Waffen der frühesten Okkupation (15–10 v. Chr.) bei Oberammergau. In Groenman-van Waateringe et al., pp. 47–52.

Zanker, P. 1990. *The Power of Images in the Age of Augustus.* Trans. A. Shapiro. Ann Arbor: University of Michigan Press.

Zeitler, W. M. 1986. Zum Germanenbegriff Caesars: Der Germanenexkurs im sechsten Buch von Caesars Bellum Gallicum. In Beck, pp. 41–52.

Zwikker, W. 1941. *Studien zur Markussäule.* Amsterdam: N. V. Noord-Hollandsche Uitgevers.

* Index *

The following words occur frequently in the text and are not indexed: Caesar, Celts, Gauls, Germans, limes, oppida.